STEAL AWAY HOME

STEAL AWAY HOME

ONE WOMAN'S EPIC FLIGHT TO FREEDOM—
AND HER LONG ROAD BACK TO THE SOUTH

KAROLYN SMARDZ FROST

HarperCollins*Publishers*Ltd

Published by HarperCollins Publishers Ltd

First edition

pp. x–xi: "Cecelia's Journey" map by Mary Rostad
p. xii: "Toronto in 1858" map, adapted from an original by John F. Moody, courtesy of
Timmins Martelle Heritage Consultants at the Museum of Ontario Archaeology.

HarperCollins books may be purchased for educational, business,
or sales promotional use through our Special Markets Department.

HarperCollins Publishers Ltd
2 Bloor Street East, 20th Floor
Toronto, Ontario, Canada
M4W 1A8

www.harpercollins.ca

Library and Archives Canada Cataloguing in
Publication information is available upon request.

ISBN 978-1-55468-251-5

Printed and bound in the United States

LSC/H 9 8 7 6 5 4 3 2 1

For my beloved Norm, who makes all things possible.
In loving memory of Alice and Duane Newby,
who shared with me their Buxton family, and of Anne Butler,
who made her Kentucky home my own.
I miss you every day.

Know all men by these presents that I
Wm Cotton of the city of Louisville have this
day sold and by these presents do bargain
and sell unto C. W. Thruston a negro woman
by the name of Mary about Seventeen
years of age, and her child called Cela about
Five months old, which I do warrant and
defend to be sound both in mind and body,
and slaves for life unto the said C. W. Thruston
his Heirs and Assigns forever — for the con=
sideration of Four Hundred dollars to me
in hand — This the 4th day of October
1831

Wm Cotton

James Th Martin

Bill of Sale, Wm. Cotton, Mary and baby "Cela," $400. October 4, 1831.

STEAL AWAY HOME

Steal away, steal away, steal away to Jesus
Steal away, steal away home
I ain't got long to stay here

My Lord, He calls me
He calls me by the thunder
The trumpet sounds within-a my soul
I ain't got long to stay here

Green trees are bending
Po' sinner stand a-trembling
The trumpet sounds within-a my soul
I ain't got long to stay here

—*Traditional*

CONTENTS

Route of Cecelia's travels

★ Places Cecelia lived

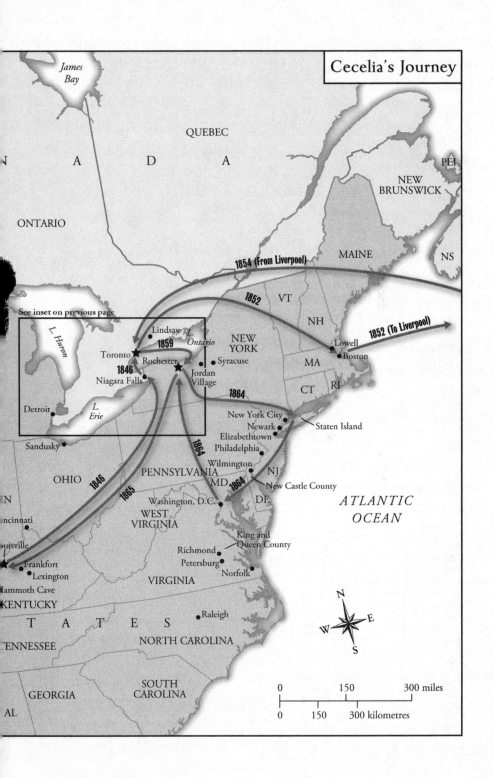

Cecelia's Journey

James Bay

QUEBEC

N   A   D   A

ONTARIO

NEW BRUNSWICK

PEI

1854 (From Liverpool)

MAINE

NS

See inset on previous page

L. Huron

Lindsay
L. Ontario

1859

Toronto
Rochester

1846
Niagara Falls

Jordan Village

Syracuse

NEW YORK

VT

NH

1852

Lowell
Boston

1852 (To Liverpool)

MA

CT   RI

Detroit

L. Erie

1864

New York City
Newark
Elizabethtown
Philadelphia

Staten Island

Sandusky

1846

OHIO

PENNSYLVANIA

1864

Wilmington

NJ

New Castle County

MD   1864

DE

ATLANTIC OCEAN

N

Cincinnati

1865

Washington, D.C.

WEST VIRGINIA

King and Queen County

Louisville

Frankfort
Lexington

VIRGINIA

Richmond
Petersburg

Norfolk

Mammoth Cave

KENTUCKY

T   A   T   E   S

Raleigh

N

TENNESSEE

NORTH CAROLINA

W   E

S

GEORGIA

SOUTH CAROLINA

0   150   300 miles

AL

0   150   300 kilometres

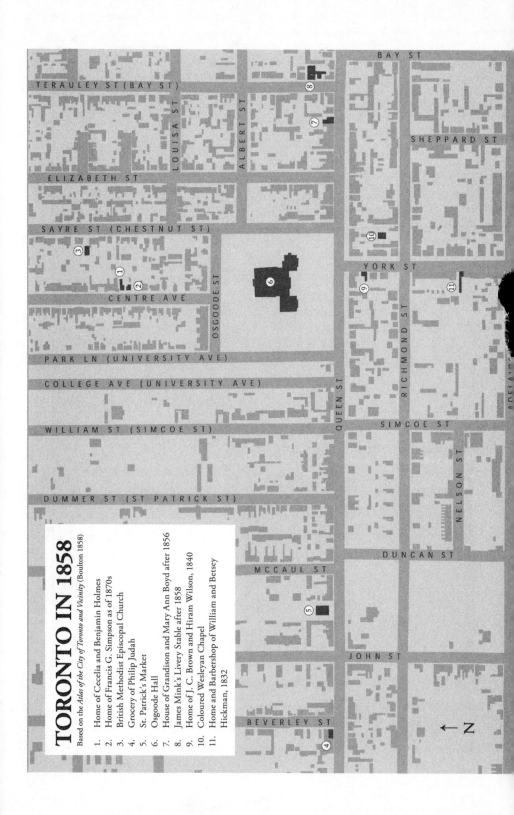

TORONTO IN 1858

Based on the *Atlas of the City of Toronto and Vicinity* (Boulton 1858)

1. Home of Cecelia and Benjamin Holmes
2. Home of Francis G. Simpson as of 1870s
3. British Methodist Episcopal Church
4. Grocery of Philip Judah
5. St. Patrick's Market
6. Osgoode Hall
7. House of Grandison and Mary Ann Boyd after 1856
8. James Mink's Livery Stable after 1858
9. Home of J. C. Brown and Hiram Wilson, 1840
10. Coloured Wesleyan Chapel
11. Home and Barbershop of William and Betsey Hickman, 1832

INTRODUCTION

MY LIFE IS IN RUINS. Sorry, that's an old archaeologist's joke. But odd bricks and stones, bits of broken pottery, rusty nails and shards of glass—stuff anyone else would think was trash—bring joy to my heart. This is why, on a chilly September morning in 2015, I found myself standing outside a tall plywood barrier in downtown Toronto, anxiously waiting to see what lay beyond. The Ontario government had commissioned a major excavation on the site of a new courthouse. Archaeologist Holly Martelle and her team were digging a full city block in what had been Toronto's first immigrant-reception neighbourhood.

Beginning in the 1830s, Toronto's old St. John's Ward received wave after wave of newcomers from all over the world. But its first residents were refugees from bondage, people whose ancestors had been torn from Africa and carried across the Atlantic in the holds of stinking slave ships to build the New World. For thousands, the little houses and tenements lining those narrow streets were the last stop on the Underground Railroad.

This densely packed city block had once been the beating heart of Black Toronto. Now soaring skyscrapers ringed the area of excavation. The makeshift gate to the site swung open. Inside lay an acre or more of dry soil covered with intersecting foundations of brick and concrete block two and three courses high, representing more than a century of building and rebuilding in this one limited space. A little to the north, in an area entirely cleared of debris, lay the foundations of the city's first British Methodist Episcopal church.

The archaeological discoveries were an unexpected gift. For the past ten years I had been piecing together clues to the life and times of one incredibly courageous fugitive slave woman named Cecelia Jane Reynolds. Now archaeologists were digging the foundations of Cecelia's first home in freedom, laid bare again to the sky after decades of obscurity under an asphalt parking lot.

How fitting that the dig was taking place in such an uncompromisingly urban environment, evocative of the experiences of a woman whose life was lived out in cities. Most people, when they think about slavery at all, see in their mind's eye enslaved men and women picking vast fields of cotton. But Cecelia was not a plantation slave. Indeed, hers was a quintessentially urban experience. Her home in slavery had been Louisville, Kentucky, a city that looked both to the North and South and shared some of the traits of each.

In 1846, conductors on the Underground Railroad helped Cecelia reach freedom in a dramatic escape via Niagara Falls. After that she resided in the cities of industrializing North America, primarily Toronto and Rochester, New York, with a sojourn in the great British port of Liverpool before returning again to Louisville.

The people with whom Cecelia was most closely associated, first in slavery and then in freedom, were also part of urban North America. Her owner, Fanny, was descended from two of the founding families of the pioneer West, both instrumental in the establishment of Louisville, her home on the Ohio River. Fanny was great-niece to William Clark of the Lewis and Clark expedition, and the great-grandmother of Rogers C. B. Morton, whom President Richard Nixon appointed Secretary of the Interior. Her people on her mother's side were the Churchills of Churchill Downs.

Although Cecelia's first husband passed his childhood in a part of the South so rural that his home county only recently acquired its first traffic light, from the age of fourteen he lived in Richmond, Virginia. The city skills he gained during his years in the state capital shaped the rest of his life. Gaining his freedom in the most remarkable set of circumstances,

Benjamin Pollard Holmes chose Toronto as his family's adopted home. It was there he learned to live as a free man.

Cecelia's second husband was also a fugitive slave, from Newark, Delaware. Fleeing first to Toronto, he was later employed on a private estate on the outskirts of Rochester, New York. William Henry Larrison became part of that city's small but very active Black community. That was where he married the widowed Cecelia in 1862. After the Civil War, he and Cecelia took their children to Louisville, where her mother was. Although he sometimes took odd jobs on nearby farms, William spent the rest of his life in Kentucky's busiest port on the Ohio River.

Cecelia's stepsons by Benjamin were urban too. Both trained in the profession their father had chosen for them in the great mill city of Lowell, Massachusetts. While they each spent time in small-town Ontario, one would end his life in Rochester while the other followed his white wife's family to Faribault, Minnesota, a boomtown on America's western frontier. His sons would break the colour bar in Minneapolis as the first Black graduates of the University of Minnesota's medical school.

Cecelia's only child to live to adulthood shared her mother's urban peregrinations, but after her mother's death she moved west. She went first to Guthrie, Oklahoma, where she remarried, and later to Kansas City when the Kansas City Monarchs of Negro Baseball fame were in their heyday. She and her husband made their home just down the street from smoky nightclubs where Scott Joplin had played ragtime and jazz musicians were inventing the Kansas City sound.

Because of her intensely urban experiences, Cecelia was at the epicentre of the social, economic, religious and political transformations of her age. In the ever-changing kaleidoscope of North American race relations both before and after the Civil War, she and her contemporaries were among the voices for change that emanated from the soul of Black America. These included a persistent drive for self-betterment, for respectability, piety and industry, to prove that people of African descent were as worthy to take up the mantle of citizenship as were their white contemporaries. Yet Cecelia's whole life was played out against a backdrop of law and custom founded on white supremacist principles.

As is the case with so many of our proud female ancestors, no documents record Cecelia's personal engagement in activism and protest. But she was among what one historian calls the "great silent army" of female abolitionists. It was women like Cecelia who provided to the refugees from bondage they found at their door the shelter, clothing, food and friendship needed to get them on their feet once they reached Canada. Working in tandem with the men they married, these women were essential cogs in the workings of the Underground Railroad. Like Cecelia, many held full-time jobs, cared for their families and still found precious hours to establish and support church-based self-help, benevolent, fraternal and self-improvement groups that were foundational to Black city life on both sides of the long border separating Canada from the United States.

Cecelia's name appears nowhere in the annals of North American antislavery. But she was there when men and women gathered at Toronto's St. Lawrence Hall to decide how best to circumvent the 1850 US Fugitive Slave Law; there in those small Black churches where Mary Ann Shadd, Henry Highland Garnet, Gerritt Smith and Dr. Martin Delany—the father of Black nationalism—thundered from the pulpit; there when Harriet Tubman was slipping in and out of Toronto collecting the funds needed to help make her audacious slave rescues possible.

Cecelia's fascinating biography demonstrates how remarkably mobile African Americans were. She lived in several parts of North America and had a long stay in Europe while her husband went off seeking his fortune on the other side of the world. During the Civil War, she, along with two small daughters (one a toddler), spent months in a Staten Island fortress while her husband cooked for troops defending New York's harbour from Confederate attack, and she and her children were in Washington, DC, while President Lincoln pursued the long drive to Richmond that would end the war.

Along the way, Cecelia and her little family encountered many of the major reforming figures of their day: George Brown, Canadian Father of Confederation; Mary Miles Bibb and Henry Bibb, whose *Voice of the Fugitive* was the first Black abolitionist newspaper published in Canada; Frederick Douglass, the greatest and most revered of all the Black abolitionists; Reverend William King, whose bright vision for a utopian African Canadian settlement on the Raleigh Plain shines on today in the eyes of Buxton's children; African nationalist Dr. Martin Delany; and Elizabeth Cady Stanton and Susan B. Anthony, whose abolitionism taught them means of protest that they employed in later years in the long struggle for women's suffrage. From African colonization to its counterpoint in slave revolt, along clandestine pathways leading northward that bore the name Underground Railroad, and on to what W. E. B. Du Bois would one day call "racial uplift," all touched her life and the lives of people Cecelia knew in her various urban homes.

As a mature woman, Cecelia's life came full circle when she returned to Louisville and struggled to find a place for her family in what was perhaps the South's most conflicted border city. Through a renewed relationship with her former owner she encountered white officials who were trying to stem the tide of anti-Black violence that gripped rural Kentucky in the wake of Emancipation. Cecelia lived and worked among outstanding Black men and women who strove to elevate African Americans to political and economic independence, if not to the seemingly unattainable goal of social equality. Cecelia and her family were there, too, when the Night Riders roamed the Kentucky countryside, punishing the state's thousands of former slaves for their new-found freedom.

During middle age this remarkable woman shared in the heady aspirations of the Reconstruction era, when the whole world seemed made new. She was also there for its failure, and to watch the rise of the "New South," which in so many dreadfully disappointing ways resembled the old one. Cecelia and her family were personally and profoundly affected by the progressive whittling away of civil rights given Black America in the Fourteenth and Fifteenth Amendments to the US Constitution. They experienced the indignities of Jim Crow segregation, but lived to see the evolution of new organizations such as the National Association for the Advancement of Colored People (NAACP), born of the struggle for the rights of citizenship and self-determination that Black Americans were still denied.

Cecelia, along with her family, never attained the levels of education and financial security that would have placed them in the ranks of Black leadership. But they were affected by the changes such efforts brought about. Cecelia was in Louisville for the streetcar strike that integrated the municipal transit system, an event that paved the way for the city's unique response to Black agitation that continued through the 1960s and beyond. She and people she knew who struggled against decades of racial division bred by slavery, coupled with Louisville's postwar adherence to the "Lost Cause," to achieve what small victories they could in a society imbued with and controlled by white supremacist thought. As a wife and mother, she was present in the city when seminal Black conventions of the late nineteenth and early twentieth centuries took place, where leading figures of African America passed resolution after resolution demanding access to educational opportunities for its youth and the right to political self-actualization, at least for its men.

For African Americans who migrated to Canada in the years of the Underground Railroad, the only story usually told of them is that of their flight. But in the overall course of their lives that was but a single moment, akin to Andy Warhol's classic fifteen minutes of fame. As Cecelia's story proves, those incredibly courageous people who broke the chains of their own bondage went on to lead complex, interesting lives. They became farmers and shopkeepers, artisans and craftspeople, ministers, teachers and students. They worked hard, raised families, led church and community activities, developed friendships, engaged in political debate, marched in Emancipation Day parades and became as full and active participants as possible within whatever society they found themselves.

When their range of action was hemmed in by the prejudice of their contemporaries, they found ways to circumvent both law and policy to achieve whatever goals they could for themselves and for their children. They created the "world within a world" that served as both scaffolding for Black culture and the fortress walls that protected it, everywhere on this continent. People like Cecelia and the two fine men she married found ways to carve lives for themselves outside the boundaries of what was expected of them. They most emphatically did not "know their place" (as defined for them by others) and they refused to remain in it. Over the course of her long life, she and her contemporaries gained education and experience. Having "made free," they worked to "use that freedom well," in the words of another famous freedom-seeker named Josiah Henson.

This biography of Cecelia Jane Reynolds took eight years to research and two to craft on paper in a way that I hope does justice to her personality and her achievements. I have sought to paint her bravery and depict at least some of the sterling character she displayed in responding to the multiple challenges that she faced. I have always been most drawn to the study of ordinary people, those whose names are not on the buildings we consider historic landmarks, but who put the bricks and mortar together so they could stand to this day. Cecelia is one of the uncounted millions who never made it into the history books but whose accomplishments demonstrate the dizzying heights of which human beings are capable when faced with implacable adversity. As Cecelia's story proves, there are no ordinary people.

Evidence for Cecelia's very eventful life and for those of the people she loved is fragmentary, but what does survive is incredibly moving. Five letters that Fanny, her former mistress, wrote to Cecelia in Toronto during the 1850s are contained in the collections of Louisville's Filson Historical Society. Also there is a typescript account by Fanny's youngest son, written in 1899, in which he describes his mother's affectionate concern for her former maid who had run away to Canada more than half a century before. R. C. Ballard Thruston's memoir provides essential information about

Cecelia's enslaved family, her precipitous flight to freedom and Fanny's rather startling response to it. But his words offer less insight into the reasons for Cecelia's return to Louisville after the Civil War, and the ways in which these two women picked up the threads of the unbreakable connection that existed between them. Too unequal to be called friendship, it endured all their lives.[1]

A rich tapestry of information is also contained in the inch-thick Larrison file in the US Pension Bureau collections at Washington's National Archives and Records Administration (NARA). It documents Cecelia's protracted struggle to gain her husband's Civil War pension and reveals much about the friendships and the hardships of her later life. Government officials went to incredible lengths to deny her the small monthly stipend due her as a veteran's widow. They interrogated their Louisville friends, old soldiers her husband had known during the war, and even people in Toronto whom Cecelia had not seen in thirty years. And there, written in her own hand, is Cecelia's autobiography, or at least the three densely written pages of it that she was willing to share with a bevy of faceless officials at a pension office in Washington, DC.

Her first husband's early life is very well documented. Reverend Hiram Wilson greeted Benjamin Pollard Holmes when he first arrived in Toronto and published a detailed account of his 1840 flight to freedom in the abolitionist press. Some of his later activities, however, are suggested mainly by the company Benjamin kept. Underground Railroad work was highly illegal and became ever more dangerous as the antebellum period wore on. What I know of the priorities that drove him is gleaned from sources ranging from British court records to the letters of Black abolitionists whom he knew.

As for Cecelia's second husband . . . well, he's an interesting case. He told his wife he had never been married before and that he was not a fugitive slave. I found neither to be true. An interesting insight into their marriage, that.

The rest of *Steal Away Home* is woven from threads scattered through public records: street directories, census and tax records, registers of birth and marriage and death. These help fill in details of Cecelia's activities but they offer no explanation as to why she made the decisions she did, and most are frustratingly lacking in historical context. In the absence of direct personal data about specific points in her life, what she did and what happened to her have been interpreted here through the lens of contemporary experience, especially the rich resource that is fugitive slave biography. I thank them more formally elsewhere, but I am deeply indebted to both community and academic historians who have shared their insights with me over the years, and whose own published works have been foundational to my evolving understanding of the social, economic, political and other influences shaping the experience of this compelling woman.

Slavery, race and discrimination are always painful topics in respect to terminology, so I would like to explain some of the choices I have made. Where historical language is contained in a quote, it remains as originally written. Otherwise, readers will find as descriptors the terms *African Canadian*, *African American* and *Black*, along with *people of African descent* and very occasionally *people of colour*. When speaking of British North America, my choices stem partly from uncertainty as to when individual formerly enslaved African Americans began to identify sufficiently with their adopted homeland to consider themselves Canadian. It is useful to remember that the term *citizenship* in the American sense does not apply; people in colonial Canada were either born British subjects or became such when they were naturalized.

The language of Underground Railroad–era North America is changing too. I much prefer the term *freedom-seeker* or even *refugee* to the commonly used *fugitive slave*, which has and always did have negative connotations. So does *runaway*, which speaks to the concerns of the slaveholder rather than the people liberating themselves. The word *slave* is extremely problematic. Slavery is a condition imposed on people; they may be *enslaved*, but no one is ever a slave. That said, despite my best efforts, all those terms appear in the following pages as a reflection of both historical and contemporary usage.

To avoid geographic confusion, I refer to "Canada" more frequently than I do Upper Canada or Canada West. Cecelia's time immediately following her escape was spent in what today is Ontario. From 1793 to 1841 much of it was known as Upper Canada, in reference to its position relative to the St. Lawrence River (as opposed to Quebec, or Lower Canada). With the 1840 Act of Union, Upper and Lower Canada were joined under a single government. After that, Upper Canada was properly referred to as Canada West, except there were always people who still called it Upper Canada or just "Canada," as did the American press. "Ontario" did not come into use until the confederation of four British North American provinces as the Dominion of Canada in 1867. If you think that's confusing, I live in Nova Scotia, where people *still* call Ontario "Upper Canada."

In closing, I would like to explain one last, very important decision that I made in choosing how to present the story you are about to read. I am by training and inclination an archaeologist. People in that intriguing profession are dedicated to exploring the hard truths of our human past. Early on we learn that while artifacts and stains in the soil tell a great deal about what people did, they rarely suggest what they believed, and never what they thought or how they might have felt about anything. We find the skeleton buried in the ground, but the voice is lost and whatever made that person unique is gone forever. Emotions, dreams and fears vanish the moment the soul departs the body.

Cecelia died just over a century ago and left no known descendants, and neither did her two husbands. But while she lived, Cecelia Jane Reynolds was both loving and very much loved. Driven by her own personal motivations and aspirations, she was a complicated soul with a depth of personal courage that both astonishes and humbles me. Cecelia deserves to be depicted in all the multiple dimensions of her character and experience. The basic facts contained in the creased and tattered letters she received from Fanny, and in official documents mouldering in a government filing cabinet, only hint at the much larger tale to be told.

So while this volume is based on a decade of research conducted in archives, libraries and community museums from Pasadena, California, to Toronto, Canada, and from Liverpool, England, to Melbourne, Australia, it is also the biography of a woman who laughed, cried, despaired, struggled and, above all, triumphed. Accordingly, in the pages of *Steal Away Home* I have largely eliminated the evidence of my own conjecture. I have chosen to write Cecelia's story as narrative, dispensing wherever possible with "perhaps," "it seems that," "one might suggest" and other artfully crafted qualifiers that scholars use to mask the inevitable gaps in our knowledge of the past. This is in no way fiction. Rather, it is a narrative based on my more than three decades of in-depth study trying to understand and articulate the African experience in North America. I have not tried to fill the gaps in what I know about Cecelia, but rather have provided some plausible links to bridge them.

Steal Away Home tells the tale of one brave and resourceful woman who fled slavery and built a new life for herself in freedom. After the Civil War, out of mingled affection and need, she "stole away home" to the place where she had spent her enslaved childhood, to reestablish a relationship with the woman who had once owned her body. Here is Cecelia Jane Reynolds as I have come to know her. I hope you find her as inspiring as I do.

PROLOGUE

SHE REMEMBERED IT AS IF it were yesterday. Each moment had been an agony of fear and anticipation until the last sliver of waning moon had left the sky. Then Cecelia and her silent guide slipped out the garden gate. Behind them loomed the huge stone bulk of the Cataract House hotel. Most guests slept. A few windows gleamed with the warm yellow of gaslight, but she imagined them as eyes, each one accusing her of abandonment, ingratitude, pride.

She wore a dark dress, as instructed, without collar or ornament whose flash might betray her. The dark-clad man led her to the river's edge, where its border of low shrubbery would mask their passage. The clamour of rushing water blocked out all other sound.

They kept close to the bushes as they crept along. The man took her hand. He had come this way countless times. To stumble here was death.

The air was saturated with moisture, the roar of the great cataract deafening as they passed its crest. She could feel spray on her face and hands. They came to Prospect Point quite suddenly. A few rapid steps took them across open lawn. Wooden railings enclosing the staircase were just visible where the land dropped away.

Three hundred stairs led down to the bottom of the gorge. Following her guide's swift descent, she counted every one. The river was eerily calm here in the little inlet where boats tied up. Just a few feet away, unfathomable quantities of falling water crashed and roiled against jagged rocks.

He left her for what seemed a very long time. She trembled, weeping a little for all she was leaving behind. Returning, he drew her still further on. There were private slips beyond the ferry dock. The man again took her hand as they felt their way down the very centre of a low dock, planks rough under her slippers. She felt disembodied as she stood right above the tumbling, churning water of the channel.

She was numb with chill and fear. Strong hands lowered her carefully into the sturdy craft. He slipped the knot and stepped in. Taking the oars, he steered the long, narrow boat away from shore and out onto the broad expanse of foaming water. The boat pivoted and tossed but he rowed steadily, keeping to his course. It seemed impossible that there was even this much calm so close to the base of Niagara Falls.

Fifteen minutes it took to cross, and then the work of seconds to stand and grasp the hands of the one waiting for her on that other shore. She turned back towards the river, but he was already pulling away. He did not see her raise her hand in farewell.

CHAPTER 1

Way Down in Egypt Land

Have you, dear reader, ever watched the slaveholder at such places
as I have, gliding through the shady groves, or riding in his splen-
did carriage, dressed in the richest attire, and with no wish
ungratified that gold can purchase; and have you ever been guilty
of envying him, or of wishing yourself in his condition? . . . Think
you, that the prayers, cries, and pleadings of the down-trodden
slave that for years have been ascending to the throne of a just
God, will never be avenged?

—Austin Steward, 1857[1]

CECELIA HAD BEEN BORN into slavery and knew no other life, but
she believed—oh, how she believed—one was possible. If all went well, that
bright vision of freedom would carry her over the river to the free soil of
Canada, her very own Promised Land.

The trip to Niagara Falls in the spring of 1846 had begun pleasantly
enough. Ostensibly it was a special treat for a beloved only daughter from
her besotted father. Charles W. Thruston, an acerbic attorney noted among
Louisville's elite for his acuity of perception and scathingly dry wit, was
seemingly a cold man in the eyes of his acquaintances and even his clients.
But within the family it was well known that he had a soft centre and that

he doted on his pretty young daughter, Frances Ann. That the trip also took his volatile son, Sam, out of harm's way while the Kentucky Volunteers were mustering at the Louisville docks for the Mexican War was an additional inducement that Charles discussed with no one.

Frances Ann Thruston was just nineteen. Known affectionately as Fanny, she was both kind and sweet-natured, but with just enough temper, coupled with a sharp intelligence, to make her wilful, the one aspect of her character her father deplored. Of the four children born to Charles and Mary Eliza Thruston, only two had lived. Fanny and her brother, Sam, had been the stars in Charles W. Thruston's sky from the day he lost their beloved mother.[2]

Cecelia was Fanny Thruston's maid and constant companion. A gift from her indulgent parents before Fanny turned fourteen, she was Fanny's personal property. While Cecelia was the one member of the Thruston party whose opinion would never have been consulted, she was quite excited about the upcoming journey. The trip north would take her to the very border of Canada. The slaves of Kentucky were well aware that on the other side of Niagara's mighty torrent lay a place where the slave-catchers could not go.

Cecelia Jane Reynolds had grown up in the Thruston household in the busy river port of Louisville, within sight of free soil. The Ohio River marked the division between slave Kentucky and the free states of Indiana and Ohio. Here in the prosperous Bluegrass region, households were run by Black housekeepers, meals were prepared by enslaved cooks, and white children were raised by nursemaids whose ancestors had been torn from their African families to create another white world, far away on the other side of the Atlantic Ocean.

Enslaved Kentuckians were highly skilled. They built gracious homes, ornamented public buildings with fine plasterwork, made bricks and pottery, dug canals and manned the steamboats that linked Louisville with New Orleans and the Gulf of Mexico. On surrounding farms they grew food, tobacco, hemp for rope and bagging—thousands of yards of which were used each year to bale Southern cotton—and corn to make the liquor for which Kentucky was justly famous. It was Black men who raised the state's beautiful racehorses, and more often than not it was Black jockeys who rode them to victory.

On October 4, 1831, when she was just five months old,[3] Charles W. and Mary Eliza Thruston purchased Cecelia and her seventeen-year-old mother, Mary, from a local dealer named William Cotton.[4] Cecelia did not remember how they came to live in the quarters behind the Thrustons' house, or the terror of their days spent in the slave trader's pen, but her mother did. Everyone at Louisville knew what it meant when the traders came. Thousands of enslaved Kentuckians were sold south each year to feed King Cotton's insatiable appetite for labour. It had been a great relief to learn they had been purchased by a Louisville family, and one with as good a reputation for the manner in which they treated their enslaved servants as Mary Eliza and Charles W. Thruston had.

Mary had even more reason to be grateful, for the purchase brought together her little family under one roof for the first time.[5] Cecelia's father already belonged to Charles W. Thruston and was a valued worker at his ropewalk and bagging factory. The Thrustons moved to a new home Charles had built on Walnut Street when Cecelia was still a tiny child. The manufacturing operations where Adam Reynolds was employed stood just across the street. Mary and her little girl were lucky that Adam was so good at twisting hemp into everything from fine cordage to steamboat cable.[6] Master Charles's gentle wife had a houseful of children and a baby son, so she needed Mary's help. Cecelia's mother became part of the household staff, and her tiny daughter the petted darling of the servants' quarters. Across Floyd Street, the ropewalk men and boys sang to the rhythm of their work, a pleasant background melody that woke Cecelia each morning and lulled her to sleep for her afternoon nap.[7]

The decision to unite the enslaved Reynolds family was rather out of character for Charles Thruston, who was by no means a benevolent slaveholder. One long-ago Christmas Eve, Charles had witnessed his father's murder at the hands of his own manservant. He was only four at the time, and the experience scarred the man for life. He had no compunction at all about occasionally brokering slaves on behalf of his clients.[8] But Charles Thruston valued both industry and reliable service. He also knew that a married man such as Adam would be a better worker, and far less likely to run away if his wife and little ones were nearby.

Thruston was an attorney but he had many other interests, one of which was the manufacturing enterprise where Adam worked.[9] It was a big operation.[10] Charles W. Thruston and his cousin Alfred went into business together in 1826, and in the year of Cecelia's birth they had advertised to purchase "eighteen or twenty negro boys, from nine to twelve years of age, and six or eight negro men from eighteen to twenty four." They also wanted to hire from other owners several "boys of the above description, for a term of years, say from five to seven for which the highest prices in cash will be given."[11] Thruston bought out his partner in 1833, after which all the slaves belonged to him, including Adam Reynolds.[12]

Cecelia was fortunate that her father was able to live with his wife and daughter. In keeping with most Louisville homes of any size, the slave quarters stood behind the airy, pleasant house in Louisville's fashionable east end. The two-storey ell had galleries overlooking the yard. This along with the property's rear fence provided a semi-enclosed place for doing laundry and other tasks better undertaken outside in the hot Kentucky summers, and it also ensured that Mary Eliza and Charles Thruston could keep their servants under constant surveillance.[13]

While she was little, Cecelia had little realization of her slave status, for she played in the Thrustons' manicured gardens with their own children. But as she grew older the rift between their respective stations became more evident. As soon as she was tall enough to see over the edge of the dining room table, Cecelia began learning how to be a slave. Brushing crumbs from the tablecloth after dinner, sweeping the porch and tidying the drawers in the nursery were all within the capability of even the smallest slave child. Sometimes her mother set her to fanning her mistress on the porch on hot summer days, or turning the spit over the kitchen fire to ensure that the meat cooked evenly.[14]

There was always a great deal to do. Master Charles was anxious about his wife's health, for she had grown ever more frail following the death of her infant son O'Fallon in 1832. Nearly three years later their youngest daughter, only six and named for her mother, was taken from them. So much tragedy had befallen that household. With her older brother, Sam, away at school and mourning the passing of her little sister, nine-year-old Fanny found some consolation in petting and playing with little Cecelia, who at four was the only other child left in the household.

A slight and sensitive girl, and deeply religious, it was Fanny's turn to try to sooth Cecelia's pain when she suffered the most tragic loss of her young life. Cecelia was barely more than a toddler when she learned that there was no safety in this world for an enslaved family. It was not death that shattered the Reynolds family but rather, at least indirectly, a decision made by Fanny's pragmatic father. On January 1, 1837, he arranged a lease–purchase agreement for his ropewalk and bagging factory. The transaction was superbly profitable, for it included the sale of twenty-seven slaves, for each of whom he received $900.[15]

The ropewalk slaves were now the property of the new proprietors. Thruston's decision to divest himself of the manufacturing operation was prescient. A steam-operated ropewalk had just opened in Lexington. It was turning out cordage at a much faster rate than Thruston's enslaved workers could. There was, too, a serious economic downturn. The Panic of 1837 would last through the mid-1840s, and partners Nicholas W. Ford and Henry W. Hawes, greatly overextended, went bankrupt.[16] Cecelia and her weeping mother watched helplessly as Adam Reynolds was sold off to the slave traders along with the rest of the ropewalk's workforce. Unwaged labour was far more valuable in the Deep South, with its long growing season and highly profitable crops of cotton, sugar cane and rice, than it was in cooler Kentucky. Uncounted numbers of Black families were shattered every year when a beloved mother or father, half-grown children or even tiny babies were taken from them. Packed boatloads full of the state's "surplus" slaves were "sold down the river." They regularly departed Louisville on their way to the crowded, raucous, terrifying auction rooms of Natchez-under-the-Hill or New Orleans, at the mouth of the Mississippi, and from there to the huge plantations of the slave South.[17]

So kindly, hard-working Adam Reynolds was lost to his family forever. Shipped down the wide Ohio, past the point where its placid green waters join the muddy Mississippi, at Cairo, Illinois, and on to the slave markets that served the Southern trade, there to be sold to another master. Meanwhile Mary and her small daughter were left behind to grieve the good man they never expected to see again in this life.

Cecelia's mother had just given birth to another child, a little boy named Edward, who never seemed to thrive.[18] Desolate, Mary clung even more closely to her daughter and new baby son, fearing that all she still had of her dear husband might also be taken from her. Fanny did her best to comfort the heartbroken Cecelia in her time of sorrow. Observing the growing closeness between their only remaining daughter and the younger child, Mary Eliza and Charles Thruston decided to start Cecelia's training as Fanny's personal lady's maid. The child's education was a matter not only of convenience but also economy. Fanny's cold-eyed father knew that a well-trained personal servant brought a premium in the marketplace. Young as she was, Cecelia was well aware that slaves were a commodity that could always be liquidated for cash.

Fanny went to school every day, her studies ranging from history and languages to fine needlework and music.[19] At home she also received the other lessons that Southern girls in comfortable financial circumstances required. Her mother and father had every expectation that their dutiful but rather strong-minded daughter would marry one day and be responsible for management of her own home, including its enslaved servants. Accordingly, Fanny began overseeing Cecelia's performance in tasks assigned to her. At the same time little Cecelia, just nine years of age, was taught to address her former playmate as Miss Fanny and refer to her as the "young mistress" rather than calling her by her first name.[20] If she forgot herself, there was always the switch to remind her, for corporal punishment was an ever-present fact of life for enslaved children like Cecelia.

Fanny also taught Cecelia to read, but heeding the caution of her parents, she did not show the younger girl how to hold a quill or form her letters. Although teaching slaves to write was not illegal in Kentucky, each was required to carry a written pass signed by his or her master or mistress when away from home. Instructing Cecelia in basic literacy was bad enough—newspapers and books gave slaves ideas—but writing was dangerous; literate slaves sometimes wrote out their own passes and disappeared altogether.[21]

Both girls had a great deal to learn. Under the tutelage of Mrs. Thruston's maid, Cecelia was taught to dress Fanny's hair in the latest styles, to care for her person and her wardrobe, and to keep her bedroom clean and tidy. It was her special duty to dress her young mistress each day and again before dinner. At night she laid out Fanny's nightclothes and helped her take off her gown, petticoats and stays, sharing with her the small pleasures and problems that had marked their days while brushing out her long hair. Cecelia slept in the dressing room in case she was needed during the night. If Fanny were out for the evening, she was expected to then wake at whatever the hour to help her young mistress to bed and then to brush and put away her finery.[22]

A high point for both girls came when Fanny Thruston, almost fourteen, was chosen Louisville's Queen of the May in 1840 and presided over parties and entertainments as well as the annual parade through the city streets. In honour of the occasion her parents gave their daughter a very valuable gift: legal ownership of her nine-year-old maidservant.[23] Cecelia, who was very fond of Fanny, was from that day forward also her personal property. Her training and her comportment, her discipline and her well-being were entirely Fanny's responsibility. This also meant that Cecelia would henceforth accompany her young mistress whenever she travelled, charged with packing and caring for her extensive wardrobe, whether it be a journey of several months' duration or a simple overnight stay at the home of one of her many relations.

Soon Cecelia learned to move among the quarters of Kentucky's slaveholding households. The Thruston relatives' names read like a *Who's Who* of the opening of the American West. Charles's grandfather had been the fabled "Fighting Preacher" of the Revolution, and his mother, Fanny's namesake Frances Eleanor Clark, "the great black-eyed beauty of the West."[24] His uncles included General George Rogers Clark, who planted the first crops on Corn Island in 1778 to found Louisville and led the defence of the western frontier during the Revolution. Two aunts had married into the Croghan and Anderson families, both of whose members gave distinguished service in the Revolutionary War and later the War of 1812. Charles's youngest uncle was William Clark, who had been dispatched by President Thomas Jefferson in 1803, along with his friend Meriwether Lewis, on a "voyage of discovery to the Pacific." Fanny's father had been at the wharf to greet the Lewis and Clark expedition when the two explorers returned to Locust Grove, the Croghan plantation on the river east of Louisville, on November 8, 1806, and again in 1819 when President James Monroe came to call.[25]

Cecelia knew that Miss Fanny was equally well connected on her mother's side. Both girls spent much time with Fanny's Churchill relations, both in Louisville at the lovely estate of Spring Grove, to the south and east of the town proper, and in St. Louis. Her great-grandfather was Armistead Churchill, who in 1787 sent his slaves on ahead from Virginia's Fauquier County to build a house for his family, and then famously drove a coach and four along the Wilderness Road from Virginia to Kentucky. Fanny's maternal grandfather, Samuel Churchill, built Spring Grove on the southeastern outskirts of the city shortly after he married Abigail Oldham, daughter of

Kentucky pioneer Colonel William Oldham, in 1803.[26] Abigail was just fourteen when they wed and produced sixteen surviving children, so Sam and Fanny Thruston had uncles and aunts younger than they were. The Churchill home was as famous for its society as it was for its fine horseflesh.[27]

Now nineteen, Fanny Thruston was coming into the fine good looks that would be her hallmark for the rest of her life. She was small, with gently sloping shoulders and a tiny waist. Her light brown hair framed an oval face with dark, haunting eyes and strongly marked brows. Although pale, she had a pretty blush that intrigued countless would-be beaux. Cecelia's young mistress was a graceful dancer and very musical, providing many an evening's entertainment as she played the pianoforte and sang the popular music of the day. Fanny's indulgent parents were sufficiently wealthy that she could dress in the latest styles. With her demure, charming manner that belied a keen intellect and determined will, Frances Ann Thruston moved easily in the highest levels of Louisville society.

Cecelia Jane Reynolds provided both foil and contrast to Miss Fanny. She too was petite, and in her early teens she was growing into the quiet beauty that would stay with her all her days. She was as dark as Fanny was fair, with smooth skin emblematic of her nearly pure African heritage. She was always careful of her appearance, and her dress was stylish, if a trifle outdated; like most personal servants in her position, she was heir to her young mistress's cast-off clothing. With the bows and rosettes removed and lacking the lace collars that embellished Fanny's gowns, her plainer dresses were easily made over to suit both Cecelia's figure and her place in the household. The younger girl was well-mannered, spoke grammatically, and was both tidy in her person and very clever. Indeed, the Thrustons placed much trust in Fanny's Cecelia, knowing her to be an excellent servant and a pleasant and ever-helpful companion to their daughter.[28]

Cecelia accompanied Fanny on family trips beginning when both girls were still quite young. It was for the sake of Missus Mary Eliza's health that they first travelled with her family to the spectacular Mammoth Cave.

Located on the Green River to the southwest of Louisville, in rural Edmonson County, it had more than three hundred miles of caverns and was one of the natural wonders of nineteenth century America. Both the cave system and the rustic Mammoth Cave Hotel belonged to the Thrustons' cousin, Dr. John Croghan. He had developed both the resort and a tuberculosis sanatorium, with huts built right inside the cave for people, like Fanny's mother, who were afflicted with "consumption."[29]

At Mammoth Cave, Fanny and her intrepid older brother, Sam, explored the vast cavern system and marvelled at the blind fish and other exotic creatures that flourished there in total darkness. Passing her own precious leisure moments in the company of the resort's many enslaved servants, Cecelia became a great favourite of two of the slave guides, a man known only as Alfred and the much-admired Stephen Bishop, who led the workers at Mammoth Cave in both knowledge and popularity. She was amused by Stephen Bishop's costume of brown slouch hat and striped trousers, but he had an air of authority; and when leading groups of tourists through the caverns, his word was law. Bishop had ventured further into the caves than any other person living, and it was he who had given most of its spectacular stalactite and stalagmite formations their fanciful names. It seemed impossible that so accomplished a man had not been granted his freedom. Self-taught, he knew some Latin and Greek and could speak credibly on scientific matters. Indeed, he was the escort of choice for European scientists, who found both the cave and its valuable guide fascinating.[30]

Mrs. Thruston had not improved in the dry, chill air of the caves, and Charles brought his adored wife home to die. There was some anxiety about Fanny's health as well, so after the funeral her father sent his son back to school and packed off his daughter and her maid to live in the country with her Churchill relatives. It was a lively household, for her relations had intermarried with Louisville's first families and with those of St. Louis, Missouri, as well, so there was much visiting between the two cities. Cecelia, of course, went along to help Fanny with her toilette. Fanny's Aunt Belle, who was three years her junior and more sister than friend to Cecelia's mistress, had a maid of her own. Sarah became a special friend to Cecelia, and it was she who put the finishing touches on her training.[31]

Fanny and Cecelia ventured further afield as well. In the fall of 1845, Mr. Thruston had entrusted his precious daughter to the care of his cousin Ann, Dr. Croghan's sister. She and her children were returning to Washington, DC, to rejoin her husband, Major General Thomas Sidney Jesup, who was Quartermaster General of the US Army, after a long sojourn at the Croghan family home, Locust Grove.[32] The occasion for the visit was to be the January 14, 1846, society wedding of Ann and Thomas Jesup's daughter, Mary Serena Eliza, to career naval officer James Blair, who was one of Washington's more eligible bachelors.[33] The decision to take Cecelia along was a fateful one, for this journey would be the catalyst for making the girl decide she was done with slavery forever.

The Jesups occupied an elegantly furnished terrace house on the south side of F Street, between 12th and 13th Streets, just three blocks east of the White House. It was said of General Jesup that "Socially his home was the most delightful in Washington, and his charming, warm-hearted hospitality was extended to both resident friends and strangers visiting the Capital."[34]

Now fourteen years old, Cecelia was kept very occupied. The Jesups had four daughters, who all needed help dressing their hair in the latest styles and ornamenting hats, gowns and dainty slippers with beads, flowers and other frippery. Her own mistress was enjoying the many entertainments and social events, each requiring her maid to prepare a fresh costume, complete with accessories. The weeks flew by in an endless round of parties and balls, musical afternoons and edifying tours of landmarks in the national capital. Moving between the Jesup and Blair homes and attending the gracious New England–style "Church of the Presidents"—St. John's Episcopal on Lafayette Square—with Fanny, Cecelia caught glimpses of many of the notables of the day.[35] Among them were Henry Clay, author of the Missouri Compromise that limited the spread of slavery in the western states; the great orator

Daniel Webster of Massachusetts; Dolly Madison with her yellow house on the square; and even President and Mrs. Polk, who were distant relatives of Fanny's father, although Mrs. Polk was a disapproving Presbyterian who usually worshipped elsewhere. With a growing awareness of her own enslaved condition, Cecelia knew also that the penny-pinching First Lady had replaced household servants at the White House with slaves and made over the basements of the presidential mansion as their quarters.[36]

While serving in the Jesup household, Cecelia Jane Reynolds came to know servants belonging to some of the neighbouring families. Behind the three- and four-storey federal-style homes lining Washington's streets, she discovered a vibrant alley life where the free and enslaved mingled. Louisville had a small community of free African Americans too, but Washington's was larger, more prosperous and sophisticated, although as Cecelia learned, only ten short years before there had been an anti-Black riot that had destroyed many businesses and burnt the Colored Orphanage to the ground. There were bold market ladies calling their wares, skilled seamstresses catering to the wives of congressmen and senators, and fine restaurants run by Black men where only white diners could partake of the fare.[37]

In the national capital the impressionable young Cecelia was also exposed to a side of Black life that shocked more hardened visitors to Washington than she. This city on the Potomac was one of the great slave markets of the eastern seaboard.[38] Visitors were stunned to observe on the streets of the nation's capital long, miserable coffles of chained men, tearful women and children following behind.[39] Ten years before Cecelia's visit, Vermont's William Slade protested to the Speaker of the House: "Sir, shall this trade in human flesh be permitted to continue in the very heart of this Republic? . . . Is merchandise to be made of men, within sight of the Capitol in which their Representatives are assembled, and on whose summit wave the stripes and the stars of freedom?"[40]

In Washington thousands of slaves were taken each year from home and family and jailed in the city's several slave pens. From there they went to the dockyards to be loaded on steamboats and coastal schooners to be carried south. It all brought back most graphically the day that Cecelia's father, Adam, had been sold away to the traders when she was just a little girl.

For Fanny her Washington visit was a heady and magical experience for a teenager on the brink of womanhood, but finally Charles called his daughter and her maid back to Kentucky. He was protective of his precious girl and had no intention of seeing her married off to a suitor in so distant a location, however ardent his attentions or advantageous the match. But for Cecelia, her time in Washington had quite a different effect. It ignited a loathing of her enslaved condition that only liberty could quench.

CHAPTER 2
That Bright and Shining Land

At that place of resort [Niagara], we stopped to view the stupendous work of Almighty God, and listen to the ceaseless thundering of the cataract. How tame appear the works of art, and how insignificant the bearing of proud, puny man, compared with the awful grandeur of that natural curiosity. Yet there, the rich from all parts of the world, do congregate! There you will find the idle, swaggering slaveholder, blustering about in lordly style; boasting of his wealth; betting and gambling; ready to fight, if his slightest wish is not granted, and lavishing his cash on all who have the least claim upon him. . . . While the wretched slave marches South with a gang, under the lash, he lavishes his funds in extravagant living,—funds gathered from the tears and blood of a helpless human being.

—Austin Steward, 1857[1]

WHETHER IT WAS THE sight of coffles of miserable people in the very shadow of the Capitol Building, or recollection of the last sight of her father being carted off to the auction rooms by dealers in human flesh, Cecelia had known enough of slavery to last a lifetime. Over the course of the next several months, that clever, courageous young woman laid the groundwork for her own escape. Exactly how she did so is lost to history, but she had the benefit of expert help, most likely from Washington Spradling, a free African American barber in Louisville. Her escape plan suggests there was a communications network stretching across the Ohio River and all the way to the borders of Canada, a "grapevine telegraph" operated by African American men and women who worked on the rivers, lakes and canals that made up the continent's inland waterways, and, as railroads progressively made their way across the continent, by those who stoked the engines and served the passengers on the trains as well.

Harbouring and assisting fugitives carried stiff penalties under both federal and state law. Underground Railroad conductors operating below the Mason-Dixon Line took the perilous secrets of routes and contacts to their graves, but in Kentucky cities and towns bordering the Ohio River there were always a few brave souls willing to help people "make free."

Cecelia already knew that it was not enough to simply cross over into a nominally free state. The southern sections of Indiana and Ohio had residents with Southern roots who might be more inclined to capture runaways for the bounty they brought than to help them get away. A secret system had evolved to take people further on up the line, out of reach of the coarse and avaricious slave-catchers who made their living roaming the borders of the slave South, capturing escaping bondsmen and women on behalf of their owners.[2] Nearly all the men and women who staffed the packet boats that carried mail, passengers and cargo between the Ohio River ports linking Louisville with Cincinnati and other northern cities were Black, and some conspired with sympathetic Kentuckians to assist people on their way north. Such vessels came back from northern places sometimes bearing with them abolitionist publications and even abolitionists themselves, who dared the perilous journey into the American South to spread the word that, as one song said, "in Canada, coloured men are free." Enslaved firemen who fuelled the steamboats; the waiters, chambermaids and porters who served their passengers; and longshoremen who loaded and unloaded cargo at the wharves whispered messages of freedom, and the slave grapevine carried the vital information far and wide.[3]

Charles W. Thruston was well aware that such a network existed. As early as 1830 he and his business partners[4] placed a runaway-slave notice in newspapers from Kentucky to Detroit. A ropewalk slave named Andrew Jones had fled, taking his wife and four children with him. The fugitive-slave notice gives details of their appearance and says that they "will probably endeavor to reach Canada," even suggesting the means by which the escape might have been facilitated: "There can be little doubt that they have forged free papers in their possession." A substantial reward of $100 was offered if the Jones family was taken in Kentucky, and $300 if recovered out of state.[5]

They were never recovered. Charles knew that his slaves had somehow acquired both means and opportunity to travel four hundred miles with the very colour of their skin flagging them as runaways, and with four small children in tow.[6] Those forged manumission papers had been supplied by someone, perhaps a free Black, who was able to read and write and willing to flout the fines and possible imprisonment in order to do so. Then word had been sent on from station to station that the family was on its way, and that they would need both shelter and assistance. (Unbeknownst to their former owners, Andrew and his family reached Canada West and settled at Windsor, on the Detroit River, where he became a prosperous farmer.)

Dozens, perhaps hundreds of Kentucky slave escapes followed a similar pattern. Cecelia's would have too, except for one fortuitous event: early in 1846, not long after Fanny and Cecelia's return from their stay in the Jesup home, Charles W. Thruston decided to take his family to Niagara Falls for their summer holiday. The sudden death of their Washington hostess, Ann Croghan Jesup, on April 10, upset Fanny very much and President Polk was about to declare war on Mexico, which meant that the impetuous Sam was itching to enlist. It seemed an excellent time for an extended journey to one of the most popular resorts on the continent. Cecelia's unnamed benefactors rejoiced, for this made arranging her flight much easier. The Thruston family's destination was the Cataract House hotel. Right across the Niagara River lay the free soil of Canada West.

More than forty thousand visitors a year flocked to Niagara Falls, which was hugely popular as one of the wonders of the North American Grand Tour. Many were well-to-do Southerners seeking to escape the heat and danger of epidemic illness that marred the warmest summer months at home.[7] At Niagara, Sam, now twenty-one and about to choose a career, and Fanny, not quite twenty, could pass their days expanding their social circle and indulging in healthful exercise against a backdrop of the most revered of all America's natural wonders. But for Cecelia the trip presented a perfect opportunity to shed the chains of her own bondage, and one not likely to come again.

Underground Railroad operators in Louisville passed word to their Canadian counterparts that the girl would be arriving at Niagara Falls in mid-May and needed their help to make her escape.[8] How the communication was effected remains a mystery, but the crux of the endeavour hinged on the courage of one man. Residing for the season on the British-owned side of the Falls, his name was Benjamin Pollard Holmes, and he was to play a very large part in Cecelia's life from that point forward.

The Thrustons had reservations at the enormous and very luxurious Cataract House hotel, which stood high over the upper rapids above the Falls.[9] The *New Orleans Times-Picayune* of August 4, 1841, warned that the Black servants of Niagara hotels were known for "abducting" enslaved men and women brought along to wait on their Southern masters and mistresses. Further, it accused the Cataract's proprietors, the "Messrs. Whitney," of being complicit in helping them escape. The *Boston Post* of August 16, 1841, took an accusatory tone: "The proprietors of the 'Cataract House' keep in their employ, as servants, a set of *free negroes* [who] have an organized plan of taking off all slaves that come to the house."

Whether or not the Whitneys themselves were actively helping slaves escape, it was certainly true that a good many enslaved African Americans who "saw Niagara" decided they might like the view of the Falls better from the other side. It was surprising, in such circumstances, that Southern tourists still insisted on carrying their servants with them to the brink of the

Niagara River, but they did it all the time, unable to imagine a circumstance without Black hands to fold their clothes or to ready them for bed after an evening's entertainment.

Fanny fussed over which of her gowns might be most suitable to pack; and Sam excitedly discussed potential battle strategies for America's coming war with Mexico, and their relatives Meriwether Lewis Clark and Thomas J. Churchill's plans to enlist. Meanwhile, Cecelia bided her time and gathered her courage for the coming ordeal. Finally the trunks were loaded and the carriage ready for the short trip to the steamboat docks. It must have been hard for a girl so young to bid farewell to the ailing younger brother she might never see again, or to know that her mother's fond farewell embrace might be her last. Did Cecelia look back one last time at the Thruston mansion on gracious, tree-lined Walnut Street, its slave quarters the only home she had ever known, and grieve to think she would never see it again?

WHILE THE THRUSTONS MADE their long journey by steamboat and then either rail or canal boat to the southern shore of Lake Ontario, in faraway Canada the pieces of the plot to free Cecelia were falling into place.

First Benjamin Holmes checked into the Cataract House.[10] His appearance on the American side of the river was risky, for Benjamin was a fugitive who had made his way to Canada only a few years earlier. A light-skinned Black man who spoke with the refined accent of the Virginia gentry, he was a dining room waiter on the *City of Toronto*, one of several steamboats that plied the waters between Toronto and the Niagara district. Benjamin wrote his name in the hotel register on April 16, 1846. He gave his address as Niagara, about twelve miles south of the Falls on the Canadian side.[11]

Benjamin had crossed the river in order to arrange for Cecelia's rescue with the hotel's nearly entirely African American staff. The main question was how and when to spirit a young woman, whom none of them had ever seen, away from her owners once she and the Thrustons arrived. Their plans had to remain undetected, and Cecelia's absence undiscovered, long enough for someone to ferry her to safety.[12]

No sooner had Benjamin Holmes departed to resume his duties aboard ship than his employer, Captain Thomas Dick of the *City of Toronto*, arrived at the hotel. In common with most officers of Canadian steamers, Dick was sympathetic to the cause of the fugitive slave and regularly conveyed them from American ports to Canadian ones at reduced fares, or no fare at all. He wrote his name in the hotel ledger on May 6.[13]

Then, on May 14, 1846, Fanny's father signed the register: "C. W. Thruston, son, daughter and servant, Louisville, Ky." Coincidentally (or perhaps not), among the hotel guests was another native Scot, the publisher of Toronto's *Globe* newspaper, George Brown, who along with his father and brother was one of the most vociferous and committed abolitionists in Canada West.

If it had been Charles W. Thruston's intent to keep his impetuous son out of harm's way by taking him to Niagara, then he was successful.[14] The Thrustons arrived at the Falls one day after President Polk's declaration of war on Mexico was ratified. Fortunately there was much to distract the young man. The Cataract was one of the finest hotels in all the northern states. By 1846 it could already accommodate some two hundred guests. Among those staying at the hotel were people from all parts of the United States and Canada, as well as several European families. It boasted the very best appointments and the most modern facilities:

> The old parlor of the Cataract Hotel, as it originally stood, was a room of French colonial design, elegant and grand in treatment. It was a very long room, having ten or twelve windows on each side. From the high ceiling hung two elaborate chandeliers, literally small forests of candles from which peeped cupids and shepherdesses of gilt and wrought iron. Flanking the doors at the center of each end of the room and opposite to each other, midway of the long walls, were enormous plate glass mirrors on marble bases,

having curved gilt legs. The frames were also of gilt, climaxing in a burst of gilt flowers and vines in high relief. Curved gilt chairs upholstered in damask lined the walls; a cream colored carpet of deep plush with a rose border covered the floor.[15]

After they settled into their rooms, Fanny, Sam and their father joined in the round of activities that made life at Niagara so pleasant.[16] British visitor Isabella Bird called Niagara an "abode of almost unparalleled gaiety."[17] Parties of languid Southern gentlemen and their beautifully dressed belles mingled with brash northerners, with confident Canadians who told all who would listen that the Falls were more beautiful from the *other* side of the river, and with distant English travellers with perfect manners and barely concealed contempt for the visitors who brought along their Black "servants" to meet their every whim. The service was superb, although it came at a price. As a reporter complained, "Niagara is an expensive place. The coloured gentleman who does you a trifling service receives a shilling (and nothing less) not because he has earned it but because he is at Niagara!"[18]

Sam Thruston and his sister delighted in the social life they found at the Cataract House. They breakfasted late in the elegant dining rooms of the hotel, chatted with acquaintances in the parlour or out on the terrace overlooking the Falls, and promenaded on the broad piazza. All this was in addition to visiting the Whirlpool, exploring the many souvenir shops and Native American handicraft stalls, and taking in the views of the Niagara River and its world-famous waterfall from multiple vantage points.[19]

Meanwhile, Cecelia was kept busy unpacking huge steamer trunks that were filled to overflowing with her mistress's extensive wardrobe. Fanny's luggage included gowns for day, evening and travel, plus shawls and cloaks, the requisite petticoats and everything else that went underneath, as well as modest nightwear appropriate for a budding belle. Each item had to be brushed, pressed and put away. Cecelia was expected to pass her evenings washing and ironing the finer fabrics and laces that trimmed her mistress's attire, and mending Fanny's clothing and perhaps that of Sam and Charles Thruston as well, as neither had brought along a valet. At Niagara, guests changed their clothing several times a day, the better to enjoy tea dances, supper parties and elegant evening entertainments. Even Cecelia would have had new things, ordered especially for the visit, and her own trunk to carry them in, for it reflected well on Master Charles if his daughter's slave presented a respectable appearance.[20]

Meals at the Cataract House were a special treat. The year before the Thrustons came to Niagara, the dinner parade—managed with efficiency and a fine sense of the theatrical by headwaiter John Morrison—was described in *Godey's Lady's Book*, a women's magazine:

> The waiters were very numerous, and of every shade of what, in their case, is denominated *colour;* black, brown, and yellow; and one or two were copper-tinted and Indian-featured. They were all dressed alike, in clean white jackets and trowsers; but their style of hair displayed a pleasing variety. It was amusing to see the manner in which this troop of well-drilled domestics brought in the dessert . . . At a signal from the major-domo (who was stationed at the upper end of the room between the tables), the waiters took up the line of march in Indian file, and proceeded round with military precision, military step, and military faces. They were armed with japan trays or servers; each holding a different article. . . . In this manner the whole dessert was placed on the tables in a very few minutes, and in the most complete order.[21]

The guests were, of course, utterly oblivious to the fact that the same John Morrison who ran the hotel dining room with such military precision was also the ringleader of Underground Railroad operations at Niagara Falls. In the off-season he resided in Rochester, New York, but his parents lived on the Canadian side of the Niagara River, in the "Coloured Village" at Lundy's Lane, a War of 1812 battle site three miles from the border.[22] It would be up to Morrison and his serving staff to help Cecelia cross Niagara's turbulent waters when the time was right.

Rescuing Cecelia was not a simple matter, for the Thrustons were well aware that taking an enslaved maidservant to the very borders of Canada was putting the girl within reach of temptation. She slept either in her young mistress's dressing room or on a pallet on the floor of her bedroom. Daytime was easier, for it was customary for Southern women to take their lady's maids along to see at least some of the sights. Fanny and Cecelia explored the footpaths of rustic Goat Island, from which the view of both the American and Canadian Falls was spectacular. One British tourist wrote: "One can sit here and think over the wonders of the place. The lofty trees of Goat Island, and the beautiful basket-like groups of shrubs which interrupt the dash of the rapids and vary its scenery, are very charming; and then one watches the water rushing to its fearful leap, observes portions of the Falls and hears all its wild tornado." It was also a popular picnic spot, and hotel servants were willing to pack wicker baskets with cold chicken, calf's foot jelly and other delicacies.[23]

The exact date of Cecelia's escape is not known, but it may well have come when Charles took his family across to the opposite, British-Canadian side of the river.[24] Most American tourists had a patriotic interest in the battlefields of the War of 1812, in the Thrustons' case particularly the Battle of Chippewa, where Major General Thomas Jesup had been wounded.[25] To get there involved taking a gallant little boat, the *Maid of the Mist*. The Thrustons had arrived just in time for her maiden voyage, on May 23, 1846.[26] The plucky ferryboat was a small but powerful steamer that passed very close to the foot of the Falls. Special weatherproof clothing was provided, and travellers remarked that the very best views were to be had from *Maid of the Mist* while in the very middle of the river. Although the passage was notoriously rough, passengers invariably landed safely. From water's edge a steep staircase wound its way to the top of the gorge, where hack drivers and coachmen jockeyed in shrill voices for the attention of new arrivals. If Charles treated his son and daughter to an overnight stay, it would have been at Clifton House, by far the best hotel on the Canadian shore, with an unequalled view of all three sections of the waterfall before it.[27]

Fanny Thruston had grown up with a beloved mother whose Episcopal faith ran deep. Her perceptions of mighty Niagara Falls were therefore coloured by her religious views. According to German-born Francis Lieber, who visited in 1834, some people were "affected in the presence of the noble aspect of Niagara, more deeply with the sensation of the power of God than they ever were in their lives before."[28] But for Cecelia the great Falls meant something quite different. One Black minister residing in Canada considered Niagara's famous rainbows a sign of God's promise to the enslaved:

> The chains seem to hang more loosely round the bondsman's limb, and through the tears of his captivity he may see the colours of the rainbow of a distant hope. That Iris shall show its colours yet more plainly, and its bow shall span the sky with bolder arch, if the supplications of the Christian church are poured forth in earnest. There's many a pious captive lifting the voice of prayer out of the hell of slavery—and just as the rainbow glows upon the spray of the Niagara, as it rises like a breath out of the abyss, so shall its hopeful tint be flung upon the incense of his prayer, as it flows out of the dark gulf of his enthralment.[29]

One day the Thrustons returned to the Cataract House only to find that Cecelia had vanished. At first Fanny feared for the young girl's safety. Cecelia was very pretty and there were plenty of wild lands around Niagara; the resort attracted its share of rough men as well as refined vacationers. Fanny's phlegmatic father may have had another opinion of Cecelia's possible whereabouts, but if so, he and his son did not immediately share it with his distressed and rather annoyed daughter. Instead, Fanny, Sam and Charles searched everywhere.

Well known at their place of accommodation after so long a stay, father and daughter inquired of every waiter at the Cataract House and questioned every chambermaid. Fanny queried sympathetic acquaintances in the dining room while her father, one of Louisville's most prominent lawyers and well versed in the arts of interrogation, badgered the personal servants of other hotel guests. Sam checked with coachmen and cabbies, tour guides and the Native Americans who sold handicrafts outside the hotel. As the hours passed and Cecelia's location could not be discovered, everyone but the incredulous Fanny became convinced that her young maid had crossed the river.

If Fanny was by turns irritated and anxious about Cecelia's defection, Charles W. Thruston was quite plainly furious. Whatever his daughter's regard for Cecelia, she was worth a considerable amount of money and he meant to recover her. Then he'd "put her in his pocket," as the saying went, and send his daughter's wayward maid down the Mississippi to the auction rooms at New Orleans. There, Charles knew, Cecelia's fresh beauty and refined manner would attract a purchaser with very specific plans for the woman he had gone there to buy.

Charles conferred with Sam, thinking long and hard about how to retrieve runaway Cecelia from her Canadian haven. Her new friends had hidden her well. Whether she was concealed in the small town of Niagara or further north at St. Catharines, or had even been put on a steamboat and sent off to Hamilton or distant Toronto, they could not ascertain.

From his own experience chasing runaways, the canny lawyer Charles knew it was almost impossible to retrieve one from British Canada by any legal method, even for someone armed, as he was, with ironclad proof of his ownership. Likewise, overt attempts to have refugees extradited on trumped-up criminal charges had been continually rebuffed by a long series of abolition-minded lieutenant-governors of the colony, and their political masters in London held similar views. Queen Victoria's government had abolished slavery throughout the Empire, and Emancipation Day was celebrated in the Canadian colony starting on August 1, 1834. British North America had no slaves and acknowledged none. No, unless Cecelia could somehow be induced to return, Fanny had lost her maid and Charles his investment.

Although her concerned father considered her delicate, Fanny was made of sterner stuff than he knew. She was very worried. She knew how clever and determined Cecelia could be, but she was still only fifteen years old and had been carefully raised in the protective atmosphere of a well-off Louisville household. Her young mistress feared Cecelia ill-suited for life in the wilds of Canada. No friends or family members that Fanny knew of awaited her there. She resolved to set aside her own anger and hurt and do her best to provide her childhood friend with what help she could.

A Southern woman through and through and the pampered daughter of the Thruston household, Fanny was still a granddaughter of Kentucky's first hardy settlers. It was now that she proved her mettle. Fanny made her own inquiries and eventually located a man who admitted to knowing where Cecelia might be found. But he would not give Fanny the address, on the grounds that Charles or Sam Thruston might dispatch bounty hunters to bring her back. Instead he promised to take Cecelia Jane's clothing to the missing maidservant. That way no secrets would be breached but Cecelia would receive her possessions, and Fanny could at least be comforted in the knowledge that the younger woman was provided for.

Hopeful for the first time in many hours, Fanny Thruston packed up Cecelia's clothing, her handkerchiefs and her few ornaments. Carefully tucked between the folds was sufficient money to help her former maid start off her new life in some comfort.[30] She entrusted Cecelia's travel trunk to her new-found acquaintance and the unnamed man vowed faithfully to deliver it to Fanny's missing servant. The box would never reach its destination. It would be years before Fanny learned what had become of Cecelia.

CHAPTER 3
Chilly Waters in the Jordan

DEAR BROTHER GOODELL,—A colored friend of mine has just called at my door, with a pleasing smile upon his brow, to introduce me to five immortal beings, just escaped from the land of oppression [including] Mr. and Mrs. Holmes and their infant son, 16 months old . . . Bro. Holmes and his wife are members of the Methodist Episcopal Church, and I doubt not are sincere and devoted Christians. He is an exhorter, quite intelligent, can read and write well. He will make a useful laborer in the field. May the Lord bless him. It is enough to melt the heart of even a colonizationist to see his joyful countenance in this land of the free, and hear him give thanks to God, and speak of his mysterious and merciful deliverance.

—Fraternally Thine, HIRAM WILSON[1]

ONCE SAFELY ACROSS THE river, Cecelia was hidden away in a series of private houses. African Canadians all, her hosts provided her with both safety and support, sharing with their nervous young guest their own food and clothing and soothing her fears as best they could. Finally Benjamin called for her and under cover of night smuggled her aboard the *City of Toronto* for the journey to the city that would be her new home as a free woman. Although Captain Dick pretended he didn't know what his dining room waiter was up to, Cecelia soon realized that her escape was part of a smoothly run routine, the result of long practice by both Benjamin and his Scottish-born employer.

As much to conceal the means of her flight as to keep her safe from discovery, Cecelia had to remain below decks until the steamer cleared port at Lewiston. Between shifts in the steamboat dining room, Benjamin visited his young guest and told her stories to while away the time and also to reassure the girl that she was no longer at risk. She learned that it had been Upper Canada's first lieutenant-governor, a veteran of the British forces in the Revolutionary War, who guaranteed the freedom she had risked so much to attain. John Graves Simcoe hated slavery and in 1793 had tried to abolish the practice in his very first parliament, but he had been stymied by slaveholders in his own executive council. The tide turned, however, when a loyal Black veteran living in British Queenston witnessed the impassioned struggles of a slave woman named Chloe Cooley being taken in a small boat, bound and gagged, across the Niagara River to upstate New York to be sold.[2]

Reporting what he had observed to Simcoe and members of his council, the outraged Peter Martin brought a white soldier along to confirm his story. The lieutenant-governor ordered Attorney General John White to devise a means for ending slavery in the new colony. Finally it was decided that enslaved Canadians would be liberated over time, with children freed at the age of twenty-five and their children considered free from birth. Although no existing slaves gained their freedom from Simcoe's Act, within a few short years most Canadian slave-owners had begun paying them wages. The brave service of hundreds of African Canadian men who enlisted in the War of 1812 to repel the American invasion rang the death knell for human bondage in Upper Canada. Simcoe's was the first law passed against slavery in all of the Empire, and it was confirmed by the British Abolition Act in 1833. Going into effect in 1834, it abolished the practice in all the lands ruled by Queen Victoria.[3]

Then Benjamin recounted for Cecelia the astonishing tale of his own flight to freedom.

AT NORFOLK, VIRGINIA, the day had dawned bright and fair. On August 3, 1840, the *Saluda* was to sail with the tide, a hopeful band of twenty-three emigrants aboard bound for Monrovia, the capital of Liberia. Among the company and looking forward to a new life on the West African coast was a young woman named Ann Eliza, her husband, Benjamin Pollard Holmes, and their infant son.[4]

The papers they carried, which attested to their very recent manumission, described Ann Eliza as twenty-two years old, "a mulatto about five feet one inch high, of good appearance, and rather spare than otherwise." Her husband was "a bright mulatto, aged about twenty-five years . . . five feet seven inches high, spare made, and of genteel appearance, [who] has no scars or marks of importance." Their little boy, Benjamin Alexander Holmes, was sixteen months old. The child's light complexion demonstrated the mixed ancestry of both parents.[5] Despite conflicting reports about the dangers they might encounter once they reached their destination, Benjamin and his wife were setting sail with joy in their hearts. Why, even the name of their new homeland spoke to them of freedom—Liberia, the land of the free.

For the young man and his little family it had been a long road to where they stood that day. Benjamin Pollard Holmes had spent his childhood at King and Queen County Courthouse, Virginia, a hamlet some fifty miles north and east of the state capital, Richmond.[6] His father was Robert Pollard, the widowed county clerk, and his mother was Pollard's enslaved housekeeper, whom Pollard had inherited from his grandmother's family. Her name was Katie Hoomes, or "Holmes," as Benjamin preferred it. Katie had an older daughter, Winnay, who had been hired away to a Caroline County farm, but Katie and her children were all educated and kept up a lively and detailed correspondence among themselves.[7]

When Benjamin was fifteen, his father's health began to fail. Robert Pollard sent the lad about twenty miles away to serve at Melville, which was the home of Benjamin's white half-sister Elizabeth (Betsey) and her second husband, a very religious Baptist planter by the name of Alexander Fleet. Fleet came from a family of considerable local prominence.[8] He was a graduate of William and Mary College, active in state politics, benevolent organizations, temperance and particularly the Sunday School movement to further the work of religious and secular education.[9] Fleet was also a committed slaveholder who routinely hired out "his people" and pursued runaways with single-minded determination. By law Alexander Fleet controlled Betsey's considerable inheritance from her first husband,[10] as well as what she would receive from her father.[11]

Benjamin had just turned eighteen when Nat Turner's slave rebellion sent terror through the Virginia countryside. Turner was a literate man and a gifted preacher whose visions indicated it was time for slaves to rise up against their masters. On August 21, 1831, he led his followers in an attack on slaveholder farms and homes that left more than fifty whites dead, a number of them children. There was little that Virginia plantation owners feared more than slave revolt, and most of the conspirators were quickly arrested. Turner eluded capture for two months but was finally caught. Before he and some of the others were executed, Nat Turner dictated his "confessions" to a local white attorney, who later published them. Such was the hysteria that gripped the South that even after Turner's death, hundreds of innocent men and women as far away as the Carolinas were tortured and killed on suspicion of being privy to the plot.[12]

Like Nat Turner, Benjamin was educated, and he was an ardent and eloquent convert to evangelical Methodism, both of which qualities might well put him under suspicion as a conspirator in the Turner revolt, so the Fleets hired out the teenager to a Richmond merchant. James T. Fisher Jr. had forty men and boys at work in his factory, which produced his excellent Orinoko brand of tobacco. He lived with his wife and eight family servants in a large brick house on the brow of Church Hill, its rich furnishings attesting to his business acumen.[13] The Fishers were devout Episcopalians and attended the nearby Church of St. John, where Patrick Henry had delivered his famous words "Give me liberty or give me death," an irony likely not lost on young Benjamin as he moved his belongings into the slave quarters behind the Fisher home. Its porches afforded him a magnificent view of the James River, the Kanawha Canal and, in the far distance and as a reminder of his own condition, the city's slave pens in low-lying Shockoe Bottom.[14] Richmond, like Washington, was a major transhipment centre for human merchandise. Every year uncounted numbers of people were sent off to Southern markets to meet King Cotton's insatiable demand for labour.[15]

The Nat Turner Rebellion did not threaten Richmond directly, but the fear it engendered inspired the Virginia General Assembly to consider doing away with slavery altogether. But slaves were valuable, and so the rising tide of Northern abolitionism was blamed instead for their discontent. These years were a watershed in Northern antislavery, and sailors coming through Virginian ports passed secretly from hand to hand tattered copies of David Walker's *Appeal to the Coloured Citizens of the World*. Published in 1829, it called for violent overthrow of the slave regime, and it was outlawed everywhere in the South. Word came too of a Black National Convention at Philadelphia in 1830, called to discuss conditions for Blacks in the United States, North and South, and to suggest remedies such as encouraging immigration to British North America. There was a newspaper called the *Liberator*, published in Boston by a white abolitionist named William Lloyd Garrison, demanding the immediate abolition of slavery.[16]

In response to the Turner incident, Virginia passed a series of laws denying education to African American children, and both enslaved and free Black people were prohibited from meeting without white supervision, even in church. Finally, in a move that tore families apart, every legally manumitted Black woman, man and child was ordered to leave the state within the year or risk re-enslavement. Even African Americans who had been free for a generation or more sold off what they could, but nearly everyone left behind still-enslaved loved ones whom they could not save.[17]

Benjamin, his own freedom promised in his aged father's will, knew he would one day have to leave Virginia too, but in the meantime the young man found urban life much to his liking. He did his best to give satisfaction in the Fisher household so they would renew his annual contract.[18] His wages went to the Fleets, but the Fishers supplied him with clothing and shoes and called in their own physician when he was sick. As the only young manservant in the Fisher household, he was butler and waiter, gardener and woodsman, and it was he who ensured that the coal bin by the stove was always full. Since he could write a fine hand and knew some arithmetic, Benjamin also tried to learn something of the tobacco business from his employer.[19]

Richmond was a revelation after Benjamin's secluded life in the country. Here slaves were everywhere, serving in the households of the well-to-do, working in industry and in the building trades, and hawking baked goods on the city streets. He also discovered Richmond's community of free people, a number of whom he would encounter in very different circumstances in his later life.[20] While most were labourers, there were among them barbers, grocers, fishmongers, seamstresses, hairdressers and milliners, along with hucksters who sold fruit and vegetables in the marketplace. Black churches were now prohibited, but most white religious establishments had African American congregants. Benjamin, who was an exhorter, or lay preacher, of some repute, began attending service in a little Methodist chapel at the foot of Church Hill. There were fraternal organizations and intellectual and benevolent societies—all now meeting in secret.[21] It was also in Richmond that, in whispered conversations in alleys and the marketplace, Benjamin learned of a place called Canada, where everyone was free.

The work in the Fisher household was not onerous, so to earn a little money, Benjamin did extra jobs around the neighbourhood during his spare time.[22] He had plans, for during his years in Richmond he had been watching little Ann Eliza grow up. Sweetly pretty, she was the daughter of a McKim family servant named Ellinor.[23] After Robert McKim's daughter died in 1833, Ann Eliza was sent to the Fisher household to help care for Elizabeth's orphaned children, and stayed on after James T. Fisher Jr. took another bride. As she matured into a young woman, she and Benjamin fell deeply in love. When they began attending the Methodist chapel together, James T. Fisher supplied coal to warm the building for Sunday service. The young couple requested permission of their respective owners so they could be married, so the Fishers made the arrangements and sponsored a small celebration to follow. Benjamin was twenty-two and his bride nineteen.[24]

But there were dark clouds on their horizon. Robert Pollard died soon after the wedding, and although Benjamin had been promised his liberty, his father's wishes were disregarded.[25] He now belonged to the Fleets, and there was nothing he could do.[26] No Black could testify against a white person in Virginia and the price of slaves was at an all-time high, with Benjamin Pollard Holmes now worth $1,200 or more.[27]

The young man was stunned and angry, the betrayal of his father's express wishes only intensifying his hunger to be free. He also knew that even if he were manumitted, any children his enslaved wife bore him would be slaves as well and belong to his wife's owner. Ann Eliza presented him with a baby son in March 1839, whom they named Benjamin Alexander Holmes. Benjamin was more than aware that any economic downturn, sudden illness or major lawsuit might force the Fishers to liquidate their assets, among which were Ann Eliza Holmes and their little boy.[28] Accordingly, the young husband devised a plan to free not only himself but also his family. They would go to Liberia.

Benjamin knew that Black Americans who were not enslaved were considered a dangerous anomaly in the southern United States. The American

Colonization Society (ACS) had been created in 1817 by genuinely altruistic clergymen, but also with the support of slaveholders such as Francis Scott Key, who wrote "The Star-Spangled Banner" but was avowedly proslavery. The objective of Key and other leading men in the society—such as Supreme Court Justice Bushrod Washington, nephew to the first president, and Kentucky's favourite son and sometime presidential candidate Henry Clay—was to solve America's free Black "problem."[29]

Sierra Leone had been established by the British on March 11, 1792, to resettle London's Black poor, including remnants of the Black Loyalists, formerly enslaved African Americans who had fought for the Crown in the Revolutionary War. More, unhappy with their shabby treatment and bereft of the land grants they had been promised in return for their service, had left Nova Scotia for Sierra Leone in 1792, and a contingent of proud Jamaican Maroons had also gone for similar reasons in 1800. Now the United States, at the urging of the Colonization Society, followed suit. In 1822 the colony of Liberia was founded, with Monrovia (named for President James Monroe) as its capital.

As a justification for removing as many free African Americans as possible from the United States, Henry Clay, ACS president from 1836 to 1849, explained in 1827: "Transplanted to a foreign land, they will carry back to their native soil the rich fruits of religion, civilization, law and liberty."[30] The ACS was very popular in Richmond, and some of the first free Black emigrants to choose Liberia as their home were Baptist missionaries from there.[31] Benjamin and his wife attended ACS lectures, and Benjamin in particular became impassioned with zeal to teach the native West Africans the ways of Christ.

Katie Hoomes was horrified when she heard that her son wanted to move his family to Africa. When the Fishers allowed Benjamin to take his wife and baby home to King and Queen County to meet his mother for Christmas week in 1839, she tried to dissuade Benjamin and Ann Eliza from such a hazardous course. Katie wrote to him after they returned to the Fisher household, employing maternal guilt as a weapon: "I am very unwell, more so than usual at this time. If you go I shall never see you again . . . I had hoped you would have delayed as long as I lived . . . my dear son, farewell, perhaps forever. Give my best love to Ann Eliza, and kiss the dear little baby for me,—your affectionate mother, Catharine Holmes."[32]

There were troubling reports from Liberia as well. Disease was rampant and the mortality rate from "acclimatizing fever" shockingly high. Incited by slave traders angered by the presence of free Black Americans on the coast, local warriors launched attacks that left settlers dead and their homes in smouldering ruins. But Benjamin and Ann Eliza remained enthusiastic. It was their one chance at freedom, and they had little Ben's future to consider.

In February 1840, Benjamin's mother tried again to intervene. She wrote a very articulate letter to her son at Richmond, urging him to consider the danger to his wife and baby and recounting what had happened to the hundred slaves freed by a local slaveholder she knew and sent to Liberia: "I think the last account I heard was that not more than twenty were alive. At one time twenty-six were murdered by the natives, many had fallen victims to the fever of the country, and those that remained were extremely anxious to return, but they cannot: when once liberated, they cannot return."[33] Addressing her son's proselytizing zeal, Katie went on to warn:

> you know that you are delicate, and besides you will have to work hard for a support. Look at the poor people about here, do not they have to work? and is not our country as good as Africa, besides if you go that you may instruct and preach to the natives, are there not many wicked people in Richmond of your acquaintance, that possibly you may be the instrument of bringing to a knowledge of the truth, by your pious walk and godly conversation. Remember, my dear son, that if you turn but one sinner from the error of his way, you will shine as the stars forever and ever.[34]

But Benjamin was anxious to begin a new life on the West African coast, and his wife supported him in the venture. They beseeched visiting ACS agent Reverend Charles Cummins to accept them as immigrants. Cummins judged them to be of "good character," "young and active" and just the type of colonists the Society was seeking, although he patently disbelieved Benjamin's claim that he was being held in slavery by his own relatives against the wishes of his deceased father. Cummins's letter to Samuel Wilkinson, the ACS director in Washington, was dated July 8, 1840:

> There is a young coloured [*sic*] man by the name of Benjamin
> Holmes and his wife who are preparing to go to Liberia with our
> next expedition. Possibly, according to the opinion of the people
> here, there have not gone to Africa coloured persons more worthy
> than this man and his wife. He will be able to pay his own way but
> his wife will have no means to meet the expenses of her case. Her
> husband will have some money left which he thinks of purchasing
> tobacco with. I have an interview with him and with his appear-
> ance and with all about him I have been very much pleased. He
> may claim connection, as report is, with one of the first families in
> Virginia but I would not say that claim [illegible] adds much to the
> respectability of the case.[35]

Between them, Reverend Cummins and Benjamin made a convincing argument. Although he had his own misgivings, James T. Fisher Jr. finally agreed to liberate Ann Eliza and their little boy, providing generously for their support once they arrived. Alexander Fleet issued a deed of manumission for Benjamin Pollard Holmes on July 18, 1840. There was a very grudging tone to the Fleet document, underlining the fact that the young man was freed only on condition that he set sail within the year for Liberia. Despite all their protestations of faith, Benjamin was the only slave the Fleets ever emancipated for the purpose of going to Liberia.

Fisher's manumission of Ann Eliza and her little boy is written in a more generous spirit, although he too insisted that their manumission was dependent on emigration. However, to his letter Fisher appended the following, quite extraordinary paragraph:

> Nothing herein contained shall be construed so as to prevent the said Ann Eliza from returning with or without her child, to my service; and, should such an event occur, I hereby bind myself, my heirs, &c., to pay to the Colonization Society the expenses of their passage, and to said society, or any one who may become entitled thereto, the expense of their passage back. Witness my hand and seal in the city aforesaid, this 30th day of July, One Thousand Eight Hundred and Forty.
> JAMES FISHER, Jr. (Seal.)
> N.B. The said Ann Eliza is about twenty-two years of age.
> JAS. FISHER, Jr.[36]

Alexander Fleet offered no fare or other support, but Benjamin had saved enough for his own passage and the necessary supplies.[37] Now, with his employer's blessing, he also purchased at very favourable rates some of James T. Fisher's stock of good Virginia tobacco. He planned to set himself up as a trader, for although he had been brought up in the Virginia countryside, Benjamin was no farmer.[38]

In July 1840, the Holmes family left Richmond for Norfolk, on the Atlantic coast, a 117-mile steamboat trip down the James River to its mouth at the Chesapeake Bay.[39] The *Saluda* was to depart on August 3 with twenty-three former slaves and some intrepid Baptist missionaries as passengers. Fervent blessings over the ship by local Norfolk clergy did not save the boat from the gale that blew up soon after it left port.[40] Five days after it set sail, the *Saluda* was in distress off Bombay Hook and taking on water, so the captain nursed her into Philadelphia's harbour for repairs.[41]

Almost immediately after the ship tied up, a well-dressed group of "black and white abolitionists" came aboard.[42] All members of the Vigilant Association of Philadelphia, they tried to persuade *Saluda*'s passengers to abandon their plans. They described in graphic detail the dangers of Liberian life, saying there were never enough supplies, that the ACS governed the colony with a despotic hand, and that agricultural production was hampered by the extremes of climate, which ranged from heavy rains to dry, very hot periods. The death rate among emigrants from the February voyage of the *Saluda* stood at an astounding 45 percent.[43]

Their fears for their child's safety taking precedence, and with Katie Hoomes's dire predictions ringing in their ears, Ann Eliza and Benjamin Holmes, with their son Ben, became the first of the *Saluda*'s passengers to abandon ship. By the time it sailed, all but five of the would-be emigrants had fled to places of concealment within Philadelphia's large and sophisticated African American community. Their short stay in the City of Brotherly Love demonstrated what African Americans could achieve when given a more level playing field than they were usually accorded. Far from free of racial discrimination and a sometime site of major anti-Black riots, Philadelphia was also home to a number of important Black institutions, including Bethel African Methodist Episcopal Church, founded in 1794 by Reverend Richard Allen. It was he who had called together the delegates of the first Black National Convention, about which news had travelled even to far-away Richmond, and a host of faith-centred, benevolent, intellectual and resistance organizations had been founded there over the years.[44]

Soon after the *Saluda* departed for Liberia, Benjamin and his little family left on the first leg of their journey to Canada.[45] Their destination was Toronto, capital of the westernmost province of British North America. There they were assured of a welcome amidst the city's thriving African American expatriate population. The Holmeses were sent secretly all the way to Rochester, New York, where they stayed a few days before traversing

Lake Ontario by steamer. When they disembarked, they were greeted by a confident, apparently quite prosperous young man named Grandison Boyd. Also a refugee from Virginian bondage, he had married a widow with property of her own and was now a successful tobacconist with a shop on Queen Street[46] and ties to both Rochester and Toronto. He whisked them off to meet the Reverend Hiram Wilson.

The warm-hearted missionary and his wife, Hannah, were devoted to serving incoming freedom-seekers. Wilson wrote a long and enthusiastic account to American abolitionist newspapers, attacking the American Colonization Society and describing the Holmes family as "important accessions to Queen Victoria's subjects, of the sable hue." He added a long description of their ownership history and recounted in some detail their disastrous experience aboard the *Saluda*. The story of their escape gained celebrity, for Reverend Wilson also sent their manumission papers to the abolitionist press, where they were published in their entirety.

The first order of business was to find the family a house and Benjamin some employment. Fortunately the entrepreneurial Grandison Boyd had his fingers in a number of pies. He was at the time serving as agent for the owner of a brand-new row of single-storey brick rental properties on Richmond Street. The Holmes family's new landlord was Silas Burnham, an Englishman who had a grocery store on King Street East that catered to Toronto's carriage trade.[47] At Boyd's urging, Burnham recommended Benjamin to steamboat captain Hugh Richardson as just the sort of refined, well-mannered young man who would make an excellent dining room waiter on one of Richardson's ships, the *Transit*.

Grandison and his wife, Mary Ann, along with her brothers Zachariah and James Patterson and her cousin Elijah B. Dunlop, who was a shoe-maker by trade, all befriended Benjamin and his family and proved to be the mainstay of their social life in their new Canadian home.[48] Benjamin learned that Boyd had arrived in 1833. His wife was the former Mary Ann (Patterson) Ross, a free-born widow from Richmond, Virginia.[49] She had moved to the city with relatives in the Waddell, Carter, Lewis, Edmunds, Gallego and Hickman families, nearly all of whom had either been forced to leave Virginia after the Nat Turner Rebellion, or were frustrated in their efforts to have their children educated because of new laws passed in its wake prohibiting schools for Black children. The intermarried clan was now scattered throughout upstate New York and Canada West, establishing links between Toronto and Buffalo, Syracuse and Rochester. Never forgetting their beloved relatives and friends left behind in slavery, they used these ties to support the Underground Railroad from both sides of the border.

One of Mary Ann's relations described his family's journey to the Town of York, as Toronto was called before the city was incorporated in 1834:

> Elisha Edmunds who has a barber shop on Yonge Street, said that he came to Little York in 1832. He was a native of Richmond Va, but was never in slavery. He was in business at first on King street opposite St. James Cathedral. When he reached Little York on the 11th of July 1832, there were only six coloured families in the place . . . The Edmunds family and collateral relatives numbered 17 persons.[50]

If Philadelphia's cultured free Black society had been an eye-opener for Benjamin and his young wife, Toronto was astonishing. There were far fewer Black faces than they were used to in Richmond, but the people they met stood tall and proud. No one stepped off a sidewalk into the city's notoriously muddy streets when a white person wanted to pass. Nor did they avert their eyes or add the ubiquitous Southern "Yes, massa" when spoken to.[51] Instead Black Canadians owned homes, stores, restaurants and one very nice hotel. Generous and community-spirited, they saw to the needs of incoming freedom-seekers as well as their own. If sickness came, one could call on the Union Benevolent Society, a self-insurance system into which men and women paid a small monthly fee. In return there was a fund to draw on in times of need and to provide a decent burial should one be required.[52]

Benjamin soon learned that Toronto played a significant role in the long struggle against slavery in which Black America was engaged, for the city was an important terminus of what had come to be called, in light of new technological advances in steam railroad transport in the 1830s, the "Underground Railroad." Never as organized or codified as some of its detractors would have had people believe, this was a clandestine and quite dangerous pursuit involving a great many people of African descent in the border cities ringing the Great Lakes.[53] Nonetheless, at least half of all those who came in search of liberty reached Canada alone and unaided. While the law protected the refugees once they had crossed over into British North America, slave-catchers were known to enter the province and kidnap people for return to their Southern owners. Each community had either a formal or informal vigilance committee to assure their mutual protection.[54]

An African Canadian–led antislavery society had been founded in the 1830s, and its banners could be seen at every celebration. The community did its best to billet new arrivals in their own homes, and churches worked with successful businessmen, both Black and white, to help them find work. Once on their feet, a few dedicated themselves, in turn, to the dangerous work of spiriting fugitives across the border to free territory, something Benjamin soon began to do as well. There was some hostility to Black immigration, but there was also support for the refugees on the part of a good many white Canadians.[55] There had been an attempt to start a white-led antislavery society in 1836, and clergymen at several city churches were there to help men find employment in a factory or workshop of one of their parishioners, or women in locating domestic positions in well-to-do households.

While Ann Eliza set up housekeeping and began to prepare for the arrival of her second child, Benjamin began regularly scheduled day trips to Niagara. He soon learned that his position as a waiter on the *Transit* was a coveted one, both because of the tips offered by grateful passengers and because it provided steady, if seasonal, employment. The steamer's western terminus was Lewiston, New York, opposite Queenston on the Niagara River below the Falls.[56] Although his fugitive-slave status posed some danger when his ship docked at ports on the American side, he kept a low profile and managed very well. Benjamin Pollard Holmes had been brought up to speak grammatically, to keep up a neat appearance and to provide prompt, efficient service. He was both ambitious and very intelligent, and soon aspired to become a steward, the ship's officer responsible for provisioning the steamers and keeping careful records of expenditures, something for which Benjamin's education made him a good candidate.

His new job was generally a pleasant vocation, although there were occasions when summary treatment and unpleasantly racist remarks on the part of passengers reminded Benjamin of his experience in slavery. Canadians were far from immune to racist sentiments, and there were enough such travellers—mainly American, but some British and Canadian ones too—to remind Benjamin how men of colour, however respectable, were treated south of the border. American newspapers were available in Toronto, helping to feed negative attitudes about Blacks, and there were even anti-Black pundits among the Canadian press who objected to wholesale African American immigration and castigated incoming refugees for their poverty and supposed propensity for criminal activity.[57]

Special trips sometimes took Benjamin away overnight, as when the lieutenant-governor or other dignitaries were aboard. Captain Richardson's vessel was a popular choice. Steamers plying these inland waterways were painted in bright colours and sumptuously appointed. Passengers enjoyed their trips aboard the *Transit*, as British author Charles Dickens did when he visited Toronto in 1842. One traveller described meals with "a service of richly coloured and gilded china, with plated covers for the dishes, fine crystal cut glass, cutlery of the best quality, and massive silver spoons and forks."[58] The fares were reasonable and there were two classes, each served with breakfast, dinner, and tea, so Benjamin was kept very busy throughout the journey. He and the other waiters were also responsible for keeping the dining room clean. Sometimes to delight Ann Eliza, who loved pretty things, he was allowed to take home a slightly chipped cup or an ornament that had developed a crack or two, for Captain Richardson tolerated no damaged goods in his salon or in the luxurious ladies' cabin of the *Transit*.

A majority of the ship's waiters were of African descent, many of whom, like Benjamin himself, had once lived in bondage in the American South.[59] Gaining confidence, on visits to Lockport, Rochester and Buffalo he would sometimes venture into town to make special arrangements to spirit freedom-seekers, whose owners were in hot pursuit, safely onto the Canadian steamer. He came to know many of the Underground Railroad operators in the Great Lakes ports. In his work he had a willing partner in the business, for the *Transit*'s Captain Richardson had been a prisoner himself in France during the Napoleonic Wars. He once told British traveller Harriet Martineau that "the sublimest sight in North America is the leap of a slave from a boat to the Canadian shore. That 'leap' transforms him from a marketable chattel to a free man."[60]

With a home established and Benjamin's employment assured, the young family joined the city's Coloured Wesleyan Chapel. Built in 1832, its founders included members of the city's Black elite, for the community was already stratified by talent and intelligence, if less so by economic status. Benjamin and his wife came to know the brilliantly business-minded Wilson Ruffin Abbott and his Baltimore-born wife, Ellen, who along with Abbott's brother-in-law, Adolphus Judah, were among the most prosperous Black people in the city.[61] Here and at the community's Baptist church, built on Queen Street after they arrived, they encountered people Ann Eliza and Benjamin knew from their days in Richmond. One new acquaintance was chapel trustee Joseph Peniel Turner, a free-born cordwainer (maker of fine shoes and gloves) from Philadelphia, who knew the people on the Vigilant Committee who had forwarded the Holmeses on to Canada.[62]

Churches were the only buildings African Canadians owned in common, and they were centres not only for faith and fellowship but also for education. There was as yet no free school in Toronto, so churches ran day schools for children as well as night and Sunday schools for working adults. There were also meeting rooms for fraternal societies, lecture halls for visiting speakers, and spaces for various entertainments and bazaars. Black Torontonians of all denominations, and people from as far away as Hamilton and Niagara, joined in the church socials at Toronto Island and excursions on steamers chartered for special occasions, weddings, christenings, musical entertainments and fundraisers. The largest annual event was Emancipation Day, held on August 1 to commemorate the end of slavery across the Empire. Speeches by the mayor and a prayer service involving clergy both Black and white were followed by a parade ending at the lieutenant-governor's grand residence at Simcoe and King Streets for a picnic on the grounds.[63]

Captain Richardson had the *Chief Justice Robinson* built at Niagara, and her maiden voyage was on Friday, April 22, 1842. Benjamin was aboard to wait tables on the swift steamer, which ran the route between Niagara and Toronto in less than three hours, although there were sometimes special, longer trips to Rochester and Buffalo.[64] Although Benjamin was still frequently away from home, Ann Eliza could be assured of support, thanks to their Boyd and Patterson family connections and their church affiliations. However, in 1843, Grandison Boyd and his wife experienced serious financial reversals and left to make a new home in Rochester, where they opened a grocery.[65] There were other changes: Reverend Hiram Wilson left Toronto for the new Dawn Settlement, an African Canadian agricultural colony in the southwestern part of the province. It was the brainchild of a formerly enslaved Kentuckian named Josiah Henson, who with Wilson was working to establish the British-American Institute.[66] Also to Dawn had gone Benjamin's good friends James and Zachariah Dunlop Patterson and Elijah B. Dunlop. After the new manual labour school was on its feet, these very cultured men enrolled at Oberlin College in Ohio to advance their own education. Oberlin was nearly unique among American schools of higher learning in accepting Black students along with white ones.[67]

It was well that the Holmes family had the support of church, fellowship and friends. One year after the family's arrival in Toronto, in 1841, Ann Eliza gave birth to a new baby; the couple named him James Thomas Holmes. But her health had never been robust, and with two children to care for, it began to deteriorate. Tragically, Benjamin's much-loved Ann Eliza had developed the persistent cough symptomatic of consumption (tuberculosis), a disease that took the lives of so many people, young and old.

Perhaps she would do better in her own home. By the spring of 1844, only four years after they reached Toronto, Benjamin had saved enough to buy real estate. The spark for this frighteningly large purchase was the seizure of their landlord's properties. To the surprise of his friends, and particularly of his creditors, Silas Burnham was found to have committed forgeries on a grand scale, and he absconded to Texas with between £5,000 and £6,000 in cash.[68] Benjamin and Ann Eliza Holmes put down their first payment on a two-and-a-half storey frame home with a fine brick front in a newly subdivided residential district called Macaulaytown. It was located on a wide double lot on the east side of Centre Street, just two blocks north of the Coloured Wesleyan Chapel. Laid out in the early 1830s as Toronto's first working class suburb, Macaulaytown had quickly become the place where most African American immigrants to Toronto made their homes.[69]

But poor Ann Eliza did not live to enjoy her fine house, with its covered porch and welcoming front parlour. Wasting away as the fires of the disease burned within her, Ann Eliza Holmes died on April 16, 1845. She was laid to rest in Potter's Field, a non-denominational cemetery that lay north of the built-up part of the city, near the village of Yorkville.[70] By the time she died, Benjamin's twenty-eight-year-old wife was so changed by her sufferings that the doctor who attended her recorded her age as forty-four. Ben Alexander, just turned six, and his three-year-old brother, James Thomas, were motherless, and their father inconsolable.

CHAPTER 4

THE LAND OF PROMISE

Tell the Republicans on your side of the line that we Royalists do not know men by their color. Should you come to us you will be entitled to all the privileges of the rest of His Majesty's subjects.

—Lieutenant-Governor Sir John Colborne, 1829[1]

NOW, A LITTLE OVER a year after his wife's death, Benjamin Pollard Holmes was returning from a trip aboard the *City of Toronto* with a wide-eyed fifteen-year-old girl in tow. Cecelia Jane Reynolds was slight and very attractive. She had a Kentucky accent, a proudly determined personality and a kindly but careful manner.

With colourful flags flying fore and aft and passengers crowded on deck in anticipation of their landing, the steamer bearing Cecelia to her new Toronto home steamed through the Western Gap, the entry to Toronto Bay. Above her, Captain Dick stood before the wheelhouse facing into the wind as he gave the order for a small cannon to be brought forward to signal their arrival. Cecelia was excited. The tale of how Benjamin and his family had reached freedom had been both stirring and inspiring, and she was very much looking forward to seeing her new hometown. Her only regret was the fact that her mother, Mary, and young Edward were not there to enjoy it with her.

The tranquil waters of the bay were partially enclosed by a long, lushly wooded sandbar that curved south and west out into the lake from the mouth of the Don River. In the harbour bobbed pleasure craft and sailing schooners, the workhorses of the coastal trade, as well as several gaily painted steamboats. The paddlewheeler was swift, its twin engines racing as it passed the lighthouse at Gibraltar Point on the tip of the peninsula, and sailed into port beneath the cannon of Fort York on the opposite shore. Toronto lay on a wide, low plain between two great rivers, the Humber and the Don. Further north, above a shallow ridge beyond the town proper, was the city's rich agricultural hinterland, and along the distant horizon, the dark green of primeval forest.

From conversations with Benjamin and her Niagara hosts, Cecelia knew that Toronto had been founded in 1793 by the same Lieutenant-Governor John Graves Simcoe who had forced through the legislation guaranteeing her freedom.[2] In patriotic British fashion he had discarded Toronto's traditional Native name and dubbed it the Town of York. Envisioned first as a shipbuilding centre because of its protected harbour, it soon became the seat of government for the new province of Upper Canada. Twice captured in the War of 1812, the town grew slowly until 1825, when the Erie Canal was completed through upstate New York. The canal ran on a series of aqueducts right through Rochester, Toronto's sister city on the other side of Lake Ontario, and gave Canadian passengers and goods more direct access east to the Hudson River and the Atlantic seaboard than the old French and British route up the St. Lawrence had. Incorporated as the province's only real city in 1834, Toronto's residents happily went back to calling it by its ancient name. Now it was a bustling industrial centre and hub of transport, with dreams of a vast continental railroad system that would ensure prosperity for generations to come.

Cecelia had learned that more than eight hundred African Canadians now lived in Toronto proper, with another hundred or so on small acreages outside the city limits. There were many more in the southwest section of the province near the Detroit River, which, like Niagara, was an important transit point into Canada for people in search of freedom.³ Toronto now had three Black churches, that provided both sanctuary and society for newcomers. Hopeful refugees arrived almost daily in groups of two or three, carrying with them little except courage and industry, but eager to embark on life in a part of North America where discrimination against people with darker skin, if not entirely absent, at least wasn't codified in law.

The *City of Toronto* slowed as it approached the docks, giving its passengers a better view of the three- and four-storey commercial buildings facing the bay. Cecelia would find much about the city that seemed familiar. Like her hometown of Louisville, Toronto was a departure point for opening up the continent's vast Western reaches. The streets were laid out at right angles to the waterfront in a grid that ignored the several minor watercourses traversing the downtown core, evidence of the British military training of Simcoe's engineers. Louisville and Toronto, with about twenty thousand inhabitants each, were also about the same size, although the latter's Black population was tiny by comparison, and both served large agricultural hinterlands.⁴ It was just now in the process of industrializing; smokestacks pierced the sky, a grey haze hovering in the air above the city streets.

As the steamer neared the shore, Cecelia spied only one or two Black faces among the dockworkers and carters awaiting its landing at the wharf. Here in Toronto she knew there were white labourers as well as Black ones, who worked at whatever job came to hand. Employment was at a premium in the growing city, so there was work and opportunity for all. There was, though, one major difference. Unlike Louisville's thousands of slaves, in Toronto the Black population was entirely and forever free.

As the *City of Toronto* pulled up to the Church Street wharf, Cecelia finally realized that once she put her foot down on dry land, she would be safe. Here no one could take away her new-found freedom. Delighted and a little apprehensive, she disembarked and waited for Benjamin on the quay as he completed his duties aboard the steamer and took his leave of the captain. Her few possessions were easily carried but it was a long walk to Macaulaytown, in the far northwest corner of the city. Benjamin's two little boys, Ben Alexander and James Thomas, boarded there with neighbours during the sailing season, and they eagerly anticipated their father's return. On their way up the bank, Benjamin and Cecelia passed cabmen and carters jockeying for passengers, and then the city's fish market with its odoriferous wares. Again, one or two were of African descent, and they waved, as Black people did everywhere when they saw one another on the streets, a familiar custom that comforted Cecelia and made her feel just a bit more at home.

As they walked along, Benjamin pointed out city landmarks and some of the homes and businesses of his friends. At the foot of Church Street stood the barbershops of two former Virginians, Elisha Edmunds and William Henderson Edwoods, the latter of whom proudly advertised "Hot & Cold Baths on Short Notice."[5] Further up, above the harbour, near the oddly wedge-shaped Coffin Block which towered over the corner of Front Street, were Black-owned restaurants that catered exclusively to a white clientele, a sop to white prejudice that Cecelia remembered well from her time in Washington. When Lake Ontario ports iced over in the winter and the steamers couldn't sail, Benjamin sometimes waited tables here and in the dining rooms of the city's better hotels. But ice and snow weren't something a girl from the warmer climate of Kentucky wanted to think about on a fine summer's day like this.

Along King Street just east of the City Hall was St. Lawrence Market. Several thriving grocery stalls there belonged to people of colour, whose soft drawl betrayed their Southern origins. Turning their heads to the west, Cecelia and Benjamin could see the lovely four-square brick house of Captain Hugh Richardson. An important man about town, he owned several steamboats, including the *Chief Justice Robinson*. Benjamin had previously been employed on the *Chief Justice*, but he had been hired on by

Thomas Dick, which was a fortunate turn of events since Captain Richardson now found himself in financial difficulty. His home and all his assets were about to be sold.[6] Past the four-storey North American Hotel, with its large livery stable backing onto Wellington Street, lay more wharves and some factories, and then along the west end of Front Street stood the mansions and town homes of the city's elite. Looking out over the waters of Toronto Bay, their manicured gardens and orchards, some with family graveyards, often took up entire city blocks.

Moving north up Church Street, Benjamin led his charge past Toronto's Court House and civic centre, and then the Mechanics' Institute with its lending library, where public lectures on multiple topics were delivered for the benefit of ordinary Torontonians. He explained that the Home District Savings Bank lay to the east on George Street, and it was there, he informed Cecelia with some pride, that working people like himself deposited their savings.[7] On King, beside the huge Cathedral Church of St. James, stood a cheerfully painted hansom cab drawn by a fine shiny bay mare. This was "The City," Toronto's first taxi. Its owner was Thornton Blackburn, and he had something in common with Cecelia: Thornton had once been the property of some of Fanny Thruston's Louisville relatives.[8]

Running west from the Cathedral, King Street was Toronto's most fashionable shopping district. At number 33 stood the livery stable belonging to James Mink, a man for whom Benjamin had a good deal of respect. A son of slaves brought in from upstate New York by their Loyalist owners after the American Revolution, he and his wife also owned the Mansion House Hotel on nearby Adelaide Street.[9] His brother George had the lucrative mail coach and livery business in Kingston, and James and George Mink were often commissioned to transport prisoners from Toronto to Kingston Penitentiary. There too was the Tontine Coffee House; its owners, Daniel Bloxom and his wife, Agnes, were Virginians who, like several other families from the old Dominion now residing in British North America, had relatives across the lake in Rochester.[10]

Looking north Cecelia could see the spire of the Catholic St. Michael's Cathedral. Next door stood the sturdy little African Baptist Chapel pastored by Elder Washington Christian, a charismatic preacher who had once been a slave; he had a regular preaching circuit through the province, founding new churches wherever he went. Next came Yonge Street, which was the city's main north–south thoroughfare.[11] At its foot lay factories where white men worked alongside skilled African American tradesmen—surprising to Cecelia's eyes, for she still saw things through the lens of the slave state where she had been brought up. Some grumbling would now and then come of that, according to Benjamin, but here in Canada West such tensions might lead to unpleasantness but rarely aroused any worse reaction.

The Richmond Street Wesleyan Methodist Church was just off Yonge on Richmond, its tall pillars shining in the early evening light. It held an astonishing 1,800 people, some of whom were African Canadians who owned their own pews. There the venerable Matthew Truss, a shoemaker by trade, brought a hush to the congregation whenever he rose to speak.[12] On the other side of Yonge were more shops and then, to the south on Bay Street facing Lake Ontario, the magnificent Georgian-style "palace" where Anglican bishop John Strachan lived. He was the reason why none of the city's churches or schools of higher education were segregated, for he was a strong-willed and stubborn Scot who had no tolerance for divisions in his flock. Further along, facing the lake, were three squat brick buildings: Upper Canada's unimpressive Parliament Buildings, now housing King's College while the government, which moved at intervals between cities in the provinces of Canada West and Canada East, sat elsewhere.[13]

The part of Bay Street above Queen was known as Teraulay, and that was where Newton Cary had his brand-new barbershop. The first of several Cary brothers who came very early from Fredericksburg, Virginia, and now made their homes in Canada, he and his many relations were in touch with Black and white abolitionists everywhere and went to antislavery meetings on both sides of the border.[14] Looking northwards, Benjamin pointed out the neat house where Wilson and Ellen Abbott lived. The best-off of the city's entire Black populace, they invested in real estate and busied themselves with making the community a better place for African Canadians to live. In the year after Benjamin first came to the city, Wilson had dared to present petitions to City Council to protest the blackface minstrel shows that mocked people of African descent and encouraged white people to think slavery was funny. He would do so again annually for the next four years. Ellen Abbott ran a benevolent society named for Queen Victoria. She and her friends helped runaway slaves when they first came to town, finding them clothes to wear, food to eat and jobs so they would soon be able to provide such things for themselves.

On the north side of King at York stood the shoemaking shop of David and Mary Cleggett. Born free in upstate New York, the Cleggetts had come to Canada with their many children some years before, but a disastrous fire had destroyed their first shop and now they were thinking of going back. Further along King, at Graves (Simcoe) Street, stood the white-painted Government House, the lieutenant-governor's home, with its many-paned glass conservatory. Benjamin and Ann Eliza used to go to Emancipation Day picnics there with their sons, so that Ben and James Thomas could learn about Queen Victoria and how she had freed every slave in the British Empire.[15] Roughly opposite stood Upper Canada College, the elite Anglican boys' prep school, where to Cecelia's astonishment she learned that the sons of men and women who had once been slaves were educated alongside the cream of the city's white elite, including sons of families that had formed the province's governing clique, the Family Compact.[16]

On Hospital Street, or Richmond, as the eastern end was called, was the modest building that housed the Coloured Wesleyan Church, Benjamin's spiritual home in the city, now because of a disagreement between its members unfortunately rented to a different congregation. Next came York Street, whose upper reaches were crowded with African Canadian homes and stores.[17] A small-frame grocery store there belonged to Willis Addison. He was a trustee of the chapel and now a pew-holder at Richmond Street Methodist Church, where he sat on Sundays amidst much of white dissenting Toronto.[18] Then came the catering business of Celestial Davis, one of the rare West Indians to make his home in Canada. Next door was house painter Carter Waddell. He was from Richmond, Virginia, and one of the Patterson-Dunlop-Ross clan related to Mary Ann Boyd.

Just across the street at 82 York lived saw manufacturer Thomas Smallwood. He had an interesting story to tell, for Smallwood had once operated his own Underground Railroad station in Washington, DC. Betrayed, he crossed the border on the *Transit* with the help of Captain Hugh Richardson, and with his family now made a home in Canada. When Smallwood published his memoirs, he wrote that it was the generosity of Hugh Richardson that enabled him to cross over into Canada West on the Fourth of July, 1842. Astonishingly, Thomas Smallwood returned to the United States to save the families of four men he had previously sent to Canada. He succeeded: "I sold my watch at Buffalo to get [the families] to Toronto, which city we reached on the 23rd of December, in 1843, on the steamer *Transit*. I mention the steamer, because Capt. Richardson, according to his usual benevolence reduced the fare for us."[19]

Philip Gallego's house was next. He came from a family freed by the owners of the huge Gallego Flour Mills in Richmond. Forced to abandon his aged parents in Virginia, he had arrived in the city with very little, but his brilliant son, Peter, was educated at Upper Canada College and then King's College, thanks to John Strachan, recently made Bishop of York. Peter Gallego had conducted a census of Black Torontonians for the reform-minded Lord Durham, sent out from Britain to examine the roots of Canadian discontent with the previous form of colonial rule. Durham's report on Canadian conditions had resulted in the union of the provinces of Upper and Lower Canada under a single government, and the former Upper Canada was now known as "Canada West."[20]

Philip Gallego's sister-in-law Betsey lived just across the street with her husband, William Hickman; they owned two barbershops and a grocery store. A community-minded couple, in their yard they put up six small cabins that they rented for little or no return to family after family of fugitive slaves.[21]

At Queen and York stood the home of Kentuckian James Charles Brown, where the good Reverend Hiram and Hannah Wilson had lived when Benjamin and Ann Eliza first came to the city.[22] A builder of considerable skill, Brown had purchased his freedom and moved to Cincinnati. In 1829 he chaired a committee to discuss how best to deal with newly imposed anti-Black laws, which so oppressed people that they decided to leave. Upper Canada's lieutenant-governor wrote a letter to Brown, welcoming them and promising them they would be accorded all the privileges of any other immigrants. So now former Cincinnatians farmed at a place north of London they called Wilberforce after the great British abolitionist William Wilberforce, who had worked so hard to end Britain's involvement in the Atlantic slave trade. These days the fearless and highly polemic J. C. Brown served as the colony's Toronto-based representative and spoke at every Black community meeting about how they could all create better lives for their children.[23]

At the top of York Street on the north side of Queen stood stately Osgoode Hall, a beautiful group of three buildings fronted by arches and columns that was home to the Law Society of Upper Canada. North and east of the Hall lay a warren of cottages, tenements, artisan shops, small factories and even a lumberyard, for Queen Street was the southern boundary of Macaulaytown, where most incoming refugees made their homes, and even at this early date was becoming overcrowded.[24] Behind Osgoode Hall stood three dwellings, each of which Robin Philips managed as a sort of halfway house for freedom-seekers. On the other side of the street was the property that Benjamin's hard work and saving ways had earned.[25]

The attractive two-and-a-half storey home that Benjamin shared with his two young sons was located in the very nicest part of Macaulaytown.

Cecelia's first impression was positive, for Benjamin's house was sturdy and well-built, with a small portico built into the red brick façade, gable ends to the roadway and a large parlour window. Benjamin had added a shed and kitchen ell at the rear, [26] but his long-term plan was to build a second home next door on the same lot, in order to provide an income so he could train his young sons in a trade. Their father received a warm greeting from little Ben Alexander and James Thomas, and he introduced the curious boys to his guest. The lads were seven and five years old.

For the present, since he was away sailing a good deal of the time, Benjamin settled Cecelia in his own home. If she looked after the children and kept house for him, it would both save the cost of the lads' board and offer her a chance to catch her breath and explore this strange city that seemed both familiar and quite foreign. Most people sounded more British than American, the weights and measures of foodstuffs and fuel were different from those to which she had been accustomed, and even the money was confusing. There were several currencies in circulation; a Halifax shilling had the same value as neither a British one nor a York shilling, and dollars and cents were also in play. She was truly, as the Bible said, "a stranger in a strange land."

Over time, Cecelia discovered that several of her new neighbours hailed from Kentucky, Virginia and Tennessee, and there were families from Baltimore up the street. Some were very poor but the community was surprisingly close-knit. Benjamin's sons played in the roadway with children from England, Ireland, Scotland and, sometimes, Italy and Germany. Everyone shared houses and married one another, or else negotiated less formal arrangements, without benefit of wedlock. Nearly everyone who lived there had arrived in Canada since 1830, when the huge old Macaulay estate that gave the district its name had first been divided up into long, narrow lots that sold for very reasonable prices.

What a change from the Thrustons' elegant Walnut Street mansion with its gardens, carriage house and stately trees. But College Road with its wide boulevard was just a couple of blocks over, and on a nice day Benjamin would take his little boys down to the waterfront to watch the ships coming in. There was swimming at Sunnyside Beach or Grenadier Pond, if a passing drayman was kind enough to give them transport, and if not there were horse-drawn omnibuses that travelled the length of Queen Street to take them to the western beaches beyond Fort York's military reserve.

As summer turned to fall, Cecelia began to seek employment. Fortunately her training as a lady's maid provided some usefully transferable skills. She was able to take in enough ironing and fine sewing work to pay her way. Little Ben and James Thomas, so sadly bereft of their mother, were beginning to become used to having someone new in the household. There was a school Ben could attend in the basement of the freshly consecrated African Methodist Episcopal Church on Sayre Street, just a block east of Benjamin's home, and the fees were manageable. When Benjamin was back from the lake, he and Cecelia would take the boys to church there of a Sunday. She found that a great deal of attention was paid to the changing politics of slavery south of the border, for everyone here had left someone they loved behind in bondage when they moved to Canada. There were charitable groups and women's societies that Cecelia could join, and she overcame her natural reserve in an effort to meet people, volunteering to help with the sales, concerts and church socials organized to raise funds to support incoming refugees in need of immediate assistance.

Sometimes Benjamin brought people he had helped come across the lake to Canada home with him after a shift on the *City of Toronto* or the *Transit*, just as he had Cecelia herself. When they arrived, she would make up beds before the fire for the tired souls and put a good hot meal in their stomachs. Cecelia and Benjamin would send them on in the morning to Robin Philips or one of the area ministers to help them find work and a place to live.

Between times, Cecelia kept up the household as best she could, bleaching and ironing the white shirts Benjamin wore waiting tables and making over his old clothes into small garments for his sons. From neighbouring women and her new friends at church she was learning to cook, to preserve the products of garden and market and, most challenging of all, to bake bread. She had discovered that, while her early training made her one of the better classes of servant in Louisville, she also needed to be able to prepare supper, harvest vegetables or learn to make candles here in Toronto. At times like this she especially missed her mother, for Mary was an accomplished cook and launderess.

Cecelia was alone with the children a good deal of the time, but she encountered her neighbours in the street and on the way to do her daily shopping. In Macaulaytown, she learned that while not everyone got along, people looked out for one another. The area had its own morality born of the previously enslaved condition of many of its inhabitants. If a man whose wife had been sold away before he left the South took up housekeeping here with another woman, or if a widowed woman with a houseful of children had rather a large number of gentlemen callers . . . well, some neighbours gossiped but most understood that people get lonely and children have to be fed. In Macaulaytown the lines that divided people were of poverty and education rather than of morality or even race. As for the rest of the city, the main division was not between Black and white but rather between Protestant orange and Catholic green.[27]

Listening to the speakers who came to lecture at the little AME church around the corner on topics of interest to Black Torontonians, Cecelia came to realize that although Canada maintained an open-door policy as far as fugitive slaves went, not everyone was uniformly delighted with having African Americans as neighbours. The kindly missionary who had greeted Benjamin's family when they arrived six years before had travelled to London for the convention of the British and Foreign Anti-Slavery Society in 1843. In his speech, Hiram Wilson said, to the dismay of his British audience,

> In certain places—as, for instance, Kingston and Toronto, and a few others, where the preponderating influence is English and Scotch, there is but very little ground for complaint; prejudice

obtains only to a faint degree; whilst in other parts, especially along the frontiers and the West, the prejudice is intolerable . . . on the River Thames there are some two or three steam-boats running, and in neither of these is a coloured man admitted as a cabin passenger, however respectable he may be; nor is he allowed, on account of his colour, to come to the first or second table . . . the coloured youth are generally shut out from the white schools; they are not suffered to be educated in common with the white people.[28]

At least it was somewhat better in liberal Toronto, but while African Canadians regularly interacted with European settlers at work and in the marketplace and everyone wanted to get ahead in this land of almost limitless opportunity, Black communities there and across the province were no more a part of white society than they had been in the Kentucky of Cecelia's youth, although at least here men had the vote and could serve on juries and in the militia.

But she had matters other than politics on her mind these days. Amidst all the welter of her new experiences, Cecelia was also a teenaged girl, and here was a fine-looking man who had managed to turn her head. For the first time in her life, Cecelia Jane Reynolds was being courted. Living in his home and taking care of his sons, Cecelia found herself drawn to the man who had saved her from a lifetime of slavery. Only a few months after Benjamin brought her to Toronto, he asked her to marry him.

There was an age gap of eighteen years between them, longer than Cecelia had yet been alive. Although she was a lovely girl, there was more than physical attraction at play. Cecelia's pluck in arranging for her own escape, and at a distance of nearly six hundred miles, intrigued Benjamin, who had freed both himself and his family through his own initiative. Cecelia was very young but well-spoken and well-travelled, and she displayed a maturity well beyond her years. Every time he set out on Lake

Ontario, Benjamin wondered what would become of his boys should he fail to return. As for his friends . . . well, the fact that a still vigorous man with two small sons needed a wife was no surprise to anyone.

Cecelia's decision to marry was not made lightly. Fond of Benjamin as she was, she was a cautious soul, proud of her relative independence and deliberate in her actions. But she also recognized that the man responsible for her rescue at Niagara had been the one with the most to lose. Benjamin, himself a fugitive, had risked his own freedom to make hers possible. He was an excellent father to his children and a very good provider, as his nice house on its big piece of land proved. Her suitor, though at thirty-three more than twice her age, was honest and very diligent; he had earned the respect of the finest captains on the lake and was well regarded in his own community. Although Cecelia was not personally very religious, Benjamin's faith, and especially his belief in the principles of temperance, was reassuring. Toronto had more taverns than churches, and she had only to look around her to see that a good many Macaulaytown families, whatever their background, suffered because of it.

Financial security was important to her. Cecelia had left behind the mother she adored along with her brother, Edward, who was only nine, both of whom she missed dreadfully. Now, with excellent prospects for full-time employment once the boys were in school, she dreamed of saving enough money to purchase her family's freedom and bring them to Toronto to live. If marrying Benjamin was a step towards that goal, Cecelia would not find it much of a hardship.

CHAPTER 5
Under the Paw of the British Lion

The population of the City of Toronto is composed of people from almost all nations . . . A few hundreds of the coloured tribe constituted part of the last census, which amounted to about 20,000 inhabitants; the generality of them appear to be a very industrious and sober race; very orderly in their conduct, and their dress on a Sabbath is of a neat and becoming description: many of those people have spent part of their lives in slavery; and as a proof of the high estimation in which they hold those in remembrance who so strenuously advocated the cause to procure their liberty . . . During the whole time I was a resident in the City of Toronto, I never heard of more than one or two dark deeds having been committed by them, to add a stain to the pages of the public record.

—James Taylor, 1846[1]

AS SOON AS NAVIGATION closed in the fall of 1846, Benjamin requested that the banns be read at St. James' Cathedral.[2] On November 19, 1846, just five months after Benjamin rescued her from Niagara's Cataract House hotel, Benjamin Pollard Holmes and Cecelia Jane Reynolds became man and wife.[3]

The ceremony was performed by Reverend Henry Grasett, a well-regarded minister with an evangelical bent and a special compassion for the city's African American refugees.[4] Although Benjamin was a devout Methodist, Cecelia had been brought up in the Episcopalian Christ Church of Louisville. For complicated reasons relating to the fact that the Church of England was the official religious institution of the British colony, none of the American-born Black ministers in the city were able to solemnize weddings.[5] Elijah B. Dunlop, who was now living in St. Catharines, made a special trip to witness their nuptials.[6] Also standing up for the couple was a Macaulaytown waiter named Francis Mullin.[7]

Cecelia and her new husband had the rest of the winter to enjoy their newlywed status and for little Ben Alexander and James Thomas to become accustomed to Cecelia's new role in their lives. As soon as the ice broke up in the spring of 1847, Benjamin had to return to his job on the lakes and, with his home life now settled, to more clandestine work in the cause of freedom. In common with most African American women living in the cities and towns of Canada West, Cecelia was expected to contribute to the family finances. With her goal of saving her mother and Edward from slavery to spur her on, she took employment that would allow her to be home in the evening with her stepsons.

Fortunately jobs were plentiful. Toronto's servant shortage was legendary.[8] Why would anyone take a domestic position when farmland was available at such reasonable rates? The city's matrons complained of the unkempt, poorly mannered help they were able to hire, and at a premium, so a well-spoken, neatly attired young woman like Cecelia, who had the soothing manner of a Southern servant about her, found herself in demand. She lacked references, of course, but the wives of Captain Dick and Reverend Cooney of the British Wesleyan Church on Richmond knew her husband and could speak to her character and moral fitness for household service. (Captain Richardson's wife, sadly, had her own troubles. His ships were seized by creditors in 1847 and she was forced to give up her beautiful home on Front Street overlooking the water.[9])

Now they were safely married, Cecelia revived her dream of freeing her family, knowing it would take a great deal of hard work and self-sacrifice to accomplish.[10] Although there is no indication that Benjamin's mother, Katie, now keeping house for Benjamin's half-brother, Robert Pollard Jr., was anxious to join her son in Canada, reuniting Cecelia's shattered family was an aspiration the Holmeses shared with many in the expatriate African American community. Nearly everyone had been forced to abandon someone they cared for when they took the Freedom Road. A courageous handful travelled the long and incredibly dangerous path back to the South and stole away beloved family members. Both Hiram Wilson's friend Josiah Henson and Thornton Blackburn, whom Cecelia had met by the cathedral cab stand, had done so, but some of those who tried to rescue family did not return. With Benjamin's boys to think of, it was not a path that she or her new husband would choose.

How to raise so substantial a sum, though? Slaves were very expensive. Nor was it in Charles W. Thruston's nature to discount the value of his excellent housekeeper and cook, or even that of her ailing son, for the sake of a young woman who had, from his perspective, been so ungrateful as to run away. As for Benjamin, his funds were limited. While he earned a good living, his first wife had been sick for a long time, depleting his savings. He and Cecelia had children to feed and clothe, and hopefully there would be more one day. Even if he wanted to sell his Centre Street property, there was not much equity there, for he did not hold the deed. The land belonged to a son of Chief Justice Robinson and would be legally transferred only when Benjamin and Cecelia had paid off its purchase price.

Benjamin was away a good deal and Cecelia found managing both home and children while working at least part of the time almost overwhelming. There was a kitchen garden on their large double lot, and with Benjamin working on the lakes, that was yet another skill she was expected to acquire. However, St. Patrick's Market had just opened nearly opposite the Queen Street home of Captain Thomas Dick, bringing the freshest meat, fish, cheese and vegetables virtually to her door. Cecelia and Benjamin also made a point of patronizing the several Black-owned shops on York Street and along Queen.[11] It was a matter of considerable satisfaction that here in Canada she was addressed as "Mrs. Holmes" by shopkeepers both white and of African ancestry, which would have been unthinkable in her home state of Kentucky.[12]

For entertainment when Benjamin had a rare day off, they could always leave Toronto for the country. A new horse-drawn omnibus service ran up Yonge Street, so they could take the boys to see poor Ann Eliza's grave in Potter's Field, the "Strangers' Burying Ground," to mourn the beloved mother they had lost too soon. While in the area they might visit some of the families who had market gardens and kept both chickens and livestock on their small acreages near the village of Yorkville. Cecelia already knew Moseby Hubbard, who spent the "season" each year waiting tables at Cataract House. In winter he lived with his wife and several children in a snug log cabin at the top of Cruikshank Lane. There was also a horse car that travelled west as far as Cooksville. There Mary Ann Boyd's former brother-in-law George Woodford Ross and his wife, Didiama, lived on a large farm about sixteen miles west of Toronto along the Dundas Road. Cecelia and Benjamin could easily take the boys there to enjoy a day of fresh air and good farm food. There were agricultural fairs in the fall, and Mary Ann Boyd's brother George was proud of the awards he won for his fine breed of cattle.[13]

With a true Scottish appreciation for profit, on American holidays, including the Fourth of July, Captain Thomas Dick ran special excursion trips across the lake to Rochester.[14] Captain Dick sometimes hired Benjamin to serve the festive meals with their red, white and blue iced cakes, and Cecelia and the children might go along for the day. While they had to be careful while on US soil, Grandison and Mary Ann Boyd or some of the Dunlop and Bloxom kin would come to visit with them at the port of

Carthage at the falls of the Genesee, which was the closest steamboat landing to Rochester. The Holmeses came to know the family of Ralph and
Margaret Francis; he was a barber in Rochester and, like Benjamin, actively
working to help freedom-seekers reach Canada. There was also a new arrival
in Rochester who was causing quite a stir. In 1847 a formerly enslaved Black
abolitionist of towering intelligence and stunning eloquence chose Rochester
as the place to begin publication of the newspaper he called *North Star*. His
name was Frederick Douglass.[15]

But holidays were few and workdays many. As Cecelia readied Ben for
his first year of school, she realized that she too had an opportunity to gain
skills she had been denied as a child. She could read but had never learned
to write. In 1846 Canada West had passed an education act and the city
had begun building common schools. Benjamin Alexander Holmes, along
with his little brother, James Thomas, attended Schoolhouse No. 12 at the
corner of Albert and Teraulay Streets, opposite the Abbott house.[16] Their
father had to pay tuition and provide books and supplies—while schools
were run at the taxpayers' expense, they were not free. However, since the
abolitionist-minded Congregationalist minister John Roaf was one of the
school's three trustees, funds were often found to assist poorer Black families. At the same time a city night school was established for working
people, and there were also church-sponsored Sunday Schools where elderly
men and women learned their letters alongside their grandchildren. In yet
another triumph over her formerly enslaved condition, by the time she
finished learning her letters, Cecelia Jane Holmes wrote a nice hand and
expressed herself on paper clearly and well.[17]

The Holmes family was reasonably comfortable financially, but like most
Macaulaytown residents they were dependent on their income. A worldwide
economic recession began in 1847. People had less money to spend on travel
and on dining out, so although Benjamin's wages were fixed, his tips
dropped precipitously. Black-owned businesses, always dependent on white
trade, suffered as Canada's timber prices fell on the world market and there

was simply less money to go around. James Brown, who owned the Prince Albert Recess at 17 Church Street, lost business, and Benjamin's friend James Mink rented his Mansion House Inn to a white hotelier.

For the unskilled majority of Toronto's African Canadian population, their employment prospects took a turn for the worse when Irish immigrants began arriving in their thousands. Fleeing the famine that blighted their homeland, they competed for jobs with those at the lowest rung of the employment ladder, all too often displacing poor Blacks and the city's more recently arrived freedom-seekers. The misery was compounded by a typhus epidemic that targeted the poorer sections of the city, where wells were often too close to privy closets, given the unrelenting heat of the Toronto summer.[18] Cecelia and Benjamin shielded their little boys from infection as best they could, but several of their neighbours died. Eventually an asylum was created for Irish widows and orphans, and in 1848 the city constructed its first "House of Industry" on Elm Street, in the heart of Macaulaytown.[19]

The Irish immigration did result in a boom in the building of inexpensive rental housing. John Meriwether Tinsley had arrived in 1842 and quickly became a leading figure in the Black community. He and his family left Richmond, Virginia, first for Ohio and then Toronto, because of the increasingly oppressive conditions for free Blacks in the United States. The Tinsleys all lived together in a pair of rambling houses at the corner of Agnes and Teraulay, from which they operated a successful construction company that provided many fugitive slaves with their first Toronto employment.[20]

Benjamin took a real interest in politics, and now Cecelia joined him, for changes in US law and policy directly affected how and when they might be able to secure the freedom of Cecelia's family. Along with the rest of Black Toronto, they were well aware of political developments relating to slavery south of the border, as well as the fissures that divided American abolitionism, and there were community meetings to discuss their implications. From travellers and the American papers that were readily available in the city, they knew that the gulf between North and South was widening and that many American abolitionists, both Black and white, had come to reject William Lloyd Garrison's adamantly apolitical and pacifistic approach to antislavery. The new Liberty League, with its champions the wealthy Gerrit Smith of Peterboro, New York, and former Kentucky slaveholder James G. Birney, was running candidates for federal office, as were the Free-Soilers, who opposed expansion of slavery into the American West. As early as 1843, violent resistance was openly discussed at an African American convention in Buffalo attended by both Elijah B. Dunlop and Benjamin's acquaintance from the Rochester underground, the outspoken Ralph Francis. Delegates saw Frederick Douglass furiously argue against Presbyterian minister Henry Highland Garnet, who favoured the use of force against slaveholders, maintaining that they had already declared war on Black America.[21]

Closer to home, Benjamin had now been in Canada West for the requisite seven years and decided to apply for naturalization.[22] Wilson Ruffin Abbott was running for alderman, so Benjamin wanted to cast the first vote of his life for the man who was also Toronto's first African Canadian candidate. Cecelia's husband joined Carter Waddell and his sons, along with Centre Street neighbour Benjamin Gross, in proudly taking the oath to Queen Victoria on December 14, 1847.[23] If Cecelia suspected that temperate Benjamin and his cronies had dropped by afterwards at the establishment of outspoken Black saloon-keeper John T. Fisher to raise a glass to their new status, there was little harm done. Most churchgoing African Canadians espoused the cause of temperance, which in its early incarnation meant moderation rather than total abstinence. Benjamin was no stranger to fine wines and liquors, for he served them to passengers on the *Transit* and the *City of Toronto* all the time. Although the *Globe* considered Abbott "altogether the better candidate," he declined to campaign and the white majority of St. Patrick's Ward instead elected two favoured sons of the Family Compact.[24]

By virtue of Benjamin's naturalization, Cecelia became a proud British subject, with all the Crown protection that implied, as did young Benjamin Alexander.[25] Concerned for her mother and younger brother in faraway

Kentucky, she watched and worried as the conditions for both free and enslaved people worsened. The United States had acquired a vast swath of land from Mexico in 1848, including Texas and California, reopening old wounds regarding the extension of cotton agriculture.[26] America's acquisition of California had another by-product: during 1848 and 1849, Benjamin and Cecelia watched as the sons of friends in both Rochester and Toronto caught "gold fever" and departed for the California gold rush. Despite the dangers presented by US travel, particularly for those who had fled slavery only a few years before, an uncounted number flocked to the goldfields from cities, towns and farms on both sides of the Great Lakes.

As African American immigration to Canada continued to escalate, newcomers faced a noticeable increase in racial discrimination. This affected Cecelia's family just as it did everyone else.[27] Some better-educated immigrants complained that Canadian racism was more difficult to deal with than American, because it was so *polite*. Learning where one could and could not go was a matter of trial and error, as opposed to the unequivocal rules of contact that governed the lives of Blacks, both free and enslaved, throughout the United States.[28]

Benjamin travelled more widely than his wife and children did by virtue of his job, and he knew that anti-Black feeling was much worse in the countryside. Toronto's relatively harmonious relations between Black and white residents was bolstered by the support for African American immigration provided by Scottish-born newspaper publisher and future reform politician George Brown, along with his father, Peter, and brother Gordon, and also by leading clergymen. From the time it was first launched in 1844, George Brown's *Globe* proved an invaluable friend to the fugitive, and an implacable opponent of American slavery.[29]

The city's cadre of sympathetic churchmen included the redoubtable Bishop John Strachan and a Presbyterian minister named Michael Willis, who had just arrived to become president of Knox College. Lacking a permanent home, the college was housed in a stately row of buildings on Front

Street constructed as an investment by Benjamin's employer, Captain Dick.[30] As a proactive measure against racism and to educate his students in the way he wanted them to go, Reverend Willis sent Knox students to teach at the new integrated grammar school at the Elgin Association Settlement, founded in 1849 on the Raleigh Plain south of Chatham, about fifty-three miles east of the Detroit River. They taught the children of former slaves Latin, Greek, mathematics, philosophy and other subjects intended to prepare them for entry into King's College and the provincial Normal School, where teachers were trained.[31]

Named Buxton after British abolitionist Thomas Fowell Buxton, the settlement was the brainchild of Scottish clergyman William King and was supported by a consortium of Toronto, Montreal and Buffalo businessmen. Investors included George Brown and Benjamin's friend Wilson Ruffin Abbott. Canada's first planned fugitive slave community, it was intended to demonstrate that, given a level playing field, Black settlers were in every way as moral, industrious, temperate and likely to succeed as European ones. There was strong local objection to siting a colony of Black Americans so close to white settlements, but Reverend King persevered. Land was sold only to fugitive slaves, but Black Toronto lost one of its most important spokesmen when Wilson and Ellen Abbott made a temporary move to property near the settlement so their very bright young son, Anderson, could attend the Buxton school.[32]

Relaxing their vigilance somewhat, the Holmeses occasionally travelled across the lake and ventured into Rochester to stay with the Boyds or the Francis family. Benjamin's friends from his early days in Toronto, the Cleggetts, were also living in the area, and the Patterson brothers had abandoned the Dawn Settlement, with its contentious politics, to open a new hairdressing salon in Rochester.[33]

The presence of Frederick Douglass, who had moved his family to the city from New Bedford, Massachusetts, in 1848, linked Rochester more firmly to the Black activism of the eastern seaboard and its leading abolitionists, such as Charles Lenox Remond, scion of an entrepreneurial African American family in Boston, who had lectured with Douglass. Dr. Martin Delany, formerly of Pittsburgh and one of the very few trained Black physicians in the entire United States, came with him to co-edit the *North Star*. Also helping Douglass as a subscription agent and later an editor was a brilliant young man named William Cooper Nell (1816–1874). The son of a prominent free Black family in Boston, Nell was active in abolitionist circles and published the first African American history. Douglass, whom Benjamin's old friend Grandison Boyd knew well, was supported in his venture by the efforts of Rochester pharmacist Isaac Post and his wife, Amy. Quakers who had left their meeting over their active engagement in antislavery, they operated a busy Underground Railroad station out of their house, where they also—most unusually, even for white abolitionists—hosted the leading figures of Black abolitionism for weeks on end.[34]

The financial Panic of 1847 lasted through the next year, and in 1849 a disastrous fire destroyed a good deal of Toronto's central business district, including the homes and shops of several African Canadians. The cathedral where Cecelia and Benjamin had been married was reduced to ash, but within a year Toronto had a new city hall and St. James' Cathedral was being rebuilt, larger and more imposing than before. A welcome addition was St. Lawrence Hall, a frothy wedding cake of a building at the corner of Jarvis and King Streets, with a gorgeous ballroom and public meeting space above and commercial space on the ground floor. The Holmes family's financial prospects began to look up too, when the Government of the Canadas moved back to Toronto and occupied the rather shabby old Parliament Buildings on Front Street, just a few blocks south and west of their home. This brought politicians and their families to the city, and Cecelia's Macaulaytown neighbours found a good deal of work in domestic service, driving coaches and doing gardening for the new households. Poorer women and those left alone with small children took in washing and ironing. With the civil service now centred in Toronto, there were many men with families living in the finer boarding houses and hotels, all in need of such services, and Cecelia herself undoubtedly benefitted from the increased trade.

Cecelia and her family now lived in a city with a population of 25,000 people; for about a thousand of them, their ancestry reached back to the shores of Africa. Thousands more set their sights on freedom in Canada after September 18, 1850, when President Millard Fillmore, under great pressure from the Southern faction in Congress, signed into law a much harsher and better enforced Fugitive Slave Act.[35] The Act made Benjamin's Underground Railroad work even more dangerous than it had been, for it was truly draconian. There were substantially increased fines and prison sentences for anyone helping or harbouring fugitives, and now magistrates and officers of the law throughout the North were required to assist slave-owners and their agents in recapturing runways. Special new commissioners were deployed with power to decide whether an accused fugitive was slave or free. They received a larger fee for sending refugees back to their erstwhile owners,[36] and anyway, the deck was stacked against Blacks. In most states they had no defence at all, for African Americans were prohibited from testifying on their own behalf. People who had been free for generations were terrified, for it was a simple matter for a bounty hunter to destroy the freedom papers that were their only safeguard, and carry them off south for sale.

In Toronto, George Brown of the *Globe* railed against the "bloodhound bill" that he said was intended to turn the whole of the United States into a "nation of slavecatchers." In February 1851 he and like-minded white Torontonians came together with African Canadian representatives at St. Lawrence Hall. In the elegant public building that had risen from the ashes of the Toronto fire they established the new Anti-Slavery Society of Canada (ASC).[37] The chair was Reverend Michael Willis and there were three African Canadians on the board, including Henry Bibb, a Kentucky refugee living in Sandwich who published the staunchly abolitionist *Voice of the Fugitive* newspaper there,[38] and Toronto's Wilson Ruffin Abbott. Recognizing that the immediate needs of the refugees had to be served first, in April of that same year Reverend Willis's wife, Agnes, along with Ellen Toyer Abbott, organized a women's auxiliary composed of both white and Black Torontonians to gather food and clothing to assist newcomers.[39] Reverend Willis always had a special fund set aside for a fearless, righteous little woman who had moved to St. Catharines, in the Niagara peninsula, after passage of the Fugitive Slave Law. She was on the board of the local ASC branch there and made frequent trips south of the Mason-Dixon Line to rescue members of her family from Maryland slavery. Her name was Harriet Tubman.

Branches of the ASC were established across the province, and in May the board invited Frederick Douglass to the city. Cecelia and her husband had the opportunity to take their boys, now twelve and ten years old, to hear Douglass speak. Having arrived from Lewiston on the *Chief Justice Robinson*, under the command of Captain Thomas Dick, Douglass commented that in contrast to his experiences as a Black man on American steamers, he had been treated in an entirely gentlemanly fashion by captain, crew and Canadian passengers alike. Doubtless he was afforded special attention by William Harney, the dining room steward and one of Benjamin and Cecelia's Macaulaytown neighbours.[40] Douglass was housed at the North American on Front Street, which was Toronto's best hotel. He had come accompanied by British parliamentarian George Thompson and Reverend Samuel J. May, an abolitionist Unitarian minister and Underground Railroad stationmaster living at Syracuse, New York. Speaking in thunderous tones, the men delivered three successive nights of lectures vilifying the Fugitive Slave Law. George Thompson berated his audience, urging them to remember that slaves were their own brothers and sisters in the sight of God, while Frederick Douglass annoyed the conservative Anglican organ *The Church* by suggesting that physical resistance to the slaveholder was sometimes justified. He also addressed the congregation at what was now the African Methodist Episcopal (AME) Church located on Sayre Street, almost in Benjamin and Cecelia's backyard.[41]

Cecelia and her family, along with most Toronto Blacks, were certainly aware of what was going on in the United States for there was a dramatic rise in Underground Railroad activity. Reaction in the North was so strong that it was said the Fugitive Slave Law created committed abolitionists out of people who had never been abolitionists before. Captured fugitives were taken, tried and returned to their owners, and a number of famous rescues were effected by local Black communities, sometimes assisted by white abolitionists. One particularly dramatic event in the farming district of Christiana, Pennsylvania, resulted in a riot; a slaveholder attempting to retrieve his human "property" was killed, sending several locals who had been involved in the event rushing for the Canadian border. They were concealed by Frederick Douglass in Rochester and then sent across the lake, where they settled at Buxton.[42] Some states passed personal liberty laws to safeguard their populations against kidnapping, while entire congregations, complete with pastors, abandoned their homes, farms and hard-won businesses and fled. Pennsylvania papers reported the loss of nearly all of Pittsburgh's African American waiters, some three hundred strong, within a six-week period.[43] At Rochester and in other harbour towns bordering the Great Lakes, Blacks engaged in Underground Railroad work came together to discuss how best to deal with the vastly increased traffic.

Benjamin was again working for Captain Dick on the Royal Mail Line's *City of Toronto*, sailing the Toronto–Kingston route. Since it stopped at ports east of Toronto and entailed an overnight stay every other day, his ability to assist freedom-seekers was more limited than it had been.[44] There was no particular danger to him personally. Thanks to Reverend Wilson's publication in the abolitionist press in 1840, his former owners were well aware of where he lived. On the other hand, Cecelia's location remained, to the best of their knowledge, unknown to the Thrustons. Both Cecelia's younger brother and her mother were entirely illiterate, so she had no safe way of contacting her family. She was afraid to do so anyway. Determined slaveholders sometimes sent their agents even to Toronto to kidnap people and take them back to slavery.

She and the other women at the AME and the little Baptist church on

Queen Street did what they could to help, but nowadays steamers brought in a dozen or more frightened, desperate people every day. The same was true at Hamilton and in harbour towns along the Niagara and Detroit Rivers. Aboard the *Chief Justice Robinson*, a fugitive slave could be in Lewiston on the Niagara River at lunchtime and in Toronto for dinner.[45] There were Canadian-owned Rochester-bound steamers as well; the *America* departed at 10:30 a.m. Mondays, Wednesdays and Fridays, with stops at Canadian ports east of Toronto such as Port Hope and Cobourg. From Rochester or Buffalo, thanks to the Erie Canal, "Passengers by this route may reach Boston or New York within 40 hours from Toronto," and of course the same was true in the opposite direction. It was fortunate for one fugitive, a man named Ben Hockley, who was pursued as far as Lockport, New York, that the passengers of the *Chief Justice Robinson* were enjoying the view one day in 1853, for they discovered him, desperate and freezing, in the chilly waters. Fearing capture, he had "lashed himself to a gate and launched himself into the Niagara River," hoping to reach Canada. The current had proven too strong for him; he was drifting far out in Lake Ontario's waters when he was spied by the passengers and brought aboard, bound for Toronto.[46]

In addition to the refugees from Southern bondage, Toronto received a steady trickle of free Blacks from the urban North. Antislavery lecturer Henry Bibb, originally from Kentucky, and his free-born wife, Mary, had moved from Detroit to Sandwich after the new law was passed. Their *Voice of the Fugitive* was Canada's first Black abolitionist newspaper, and had multiple subscribers in Toronto. Bibb wrote on October 22, 1851: "Men of capital with good property, some of whom are worth thousands, are settling among us from the Northern states." Some bought farms near the Elgin Settlement at Buxton, but people with skills more suitable to city living, like Newton Cary's nephew John J. Cary, came to Toronto from Cincinnati in 1850. He was already committed to the Underground Railroad and political abolitionism and a participant in the Black convention move-ment.[47] More people passed through the city than stayed, and Cecelia and

Benjamin from time to time would encounter someone from Louisville, Richmond or even little King and Queen County, Virginia, who could tell them how "their people" were when last they saw them.

Much of the work entailed in welcoming fugitive slaves fell to women, although the city now boasted a single Black doctor. Alexander Thomas Augusta arrived late in 1850, flush with profits from the California gold rush. He enrolled at the Toronto Medical School and opened an apothecary shop on Yonge Street, on the eastern fringe of Macaulaytown, while his wife launched her "New Fancy Dry Goods and Dressmaking Establishment" on York Street between Richmond and Adelaide.[48] Homemakers such as Cecelia, who had both the room and some means (especially with Benjamin out of town so much), billeted entire families, sewed or collected garments for their use, and cooked endless meals. The limited resources of African Canadian self-help and charitable organizations were soon overwhelmed by the need, as hundreds of people, some of whom had lived for years in Northern states, abandoned all they had to preserve their freedom.[49]

Groups such as the Queen Victoria Benevolent Society, operating out of the AME church, worked closely with the wives of white clergymen to find situations for their charges. Most of the incoming women went into service, at least temporarily. Toronto's elite, merchant and even artisanal classes had ample employment for either live-in or day help, although Irish servants were providing some competition.[50] The city was oversupplied with washerwomen, and Cecelia watched men whose families filled every possible nook and cranny in Macaulaytown going out at dawn to the city's outskirts to chop wood for a few cents a day.

More formal reception services were provided by their neighbour Robin Philips. His three houses behind Osgoode Hall were the first Toronto destination of dozens, if not hundreds, of fugitive slaves. The Philipses served as Toronto agents for William Still, the Philadelphia-based secretary of the Pennsylvania Anti-Slavery Society, and connected men with employers such as the Smallwood saw manufactory and the Tinsley construction company.[51]

In a proactive attempt to make sense of all the upheaval, Henry Bibb used the pages of his newspaper to send out a call for a convention to discuss how best to both help the free people of the Northern states, and succour the freedom-seekers whose only safe haven was now in British North America or what remained of Mexico. Benjamin's job prevented his attendance at the North American Convention of Coloured Freemen, held at Toronto's St. Lawrence Hall from September 11 to 13, 1851. However, Cecelia, with the other churchwomen, would have been present to serve the meals provided by the city's several excellent African Canadian caterers. Delegates came from all over the Great Lakes region and some from as far away as Jamaica and England. Elijah B. Dunlop was there for St. Catharines, along with Benjamin's old mentor Reverend Hiram Wilson, who had left the British-American Institute and moved to the Niagara peninsula in 1849 to open a school and reception centre for fugitive slaves.[52] Also there was Josiah Henson of Dawn, fresh from a trip to display the settlement's finely sawn and polished hardwood boards at the British Industrial Exhibition in London.[53] John M. Tinsley and his talented musical son James D. Tinsley took part; the latter was appointed, along with saloon-keeper J. T. Fisher and conference organizer Henry Bibb, to summarize the resolutions passed during the proceedings.[54]

Also participating were Thomas Smallwood, J. C. Brown (now living in Chatham, as was Dr. Martin Delany) and Wilson Ruffin Abbott, accompanied by his wife, Ellen Toyer Abbott, although no women's names appear in the proceedings, for they were excluded from being delegates. The Abbotts were living again in Toronto while their son Anderson completed his education at Ohio's Oberlin College. Reverend Samuel Ringgold Ward arrived by steamer via Buffalo; he pastored a church in Syracuse, where he ran his own flourishing Underground Railroad operation. Abraham D. Shadd, secretary of the first Black National Convention, came from Pennsylvania with his intelligent, outspoken eldest daughter, Mary Ann.[55]

One of the conclusions of the conference was a plan to establish a consortium to build a mill, sawmill and general store at the Buxton Settlement to provide immediate employment for the large numbers of incoming fugitives. Cecelia was proud to learn that Thornton Blackburn, the fugitive slave and Toronto taxicab owner whom a relation of Fanny Thruston's had chased all the way to the borders of Canada, was appointed vice-president.[56]

Of all the people there, Cecelia was most interested in the Detroit delegation.[57] It included a white Presbyterian minister named Charles C. Foote. A graduate of Oberlin like the Reverend Hiram Wilson, he had a somewhat chequered reputation among Black people on both sides of the border.[58] A formidable opponent of slavery, he lectured widely on the desperate plight of the fugitive, arousing the ire of proud Black Canadians by painting an unflattering image of their conditions in order to encourage donations.[59] On the other hand, Reverend Foote did receive and transport across the border (thus avoiding customs duties) large quantities of clothing and books donated by American organizations to help the refugees.[60] As well, he collaborated with the Bibbs in a land-distribution scheme called the Refugee Home Society, intended to settle refugees on independent farms in the far western part of the province.

Between heated conference sessions wrestling with such questions as whether or not Canada remained the best place to send freedom-seekers and how to unify the multiple Black antislavery groups in the American North and Canada into a single, more effective organization, Cecelia made a point of attracting Reverend Foote's attention. Detroit seemed far enough away that Charles W. Thruston would not suspect her Toronto location. Foote agreed to be Cecelia's go-between in establishing contact with her former owners in Louisville. She and Benjamin had carefully hoarded their savings against the day when they could buy her family out of slavery. Now was the time to put the first piece of their plan into place. Using her newfound literacy skills and gathering every ounce of her courage, Cecelia wrote a letter to the slaveholder in whose household she had grown up. Charles W. Thruston never replied.

CHAPTER 6
GOT MY LETTER

Pa received a letter from you, Celia, a few days ago, in which you
make affectionate inquiries about all your family. He has received
other letters from you at different times, all of which I read to your
Mother and Brother; and should have answered your last to him,
but you said in it, that you expected to leave Canada soon for
Europe in pursuit of health, so I reasonably concluded you could
not receive my reply before your departure.

—Fanny Thruston Ballard to Cecelia Jane Holmes, March 11, 1852

OVER THE NEXT MONTHS, Cecelia addressed several more letters to
the Thruston household, but it was not until the spring of 1852 that she
received her first response. Rather dreading what Charles W. Thruston
might have to say, she was delighted to see that it came from her former
mistress, via Reverend Foote's Detroit address.[1]

Fanny began her letter with an apology for not replying sooner. She
said she had been uncertain where to write because, she wrote, Cecelia's
most recent letter had said she was on her way to Europe "in pursuit of
health."[2] Informing Cecelia that she had read her earlier letters aloud to
Mary and Edward, she then described her own circumstances:

There have been many changes in my family since you lived with
us: in the first place I myself have been married almost four years
and have two little boys—the first I call Charles Thruston[3] and the
second Bland Ballard.[4] Charley is not yet two years old, Bland is
not quite five months. My husband (Andrew J. Ballard) is a lawyer
and native of Kentucky and we still live at the old homestead on
Walnut Street.[5]

Cecelia would have found it interesting that Fanny's family was living
in her father's home. That Charles would be loath to part with his only
remaining daughter when her time came to marry was no surprise to anyone. He had apparently managed to both marry her off and keep her at
home under his watchful eye.[6]

Six years had passed since she and Fanny had seen one another.
Although there was a reassuring warmth underlying her words, Fanny's
tone was formal and a bit stiff, and Cecelia could see that the woman who
still was, under American law, her owner was delicately aware of the change
in their relative circumstances. Cecelia was no longer her little slave girl but
rather a respectable married woman of twenty-one with husband, home
and family of her own. Free to come and go as she chose, she owed no one
her service and answered to no mistress.

Fanny herself was now twenty-six. She had grown up to fill the role of
Louisville society matron for which her education and upbringing had
groomed her. Cecelia knew Fanny would now be mistress and chief manager of her husband's slaves, and also those of her father, hopefully still
including Mary and Edward Reynolds. She had been careful so far only to
ask after the health of her mother and especially her frail young brother,
but Fanny understood her old friend and companion better than she knew.
She answered both her questions about Mary Reynolds, and one she had
not asked but to which she very much wanted to learn the answer:

I will first write of those in whom you are most interested and begin with your Mother. She was here yesterday; is beginning to show age a little, but is in most excellent health. She does not now belong to Pa. After my marriage she desired to be sold; but she frequently visits us and is exceedingly anxious that I should buy her, and bring her home to live again. She seems to be so much attached to us and always so good a servant that I wished to do so, but her present owner was unwilling to part with her.

So Mary had been sold out of the family. That alone was crushing news, with some nasty implications besides. All freedom-seekers who left family behind knew that they risked their family's suffering in retaliation. Cecelia had pinned her hopes on the fact that the Thrustons considered themselves good slaveholders who ensured that their enslaved servants appeared well cared for and happy. Whippings were infrequent, although she could remember a time when the lash rang out regularly from the old ropewalk next door. How angry had her sudden departure made Charles? Did he suspect that her poor mother had been aware her daughter was plotting to escape, even before she left Louisville? Mary must have been somehow mistreated if she had abandoned her only son to his fate and asked to leave the household.

Although Mary Reynolds lived elsewhere, Fanny had made a point of reading Cecelia's letters aloud to her, and she longed to see her daughter. Cecelia found it interesting that when Mary begged to come "home to live again," it was Fanny and her husband she wanted to buy her, rather than her former master, Charles W. Thruston. Mary evidently believed that the kind-hearted and devout Fanny was more likely than the harsh and uncompromising Master Charles to help her make arrangements to free herself so she could join her daughter in Canada. Fanny's words were laden with hidden meaning:

I told [Mary] however that I would always feel interested in her and would at any time be glad to have her live with me. She says she has a good home but would rather live with me than any one else. She frequently talks to me about you and always in tears expresses a hope to see you once more.

Though Cecelia knew her former mistress very well and understood that she was not above eliciting a little guilt for what she perceived as Cecelia's betrayal, Fanny was suggesting that she herself might be willing to help place Mary in her daughter's hands, should an opportunity present itself. As for Edward, Fanny intimated that he would never see his older sister again:

Your brother Edward, Pa still owns; he is still afflicted with Scrofula; has never outgrown it as we once hoped, and is now under medical advice, as he has at different times since his birth. He has grown very much, but I think you would know him were you to see him for his face has changed very little tho' he is now in his sixteenth year.[7]

Cecelia's husband, Benjamin, understood the implications of this instantly, if Cecelia did not. If he was somewhat relieved that they had to raise only Mary's purchase price rather than that of both her and Edward . . . well, as a twice-married man he wisely kept his feelings to himself.

The rest of Fanny's letter was full of family happenings. In the oddly intimate interpersonal relationships that slavery and slaveholding bred, Cecelia had at one time known most of Fanny's extended family nearly as well as Fanny did.

My Brother Sam has been married about eighteen months, has never had a child and is for the present in business in St. Louis, Missouri.[8] I frequently hear from St. Louis, none of my relations have died there except Uncle Dr. Farrar[9] and Aunt Abby Clark, the first of Cholera, a year and a half ago; and Aunt Abby last January leaving seven sons.[10]

Cecelia had grown up alongside Sam Thruston, who was the Thrustons' only son to survive childhood,[11] and also knew Fanny's Clark relations in St. Louis for she had worked in their homes alongside their servants during family visits. She shuddered at memories of Charles W. Thruston's O'Fallon half-brothers, who had at one time kept specially trained bloodhounds to track any of their slaves who might try to escape.[12] The young woman was interested to hear about her old friend Sarah, who had been lady's maid to one of Fanny's more youthful aunts:

> Isabelle Churchill married a merchant of St. Louis; and Sarah your old friend still lives with Belle in St. Louis.[13] Thomas & Charles Churchill have also married.[14] Tom married a lady from Arkansas and lives in that state. Julia Churchill[15] whom we call Puss, is now a grown young lady with many admirers. Aunt Emily Zane has three children, two girls, whom you have seen, and one boy.[16] Aunt Malinda & Uncle John Oldham I see occasionally, both are well.[17] John Bullock is married and has a young child.[18]

Cecelia was momentarily amused at the thought of Fanny's "Uncle John Oldham." She wondered what that rather severe man would think if he knew that his former slave, Thornton Blackburn, now owned a successful cab business and was a well-respected businessman in Toronto.[19] In closing, Fanny expressed herself willing to continue corresponding with Cecelia, ending with a blessing evocative of her profound Episcopalian faith:

> I can think of no other news concerning your friends that would interest you; but if you have any inquiries to make about a partic-

ular person or persons, I will at any time willingly inform you.

I hope Cecelia you are happy; much happier than when you were my property; and I trust you may always be surrounded by every comfort and blessing. If it should be never your lot to meet your parent on earth may God in his mercy and love gather you together in Heaven.

Cecelia sorrowed to think of Edward's condition, but in fact Mary's situation was more urgent than it had been. Since she no longer belonged to Fanny's father, her new owner was perfectly free to sell her away, even to the Deep South, just as Adam Reynolds had been so long ago. The cost of buying Mary was, however, more than Benjamin and Cecelia now realized they could ever save from their earnings. To that end, Fanny's letter had arrived in the nick of time, for Benjamin and Cecelia were indeed planning a major trip abroad.

They had been carefully considering their prospects over the past winter. On the one hand, they were doing well enough. With both boys in school, Cecelia had been more able to work, and Benjamin had again been hired by Captain Thomas Dick for the sailing season. Dick was now sole owner of the *City of Toronto*, running the old Toronto–Niagara route that had brought Cecelia to Toronto six years before. The *Transit* was no more: the consortium that seized the ship from Hugh Richardson during his financial troubles in 1847 had run her aground on the shoals of the St. Lawrence.[20]

The Holmes family's commitment to fugitive slave assistance was as great as ever. With steamers now sometimes depositing a dozen or more refugees at a time at Toronto and other Canadian Great Lakes ports, Benjamin's clandestine efforts to save those he could had not gone unnoticed by some of the most important Black abolitionists of the day. Underground Railroad conductors were almost never identified by name, lest they be taken up by American authorities and their routes compromised, but in a letter published in Frederick Douglass's newspaper, Samuel Ringgold Ward expressed particular admiration for the untiring assistance undertaken at Toronto by "good brethren like brother Francis, brother Holmes and brother Brown."[21] Although Cecelia's efforts were not mentioned, Ward's was a rare and important tribute to Cecelia's husband.

Reverend Ward's acknowledgement suggests that Benjamin Pollard Holmes's Underground Railroad efforts were known to the leaders of contemporary Black abolitionism. Samuel Ringgold Ward and Jermain Loguen, both ministers and committed Underground Railroad stationmasters, had been forced to relocate to Canada West with their families after being involved in the successful rescue of "Jerry" McHenry in Syracuse, New York. Reverend Ward was hired on as the travelling agent for the Anti-Slavery Society of Canada, and soon after his arrival he was approached by Mary Ann Shadd to help her publish a new African Canadian paper.

After the Convention of Coloured Freedmen, Shadd had moved to Canada to help Mary and Henry Bibb with their newspaper. Establishing a school for Black children at Sandwich, on the Detroit River, she soon had a falling out with the Bibbs over the issue of "begging," or soliciting funds, used clothing and other supplies on behalf of the fugitives living in Canada. She reserved a special dislike for Reverend Charles Foote, who had facilitated Cecelia's correspondence with Fanny. He was noted for his lurid descriptions of the privations suffered by freedom-seekers. After a particularly bitter exchange with Foote and the Bibbs over the Refugee Home Society land-distribution scheme, the American Missionary Association rescinded funding for her school. Mary Ann Shadd resolved to start her own newspaper, which she named the *Provincial Freeman*. Its masthead trumpeted Mary Ann's views on Black immigration to Canada: "Self-reliance is the true road to independence."

The *Provincial Freeman* had Reverend Samuel Ringgold Ward on its masthead as publisher, in deference to contemporary sensibilities regarding the proper role of women in society.[22] She could not have had a better associate. Describing Ward, Frederick Douglass said: "As an orator and thinker he was vastly superior, I thought, to any of us . . . In depth of thought, fluency of speech, readiness of wit, logical exactness, and general intelligence, Samuel R. Ward has left no successor among the colored men among us."[23] It was fortunate that the paper began when it did, for in 1854 Henry Bibb died suddenly, and the *Voice of the Fugitive* with him.

The presence of a Black press was important. It kept African Canadians, including Benjamin and his wife, aware of the widening divide between North and South as pro- and antislavery positions became ever more entrenched. They were dismayed by the disarray into which organized abolitionism had fallen. William Lloyd Garrison and his followers were distracted by issues of women's rights and prison reform that had little relationship to helping free the South's millions of slaves, while African American abolitionists struggled to provide what aid they could to thousands seeking to escape their bonds. Out of this volatile crucible came the astonishing public response to a serialized novel published in the *National Era* in Washington, DC, between June 1851 and the first of April, 1852. A New England schoolteacher named Harriet Beecher Stowe was taking the world by storm. Rumoured to be based in part on the autobiography of Dawn Settlement founder Josiah Henson, it was called *Uncle Tom's Cabin* and brought thousands of readers into the abolitionist fold, at least as armchair activists. On the political front, Black Canada now had a highly placed friend in Parliament, for George Brown had been elected, with the support of many previously conservative African Canadian voters. His "Clear Grits" were a new political party that promised reform.

The Anti-Slavery Society of Canada opened an employment office on Toronto's Front Street to help newly arrived fugitives, while the ladies' auxiliary collected goods to distribute to those in need. There would soon be an easier path by which to transport the refugees as well. The past October had seen the ground-breaking for a new railway, the first in the province, that would link Toronto with Montreal and then the Upper Great Lakes.

Rail service had already begun between the port of Oswego as far as Syracuse, New York, greatly facilitating Underground Railroad traffic. At Rochester, as was true across the full sweep of Lake Ontario's south shore, Underground Railroad business had increased to an all-time high.

Despite his commitment to his clandestine work on behalf of the fugitives, Benjamin and Cecelia were anxious to take charge of their own fortunes, particularly in light of what they now knew about Mary Reynolds's changed circumstances. Fortunately there was a bright spot on the horizon and it shone with an aureate gleam. Alluvial gold had been discovered in New South Wales, Australia, in early 1851. Within months strikes were made at Ballarat and also Bendigo, where a tent city, then a nascent town, sprang up to the northwest of Melbourne. The rush was on.

The Black abolitionist press became caught up in the fever. On October 9, 1851, Washington's *National Era* reported on finds near Bathurst: "quantities as great as those which, on the average, are obtained in California. About a thousand pounds' worth of the metal had been received at Sydney in the course of only a few days." On May 13, the same paper reported: "We have glowing accounts from the gold region of Australia. The ship *Brilliant* had arrived in England with £217,000 in gold, and the ship *Statesman* was on her way with 80,000 ounces. Twenty-one vessels, with emigrants from the adjacent colonies, were entering the harbor of Port St. Philip when the *Brilliant* sailed."

In Canada, special sailings destined for Australian ports were announced in the Montreal, Halifax and Toronto newspapers. Travel agents opened offices at Front and Wellington Streets, and outfitters touted the availability of rough, durable clothing and luggage designed for the long journey. While a sea voyage on one of the fast new Atlantic packet boats to British ports lasted twelve to fifteen days, the trip from Liverpool to Australia took three months or more, and that in fair weather. Undeterred, the men who left for the goldfields included the sons of some of Benjamin's oldest Toronto friends.

The names Tinsley, Cary and Hickman appeared on ships' manifests, all Australia-bound. Among those going was Elijah B. Dunlop, who left a wife and children behind in St. Catharines. William and Betsey Hickman entrusted to his care their younger son, Henry, aged twenty-six; both men booked passage on the *Madison* and landed on December 22, 1852, at Melbourne.[24] On the same ship went Lewis Gross, whose father had taken the naturalization oath with Benjamin five years before, and thirty-one-year-old James Dunlop Patterson, with brother Zachariah to follow on a later ship.[25] James D. Tinsley, son of builder John M. Tinsley, also went, with his brother John Henry. On July 31, 1852, the Tinsley brothers and four of their friends left Toronto. They had booked passage on a fast and comfortably appointed three-masted schooner, the *Epaminondas.*[26] The six men first crossed Lake Ontario, headed for the port of New York to take ship, and arrived in Melbourne, Australia, in November 1852. All free-born Virginians who had lived in Canada for years, they were listed as "coloured" in the ship's manifest.[27]

Grandison Boyd went too. Since the Fugitive Slave Law began to endanger his home and business in Rochester, he had been trying to buy himself out of slavery. Both to conceal his location from his legal owner and to raise funds to purchase his freedom, he asked Frederick Douglass for help. Douglass in turn approached Sidney Howard Gay, who published the *National Anti-Slavery Standard* in New York, in a letter dated June 12, 1852, on his behalf:

My Dear Sir

My friend Boyed called upon me to day and informed me, of his purpose to ransom himself. He also told me of your kind offices in the matter. Thinking that you might feel more assured in the undertaking on his behalf, if you knew something of the man, I take the liberty to say a word to you respecting him. When I came to Rochester five years ago among the first colored persons to whom I was introduced was Mr. Boyed. He was then a respectable grocer keeping his shop on Maine Street. I found him an upright industrious and interprizing man greatly respected by the white people—and loved among the intelligent colored people.

I am sure Sir—that whatever service you may render Mr. Boyed will be service rendered to a worthy man.

Very truly yours,

Fred Douglass[28]

It was an extraordinary step and spoke to how much regard Douglass had for Grandison Boyd, for he and Sidney Howard Gay detested one another. When Boyd's attempts to raise the necessary funds failed, he left his wife with her family at Toronto and he too set sail for Australia.

Caught up in mutual enthusiasm, Cecelia and Benjamin rented out their house to a man named George Browne, with neighbour George Washington delegated to act as "agent" to pay the taxes and collect the rent of £12 annually.[29] They expected to be gone about two years. The only sticking point was what to do with the children. Ben was already at an age when most youths began to apprentice in a trade. James Thomas was a little young for that, but the boys were so close they could hardly be separated, and they could at least look after one another while their father and step-mother were out of the country.

The dilemma resolved itself in an intriguing fashion. In Lowell, Massachusetts, a group of prominent Black barbers were offering an informal barber training program. Several of them were members of families that had been engaged in generations of protest in abolitionist Boston, including founders of that city's oldest African American institutions. Such men could be trusted to keep Benjamin's boys safe while providing them with solid training leading to an excellent career.

That Lowell also boasted the only integrated public education system in the United States, with an excellent secondary school. This was a deciding factor, for at Lowell Ben and James Thomas would have the benefit of as good an education as they could receive in Toronto.[30]

Benjamin and Cecelia's choice of Lowell was perhaps influenced by a man, a cordwainer by trade, who had left Toronto before Cecelia arrived. Benjamin and his first wife had known him well. In earlier years a trustee of Toronto's Coloured Wesleyan Methodist Church, Joseph Peniel Turner was now an ordained minister living thirty miles from Lowell, Massachusetts.[31] Turner moved in the same antislavery and denominational circles as Lowell's master barbers, and it may well have been he who explained Lowell's advantages to the Holmes.[32]

Still, taking the boys to Lowell first and then sailing for Europe from either Boston or New York presented considerable danger. There had already been celebrated attempts to rescue fugitive slaves from being sent back to their owners under the Fugitive Slave Law, including one at Lowell. Whether or not Benjamin and Cecelia's status as British subjects would keep them and the boys safe was anyone's guess, but they decided the benefits outweighed the risk. Benjamin was nearly forty, hardly a young man, but his sense of adventure was unabated, and Cecelia's goal of rescuing her family could not be met by remaining in Toronto.

They could easily work their passage, Benjamin as a waiter and Cecelia as a stewardess.[33] Women stewardesses were common on oceangoing steamers and, like Cecelia, they were often the wives of male servants. Experienced employees such as Cecelia spent their time on board in service to the captain's family and the female portion of the first-class passengers. There was also the prospect of employment for either or both of them in Australia if a fortune in gold was not forthcoming from mining. Such was the hunger for riches that after arriving in Australian ports, entire ships' crews, along with their captains, would abandon ship. Fifty derelict vessels were reportedly lying at anchor in Hobson's Bay by June 1852, and seamen's wages went through the roof in an effort to keep at least the mail runs operating. Servants were not to be had for any price and it was widely reported that the governor of Australia was obliged to groom his own horse. Foodstuffs became incredibly expensive, and those who provided them charged exorbitant rates.[34]

The decision to leave Canada would prove fateful. Cecelia was to return to Toronto two years later, but she would come back alone, and in circumstances that caused an estrangement from Benjamin's sons that never healed. Ben Alexander and James Thomas Holmes would return to Canada only as grown men, and they would make their homes away from Toronto. As for Cecelia's Benjamin, he would not see his little house on Centre Street until 1856, and then it would be in the saddest of circumstances. But that was all in the future, which must have seemed very bright in the early summer months of 1852.

CHAPTER 7
Go Down Moses

Black barbers fended off white competitors by preserving the artisan system, inventing first-class barber shops, and catering to the racial stereotypes of their white customers. Of these elements, the artisan system formed the cornerstone of the black barbers' tradition of enterprise. It ensured work and decent prices for all through a system that took care of barbers from the moment they entered the trade until their death. Graduating through a series of reciprocal relationships, barbers started out as apprentices living under the roof and supervision of a master barber until they were eighteen or twenty-one.

—Douglas W. Bristol Jr.[1]

THE HOLMES FAMILY EMBARKED on the first leg of their journey six years almost to the day after Cecelia's Niagara rescue. It was now possible to travel by steamship and rail all the way to New York or Boston. One of the oldest rail lines in the nation ran from Boston to Lowell.

Lowell, with a population of 33,000 people, was the second largest city in Massachusetts.[2] Fully one-third of them worked in its multi-storey red-brick textile mills. Fuelled by unfathomable amounts of slave-produced Southern cotton, by the time Cecelia and her family got there the mills were producing enough fabric annually to encircle the globe twice over.

Benjamin wanted his sons, aged thirteen and eleven, trained to the level of master barber, with all the degrees of specialization in the field made available to them. The preponderance of "first-class" barbers in Lowell and its environs, and the community's strong ties to Boston's complex and sophisticated Black abolitionist community, promised the boys an excellent vocational education, as well as entrée into what amounted to a guild composed of master barbers. These "knights of the razor," as one writer styles them, provided professional assistance and employment opportunities for one another, as well as support in times of illness or trouble.[3]

Benjamin's choice for his sons' future career was strategic. Barbers were among the most prominent members of Black communities everywhere on the continent. Independent businessmen who often employed others in the trade, African American hairdressers, shavers and barbers earned both financial security and prestige. This placed them very close to the pinnacle of African American and African Canadian society. Only the clergy and a bare handful of professional men—doctors, lawyers and the like—stood higher. Barbers provided indispensable personal services to European Americans and they were, as Cyprian Clamorgan of St. Louis, a barber himself, put it, Black "aristocracy."[4] It was also a portable trade: a barber carried his tools with him and could set up shop anywhere. This placed him in charge of his own destiny as much as any Black man in North America could hope to be, given the racial climate in which Cecelia's stepsons were growing up.

Ben and James Thomas had of course been in and out of barbershops owned by Toronto community leaders such as John J. Cary, William Hickman and the Edmunds brothers since they were tiny children. They knew shaving was more important than haircuts; it was a remarkably intimate act, and some well-to-do business and professional men were shaved every day—except for Sundays, because of Toronto's strict Sabbatarian laws.[5] A first-class barber with his own shop had several apprentices and provided multiple services. Some sold dyes and pomades or promoted their own shampoos and special hair tonics that promised to ensure rapid regrowth on balding pates. It was common for each shop to employ a shoeshine boy who polished each patron's footwear, and apprentices were assigned to spot-clean clothing as required.

Some barbers had special cupboards built to house the personal shaving mugs of favoured customers, and there were those who provided smoking rooms, sold fine tobacco and candy or—for those who were not strict adherents of the temperance code—offered a dram of whisky or two to ease the grooming process. There were specialists in dressing children's hair and in catering to the female trade, although most women had their hair styled at home by their maid or by a specialized hairdresser who came to the house. Barbers who served a less affluent clientele and those in rural communities that lacked doctors acted as common surgeons too, doling out medical advice and, as often as not, pulling teeth.[6]

There was a great deal to learn. African American barbers hovered between the Black and white worlds and, because of the personal nature of the services they provided, were in a delicate position. Apprentices like Ben and James Thomas Holmes needed to learn the specialized manners, decorum and conversational style—friendly but always deferential and not too familiar—that would ensure a smooth relationship with their clients.[7] Entertaining stories and even light gossip were permissible, but political discussion of any kind was not, at least on the part of the barber. One might develop a closer relationship with certain customers that led to a form of patronage, and this sometimes provided protection for a barber and his family in times of trouble. People talked to their barbers, and they conversed with one another in their shops. Barbers, many of whom had learned their skills in slavery, were therefore conduits of crucial information from white society to Black, and this was as true in Canada as it was in the United States, North and South.[8]

Lowell was as famous for innovative labour management as it was for its vast brick textile mills constructed in the 1820s. It had been a grand social experiment. Since textile weaving was more effectively carried out by small hands, women and children made up the initial labour force. To reassure anxious parents of New England farm girls, the companies promised strict religious and moral oversight and to provide a safe and respectable living environment in pristine boarding houses. To the same ends, Lowell's industrialists encouraged the values of self-improvement and social reform. Temperance was a watchword, as were Christian faith and action.[9] Lowell used vast quantities of Southern cotton and produced much of the "negro cloth" that was made into jeans and rough work shirts for the slaves of the American South, but, perversely, abolitionism was very popular there. Lectures and antislavery meetings packed churches and halls, and the city had its own antislavery society, with mill girls pledging a few pennies from each salary package to aid the cause.[10]

Massachusetts had been among the earliest states to rule against slavery. Benjamin's own experience echoed that of Revolutionary-era Quock Walker, who had been cheated of the liberty promised him by a deceased master and mistress. Walker challenged the state's new constitution that in 1780 had declared all men free and equal, and by 1783 slavery had ended within state boundaries. Lowell's African American population harkened back to the early eighteenth century, and the advent of the vast factories whose thousands of workers needed such services had attracted a contingent of politically engaged former residents of Boston and Cambridge in the 1820s. Among them were founders of Boston's African Baptist Church (1805), the Massachusetts General Colored Association (1826) and, along with William Lloyd Garrison, whose *Liberator* was published in Boston, first the New England Anti-Slavery Society (1831) and then the American Anti-Slavery Society (1833).[11]

The families who received Cecelia's stepsons in Lowell retained their links with Boston and continued their political and community organizing work not only locally but also at the state and national levels. They formed branches of antislavery and self-insurance societies in Lowell, which also had its own Prince Hall Masonic Lodge. The order had been founded after the American Revolution and chartered out of Britain because of American racial exclusion. Now there was a lodge in Hamilton, Canada West, and it would not be long before one started in Toronto too. Benjamin and Cecelia were aware that membership in fraternal societies such as the Masonic Lodge, the Grand United Order of Odd Fellows, the Sons of Temperance and a host of others, most mirroring white orders from which Blacks were excluded, would give his sons both place and protection wherever they chose to settle once their training was complete. It was important that Ben and James Thomas behave both respectably and respectfully, so they might be invited to join when they reached the appropriate age.[12]

Public spaces in Lowell, as was the case in Toronto, were not segregated. Ben and James Thomas could take part in activities intended by the textile companies for the ethical and intellectual edification of their workers.[13] There were museums, theatres, a library and a Mechanics' Institute. Parks were laid out to encourage healthful exercise and enjoyment of nature. Most important, Lowell townsfolk could proudly declare that in Lowell's elementary and secondary schools "the children of colored parents [sit] side by side with those of white parents, a living evidence of toleration and respect."[14] In 1843 Caroline Van Vronker, the daughter of a barber in the town, had been Lowell's first African American high school graduate.[15]

Benjamin's boys would also be relatively safe. Black Lowell had followed the lead of Boston, New York and Philadelphia in establishing a vigilance committee to protect both runaways and those who aided in their flight. Lowell had attracted much publicity when fugitive slave Nathaniel Booth, who had operated his own barbershop there for a time, was captured in 1851 after the passage of the Fugitive Slave Law the year before. A bloody confrontation with local abolitionists was avoided only when Linus Child, agent for the Boott Milling Company, managed to arrange for Booth's purchase at a price reduced from $2,000 down to $700.[16]

There were sixteen barbershops at Lowell in 1852.[17] Benjamin and Cecelia applied their usual careful consideration to choosing a household where Ben and James Thomas would be placed. The most likely candidate from their point of view was Walker Lewis, who had aided Nathaniel Booth during his time of trouble.[18] He was out of town when the Holmeses arrived, but his brother-in-law John Levy, or another member of his extended family, could deliver initial instruction until he returned.[19] Walker Lewis already had apprentices in his shop, and an excellent reputation. His father had been a founder of Boston's African Meeting House, and Walker himself as a young man had worked with Boston used-clothing dealers to sew copies of David Walker's incendiary 1829 *Appeal to the Coloured Citizens of the World* into the garments of sailors. As Benjamin knew from his early years in Richmond, mariners' work on coastal vessels enabled them to distribute the *Appeal* all along America's eastern seaboard.[20] Lewis was also a member of African Masonic Lodge 459 in Boston and risen to become Most Worshipful Grand Master in 1829.[21] With David Walker and William C. Nell, Lewis was a founder of the Massachusetts General Colored Association in 1826 and president of the African Humane Society; he had also served as an agent for the first Black-owned newspaper in the United States, *Freedom's Journal*, before moving to Lowell.[22]

Walker Lewis, who had converted to the Mormon faith (one of few African Americans to do so) was also an agent for the Massachusetts Anti-Slavery Society and ran an Underground Railroad station out of his home in Lowell. Along with local barbering families such as the Cuffs and Lews, who traced their tenure back to the time of the Revolution, Lewis was engaged in the highly illegal work of forwarding refugees on the Freedom Road, just as Benjamin did on the Great Lakes steamers. Some passed through Lowell proper, but most travelled an Underground Railroad route that ran from Concord, Massachusetts, to the Merrimack River by way of the nearby village of Dracut, or "Black North."[23]

Apprenticeships were not free, and Cecelia and Benjamin were expected to provide a substantial sum up front. There remained something of the medieval about it all, with "masters" having the right to dole out corporal punishment to their apprentices. The choice of master was therefore an important one. Cecelia's stepsons would grow to manhood in Lowell, half a world away from the influence of their father and stepmother.[24]

Training programs followed the age-old artisanal model, with boys going to live in the household of a master barber. At any one time Walker Lewis and his wife might have three or four boys between the ages of twelve and fifteen with their family, each at a different stage of his training, along with journeymen. In the place of their father and stepmother, Lewis and his wife would be responsible for Ben and James Holmes's care and upbringing, providing them with clothing, discipline and medical attention as required. Cecelia's stepsons were to eat their meals and receive religious instruction in the household. As apprentices it was expected that they would go to school and then help with the business of their employer in their off-hours. This included tidying the shop, cleaning equipment and sweeping floors before graduating to greeting customers. Youthful apprentices carried away hats and coats and gave them a brush-down while the client had his shave and haircut at the hands of the shop owner or one of his assistants.

If their apprenticeship was deemed successful, the Holmes brothers would pass on to the journeyman stage. They would be considered wage-earning full-time employees and might move on to another barber-shop, living in the home of the barber with whom they worked.[25] Only after gaining sufficient experience in handling money and shop management would Cecelia's stepsons be considered prepared for their own establishment. Their father Benjamin knew it was the master barbers who controlled access to the trade, through a sort of informal guild that worked to limit the number of "first-class" barbers in a specific locale in order to keep down competition.

Cecelia was reassured to learn that barbers established associations to aid one another in times of trouble or to offer burial services to their members. They also provided direct assistance to help young men become established in their own shops.[26] The barbers' association would scout out appropriate locations for such a venture, often somewhere different from the town or city where the youth had apprenticed, to ensure that there was sufficient clientele to support a new hairdressing establishment. Hopefully the newly minted master barber would in time take apprentices into his own home so the process could continue.

With the boys' future in good hands, Cecelia and her husband departed for Boston. Leaving his two young sons must have been painful, for sea travel was subject to the whims of wind and tide, and living conditions in the Australian goldfields were reportedly dreadful. Whether or not the little family would ever be together again was something none of them could predict.

Ben and James Thomas were now settled, however, and the couple was excited to embark on the next stage of their grand adventure. It was but a short train trip from Lowell to the great port of Boston. Cecelia and her husband did not book passage for Liverpool; their names appear on no passenger manifests, as they chose to work their passage across the Atlantic.[27] The main objective of the trip, after all, was to acquire sufficient funds to ransom Cecelia's mother from a life of slavery. This way they both avoided paying the fare and added to rather than depleted their savings.

Steamers built for the transatlantic trade were quite different from those on which Cecelia had travelled with Fanny on the Missouri and Ohio Rivers, and the *Transit* and *City of Toronto* with which Benjamin was familiar. To ensure that the ships could continue on their way even if something went wrong with the boilers or the steam-driven propulsion systems, they were also rigged for sailing. The passage from Boston to Liverpool took between twelve and fifteen days in good weather. An American journeying to London via Liverpool around the same time as Benjamin and Cecelia described his first view of the British port:

> finally Liverpool looms up in the distance, with her steeples, her great forest of ships and steamers, and her gigantic docks. We are . . . fairly abreast the town, and our anchor goes hissing down

to seize upon reality once more. There is a noise of cheering among the crew, and we transfer ourselves and baggage to the little Tug and steer for the Custom House. Here we are detained for an hour, perhaps longer, and undergo an unpleasant examination, but at last it is all over and we stand free in the streets of Liverpool—we are in the Old World![28]

Vessels from North America tied up at the Waterloo docks. There were many Black faces at quayside and in the city streets, for Liverpool had the oldest African community in Britain. Despite its earlier strong connections to the Atlantic slave trade—abolished in Great Britain, along with the rest of the Empire, in 1833—Cecelia and her husband found Liverpool a hospitable place.[29] Sailors liked it, for they were treated with at least some degree of British egalitarianism, and those of African descent found themselves welcome in most taverns and dining establishments, at least in the dockyards. There was a good deal of intermarriage between Black seamen and English and Irish girls in the town, something that would have aroused mob violence in most US cities.[30] Samuel Ringgold Ward, who had written so glowingly of Benjamin's commitment to the antislavery cause, wrote of his own experience there:

> I seemed to be simply in a neighbouring town, when in Liverpool. I could see in this town, and in the appearance of many of its inhabitants, some resemblance to Boston and the Bostonians. Nothing wore, to my view, the strange aspect which I had expected [owing] partly to the strong resemblance of the New England people to those of Liverpool; but, more than either, to the fact that in Canada, especially in Toronto, we are English in habits, manners, &c.[31]

Nor was he alone. Frederick Douglass, William Wells Brown and other African Americans who came to England wrote that for the first time in their lives they were treated as human beings. Benjamin, a former slave, could echo their words: "No sooner was I on British soil than I was recognized as a man and an equal." Cecelia could expect her experience as a Black woman in England to be equally positive. Fugitive slave Harriet Jacobs spent seven years living in the attic of her free Black grandmother in Edenton, North Carolina, before she found a ship to carry her north to freedom. She had been to England in 1845 and found that "For the first time in my life I was in a place where I was treated according to my deportment, without reference to my complexion."[32]

Although Cecelia and Fanny continued their correspondence over many years, exactly what happened to the Holmeses after Benjamin's sons went to Lowell remains something of a mystery. The most likely scenario is that Cecelia and her husband sought lodgings at a well-known boarding house for Black sailors, run by transplanted African American abolitionist William P. Powell. He and his wife, Mercy, were well acquainted with people in Benjamin's circle of friends through their abolitionist connections and knew Grandison Boyd as well. The couple had run similar establishments in New Bedford, Massachusetts, and after 1839 at New York. Unlike most seamen's boarding houses, the Powells' was a bastion of temperance. There was an antislavery library for use by the sailors, as well as a bin containing used clothing gathered for the benefit of those who had fallen on hard times. Both of the Powell boarding houses were known stops on the Underground Railroad and William was regularly published in the abolitionist press and chaired meetings protesting abuse and discrimination against Blacks.[33]

An advertisement for the Powells' "Colored Seamen's Home" in the *Liberator* of December 18, 1840, ends with this assurance: "Cooks, stewards and seamen, who come to this house, will have their choice of ships and the highest wages." The family also opened their doors to travelling abolitionists:

After a visit in February 1848, Frederick Douglass praised Powell's Colored Seamen's Home as "an *Oasis* in the desert, when compared with many houses where seamen usually congregate." The banner of temperance floated conspicuously throughout the establishment, and an excellent library and other reading room facilities were available. At meal times and on every other occasion, Powell led discussions of the issues confronting blacks. Douglass himself had escaped from slavery with the aid of a black seaman . . . [He] was very much impressed with the discussions held at Powell's home concerning slavery and the need for conducting a continuous struggle against it.[34]

On October 13, 1851, the *National Anti-Slavery Standard* reported that William P. Powell had chaired a meeting of New York's Committee of Thirteen, a vigilance committee, to protest the new Fugitive Slave Law. Refusing to live in a country that would pass such legislation, Powell and his wife packed up their children and moved to England.[35] There he found employment with a Liverpool customs broker, sent his sons to university, and with his wife opened their third boarding house for Black seafarers.[36] They maintained their American ties, and Mercy Powell, in addition to many other duties, made handicrafts for sale at bazaars organized by women's antislavery organizations in Boston and elsewhere.[37] The Powells hosted travelling abolitionists both white and Black, provided reception services for fugitive slaves who managed to reach Britain and—most important from Benjamin and his wife's point of view—hosted African Americans and African Canadians en route to the Australian goldfields.[38]

When Benjamin and Cecelia arrived in the fall of 1852, Grandison Boyd had been there before them. William Powell wrote to the *National Anti-Slavery Standard,* edited by Sidney Howard Gay in New York, about his many visitors:

The many friends of WMP. POWELL . . . will be glad to hear of
his success since his removal to Liverpool. His eldest son is studying with a physician and surgeon, two others are fitting themselves
for engineers, and Mr. Powell himself is a Custom-House clerk in
a large mercantile house. . . . [He writes] "part of my time is
devoted to waiting on passengers often arriving in Liverpool by the
Underground Railroad . . . No less than five have visited me within
the last five months; namely Grandison Boyd, Charles Hill,
George Washington, Alexander Everett, and Ananias Smith; the
first you know; the second is from Maryland, formerly owned by
Dr. Alan; the third is from Georgia; the fourth from Virginia; and
the fifth, from New Orleans, was stowed away on board ship there,
among the cotton bales, by the sailors." Mr. Powell's friends cannot fail to consider this as a good account of himself.[39]

The fact that Boyd had been on his way to Australia likely bolstered
Benjamin's enthusiasm for the next leg of the journey, but exactly what
happened next is not entirely clear. The Powells may have urged Cecelia to
remain in England, where there was a call for well-trained domestic servants
such as herself. Fanny's letter regarding Cecelia's European travel plans
raises the question of whether her former maid had ever intended to accompany her husband as far as Australia. Since the objective of the trip was to
earn rather than to spend money, she would have sought employment,
either as a servant in a well-to-do household, or with the Powells.[40] Mercy
Powell ran the Coloured Seamen's Home with the assistance of servants
while William went out to work, and there was always a great deal to do.

There were good reasons for Cecelia not to go to Australia. Returning
sailors described conditions in the goldfields, where they lived in tent cities
devoid of comforts and even basic sanitation. Food and other supplies were
astronomically expensive. Miners eked out a hardscrabble existence moving
from place to place as new strikes were announced, and many returned

empty-handed. There was a good deal of drink and hard living, so some didn't return at all.

Benjamin would have encountered no difficulties finding employment on a ship leaving Liverpool, but whether or not he ever reached Australia is not recorded. Letters to a man named Benjamin Holmes sent to the Adelaide post office were never claimed. The voyage to Australia was frequently plagued by dangerously rough weather; sometimes ships were blown far off course or forced to put into port along the way for repairs, delaying the journey for months. And Cecelia well knew that sailing vessels could be lost at sea, while steamers were notoriously unstable—if their boilers blew out of sight of passing vessels, there was no hope of rescue. While they were parted, British and Australian newspapers published worrisome reports about life in the mining camps. Men worked long hours in the broiling sun, often with little or nothing to show for their labour. Alcohol was endemic, as was gambling, a volatile mixture. Fights broke out, fuelled by drink and either triumph or despair. Men died of illness or injury with no record of their passing. If something happened to Benjamin, Cecelia would have no way of knowing her husband's fate unless it was sufficiently unusual to be reported in the Australian press, or if a friend wrote to her at the Powells' with the news.[41]

There were, however, newspaper accounts that named some of Benjamin's friends. Even in the goldfields there was cultivated company, for gold's yellow gleam attracted people from all classes of society and all walks of life. Some camps had a tent fitted up as a reading room equipped with books and newspapers. Men like James D. Tinsley of Toronto found solace from their labours in their faith and worked with other like-minded miners to establish Sunday schools. In such places the Sabbath was strictly observed; few men worked their claims on Sundays and the tent cities had shelters for use by various denominations for church services. Ballarat seems to have been the most civilized; there were so many British North Americans there that one of the richest claims was called Canadian Gully.

Giving up on dreams of striking it rich, some African Canadians and African Americans in Australia chose other ways of making a living. Goods and any sort of service were very expensive, and they did very well working as domestic servants, carters, laundresses, gardeners or cooks. A few opened small restaurant operations in the tent cities. By and large, apart from the Americans, who imported their prejudices with them, the treatment of Black North Americans there was refreshingly unbiased, and they also had the protection of British colonial law. The Melbourne *Argus* published the proceedings of a court case in which Zachariah Dunlop Patterson, who operated a barbershop with his brother, James D. Patterson, in Ballarat opposite the Rising Sun Hotel, sued a white American for refusing him service at his bowling alley. Patterson won the case.[42]

John James Cary of Toronto opened a barbershop and eventually returned home with well-padded pockets. He would for the rest of his life regale customers with tales of his adventures in Australia.[43] Like the Patterson brothers, Henry Hickman, son of Benjamin's friends Betsey and William of Toronto's York Street, chose to make his home in Australia.[44] While James D. Tinsley always intended to return home to his family, his younger brother John found the less restrictive lifestyle of Australia more to his liking, and stayed to marry and raise a family.[45]

Ship after ship left Liverpool for Australia, and that was from only one of several ports. Not all were bound for the goldfields. The gold rush had greatly stimulated emigration from Great Britain to Australia, and the British government subsidized the passage and start-up costs of tens of thousands of the British, Irish and Scots poor.[46] Meanwhile, a steady stream of interesting people passed through the doors of William and Mercy Powell's boarding house.[47] Some Cecelia knew, like Reverend Samuel Ringgold Ward, who had relinquished his role of publisher for Mary Ann Shadd's *Provincial Freeman* to lecture in the British Isles on behalf of the Anti-Slavery Society of Canada.[48] Another was William Wells Brown, the former slave and Underground Railroad conductor who in his memoirs, published in 1847, had written damning description of the brutal slaveholding practices of Charles W. Thruston's O'Fallon half-brothers in St. Louis.[49]

Harriet Beecher Stowe arrived on the *Canada* in April 1853, to be greeted by thousands of fans gathered at the Liverpool docks. *Uncle Tom's Cabin* had come out in book form thirteen months earlier and had sold many thousands of copies. In Britain her antislavery novel appealed equally to Victorian sentimentality and the British sense of fair play. Twice as many copies sold there as in the United States and a play based on the novel was making the rounds.[50] Savvy European manufacturers capitalized on its popularity: everything from Staffordshire figurines to matchbooks, handkerchiefs, candelabra and fireplace screens depicted scenes of Eliza crossing the ice, Uncle Tom and little Eva, and Topsy.

There was also entertainment. After arriving at Liverpool, Elizabeth Taylor Greenfield, whom Cecelia may have already heard sing in Toronto, was introduced to British audiences by Stowe; the immensely talented African American vocalist, known as the "Black Swan," had been born into slavery. Also performing at the time was Henry "Box" Brown, originally from Richmond, Virginia, who had famously made his way out of slavery by having himself nailed up in a crate and shipped by train to Philadelphia. Public interest in Brown and in other fugitive slaves travelling in Britain had taken a great leap forward with the fame surrounding *Uncle Tom's Cabin*.[51]

The tide of immigration and emigration to and from the British Isles was stymied, starting in October 1853, by the outbreak of the Crimean War. Steamers and sailing vessels alike were commandeered to carry troops and materiel. The mails were completely disrupted, and even if Benjamin had written, his letters would have had little chance of reaching his wife. Anxious and alone, Cecelia had by this time completely lost touch with her Benjamin.

Cecelia's time in England ended abruptly in the winter of 1853. She had a very strong reason for returning to her Canadian home. She was pregnant.

CHAPTER 8
Don't Be Weary, Traveller

I often think of you Cecelia; oftener, since the death of my brother; you were the companion of my childhood, I can never forget you, and far from reproaching you for leaving me, I think and always thought it a very natural desire of the slave to be free. . . . I am and always will be a friend to the slave, and denounce the system of slavery as diabolical, at variance with Christianity.

—Fanny Thruston Ballard, August 2, 1855

THE DETAILS OF HOW Benjamin became separated from his wife are now lost, but he was out of touch for a sufficient length of time for Cecelia to believe that he had died somewhere overseas. The only clue lies in several letters to a Benjamin Holmes in Australia that went unclaimed. Postal service in the goldfields was irregular, particularly after the outbreak of the Crimean War, and people travelling between the mining camps and the towns that sprang up to service them often lacked a means of reliable communication for months at a time. Poignantly, death announcements in the Australian press often included "Canadian papers please copy" so families of loved ones lost on the other side of the world would be informed of their passing. Unclaimed letters in the Adelaide post office for Benjamin Holmes were recorded in the *South Australia Register* in late summer 1853, and again early in 1854.[1]

Cecelia was six months pregnant when she left Liverpool.[2] That the child could not be her husband's was obvious to everyone, including the very moral Mercy and William P. Powell. Benjamin had been away since the fall of 1852; her baby was conceived sometime in June of the following year. She worked in some sort of service position, and Liverpool was a port town with its rough-and-tumble side, so she may very well have fallen prey to unwanted advances on the part of either an employer or one of the sailors who frequented the Powells' boarding house. The former was a common hazard for any woman in a domestic situation, while the risks to a young and very attractive woman living near the dockyards of one of England's busiest harbours need no explanation.

Whether the pregnancy was the product of a consensual relationship or sexual assault, Cecelia did have one piece of luck: she was not travelling with John M. Tinsley's eldest son, James. He had taken part in religious and community life in Melbourne, lecturing at the YMCA, teaching Sunday School and producing a "very graphic and interesting document written by one of the members [of the Young Men's Christian Association], James Tinley [sic], a native colored man of Virginia, depicting the horrors of slavery" and rivalling *Uncle Tom's Cabin*. He returned to England in February 1854, en route to Toronto, carrying with him enough gold to set his family up for life. His younger brother, John Henry, had elected to remain in Australia.[3]

The young man arrived in England armed with letters of introduction from Australian officials and clergymen. He contacted Samuel Ringgold Ward in London and the two men passed several enjoyable days making the rounds of their English abolitionist acquaintances. They then went on to Liverpool to visit with William and Mercy Powell before Ward returned home. Tinsley had originally intended to sail on February 25, but for some reason he delayed his journey until March 1, when he boarded an American steamer named the *City of Glasgow*, bound for Halifax via Boston.[4]

Long after Cecelia reached Toronto, the *Provincial Freeman* of May 13, 1854, reported "No News Yet, of the 'City of Glasgow.'" Everyone's fears were well founded. The *City of Glasgow* had sunk, with 480 passengers and crew. It was Samuel Ringgold Ward who eulogized John M. Tinsley's beloved elder son in the *Provincial Freeman* of August 5, 1854.[5]

If the unclaimed letters were indeed intended for Benjamin Pollard Holmes, the timing is interesting, since they would have been written about the time Cecelia left Liverpool for her sea voyage back to Canada. After she arrived home on the St. Lawrence steamer, by way of Montreal, to find no correspondence from Benjamin awaiting her, she was presented with a dilemma. If Benjamin had met with misadventure and was indeed never coming home, she needed proof that would allow her, as a woman, to conduct business regarding his property on her own behalf. Reluctantly she came to the conclusion that her husband had either been lost at sea or had met with some fatal accident in the goldfields.

Heavily pregnant with another man's child and with profoundly mixed emotions, she was in need of financial support. Cecelia arrived home just in time to deliver her baby girl, in March 1854. She named her Mary, after her mother, although from the beginning the little girl was known to everyone as Mamie.[6] Her surname was Holmes because Benjamin was married to Cecelia and Mamie was thus legally his child.

Cecelia began listing herself as "Cecelia J. Holmes, widow" for property tax purposes, starting in April 1854.[7] If Benjamin was indeed lost to her forever it was important for Cecelia to establish her widowed status legally. In the same month that her baby was born, James Lukin Robinson finally transferred the ownership of their Centre Street land. It passed into the name of Benjamin Pollard Holmes, its original purchaser. Now listed as a freeholder for tax purposes, Cecelia could not use the house and land as collateral unless she could prove herself Benjamin's widow.[8] It might take years to convince a court to transfer title in the absence of proof that her husband was actually dead. Also her stepsons, now fifteen and thirteen, had claim to the land, if not the house.

Worries about property and finances paled in comparison to the terror Cecelia felt when the first heat of summer brought cholera to Toronto. Carried on immigrant ships to Quebec City and thence to the Lake Ontario ports, it spread like wildfire. On some of Toronto's more densely populated streets, the infection rate neared one hundred percent. She was less afraid for herself than for her baby girl, Mamie, but the illness passed when the chill of autumn calmed the epidemic, and they were spared.[9]

Although her absence had been brief, the Toronto to which Cecelia returned was changing. The population now approached 55,000 and the city was undergoing an unparalleled growth spurt, with houses and commercial blocks, many of them brick, going up everywhere. Advancing industrialization and the digging of sewer lines on most main streets caused a veritable boom in available employment.[10] The 1854 Reciprocity Treaty had been signed, permitting free trade between the United States and Canada in a wide range of products, from lumber and grain to such diverse items as livestock, butter, gypsum, raw tobacco and vegetables, enhancing the prosperity of both nations.[11] Rail service was opening up access to the Upper Great Lakes, and freedom-seekers would soon be able to take advantage of the 1855 rail link between Toronto and Collingwood, on Georgian Bay, where grain boats from ports such as Chicago soon brought in hundreds of newcomers. A second Welland Canal, this one of stone, greatly facilitated the transport of goods and passengers between Lakes Ontario and Erie. The Great Western Railroad connected Toronto to Hamilton, and by 1856 the Grand Trunk Line would provide Toronto with regular passenger service east to Montreal (a journey of only fourteen hours) and west to Sarnia, on the Detroit River border. The Underground Railroad in which Benjamin had been so instrumental now had a new means of transporting refugees, and in larger numbers than had hitherto been possible. This one ran on steel rails and was powered by steam.

Francis Mullin and his wife had witnessed Cecelia's wedding to Benjamin, and Francis had worked on the lakes with Benjamin as well, but they were now living elsewhere. Benjamin's old friend Daniel Bloxom was still at 215 King Street East, near Berkeley. Daniel Bryant, who had sailed with Benjamin, was now headwaiter at Beard's, one of the city's best hotels, which was at the corner of Church and Colborne Streets. John James Cary, already back from Australia, was operating a barbershop on Yonge Street. Like the rest of the Cary brothers, he made his home on the upper reaches of Church Street near Gerrard.[12] William Hickman had grown very prosperous, owning a barbershop at 15 Church Street and one by his York Street home; his remaining son, William Hickman Jr., operated a grocery store at 75 King Street West. Beverly Snow, who in 1835 had been forced to flee Washington through the sewers when his restaurant was torched during the Snow Riots, the same ones about which Cecelia had learned as a visitor to the US capital in 1840, had given up the Epicurean Recess (named for his old Pennsylvania Avenue oyster house). He now operated the Phoenix House, in partnership with John T. Fisher, at 70 King Street West.

Carrying her little daughter through the city streets, Cecelia could see Toronto growing in all directions. The huge estates of an earlier era were being broken up and development was reaching northwards as new roads were cut along the old divisions between them. An elegant hotel built by one of the city's few Jewish families, the Rossin brothers, was going up at the corner of King and York; there would be jobs for the waiters, chambermaids, cooks and porters, mainly benefitting the Black population of St. John's Ward. There were two new railway stations located near the Queen's Wharf, which served Fort York. As for public buildings, the Lunatic Asylum at the western end of Queen Street, near the Fort, was most impressive, and a Provincial Normal School had risen east of Yonge Street. At the top of College Avenue, just west of Cecelia and Benjamin's house, the University of Toronto was under construction.[13]

African Canadian Toronto was also transformed. Benjamin and Cecelia's neighbourhood had been divided off and renamed St. John's Ward. It was filled to overflowing, and now tenements and substandard shacks were being added in the rear yards of houses to accommodate still more people. The Fugitive Slave Law, coupled with well-publicized attempts to rescue captured freedom-seekers in Syracuse, Boston and elsewhere, had galvanized Underground Railroad operations throughout the American North. Stationmasters sent an ever-increasing number of "passengers" to Canada West.[14]

People with experience of city life and marketable skills favoured Toronto, Hamilton and other urban centres, while others moved to the fugitive-slave colonies at Buxton and Dawn or worked until they earned enough to purchase one of the farms east of the Detroit River offered by the Refugee Home Society. There were Blacks living in all the Lake Ontario ports, both east and west of Toronto. An adventurous few penetrated the interior as farmers or to offer their skills as settlement expanded beyond the lakeshores and major river systems that had been the transportation conduits of the pioneer era.

Cecelia noted the cultural changes that influenced Black life in her city. African Canadians were well aware of the contradiction that their respectable behaviour, industry and economic success posed to slaveholder propaganda. This fuelled their drive to become better Christians and citizens and thus show that Black people were as equally fit as whites to participate fully in civil society. Moneyed free African American families from the larger and more sophisticated Black communities of New York, Cincinnati, Chicago and Boston brought new leadership to organizations devoted to charity, refugee reception and protest, and efforts aimed at moral and intellectual uplift flourished.[15]

There were now four churches serving the community. The old Wesleyan Chapel had been rented to a Baptist congregation and a new Baptist church built on Teraulay north of the Abbott home. Cecelia would have noted with pride the growing list of societies serving Black Toronto: the Toronto Excelsior Young Men's Literary and Debating Society; the Mental and Moral Improvement Society; and the Provincial Union Association, organized in August 1854 by a committee made up of nearly all of Benjamin's old friends in the city. It was dedicated to encouraging education and loyalty to the Queen.[16] There were also the Provincial Association for the Education and Elevation of Coloured People and the Provincial Freeman Association, the latter created to support Mary Ann Shadd's *Provincial Freeman*. The paper was published first in Windsor and then Toronto. But Mary Ann was to marry Toronto barber Thomas Cary in 1856 before again taking up the helm of the *Provincial Freeman* at Chatham, where her brother Isaac could aid in managing its production.[17]

America's loss was Canada's gain. People experienced in community-building and in touch with abolitionists across the United States and Europe forged new links between Toronto groups and both American and British antislavery.[18] From Baltimore, New York, Cincinnati, Boston and Philadelphia they brought with them traditions of resistance to racial oppression and of community development that greatly advanced African Canadian efforts. The cultivated William J. Watkins, in whose Baltimore home the popular poet Frances Ellen Watkins Harper had grown up, abandoned his much-admired Watkins Academy for Negro Youth in Baltimore and opened a grocery business on Toronto's Church Street. He wrote for the *Frederick Douglass' Paper* (which replaced the *North Star*) under the byline "A Colored Canadian."[19] Along with newcomer Francis Griffin Simpson of New York State, saw-maker Thomas Smallwood and others, Watkins encouraged Black voters to abandon long-held Conservative values and embrace the reforms promised by George Brown and the Clear Grits.[20]

Just as Cecelia had learned to write after she reached Toronto, others took advantage of the educational opportunities that Canada West offered, which were all but unique in antebellum North America. Both people who had suffered under slavery and free Black immigrants—fleeing oppressive laws and the ever-present threat of being kidnapped and sold away, as poor Solomon Northup had been—flourished in an atmosphere where racism, while not absent, was not justified in law.[21] Visitors to the Buxton school marvelled at students whose fathers and mothers had worked the fields of the plantation South declaiming in flawless Greek and Latin. A young man named Alfred Lafferty, whose father was an illiterate carter, was one of the first six students to graduate from the Buxton school; he went on to take a double first in classics and mathematics at the University of Toronto. Likewise Mary Ann Shadd's sister Emeline learned to be a schoolteacher at the Provincial Normal School, earning top honours, and later became the wife of Francis G. Simpson's clergyman brother, Reverend Henry Livingston Simpson.[22]

Dr. Alexander T. Augusta, who had made his money in the California gold rush, graduated from the Toronto Medical School in 1856. A year later he gained hospital privileges, becoming physician to the House of Industry. He also served as preceptor, or personal tutor, for the Abbotts' son Anderson, who had left Oberlin College to study medicine in Toronto and was destined to become the country's first Canadian-born Black doctor.[23]

As for Cecelia, once she had recovered from the birth of her child and resigned herself to the loss of Benjamin, she resumed her correspondence with her former owner. She wrote in January 1855 to tell Fanny about the birth of her baby girl. Fanny responded from Mammoth Cave on August 2, apologizing for her delayed response.[24] She had been delivered of a child in February. Her beloved grandmother Abigail Oldham Churchill had died the preceding year, and her comments suggest postpartum depression, in part brought on by the loss of her little boy Bland, and then the very sudden death of her brother, Sam, the year before. Cecelia too mourned the impulsive youth who had teased her when they were little and so wanted to be a soldier. He had been

> killed by lightning last April a year ago. My brother had married and was settled on a farm about twenty miles from Louisville where we were, on a visit to him at the time of his death. He had been fishing with Pa and on his return home was struck by lightning and instantly killed; he had been married about two years and a half, left no children.[25]

Fanny's sorrow over her brother's passing was made all the more poignant because Sam's funeral was held in her home.[26] And there was even more sad news from Louisville:

> You made inquiries in your letter about your Mother & Brother.
> Your Mother was well when I saw her about ten days ago; tho' she
> looks much older than when you saw her. . . . Your brother Edward
> never recovered from scrofula, it finally settled upon his lungs and
> he died last Christmas. Mary says he was resigned and died a christian's [*sic*] death. I read your letter to your Mother, she is always
> delighted to hear from you, and was much pleased to hear you had
> a daughter. I hope you have named her for your Mother.

Cecelia's family's news dutifully delivered, Fanny turned to other subjects. Writing from Mammoth Cave reminded Fanny of her earlier visits there in Cecelia's company. She wrote that the resort's famous African American guides were asking to be remembered to the young servant girl whom they had befriended so many years before. They had exciting plans for the future, too: "Stephen says he is going to Liberia next year." When Fanny's uncle Dr. John Croghan died in 1849, he left the cave to his many nieces and nephews. His will dictated that Stephen and Charlotte Bishop, along with their son, Thomas, were to be freed seven years after Croghan's death. In 1856 the estate was to provide them money equivalent to the last three years of their labour, along with their passage on an American Colonization Society ship bound for Liberia.[27]

Fanny closed her letter in sentimental and—for a Southern woman raised in a slaveholding household—utterly remarkable fashion:

> I often think of you Cecelia; oftener, since the death of my brother;
> you were the companion of my childhood, I can never forget you,
> and far from reproaching you for leaving me, I think and always

thought it a very natural desire of the slave to be free. You need have no fear for your freedom from me; I should never assert any claim to you if you were in my house. I tell you now that I relinquish all claims to you forever, and only hope that the fear and love of God may always be with you and that he will bless you and make your family prosper. I am and always will be a friend to the slave, and denounce the system of slavery as diabolical, at variance with Christianity.[28]

I am away from home, and your Mother does not know that I am writing to you else she would probably send you some affectionate message.

I shall always be glad to hear from you. Farewell Yours

Fanny T. Ballard

Cecelia's former mistress certainly seemed sincere in her new-found aversion to slavery. Although this fell far short of legal manumission (as later events would prove), Cecelia was sufficiently comforted to believe that Fanny would not pursue her arrest, even on American soil. This was a great relief, especially since Mamie, now fourteen months old and the daughter of a woman legally a slave, was technically Fanny's property too.[29]

Between Fanny's letters, Cecelia kept an ear out for intelligence from Louisville that might affect her still-enslaved mother, Mary; cared for her baby daughter; and worried about ominous signs from south of the border.[30] Every band of freedom-seekers arriving at the city docks and railway stations brought news of escalating tension. The Liberty Party, founded in 1840 to promote the abolitionist cause, had foundered. In 1854 abolitionist William Lloyd Garrison gave one of his most ominous speeches, "No Compromise with the Evil of Slavery," summing up the American political scene as a struggle between "the South [where] the preservation of slavery is paramount to all other considerations, above party success, denominational unity, pecuniary interest, legal integrity, and constitutional obligation" and "the North, [where] the preservation of the Union is placed above all other things, above honor, justice, freedom, integrity of soul, the Decalogue and the Golden Rule, the infinite God himself."[31]

A new and ominous piece of legislation had been passed by the US Congress after Cecelia came home. The Kansas-Nebraska Act of 1854 ignored the Missouri Compromise and left the new states of Kansas and Nebraska to decide "by popular sovereignty" whether to permit slavery within their borders. Settlers with hardline opposing views ignited a localized civil war, and a fierce middle-aged abolitionist named John Brown went west to help his pioneering sons keep Kansas free of slavery.[32]

Then, on October 16, 1854, in a speech at Peoria, a gangly Illinois politician named Abraham Lincoln stated that in passing the Act, Americans "declared indifference, but as I must think, a covert real zeal for the spread of slavery. I cannot but hate it. I hate it because of the monstrous injustice of slavery itself. I hate it because it deprives our republican example of its just influence in the world." He expressed support for the gradual abolition of slavery and echoed the old position of the American Colonization Society: "If all earthly power were given to me . . . my first impulse would be to free all the slaves, and send them to Liberia,—to their own native land." Lincoln acknowledged the immense difficulties and expense inherent in such a course: "But a moment's reflection would convince me that whatever of high hope (as I think there is) there may be in this, in the long run, its sudden execution is impossible."[33]

One thing evident to Cecelia and her contemporaries was a new hardening of racial attitudes, in part due to the rhetoric that spewed north into British Canada in the pages of American newspapers and on the tongues of American travellers. It was also a reaction to the large influx of fugitives after the US Fugitive Slave Law was passed. The Black community's hard-won prohibition against the blackface performances that so demeaned people of colour was ignored; advertisements for minstrel shows were once again posted in the Toronto papers, including George Brown's *Globe*. This appeared on March 9, 1855:

The Stanley Minstrels! Concert! The Stanley Minstrels in returning their sincere thanks for the very liberal patronage, approbation, and applause, which was bestowed upon them at their two last Concerts, beg leave to announce, that they will give their third concert at the Saint Lawrence Hall, on Monday Evening the 12th March, 1855, On which occasion they will introduce an entire new programme, consisting of New Ethiopian melodies, witty sayings, jokes, black blunders, dancing, &c. To conclude with the Burlesque Ball.

Meanwhile Cecelia was experiencing real financial hardship. She owned her home in all but name,[34] but the Holmes family had lost its main bread-winner. Like most widows of her acquaintance, she made a little money by renting out a room or two, but by 1855 Cecelia Jane Holmes was forced to seek employment. If she took a live-in position as a children's nurse, for instance, she could rent out the Centre Street house. Fortunately the itin-erant Government of the Canadas returned to Toronto in December that year, so many families of newly displaced politicians and civil servants needed household help.[35] She found a live-in position where her child would also be welcome, along with a reliable tenant to cover the cost of taxes and relieve her of the maintenance of her Centre Street house.[36]

Cecelia took her year-old daughter and moved into the home of a well-to-do family living about three miles outside the city centre. There was transportation now, for the ever-ambitious Mink brothers, James and his Kingston-based brother George, had started a horse-drawn omnibus (a sort of elongated coach) that ran between Yorkville and St. Lawrence Hall for the meagre fare of a York shilling, giving Cecelia and her baby girl an opportunity to attend the AME church on Sayre Street, visit old friends and keep an eye on her comfortable little house behind Osgoode Hall.[37] Cecelia neglected to leave a forwarding address, so when, at Mary Reynolds's request, Fanny wrote to her in October 1856, the letter did not reach her. However, Fanny wrote again the next January, saying she understood the mix-up, for Cecelia's most recent note had explained her removal from the city: "I see that you now live in the country three miles out from Toronto."[38]

It was while Cecelia was living at her employer's suburban home in the summer of 1856 that she received the shock of her life—her long-lost husband Benjamin came back to Toronto. Though it must have seemed to her that he had virtually risen from the dead after all this time, his health was actually very precarious. For that reason and because he felt it was time to reconcile with his wayward wife, he had come home.

BENJAMIN POLLARD HOLMES HAD returned to England from his Australian adventures in the spring of 1854. Apparently his own letters to Cecelia had gone astray, probably because of disruptions brought on by the continuing war in the Crimea. He arrived to learn that his wife had departed for Canada. More distressingly, he learned that she had been quite visibly with child when she left. Whatever he believed about the circumstances of her baby's paternity, instead of making his own way back to Canada, Benjamin took a position on a steamer, the *Black Eagle*. He spent 1855 and the first part of 1856 as ship's steward. Sailing out of Liverpool, he most likely hung his hat at William and Mercy Powell's boarding house while in port.

There were in Liverpool a great many Black seafarers from all over the globe, and ships' crews were often integrated. Benjamin Pollard Holmes chose the *Black Eagle* because it usually plied the waters of the Indian Ocean, rather than risking his freedom on an Atlantic vessel that might stop in at the West Indies or North American ports.[39] Black seamen were routinely imprisoned while their ships waited at anchor in ports below the US Mason-Dixon Line, ostensibly to prevent them from fraternizing with the enslaved and giving them ideas about freedom. Tales were rife of men unable to pay their prison board who were sold into slavery to cover the "debt."[40]

Aboard the *Black Eagle* Benjamin had finally attained the position of steward, and it was exacting. He oversaw all matters pertaining to service aboard the vessel. He answered only to the captain, and it was his responsibility to hire and maintain discipline among the waiters as well as the stewardess and her maids. He personally served at the captain's table and was responsible for care and cleaning for first- and second-class passenger cabin. Along with the cook, he stood somewhere between the ship's officers and the crew. It was his particular job to ensure that the vessel was well supplied with water and foodstuffs, and at the most reasonable possible cost. That meant Benjamin had to develop contacts with ship suppliers in each of the ports the *Black Eagle* entered, from Peru to Tasmania and throughout the Indian Ocean. At its home port of Liverpool, he had to make arrangements for fresh eggs, meat, fruit and vegetables to be ready at the docks for when the *Black Eagle* made its return journey. It was in his own interests to inspect every barrel and bottle coming aboard to ensure that cheap substitutes had not been made, for Benjamin would have to answer to the captain and the chief clerk (if there was one aboard) for all the accounts related to victualling.[41] The position also carried a higher salary than he had previously commanded: a steward was usually paid at the same rate as the second mate.[42]

Both a cargo and a passenger ship, the *Black Eagle* had no regular schedule, but most often it carried emigrants leaving the British Isles for a fresh start in Australia or New Zealand.[43] The vessel was quite large for its day, described as having "1600 tons register, 188 feet long in the keel and 100 feet long over all"; its hull was sheathed in a yellow metallic alloy to make it more seaworthy and repel marine parasites. Like all seagoing steamships of this era, it was also supplied with full rigging in case of failure of an engine or some other calamity.[44]

Benjamin had visited a good deal of the world since the last time he saw his wife. In a typical voyage the *Black Eagle* left Liverpool on June 24, 1854, arriving on October 19, as announced in the *Argus* of Melbourne, Australia, in the October 20 edition. Three days later, the *Argus* announced that the

Black Eagle was at anchor with 497 passengers aboard in Hobson's Bay, Tasmania. The ship must have been both well provisioned and well run, for only two people died en route. However, the vessel had been delayed by a sprung mainmast that required stopping at Milford for repairs, according to the London *Times* of July 5, 1854.[45] It carried a quite varied cargo earmarked for a number of different merchants:

> 30 casks plaster, J. G. Martin; 1 cask soda, 41 bags whiting, W. W. Wakefield; 3 cases bedsteads, 6 bundles doors, 1 case, B. Tonks and Co.; 6 cases, B. Amsberg and Co.; 1 box apparel, Heape and Grice; 3817 pieces deal, 11,210 slates, 22,000 ladies do.[?], 275 casks bottled porter, 25 half-barrels cement, 14 barrels whiting, 30 bags do [ditto], 250 tons coal, 2 bags coffee, 2 casks sugar, 4 cases sherry, 4 do. port, 12 do. claret, 2 do. champagne, 1 cask whiskey, 14 cases, 46 crates, 8 [hogsheads], Order.[46]

When Benjamin Pollard Holmes sailed in it during the mid-1850s, the *Black Eagle* made regular stops at the island nation of Mauritius. This was a provisioning point on shipping routes between the British Isles and Australia. However, during his time on board, the ship also carried cargo and passengers to South America.[47] On October 14, 1856, *Allen's India Intelligence* recorded the arrival of the *Black Eagle* from Liverpool. However, by that point the ship was sailing without its steward.

What prompted Benjamin's return to Toronto, despite the unhappy situation that awaited him at home, was the loss of his health. Bristol, Manchester and Liverpool papers and eventually the *Belfast* (Ireland) *News Letter* variously published articles titled "A Warning for 'Quack' Doctors," detailing a case underway in the Marine Court:

> At the Liverpool Court of Passage, a day or two ago, a man of colour, named Holmes, sued the well-known quack doctors,

Messrs. Startup & Brown, to recover compensation for the injury and loss sustained by him through improper medical treatment . . . the plaintiff, returning from a voyage, some time since, felt unwell, and went to consult the defendants in his case. They undertook to cure him of his illness, the bargain being "no cure, no pay," and the plaintiff paid into their hands as a deposit £1 10s. They at once put him under the influence of an active drug, though his ailment did not require so dangerous a medicine, and the result was, that instead of being relieved of his sickness, his constitution was so impaired by this improper treatment, that when Dr. Hutchenson, of Parliament Street, was called in, he for some time considered the plaintiff's life in danger. The jury returned a verdict for the plaintiff for £30 damages, with costs.[48]

Benjamin's medical problems had begun the year before, when he was forty-two. He had returned from a voyage to Mauritius with a severe cold that resulted in pain in his hips. After reading a handbill describing his very ailment, he consulted its authors at the shop of Startup and Brown. Apparently Dr. Startup and his colleague were well-known amateur physicians who sold dubious wares with great fanfare from a marketplace stall near St. George's Hall, and who had long histories of run-ins with the law. A February 1855 advertisement in a Bristol paper boasted that they were "American doctors" who employed "Herbs, Roots, Barks and Flowers" in the preparation of "botanical" medicines, and stated that they had offices in Liverpool and Glasgow as well as a newly opened shop in Bristol.

Benjamin was treated for "syphilitic rheumatism," and although he insisted that he did not have syphilis, he was given the usual "cure." Both the pills and the ointment he was prescribed contained a good deal of mercury. By February 6, 1856, he was so ill he "could not raise his head from his pillow." Benjamin's complaint was actually a form of rheumatism that had settled in his hips and pained him greatly, probably a result of his long years of standing in steamboat dining rooms in all weather on the Great Lakes. The mercury in his medications attacked the tissues of the mouth, causing excessive salivation to "a fearful extent." "And the plaintiff's mouth was in [such] a state of incipient mortification" that Dr. Hutchenson was called in to see what could be done for the poor man.

Feeling somewhat better under the good doctor's ministrations, Benjamin retained a local barrister, Tindal Atkinson, and brought suit. Although the lawyer for Startup and Brown accused him of having misstated his case to the "doctors" and of being a "man of loose habits," Benjamin won his case. But it was a pyrrhic victory. The physician reported that the prolonged use of mercury had caused such swelling of the tongue, and poor Benjamin's mouth and gums were so ulcerated, that he could hardly speak. Ultimately the mistreatment damaged his jawbone permanently, leaving him in constant pain. Benjamin Pollard Holmes was only forty-three.[49]

Yearning for home and knowing that he was not long for this world, Benjamin set his sights on returning to Toronto and whatever he might find there. The exact date of his sailing is lost, but he left Britain in the spring of 1856. He likely travelled by way of Boston to visit with his two sons in Lowell. Cecelia's husband was back in Toronto and living in the couple's Centre Street home by the summer of 1856.[50]

CHAPTER 9
I Ain't Got Long to Stay Here

The large and thriving City of Toronto contains a more numerous colored population than any other town of Canada. Out of its 50,000 inhabitants, from 1200 to 1600 are estimated to be colored . . . One of them, a man of wealth, lives upon his means . . . one is a regularly educated physician; three are studying law; one medicine; two at least are master builders . . . one keeps a large livery-stable, one of the best in town, and is employed to take the mails to and from the Post office to the railroad depots . . . and the barbers and waiters in hotels and private families are almost exclusively colored men . . . many of them have accumulated considerable property [especially] among the older residents [in] real estate.

—"The Negroes of Toronto," *New York Tribune*[1]

CECELIA AND HER DAUGHTER did not go back to the family's Centre Street home for some time after Benjamin returned to Toronto. A letter that Fanny sent to Cecelia in October 1856 never reached her; she wrote again to Fanny early in January of the next year from her employers' address,[2] asking for clarification on some questions she had posed about her mother's situation and noting that her financial situation had somewhat improved. Fanny responded right away. Her letter of January 25, 1857, was addressed to Cecelia's temporary home outside Toronto, and began:

> I received your letter of the sixteenth, Cecelia, two day since; and was surprised to learn that you had not received one from me since I was at the Mammoth Cave. I wrote to you about three months ago by your Mother's particular request, directing my letter to "Centre St No 8." I see that you now live in the country three miles out from Toronto, which of course is the reason why you did not receive it. Your Mother some time afterwards, told me she heard that you had moved to Chicago in Illinois.[3]

There is no evidence that Cecelia had removed to Chicago, unless she and her little girl accompanied her employers on a visit to the Illinois city. If she had indeed sent word to her mother by way of an unnamed intermediary that she would be crossing the border, she was taking a terrible risk with not only her own freedom but also that of her daughter.[4] Whatever her assurances, Fanny had not legally manumitted Cecelia or her child, even though it would have been an easy matter to accomplish, given that her father and her husband were both attorneys.

Employing the delicately euphemistic language of genteel slaveholding, Fanny conveyed some momentous news. She and her husband, A. J. Ballard, had arranged to purchase Cecelia's mother, Mary:

> About thirteen months ago your Mother, whose master intended to move to New York, was offered for sale. She came to us repeating her desire to live with us; and requested us to buy her.[5] She had always regretted leaving us; and we were willing to receive her again into our family; Mr. Ballard became her purchaser for the sum of six hundred ($600) dollars, telling her at the same time, that he would bestow upon her, her freedom, at the end of six years.

Now Mary Reynolds was asking directly for her daughter's help. While A. J. Ballard was offering to free her in another five years, she wanted her liberty immediately, and she had an idea of how she might accomplish such a goal:

> One of the six years has now expired, and she is very anxious, very impatient to see you, whom she expected to visit at the expiration of her service and requested me to make the following proposition to you—which is—that you will assist her in raising the sum of $500 necessary in securing her immediate freedom.

Her mother was now offering to pay back her own purchase price if Cecelia and her husband could see their way clear to putting up the money to buy her from the Ballards right away. It was a time-honoured method of gaining liberty, and one commonly employed in Louisville. Indeed, it may even have been suggested by Washington Spradling, the enterprising free Black barber most likely to have put in place the complicated arrangements to secure Cecelia's freedom ten years before.[6]

> She is a superior cook & laundress and would soon be able to earn that sum at a hotel, or boarding house when, she says she would repay you. She enjoys good health and is a fine servant, and nothing but her desire to be free, to live with you, would induce me to part with her. I should like to hear from you as soon as possible on this matter.[7]

The letter closed with an update on Fanny's own children, her youngest just turning two and "our little daughter is of course the life of the house." There were also reports of the doings of Fanny's aunts, both her near contemporaries, with whom Cecelia had been well acquainted before she fled to Canada.[8]

Cecelia had been planning for years to free her mother and bring her to live with her family in their Toronto home. At least in part, her and Benjamin's dreams of striking it rich in the Australian gold rush had been engendered by her desire to raise enough money to buy Mary's freedom. But now everything had changed. She had not seen her husband since their parting in Liverpool, and she was now the sole support of a child who could not possibly be his.[9] With Benjamin living in the Centre Street house, there was no longer rental income to be had either. For her own sake and for her child's in the immediate future, and for the purpose of obtaining freedom for her mother in the longer term, she would need to reconcile with her husband, and soon.

From Benjamin's point of view, all was perhaps not quite forgiven, but he had arrived back from his global travels chronically ill. Although he was well enough to work, the damage to his mouth and jawbone was so extensive that his health was permanently compromised. His sons were far away and his wife was estranged. Furthermore, he had legal reasons to try to sort out his uncomfortable marital situation, for any changes he wanted to make regarding the Centre Street land would require his wife's signature. Fortunately he no longer had to send much money to Lowell. His sons, now seventeen and fifteen, had reached a point where they were earning at least their own room and board through their work in the master barber's shop.

It is uncertain how much of the reconciliation of Benjamin and Cecelia was based on real affection and how much was sheer practicality. Benjamin's first priorities were to secure an income against the day when he could no longer work and to ensure his sons some sort of legacy. It is difficult to know how much regular contact he had with his boys. They were all educated people, so they certainly corresponded, and train service had so improved between Toronto and the eastern seaboard that it would have been a simple matter, if expensive, to bring his sons home for a visit now and then. He was concerned that they would always have a Toronto home. His wife, still living in the suburbs and working as a domestic servant, was all but certain to outlive him, and as his legal wife Cecelia would have a claim on his existing house in the event of his death.

Cecelia too must have been mindful of the long view, for on September 12, 1856, she and Benjamin mortgaged their double lot for £100, the same amount Benjamin had paid for the land in 1844.[10] This was the equivalent of about $400 American. In other words, one could build a good house in Toronto for two-thirds of the amount the Ballards had paid to purchase Mary Reynolds from her previous owners.[11]

But Benjamin's immediate purpose was not to ransom Cecelia's mother. She was, after all, safe in the home of Fanny and A. J. Ballard, and thanks to their generosity, due to be freed in less than five years in any case. Instead he was anxious to build a second house at the southwest corner of their Centre Street lot.[12] Cecelia must have agreed to the loan, for as Benjamin's wife her signature was necessary on the application documents. By the next spring a rental home had been constructed just south of the house in which they lived. It was of frame construction with a brick front and built with the shorter side to the street, as was usual in Toronto, where property taxes were based on street frontage. There was a kitchen extension at the rear, just as there was on their own home. It was probably the work of builder James Buckner Lewis, who had arrived in the city in 1851 and become acquainted with the couple through his friendship with Francis G. Simpson. In later years he would confirm his knowledge of Cecelia and Benjamin's marital relationship in a legal document.[13]

Benjamin had built 7 Centre Street, but the house numbers were recalibrated the next year and the Holmes properties were renumbered 29 and 31 Centre Street, with 29 being the newer of the two. Their first tenant was Alfred August, a British-born carpenter, aged twenty-seven. In liberal Toronto it was not unusual for Black landlords to have white tenants and vice versa, but all Benjamin and Cecelia's tenants were either British or Irish, suggesting that they were charging market rents or better. It was, after all, a brand-new house, and Benjamin's goal was to both supplement their income and put something aside against the day when he could no longer seek work. Living apart as they were, the Holmes family was in no position to provide low-cost rental housing for incoming fugitives, as some of their old friends were doing.[14]

Benjamin's former employer Captain Thomas Dick hired him on as steward on the *Chief Justice Robinson*.[15] This was a promotion over his last Toronto position and reflected Benjamin's experience aboard the *Black Eagle*. Considering the state of his health, it was as much kindness to a long-time faithful employee as it was a need for a new steward that prompted the promotion. In any case, his job would have been both easier and more pleasant than when he was travelling the globe. The *Chief Justice Robinson* was a packet boat with established suppliers in its home port of Toronto. The higher rate of pay was welcome and, even better, the unusual construction of the *Chief Justice* meant that his employment was not limited seasonally. A wooden side-wheel steamboat built for Captain Hugh Richardson at Niagara in 1842, it had a long, sharp bow that acted as an icebreaker so it could run through the winter. The winter journey was sometimes harrowing; when the harbours were choked with ice the passengers had to disembark from the ship directly onto the ice and walk to shore.[16]

The trip from Niagara to Toronto took about two and a half hours in fair weather, and the steamer serviced Lewiston, Queenston and, at the western end of the lake, Hamilton, Oakville and other ports. Ten years earlier Sir Richard Bonnycastle took the steamer from Lewiston and remarked, "the stewards and waiters are coloured people, clean, neat, and active; and you may give seven pence-halfpenny or a quarter dollar to the man who cleans your boots, or an attentive waiter, if you like; if not, you can keep it, as they are well paid."[17]

Still the matter of Cecelia's mother lingered. Apparently Cecelia had been able to put something aside over the winter against Mary's purchase price, for on February 23, 1857, Fanny Thruston Ballard wrote again to her former lady's maid at Toronto. Her letter's businesslike tone was a sharp reminder to Cecelia that Fanny was, after all, her father's daughter:

Louisville, Feb. 23rd '57

I received your letter a few days ago Cecelia in which you inquired how the money for your Mother's freedom could be sent to Mr. Ballard. You can purchase from some of the bankers of your town a draft on New York payable to the order of A. J. Ballard and send it to me by mail.

If you cannot raise the entire sum necessary to secure Mary's freedom now you may send whatever sum you can afford, and we will credit Mary with it by hastening the time of her freedom. You may be able to procure the draft in Buffalo if not in Toronto.

Mary is very anxious to see you and of course anxious to be free, and I am willing to do all I can to gratify her.

We are all well. Yours respectfully

Fanny T. Ballard[18]

Whatever sentimental recollections of her years with Cecelia that Fanny might retain, it is clear that the Ballards had no intention of simply liberating Mary Reynolds, or even discounting her price. There is no mention of Cecelia's husband in Fanny's letter, although it is clear that A. J. Ballard is transacting the sale on his and Fanny's behalf.

By the next spring Benjamin and Cecelia had come to some sort of an arrangement. It was as well that they had secured their finances, as 1857 saw the beginning of a worldwide financial panic that played havoc with the banks and caused many businesses to fail across North America. City services were reduced and the House of Industry and private charitable organizations were overwhelmed by need because of widespread unemployment. In Massachusetts the Lynn shoemakers went out on strike in force.

In Lowell, where Benjamin's sons were training to become barbers, the looms were largely silent, bringing about much local hardship.[19]

Benjamin continued working on the *Chief Justice Robinson* through the spring of 1857. Then he moved to the employ of Captain Andrew Heron, owner of the *Peerless*. The timing was fortunate, or perhaps Captain Thomas Dick, who was fond of Benjamin, had suggested the move.[20] As for Toronto, competition from the new railroad coupled with the economic downturn meant that a number of important lake vessels went bankrupt. The *Chief Justice* was broken up in April 1857. The *Peerless* offered daily service on the Toronto-Niagara-Hamilton route and was one of the few lake steamers to survive the economic crisis relatively unscathed.[21] Things were not looking up. The *Toronto Leader* remarked on April 2, 1858: "It is matter of regret that in the outset we must speak of the prospects of this branch of our trade as much darker than usual. The present season of navigation opens before business men have recovered from the prostration of the late commercial crisis."[22]

When the tax assessor inspected their properties on March 8, 1858, Cecelia and her little girl, now four, were again residing with Benjamin in their old Centre Street home. They were just then taking out another small mortgage, this one for £25.[23] Resuming family life meant an adjustment for both of them. Their social situation was rather different than it had been as well. Benjamin could renew his acquaintance with the Rosses, the Carys, the four Edmunds brothers and Toronto's other early Virginian settlers, but one wonders how Cecelia was now regarded. Once her husband returned to the city, after Cecelia had been saying that she believed he had met with misadventure during his travels, it must have been obvious to everyone that Benjamin was not little Mamie's father. Nor would Benjamin's perceptive friends have missed the fact that he and Cecelia had also been estranged for some time after his return.

As for the Australian adventurers, James D. Tinsley was dead and a number of Benjamin and Cecelia's Toronto and Rochester friends had decided to make their homes in Australia. Tinsley's brother stayed there, as did Henry Hickman. Mary Ann Boyd's brothers also remained and started families there. To everyone's dismay, Elijah B. Dunlop abandoned his wife and children in St. Catharines for a life of derring-do in the Australian outback. His wife is listed in the St. Catharines, Canada West, directory for 1865 as "Dunlop, Mrs. Elizabeth (widow Elijah), seamstress."[24] As for Benjamin's oldest Toronto friend, Grandison Boyd made his own voyage back to Liverpool early in 1854 but landed soon after Cecelia's departure from British shores. On February 5, the *New York Times* published the following interesting article:

> A runaway slave named GRANDISON BOYD who had taken refuge some years since in Rochester, left the country, as so many others did, at the time of the passage of the Fugitive Slave Law, from fear his owner might reclaim him. He went to Australia and commenced work in the gold mines. When he left he was indebted $200 to a crockery merchant in this city, who had no very strong hope the debt would ever be cancelled. A few weeks since, however, he received a letter from Boyd stating that he had just arrived at Liverpool from Australia, where he had made $8,000, and enclosing a draft for £40 ($200), the amount of the debt.[25]

Some of the African Canadians who had tried their luck in the goldfields returned with money in their pockets, but it was generally earned from barbering or providing other necessary services. Only Grandison Boyd brought back a veritable fortune in gold, although James D. Tinsley would have as well, had he lived. Grandison had rejoined his wife, Mary Ann, in Toronto and the couple opened a grocery store on Queen Street, very close to the Holmes house. Perhaps it was they who had assisted Cecelia when she gave birth to her baby girl. The Boyds were both benefactors and canny businesspeople. For instance, Grandison and his wife paid to move the remains of a beloved Baptist minister, Elder Washington Christian, to a new place of rest in the Toronto Necropolis. The non-denominational cemetery had opened in 1850 to replace the old Strangers' Burying Ground above Bloor Street, where so many of Toronto's early Black residents had been interred.[26] Despite the economic downturn, the Boyds, who had successfully invested in bank stocks, were planning a move to Chatham, where they hoped to construct a commercial row in the downtown core.[27]

In Benjamin's absence Cecelia had made more recent acquaintances, to whom she now introduced her husband. A particular friend was Francis Griffin Simpson, most probably his tenant in 1855. Born free in New York State, he had arrived in Toronto in 1854. While training as a shoemaker, Simpson managed the fugitive-slave employment offices run by Thomas Henning, secretary of the Anti-Slavery Society of Canada and brother-in-law of George Brown of the *Globe*. Simpson was a very intelligent man with a superior education. He soon became a spokesperson for the Black community and often served as secretary to take minutes for meetings. He joined existing African Canadian benevolent, self-help and fraternal organizations and was a founder of the African Moral and Mental Improvement Society to supply poor children with the necessary books and supplies to attend school.[28] As a Liberal Party organizer he, rather unusually, served on the executive boards of predominantly white political organizations.[29]

There were also the couple's fellow Methodists. The old chapel on Richmond now served a Baptist congregation, so the Holmes family, along with other members of that congregation, were again attending the little African Methodist Episcopal church on Sayre Street, one short block east of their home. In 1856 it had become part of a new denomination, the British Methodist Episcopal Church, reflecting both the loyalty of its congregants to Queen Victoria and the fact that most AME ministers were former slaves who, in light of the Fugitive Slave Law, could not safely attend AME conferences held on US soil.[30]

Torontonians who had fled slavery were sometimes subjected to rather unpleasant reminders of their earlier condition by the arrival in the city of members of their former owners' families. Toronto had both commercial and intellectual ties with the American South, and there were always a few Kentucky and Virginia lads enrolled at Upper Canada College and at King's College, the Anglican school that was the progenitor of the more secular University of Toronto. Cecelia's own experience was no exception. In August 1858, George R. R. Cockburn, the Scottish-born and extremely right-wing principal of the new provincial Model School attached to the teachers' college (Normal School), was feted both in the press and by the city's white elites. He would one day marry Mary Eliza Zane, born in Louisville, Kentucky, two years before Cecelia's precipitous flight to freedom. Her mother was Fanny's favourite aunt, Emily Ann Churchill, wife of Hampden Zane. The couple had resided in Washington but made frequent visits home to Kentucky. Cecelia may well have rocked little Mary Eliza to sleep while she was an infant, only to rediscover her as wife of the headmaster of Canada's most prestigious boys' school, one that accepted Black students on an equal footing with white ones.[31]

It all reminded the Holmes family of their own days in slavery. As Cecelia and her ailing husband resolved what differences they could between them and re-established themselves in African Canadian society, the news from south of the border was grim. In March 1857, Judge Roger B. Taney delivered his fateful verdict in a court dispute launched by a man who had been taken to live in a free state by his owners and then brought back. The case of *Scott v. Sanford* was explained in the Toronto *Globe*. In the Dred Scott decision Judge Taney ruled that Scott's owner could retain his slave because Blacks in the United States "had no rights a white man was bound to respect." More, laws limiting slavery in any state or territory were unconstitutional, negating the Missouri Compromise of 1820. This dashed any hopes that African Americans would one day be accorded citizenship rights and denied them protection under law, further heightening Cecelia's anxiety over her mother's situation and increasing her desire to bring Mary to Canada to live.[32]

The turmoil roused Abraham Lincoln to one of the feats of eloquence for which he was becoming known. The *Globe* reported on the Springfield, Illinois, convention of June 16, 1858, where Lincoln accepted the Republican nomination for the position of US senator. No one knew it yet, but the words of that practical, plainspoken statesman were prescient.

> A house divided against itself cannot stand. I believe this govern-ment cannot endure, permanently, half slave and half free. I do not expect the Union to be dissolved—I do not expect the house to fall—but I do expect it will cease to be divided. It will become all one thing or all the other. Either the opponents of slavery will arrest the further spread of it, and place it where the public mind shall rest in the belief that it is in the course of ultimate extinction; or its advocates will push it forward, till it shall become lawful in all the States, old as well as new—North as well as South.[33]

Closer to home, in the spring of 1859, Boston abolitionist William Cooper Nell toured Canada West. The *Liberator* of June 17, 1859, published Nell's letter to William Lloyd Garrison about his Canadian journey, and it provides a fascinating snapshot of conditions in Toronto that affected Cecelia, her husband and her daughter in the late 1850s. It also mentions people they knew, and they may have been acquainted with Nell as well, for he was a friend of William P. Powell's. Nell's sister was married to Benjamin Cleggett, the son of Benjamin's old friend David Cleggett, who had gone back to live in Rochester about ten years before. It caused a scandal there when white abolitionists Isaac and Amy Post hosted the Cleggett-Nell wed-ding on September 5, 1849. The union produced eleven children.[34]

William C. Nell first visited the thriving Black community of Malden, where he met an African Canadian justice of the peace, a concept unthink-able in the United States. In Sandwich Nell mentioned the groundbreak-ing significance of the now-defunct *Voice of the Fugitive*. He was delighted by the prosperous community of Black people he encountered in Chatham, including the local express agent, who was responsible for carrying "His Majesty's mail from Chatham to Detroit." In his account of the visit, Nell expresses his admiration of construction company owner James Madison Bell, who was a well-known poet, and also mentions Mary Ann Shadd Cary, who was publishing the *Provincial Freeman* there with help from her family.

Nell paid a flying visit to the Dawn Settlement; he writes that its founder, Josiah Henson, was "now traveling through the United States as Uncle Tom." With Dr. Martin Delany, now practising in Chatham, he visited the Elgin Association Settlement and inspected the sawmill, built with the help of Thornton Blackburn, George Brown and John M. Tinsley to supplement the colony's agricultural income. He also met William Parker, hero of the Christiana Riots, but reserved special praise for the Buxton school, where, he was proud to report, children of couples who had once been enslaved studied Virgil and were being prepared for entrance into the University of Toronto.[35]

Visiting Toronto just before the great Provincial Exhibition, which included the opening of a replica of Prince Albert's Crystal Palace, William Nell comments favourably on the churches and St. James' Cathedral, and writes of the prosperity and high culture he observed in the Black community. Nell may well have brought news of Benjamin's sons in Lowell, for he was frequently in and out of that city on speaking tours and to visit with the local abolitionists there. He mentions Dr. Alexander T. Augusta, who was not only a university graduate but also a member of several African Canadian–led societies. At another time the well-educated Benjamin Pollard Holmes might have joined the new organization formed by Dr. Augusta, Wilson Ruffin Abbott, Isaac N. Cary and others. It had just been incorporated by the Legislative Council.[36]

> Resolved, That the British Constitution knows no man by his color
> or creed, and that her colleges wherever established are open to all

without distinction, it is expedient that encouragement should be given to young men, to enable them to enter the different schools, academies, colleges, and universities that thereby they may be prepared to fill any station which circumstances hereafter may assign them, either in or out of this province.

But whatever else was happening in the province, Cecelia's fortunes hinged on the economy and on her husband's ability to work. On April 13, 1858, a huge storm cut through one end of Toronto harbour, creating the permanent Eastern Gap where none had before existed. This materially altered steamer routes, which took advantage of the passageway to access the port towns of Colborne, Newcastle, Brockville and Kingston, routes on which Benjamin had been occasionally employed. He was kept very busy in the fall of 1858, as, mimicking the success of Prince Albert's Crystal Palace at London, Toronto had built an enormous iron and glass cruciform structure to showcase the latest agricultural and industrial advances of the day. Thousands of visitors were ferried back and forth from Lake Ontario ports as both Americans and Canadians flocked to the city to attend the exhibition.[37] As for the city, a real revival in fortunes was underway by 1859, in part because of the imposition of a protective tariff on Canadian products.[38] But times remained hard for Toronto's African Canadian community, many of whom were reduced to asking for aid from the House of Industry.

Benjamin's health was deteriorating badly. While the tax records and the *Canada Gazetteer* for 1858 list him as a waiter, the next year's city directory describes him as a labourer, suggesting that he was only doing day work when and if he was able.[39] Perhaps he was able to accompany Cecelia to the Provincial Exhibition held in September on military reserve lands south of the provincial lunatic asylum, but he continued to suffer from the after-effects of Dr. Startup's mercury "cure." The new Toronto General Hospital had been established in the city's east end in 1856, and Dr. A. T. Augusta operated his apothecary shop right around the corner from the

VIEW OF MAIN STREET, LOUISVILLE, IN 1846.

1. Main Street, Louisville, in 1846, as it was when Cecelia was planning her escape to Canada.

2. Charles W. Thruston and Mary Eliza (Churchill) Thruston, who purchased Mary Reynolds and baby Cecelia on October 4, 1831.

3. Fanny Thruston was nearly fourteen when she was given nine-year-old Cecelia as a lady's maid.

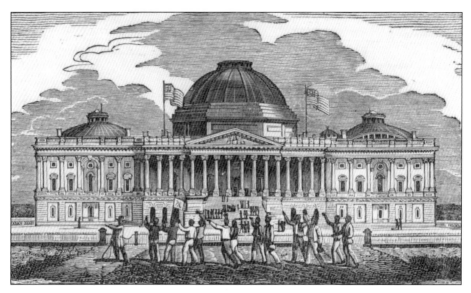

4. The sight of slave coffles passing in the shadow of the Capitol Building, Washington, DC, may have inspired Cecelia to plan her escape.

5. The elegant Cataract House hotel at Niagara Falls ca. 1860, from which Cecelia made her escape in May 1846.

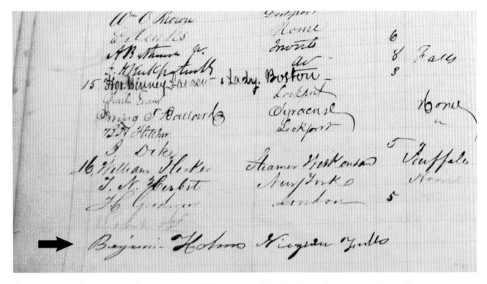

6. Benjamin Holmes, a steamboat waiter and Underground Railroad conductor, signed the Cataract House register on April 16, 1846. This was four weeks before Cecelia was due to arrive. Note there is no stateroom number listed beside Benjamin's name: Black guests were housed together in dormitories in the hotel's lower levels.

7. Captain Thomas Dick of the *City of Toronto* steamer, Benjamin's employer, signed the Cataract House register on May 6, 1846, eight days before the Thrustons were to arrive from Louisville.

8. Charles W. Thruston signed the Cataract Hotel register on May 14, 1846. With him were his son, daughter and "servant" Cecelia Jane Reynolds.

9. This 1882 bird's-eye view shows the Cataract House overlooking the rapids above Niagara Falls, and Prospect Point with the staircase Cecelia descended so she could escape across the river.

10. View of Richmond from Church Hill (1851) overlooking the slave-dealing establishments in Shockoe Bottom, as Benjamin would have seen them from the slave quarters where he lived in 1831 while hired out to tobacco merchant James Fisher Jr.

11. Robert Pollard Sr., clerk, King and Queen County Court, Virginia, who was both Benjamin's father and his first owner.

12. *View of King Street* by John Gillespie, looking west from Jarvis ca. 1844. Thornton Blackburn's cab is in the lower centre, travelling towards St. James' Cathedral, where Cecelia and Benjamin would be married in 1846.

13. York Street, where lived the Hickman, Gallego, Waddell and other Virginia-born families who were Benjamin and Cecelia's closest friends in Toronto. Osgoode Hall, home to the Law Society of Upper Canada, stands at the north end of York Street in this rare photo ca. 1856, by Armstrong, Beere & Hime.

Louisville Feb 23rd '57

I received your letter a few days ago, Cecelia, in which you inquired how the money for your mother's freedom could be sent to Mr Ballard. You can purchase from some of the bankers of your town a draft on New York payable to A. I. Ballard and send it to me by mail. If you cannot raise the entire sum necessary to secure Mary's freedom now, you may send whatever sum you can afford, and we will credit Mary with it, by hastening the time of her freedom.

You may be able to procure the draft in Buffalo if not in Toronto.

Mary is very anxious to see you and of course anxious to be free, and I am willing to do all I can to gratify her.

We are all well. Yours respectfully
Fanny I. Ballard

14. On February 23, 1857, Fanny wrote to Cecelia regarding the purchase of her mother, Mary Reynolds. "If you cannot raise the entire sum necessary to secure Mary's freedom now, you may send whatever sum you can afford . . . Mary is very anxious to see you and of course anxious to be free, and I am willing to do all I can to gratify her."

15. Charles W. Thruston, who owned Cecelia's family and to whom she had first written to ask about her mother's and brother's purchase price in 1851.

16. The British Methodist Episcopal Church on Sayre (Chestnut) Street, where Cecelia and her family were members. Benjamin's funeral was held here on Sunday, August 28, 1859, Reverend Isaac L. Christine officiating, before his cortege wound through the city streets to his grave at the Necropolis.

17. John M. Tinsley, aged 107. He was a builder from Richmond, Virginia, and a leading figure in Toronto's Black community. His son James was a close friend of Benjamin and Cecelia's and lost his life on the *City of Glasgow* while returning from the Australian Gold Rush.

DIED

On Thursday, the 25th instant at her parent's residence, 623 Yonge-st., Yorkville, MARGARET SARAH, the only child of Frederick and Maria Luaster, aged 8 years and 8 months.

☞ Friends and acquaintances are requested to attend the funeral on Sunday next, at 4 o'clock.

On Friday the 26th August, Mr. Penjamin Pollock Holmes, aged 46 years

☞ Friends and acquaintances are requested to attend the funeral, to-morrow (Sunday) afternoon, at 3 o'clock, from Sayer-street Church, to the Necropolis.

18. Obituary of Cecelia's husband, Benjamin Pollard Holmes, after his tragic death at the age of forty-six.

19. Wilson Ruffin Abbott was a leading spokesperson for the city's African Canadian community and Toronto's most successful Black businessman. He was a founder of the Coloured Wesleyan Methodist Chapel, which Benjamin and his first wife, Ann Eliza, attended when they arrived in Canada. Wilson and his wife, Ellen Toyer Abbott, were close associates of Cecelia and Benjamin Pollard Holmes after they married in 1846.

20. Frank Simpson (1859–1936), seen here with his wife, Laura, and children, Francis, Jeannette and Gordon. Frank was the son of Francis Griffin Simpson, who was Cecelia's closest Toronto friend. Frank lived in Cecelia's house for a time after his father purchased it in 1889.

house Benjamin and Cecelia again shared, but there was little that physicians could do to help Cecelia's ailing husband except provide opiates to help alleviate the pain.[40]

Benjamin's medical condition reached its lowest ebb in the summer of 1859. He wrote his will on July 30, 1859. The witnesses included two of the couple's Irish neighbours: Alexander Fleming was a court crier and the tax collector for St. John's Ward, while Thomas Mann was a shoemaker whose shop at 47 Richmond Street East was very near Benjamin and Ann Eliza's first Toronto address.[41]

The executors Benjamin chose were interesting. Both lived within a few blocks of the Holmes house at 31 Centre Street. They included Benjamin's former employer, Captain Thomas Dick, who still resided at his Queen Street West address in Toronto. He was now in partnership with his brother in a fleet of steamships on the Upper Great Lakes, as well as running the mail route to the Red River Settlement. The other executor was James Mink. Although he had experienced hard times when an arsonist burned his livery stable to the ground in 1858, he had built a new one on Teraulay at the edge of St. John's Ward and was still one of the city's most prosperous African Canadian businessmen.[42] Mink was illiterate, signing the documents associated with Benjamin's estate with an X, although his wife, born in Canada, could sign her name.[43]

While Benjamin was ensuring that his affairs were in order, Cecelia received another letter from Fanny Thruston Ballard. It is dated August 11, 1859, and is the last surviving piece of correspondence between these two interesting women. The timing of its arrival was propitious, for 1859 signalled major changes in the lives of both of them. Fanny apologized for her delay in answering Cecelia's previous letter, "since [I] have had an attack of fever which confined me for some time, but I am quite well again . . . I believe I have not written to you since the birth of my last child. I now have four children: three boys and a girl; my baby we named Rogers Clark—two family surnames combined."

The letter brought Cecelia up to date on a good deal of Thruston and Churchill family news, and then: "You inquired in your letter if your Mother still lives with us. She does and is very well. You spoke of 'raising money to get her,' let me know in your next how much you think you can raise." This last suggests that the Ballards were perhaps willing to relent on the matter of how much they thought Cecelia and her husband might realistically be able to come up with, given the current financial situation. She seems to have been unaware of Benjamin's condition, for she closes:

> I regretted to hear your health was so delicate. I imagine the cold climate in which you live is not favorable to you. You must not give up, but take care of yourself, for the sake of your child. Your Mother wishes to know the name of your daughter, you can let me know in your next letter. We are all well. Your Mother sends you much love.
>
> Yours respectfully,
> Fanny T. Ballard[44]

Sadly, there is no further information on Cecelia's mother, Mary. She presumably continued in slavery until she received her promised freedom in 1861, which was also the first year of the Civil War. Mary Reynolds would have been about forty-seven or forty-eight when she was emancipated.[45]

But Cecelia's attention was on other things. On August 26, 1859, less than a month after writing his will, Benjamin Pollard Holmes passed away. His death notice was published in the Toronto *Globe* of Saturday, August 27, 1859, a rarity for residents of St. John's Ward. According to the records, for some years, in addition to his oral difficulties, Benjamin had suffered from dropsy. Probably also a result of mercury poisoning, this painful and incurable illness resulted from kidney failure, which forced fluids into the soft tissues of the body and caused swelling in the extremities. Benjamin was forty-six years old and his widow twenty-eight.[46]

Benjamin's funeral was held at three p.m. at the Sayre Street Chapel of the British Methodist Episcopal Church, Reverend Isaac L. Christine presiding. Benjamin Pollard Holmes, fugitive slave, eloquent Methodist "exhorter," steamboat waiter, world traveller, husband and father, was laid to rest on Sunday, August 28, at the Toronto Necropolis cemetery. His funeral would have resembled one described by a mid-nineteenth-century visitor to the city: "I attended the funeral of one of the coloured inhabitants. The assemblage of brethren at the place of interment appeared respectable and numerous. On the coffin being lowered into the grave, a fervent prayer was offered up by one of the coloured class of the community, after which a contemporary exhortation was devoutly delivered, which closed the mournful scene."[47]

Benjamin's estate, including household furniture and Lot 7 on the east side of Centre Street in downtown Toronto, passed to his heirs. His two sons, Benjamin and James Holmes, jointly inherited the rental home at 29 Centre Street and an interest in all of Lot 7, which they shared with their stepmother. As for Cecelia, it is unusual that her husband's will does not add the customary clause to deprive his widow of her bequest should she remarry. Perhaps that had been the price of her returning to nurse him in what both knew would be his final illness.

> I give and bequeath unto my beloved wife Cecelia Jane Holmes the house and lot situate on the East side of Centre Street and North of the one already devized to my two sons[48] together with all my household furniture and effects to have and to hold the same to her own use and benefit during her life and upon the demise of my said wife it is my will and I order that the said house and lot and household furniture be given to my said two sons Benjamin Alexander and James Thomas Holmes to have the same to their own use and benefit forever. As Witness my hand and seal, this thirtieth day of July in the year of our Lord one thousand eight hundred and fifty nine.

It is telling that Benjamin's will does not mention Mamie Holmes at all, nor would any of his property pass to her at Cecelia's death. The child was now five years old and lived in his household along with her mother, who was Benjamin's legal wife. Whatever the identity of her father or the circumstances of her birth, she considered herself Benjamin's child. For the rest of Mamie's life she would list her birthplace as Toronto and her father as Benjamin P. Holmes.[49]

As for Cecelia, the decisions she made in the immediate aftermath of her husband's death were dramatic and had profound consequences for both herself and her five-year-old daughter. They would be living in the United States when the Civil War broke out, and Cecelia's choices would carry them both into the very heart of the conflict.

CHAPTER 10
I Am Seeking for a City

[Rochester is] the center of a virtuous, intelligent, enterprising, liberal, and growing population. The surrounding country is remarkable for its fertility, and the city itself possesses one of the finest waterpowers in the world. It is on the line of the New York Central railroad—a line that, with its connections, spans the whole country. Its people [are] industrious and in comfortable circumstances—not so rich as to be indifferent to the claims of humanity, and not so poor as to be unable to help any good cause which commanded the approval of their judgment.

—Frederick Douglass, 1882[1]

SOON AFTER BENJAMIN DIED, the widowed Cecelia packed up a few possessions and took Mamie with her to Rochester, New York.[2] Trusting in Fanny's assurances that the Ballards of Louisville had no designs on her freedom, Cecelia thought the American city might provide new horizons of possibility for herself and her daughter. It was also far away from the sad reminders of Benjamin's last, painful illness.

Cecelia already had some acquaintance with the city, for she had occasionally visited Rochester while Benjamin was working the lake boats and assisting local Underground Railroad conductors helping freedom-seekers make their way to Canada. On a clear day the city skyline was visible from the Toronto shore. America's first planned boom town, Rochester was a vibrant and vital place, blessed with ample water power from the falls of the Genesee River and profiting greatly from its privileged position on the Erie Canal. The urban centre had rebounded more quickly than Toronto after the Panic of 1857, and two years later it was in the process of transforming itself. The milling capital of the Great Lakes, the "Flour City" (there was even a bank of that name) was becoming the "Flower City." Rochester's many nurseries and seed houses were just beginning to develop mail-order businesses whose customers spanned the nation.[3]

With the new improvements in transportation, Cecelia and her daughter were able to take a steamer to Rochester's main port, Charlotte, at the mouth of the Genesee, where they boarded the New York Central Railroad for passage downtown.[4] Taking her daughter in hand, Cecelia explored the city. The central business district ran along Buffalo Street (called Main east of the river) on either side of the falls that bisected the oldest part of downtown and had been the source of Rochester's early prosperity. Though there was a good deal of older housing stock, by mid-century real wealth accumulated by the industrial and commercial classes, coupled with civic pride, had resulted in construction of some impressive architecture. Rochester's beautifully classical Corinthian Hall stood just behind the Reynolds Arcade. It was there that on July 5, 1852, Frederick Douglass had given one of his most lauded speeches, "What to the Slave Is the Fourth of July?"[5]

Concerned for her daughter's future, Cecelia took some time to make her decision, and she and her little girl travelled back and forth between Toronto and Rochester several times before finally deciding to move there. She already knew the main Black residential area of Cornhill, a district nestled into the river's curve west of downtown and the site of the first African American church in the city. There stood Black-owned shops and businesses, but most of the area's residents worked as seamstresses, coachmen, hostlers, gardeners, porters and household servants to wealthy whites with homes in the Third or "Ruffled Shirt" Ward. However, well-to-do white families had in the past few years begun moving across the Genesee to the newly fashionable rural suburb of East Avenue. The city's Black population had also spread into other parts of the city as employment prospects expanded. Across the river and north of East Avenue, in the Fifth Ward (known locally as the Near Northeast), members of the city's working class, both Black and white, occupied modest homes and tenements on small streets that ran between blocks of factories hugging the riverfront and rail lines.[6]

Arriving first in the fall of 1859, Cecelia found conditions relatively good. Despite African Americans' exclusion from many employment, entertainment and educational opportunities, as was typical of most Northern cities, there was now a second church along with the shops of barbers and blacksmiths, milliners and tailors, butchers and bakers, grocers and shoemakers, as well as sailors and stevedores, and one formally trained African American physician.

There were only 410 persons of African descent in the city proper, and 157 more in nearby towns and villages.[7] There had actually been more in Rochester in earlier years, but the Fugitive Slave Law had sent much of the city's fugitive population—including Grandison and Mary Ann Boyd— scrambling for the border after 1850.[8] Still, there were many people who had been free from birth, and Rochester's African American community was closely linked with that of Toronto, where a good many local people had relatives. Fewer people crossed the lake for church and social events these days, but there were plenty of free-born people in both cities who risked less than fugitive slaves did by entering the United States.

Now entirely alone and with a little girl to support, Cecelia's first priority was to find a job. She had found a good tenant for her Toronto house, but Benjamin's protracted death had left her without much in the way of resources. The savings she had so carefully hoarded for her mother's release were depleted, and she found that she could neither sell nor mortgage the Toronto home her husband had left her, because the land on which it stood was tied up with her stepsons' legacy from their father.[9] Mary's eventual freedom had been assured by the Ballards in any case; she would be manumitted within a couple of years, so Cecelia set that long-wished-for goal aside to attend to the more immediate problem of finding employment and securing her small daughter's future.

Fortunately, servants were in short supply and wages substantially higher than in most parts of the urbanized North. Early in the spring of 1860, Cecelia secured a live-in position with the family of John Craig. Born in New Hampshire in 1797, he had lived with his family in Middleport, Niagara County, until 1855, when he chose Rochester as a home. By the time Cecelia came into his household, John Craig was an attorney with substantial holdings in local real estate, as well as president of the Rochester Exchange Bank. Some influence may have been brought to bear in Cecelia's rapid hiring by the Craigs. Abolitionists often met at the Reynolds Arcade, where Mr. Craig had an office, and while not active abolitionists themselves, John Craig and his wife, Rhoda, were generous contributors to local charities and knew all the prominent people in the city who were involved in antislavery.[10]

With the Craigs lived with their niece, Martha T. Craig, still unmarried at thirty-two, and their daughter Helen and her husband, Daniel W. Powers. Powers was a brilliant banker and financier who had arrived at Rochester with the proverbial ten cents in his pocket, and now he was busily working towards millionaire status.[11] The Craigs' spacious home stood on the north side of broad East Avenue, which was lined with stately elms and the equally stately mansions of the rich and fashionable set. Cecelia was hired to work as a nursemaid to the Craigs' small granddaughter. Little Helen Powers, named after her mother, had just turned three.[12] Excellent with children, at this stage of her life Cecelia had for the most part abandoned her early vocation as a lady's maid and preferred to work with babies and toddlers. In later years friends described her as "a proud, particular woman" and a faithful and reliable servant who rarely searched long for a position.[13]

What little leisure time Cecelia had was devoted to her daughter, now six and about to start school.[14] One of the deciding factors in moving to Rochester was that there Mamie would have access to an education equal to the one she would have enjoyed in Toronto. Although Frederick Douglass had been forced to home-school his own children—a task he accomplished with the help of Phoebe Thayer, a New England teacher with strong abolitionist roots who moved into the house with the family—he had led the charge to have Black children educated in the public system. Rochester's schools were desegregated in 1857.[15]

Living out on East Avenue put Cecelia far from Cornhill and the centre of African American religious and social life, but a horse-drawn omnibus ran at regular intervals along East Avenue, between Conner's Tavern at the eastern city limits to the corner of Main and St. Paul Streets downtown.[16] This made it easy and inexpensive to visit friends she had known from earlier years, as well as to make new acquaintances within the community. It was also possible for her to attend church services and at least some of the events hosted by the city's African American population, but as a woman engaged in household service, Cecelia worked long hours and lived very much under the scrutiny of her employers.

Along with the relations of Toronto restaurateur Daniel Bloxom and Grandison and Mary Ann Boyd's friends and relatives in the area, she had a chance to renew her acquaintance with Benjamin Cleggett. Only three years younger than Cecelia, Cleggett had grown up in the Toronto home of his parents, shoemaker David and his wife, Mary Cleggett, but the family had moved to Rochester about a year after Cecelia landed at Toronto. Mary Cleggett was now a widow living on Rochester's Jefferson Street. Her son Benjamin was a member of the younger generation of Black community leaders in Rochester. He had married into one of the leading African American abolitionist families of the eastern seaboard: his wife was Frances "Frankie" Nell. Daughter of a prosperous catering family, she was the sister of William Cooper Nell. Nell was not only a regular visitor to Lowell and well-known to the Black barbers' guild where Benjamin's sons had trained, he was also very active in upstate New York abolitionist politics. This was the man who had helped Frederick Douglass in 1847 when he first opened the *North Star* in Rochester, and who had recently reported on the conditions of formerly enslaved residents of Canada West.

Another Cleggett son was James, who had a hairdressing business at the Reynolds Arcade that he had previously run in partnership with Ralph Francis.[17] After the Fugitive Slave Law was passed, Francis and his wife, Margaret, had taken over management of the main hotel at the Carthage wharf in order to enable smoother, more secure transfers of Underground Railroad passengers onto lake steamers there. Up to when the railroad link was constructed between Charlotte and Rochester proper, steamers crossing Lake Ontario had to be towed upstream to Carthage, where the passengers descended to be taken overland by a horse-drawn omnibus into Rochester. Carthage's port became redundant after 1853, but in the meantime the traffic in fugitive slaves had grown exponentially.[18] The work became so dangerous that Francis, along with his wife and daughter, left for Canada and opened a restaurant in Port Hope, east of Toronto.

By the time Cecelia came to live in Rochester, the Francis family was living in the market and milling town of Peterborough, about ninety miles north and east of Toronto. Boarding with Ralph and Margaret and their tiny grandson Ralph L. Johnson was the younger of Cecelia's two stepsons. James Thomas Holmes had completed his barber training in Lowell and chose Peterborough as the place to open his first shop. Cecelia had little contact with her stepsons, although having reached the age of his majority, Ben had now taken charge of the Centre Street properties, collecting the rents, paying the taxes and, for a short time, maintaining the northernmost of the two homes on his stepmother's behalf.[19]

An early community leader in Rochester was local grocer Austin Steward, who had at one time operated an important school in the basement of the African Methodist Episcopal Church Zion, before he departed the city for Canada to help manage the Wilberforce Settlement in 1830.[20] Cecelia was even more familiar with Rochester's most famous adopted son, Frederick Douglass. His autobiography, detailing his 1838 escape from Maryland and subsequent conversion to the antislavery cause, had been first published in 1845. First taken under the wing of William Lloyd Garrison, he was a brilliantly successful campaigner for the abolitionist cause. However, differences with Garrison led Douglass to consider other locations for his publishing venture. At the urging of Quaker abolitionists Amy Post and her pharmacist husband Isaac, he moved to Rochester.

With the assistance of William C. Nell and Dr. Martin Delany, who had given up his own Pittsburgh paper, the *Mystery*, Douglass began production of the *North Star* while staying with the Posts in their Sophia Street home. He brought his family to Rochester in 1848.[21] He supported Susan B. Anthony and Elizabeth Cady Stanton, both staunch abolitionists, in their crusade for women's rights, and was one of few men and the only African American man at the landmark Seneca Falls Convention in July of that same year.[22] Fittingly, the masthead of Frederick Douglass's *North Star* newspaper read: "Right is of no Sex—Truth is of no Color—God is the Father of us all, and we are all Brethren." It was through his influence, Cecelia learned, that the National Convention of Colored People was held at Rochester on July 6, 1853.

In fact, Cecelia found that reform of all kinds was very popular in Rochester, which lay within the "Burned-Over" district of upstate New York, so called because there had been so many religious revivals there during America's Second Great Awakening of evangelical Christianity. With the old constraints of formalized church discipline and concepts of original sin washed away, the whole region was optimistic about the possibility of positive change, both spiritually and socially.[23] There was, however, also a strong Unionist and a proslavery faction in town, and abolitionist meetings such as the one held by Susan B. Anthony and Frederick Douglass in 1858 at Rochester City Hall, just before Cecelia and Mamie came to live there, sometimes erupted in violence.

When Cecelia brought her daughter to Rochester, Frederick Douglass was not actually in residence. The city was in a furor over John Brown's failed raid on the military arsenal at Harpers Ferry, Virginia. Early in the year before, Brown had been a guest of Anna and Frederick Douglass. In their Rochester home Brown crafted his manifesto for establishing a new government in the mountains of western Virginia. Douglass declined to participate, even after meeting again with Brown at Detroit. He had arrived with eleven freedom-seekers in tow, en route to Canada, where he had held his landmark convention at Chatham in May 1858. There he stayed with Mary Ann Shadd Cary's brother and partner in her newspaper, Isaac Shadd, and met with Black supporters from as far away as Toronto, St. Catharines and Detroit. Dr. Delany, who was now practising medicine in Chatham, went to Brown's constitutional convention in 1858, as did many men from the Buxton Settlement. After conferring with Reverend William King, who, like Douglass, believed the venture had no chance for success, not one of the latter joined Brown's ragtag force.[24]

After the raid of October 16–18, 1859, failed, incriminating papers linking Frederick Douglass to John Brown's plans were discovered. Douglass fled to Canada West and published a letter in the Toronto *Globe* attesting to his innocence before departing on a hastily organized speaking tour of Great Britain. John Brown was executed at Charles Town, Virginia, on December 2, 1859.[25] Across the lake in Toronto, bells tolled and a service of remembrance in Brown's honour was held at the city's newly rebuilt St. James' Cathedral, and Black Torontonians held a special commemorative event that Grandison Boyd and Francis G. Simpson were instrumental in organizing.[26]

When Douglass returned to Rochester, he began again to operate his family's Underground Railroad station out of their home on the outskirts of the city. This was an effort that gave him much satisfaction and may in earlier days have brought the Black abolitionist into contact with Cecelia's Benjamin, while he was still working the lake boats. Douglass wrote of the business of conducting fugitives on the road to Canada:

> I can say I never did more congenial, attractive, fascinating, and satisfactory work. True, as a means of destroying slavery, it was like an attempt to bail out the ocean with a teaspoon, but the thought that there was *one* less slave, and one more freeman—having myself been a slave, and a fugitive slave—brought to my heart unspeakable joy. On one occasion I had eleven fugitives at the same time under my roof, and it was necessary for them to remain with me until I could collect sufficient money to get them on to Canada. It was the largest number I ever had at any one time, and I had some difficulty in providing so many with food and shelter, but, as may well be imagined, they were not very fastidious in either direction, and were well content with very plain food, and a strip of carpet on the floor for a bed, or a place on the straw in the barn-loft.[27]

Many of the other people in town, Black and white, were also engaged in this dangerous work, for Rochester was one of the most important conduits through which freedom-seekers on their way to Canada flowed. One who befriended Cecelia soon after her arrival was Sarah Powell, the much younger wife of community leader Harrison Powell. Harrison had worked with Mary Ann and Grandison Boyd to found the city's Ford Street Baptist Church, as noted in the *North Star* of March 9, 1849.[28] In Rochester Black abolitionists, Cecelia was to find, were very active. The Western New York Anti-Slavery Society, of which Ralph and Margaret Francis were founders in 1842, along with the Rochester Vigilance Committee, had some members whom Cecelia's deceased husband had known well. The Society was open to both men and women and was racially integrated.

Cecelia had little personal involvement in antislavery at this point, although she would have been familiar with Isaac and Amy Post; their living room was a place where both Black and white abolitionists and community members were always welcome. Amy Post was a founder of the Rochester Ladies' Anti-Slavery Society, originally established as a sewing circle in 1851. By 1852, in response to the passage of the Fugitive Slave Law, its members were running an annual bazaar of handicrafts, some acquired from as far afield as Great Britain.[29] They also sold antislavery literature to support *Frederick Douglass' Paper* and organized lectures. The group helped Harriet Tubman, who until 1859 had been living in St. Catharines but had just moved with her brothers and aged parents to Auburn, New York.[30]

Harriet Jacobs had spent a year living with the Posts and helping her brother John S. Jacobs, who assisted Frederick Douglass with his paper, operate the antislavery book room. She then returned to New York City to write a frank autobiography about her experiences in Edenton, North Carolina, *Incidents in the Life of a Slave Girl.* (Her brother John subsequently joined Grandison Boyd, the Patterson brothers and Elijah B. Dunlop in the Australian goldfields.) The Posts were also great friends of Sojourner Truth, the former Isabelle Baumfree, who had been a slave of one of the early Dutch settler families of New York State. Truth was both a civil and women's rights activist. She formed a deep friendship with Amy Post and was a frequent guest in her home. Her steady correspondence with Amy was maintained via intermediaries, for she had been unsuccessful at learning to read and write.[31]

But Cecelia was both a single parent and a live-in nursemaid for the Craig family. Like most African American household servants she worked more than ten hours per day, and often as many as fourteen. Living in also meant that both she and little Mamie were continually subjected to the whims and tempers of her employers, which was irksome and limiting. However kindly and charitable they might be, Cecelia's situation as a domestic servant was little better than that of a slave without a master.

One blues song put it eloquently: "Black gal, Black gal, got some work for you / Tell me, white folks, what you want me to do? / Got a big house to clean and scrub / dishes to wash and floors to mop and rub / White folks tell me how much you going to pay? / Well lemme see now, seeing as it's a rainy day . . ."[32]

This is likely why Cecelia belonged to "no church or society" while at Rochester.[33] There were both Baptist and African Methodist Episcopal Zion congregations in Rochester, the latter founded by Reverend Thomas James. Taught to read by Austin Steward, this formerly enslaved community organizer, author and inspiring antislavery lecturer had for a time pastored a church in New Bedford, Massachusetts, and it had been he who first encouraged the young Frederick Douglass to speak out publicly about his experiences while enslaved. James had returned to Rochester in 1856.[34] Cecelia would come to know the Reverend James again, under very different circumstances. Having attended church regularly, she must have missed the support and society of other Black women. As wives, mothers and widows, women like Cecelia were the mainstay of the self-help, benevolent and charitable organizations. Because they were breadwinners, any illness or injury they might suffer would have a dramatic impact on the welfare of their families. The self-insurance schemes offered by various societies, including the female branches of fraternal orders such as the Masons and the Grand United Order of Odd Fellows, helped shield employed women through the worst of such crises.

Cecelia very much wanted her own home again, and a family on whom she could depend. Amidst the upheaval surrounding the very contentious federal election taking place in the fall of 1860, she found herself being courted, and by a much younger man. Some years before she moved to Rochester, Cecelia had met William Henry Larrison in Toronto, probably at the British Methodist Episcopal Church. William was short and stocky, with what Cecelia called "Madagascar" hair and a "ginger"complexion,[35] and he had a personable and cheerful demeanour. Despite his youth, once she moved to Rochester he and the now-widowed Cecelia developed a very satisfactory mutual attraction. Cecelia was, however, careful not to admit she had known William while Benjamin was still alive, for she later said of their relationship:

> I went to Rochester not long after my first husband, Holmes died
> and had been there, not quite two years when I was married to
> Larrison. I got acquainted with Larrison soon after I went to
> Rochester. He was nothing but a young boy and he had never been
> married before his marriage to me. He had no relatives there. His
> people were at Wilmington, Del. [Delaware]. I think he had been
> at Rochester 3 or, 4 or, 5 yrs. at the time of our marriage. He came
> to Rochester with a white gentleman that lived at the edge of town
> on East Ave. I forget his name. [He] was working for this man
> when I married him.[36]

William had indeed been married before, and was, like Cecelia and Benjamin, formerly enslaved. Shortly after he took a bride, he was threatened with sale and fled his New Castle County, Delaware, owner. He walked all the way to Wilmington, to the home of Thomas Garrett. Garrett was a fearless Quaker Underground Railroad stationmaster who passed a remarkable number of freedom-seekers through his busy station. Garrett forwarded Larrison on to William Still in Philadelphia, who sent him via Sidney Howard Gay's station in New York City to Canada.[37] Still kept careful notes of everyone who passed through his busy Underground Railroad station, but he mistook William's name. He called Cecelia's beau, who arrived on January 17, 1856, "William Henry Lamison" and recorded his age as twenty-one, saying that Larrison "had belonged to Francis Harkins, and was worth $1,000 in the marketplace."[38]

William stayed in Toronto for a time, but the financial recession of 1857 severely reduced employment opportunities for the less skilled freedom-seekers. In February 1858 he was forced to seek assistance from the House of Industry, which listed him in the record as "W.H. Lawrison, American-born, poor, Methodist." However, by the time William and Cecelia reconnected at Rochester, he was working at the home of the elderly William and Siba Slocomb, New Englanders by birth, who lived on the outskirts of Rochester at Grove Place, at the end of East Avenue. The Slocombs had an adopted daughter named Eliza Carter who was, like William, from Delaware.[39] She was the wife of Joseph Buell Ward, son of the immensely wealthy local merchant Levi Ward Jr. Eliza and her adoptive parents lived with her husband in a large and beautifully appointed house his father had built for them in 1855.[40] William farmed their fields of wheat and barley and helped care for the orchards. "An extensive garden covered the space to the south and east of the homestead, wherein were all manner of flowers, vegetables, fruit trees, bushes and vines. . . . The portion of land lying next to Scio Street and extending well up towards the old house was laid out in farm and meadow."[41]

William and his lady friend spent what time together they could, but they had fallen in love in times full of upheaval and conflict. The outside world could not help but intrude on the couple's happiness, for the political situation, which had been very worrying, was now dire. On November 6, 1860, Abraham Lincoln was elected sixteenth president of the United States. With Rochesterians casting 975 out of 1,032 votes in his favour and with a majority in every Northern state, his election lit the fires of rebellion in the restive American South. On December 20 the secession of South Carolina from the Union began a cascade of rejections of Lincoln's presidency, and with it the Union. Early in 1861 the defection of South Carolina was closely followed by those of Mississippi, Florida, Alabama, Georgia, Louisiana and Texas. In the midst of it, Abraham Lincoln, now president-elect, made a whistle-stop tour on his way from Buffalo to Albany.

Lincoln stopped at Rochester on February 18, 1861, and spoke to a crowd of eight thousand from the rear platform of his train. Black

Rochesterians were well aware of the causes that had finally sundered the industrializing North from the slave South. A contemporary sketch of Lincoln's speech shows several African Americans in attendance, including at least one well-dressed and very respectable looking couple.[42] On that very day, another Kentucky-born politician, Jefferson Davis, was inaugurated as president of the Confederate States of America.

President Lincoln took office in March and Confederate troops fired on Fort Sumter in Charleston harbour on April 12, ushering in the Civil War. Cecelia would have recognized the name of the man who surrendered Fort Sumter thirty-four hours after the attack began, for it was Fanny Thruston's cousin from Louisville, career military officer and staunch Unionist colonel Robert Anderson.[43] On April 17 the state of Virginia separated from the Union, followed in close succession by Arkansas, North Carolina and Tennessee, which declared for Jeff Davis and left the Union on June 8, 1861. Rochester, with its population of fifty thousand, responded to the challenge by supplying thousands of young men to the cause. On May 3 more than twenty thousand people lined the downtown streets to see off eight companies of the Rochester Regiment—officially the 13th Regiment, New York State Volunteers—who would soon be deployed in defending the nation's capital.[44]

At the eastern end of East Avenue, away from the furor of wartime preparations, William Larrison cultivated his employers' extensive properties, all the while keeping company with the petite and comely widow who worked in the Craig and Powers household just down the road. Across the street from the Slocomb house stood St. Peter's Church, its construction funded by the devout Levi Ward Sr. so there would be a Presbyterian church near his home. William Slocomb served as an elder there for the rest of his life, and it was in this church that on April 3, 1862, William and Cecelia were married by Reverend John Townsend Coit.[45] At the time William Henry Larrison was supposedly twenty-four years old (if Still was correct, he was actually twenty-seven) and Cecelia Jane Holmes was nearly thirty-one. For the second time in Cecelia's life she was wed after a formal calling of the banns, which meant that no licence was needed. Because of the prominence of their employers, but rather unusually for an African American couple in Rochester, their marriage was announced in the Rochester *Daily Democrat* on April 4, 1862: "Lorrisen, William Henry Married Mrs. Cecelia Jane Holmes. At St. Peter's parsonage, April 3rd by Rev. J. T. Coit, Mr. William Henry Lorrisen, and Mrs. Cecilia Jane Homes [*sic*], both of this city."[46]

Although their nuptials were sponsored by William's employers—which is why they did not take place in one of the local Black churches—the only witnesses to the wedding were "Harrison Powell and his wife, colored, residents of Rochester, and a white gentleman named Smith who was present at Mr. Coit's parlor at [the] time of the marriage."[47] Harrison and Sarah Powell were there to support Cecelia, and both members of the couple were well respected locally despite their relatively humble station in life. Powell's name appeared alongside that of the educated and sophisticated Boston abolitionist William C. Nell at meetings of the community, and he along with Ralph Francis and Elijah B. Dunlop participated in the Buffalo National Convention of 1843. Originally from Virginia, Harrison Powell and his wife owned a home on Tappan Street in Rochester's Tenth Ward.[48]

William Larrison and his new bride set up housekeeping in a rental house on the northern edge of town near the Powells, but Cecelia continued to work as a daily for the Craigs for a few months after she established her own household. As Cecelia would inform the Pension Bureau some thirty-four years later, "I used to work for the Craig family. D. W. Powers was a son-in-law of the Craig family. After our marriage we kept house on Tappan St., Rochester. [We] Rented from Mrs. Maud Bailey, colored and lived next door t[o] a gentleman named Ungling[?]." The district was an integrated one with an admixture of recently arrived European immigrants. The "Unglings" were newcomers from Germany headed by carpenter Jacob, whose surname was actually Unglink. Relations between the Larrisons and other residents of the neighbourhood were cordial, and

Cecelia would in future use the Unglinks as a reference for dealings with the federal government.[49]

The Larrison wedding must have been a rather hurried affair, for a little too soon after her marriage to William, Cecelia gave birth to her second daughter. She named her Sarah, after the maid of Fanny's youthful Aunt Belle who had been her best friend in her slavery days.[50] William remained with the Slocombs, but when Cecelia's pregnancy became advanced, she gave up her own employment for the sake of the coming child. She had private income from her Toronto property and, thanks to Benjamin's foresight, this remained available to her even after her remarriage. The income from the rental was between $42 and $50 in the 1860s, about the same as she and William were paying on their Rochester accommodation, so it was very helpful.[51] Cecelia's daughter Mamie was very fond of her stepfather, and at age eight she began to use the surname Larrison.

Cecelia's new family was snug in their little house. But as was often the case for poor Cecelia, their happiness was to be short-lived. The Civil War would consume all before it.

CHAPTER 11
THE TRUMPET SOUNDS WITHIN MY SOUL

Once let the black man get upon his person the brass letter, US, let him get an eagle on his button, and a musket on his shoulder and bullets in his pocket, there is no power on earth that can deny that he has earned the right to citizenship in the United States.

—Frederick Douglass, June 17, 1863

ACROSS THE STREET FROM the Craig house on East Avenue stood the huge Federal-style brick house of Aaron Erickson and his wife, Hannah.[1] An immensely wealthy wool merchant and banker, he and his wife had filled the stately brick mansion, fronted by Corinthian pillars, with eight children, including the mischievous and spritely fourteen-year-old Hannah Viola Erickson, named after her mother.

Cecelia had gone back to work soon after baby Sarah was born, and through the Craigs she became acquainted with the servants of the Erickson household. She worked hard and cared for her children, but though her young husband continued to work for the Slocombs of Grove Place, he, along with most of Rochester's male African American population, was seething with frustration. Although war was raging in battlefields far from the Genesee River Valley, Black men were not allowed to fight.

Meetings of protest were held at Boston and New York, Chicago and Cincinnati. Frederick Douglass railed in the pages of his newspaper that African Americans were being left out of a war that, whatever President Lincoln said, Black Americans knew was about slavery. In Canada West they were just as anxious to fight. Josiah Henson—who was becoming ever more identified with the character of Uncle Tom from Harriet Beecher Stowe's sentimentalized but immensely popular antislavery novel, which President Lincoln himself considered one of the causes of the war—itched for battle. He began drilling the men of the Dawn Settlement against the day when they could cross the border and enlist. In doing so he was risking arrest, for under the Foreign Enlistment Act it was illegal to recruit British subjects for wars in which Great Britain was not a combatant.

All over the South, enslaved Black men, women and children saw the declaration of war as an opportunity to create their own freedom. Thousands headed for the Union lines, where officers and men alike were ill prepared to receive them. These "contrabands" were often poorly treated and ill-fed, and some Union officers felt bound to return them to the masters they had fled.[2] Yet their service proved invaluable to the Northern war effort: they took on work as builders, hostlers, seamstresses and laundresses and provided a host of other services needed by the Union troops, thereby depriving the Confederacy of their labour.

Cecelia's friends the Harrisons and the Bloxoms, along with the rest of African American Rochester, felt the loss when the beloved Reverend Thomas James left to join the war effort. He was commandeered by the US Army in Louisville while travelling south to an American Missionary Association posting in Tennessee. Instead he was given the charge of protecting and caring for both escaping slaves and free people there.[3]

Anxious that William might be drawn into the fight, Cecelia was fearful of being left behind in the city with two young children to care for, but the US Congress resisted the idea of African American men fighting for the

Union. Frederick Douglass complained that after the first disastrous Battle of Bull Run, where the popular Rochester regiment the "Bloody Thirteenth" had fought, there were Black men in the Confederate forces but none in Union blue. Although these were usually personal servants who accompanied their owners to the front, the point rankled with African Americans who were anxious to prove their devotion to the cause of freedom on the battlefield.[4] However, their chance—and William Larrison's—came in the spring of 1863, following Lincoln's Emancipation Proclamation of January 1, 1863. The proclamation freed slaves only in the rebelling states, but it finally made way for the recruitment of Black soldiers into Union ranks. For a time Cecelia managed to convince her young husband to remain at home and take care of his family, but it would be her own actions that ultimately plunged both William and herself into the midst of the conflict.

Meanwhile, on March 2, 1863, Frederick Douglass published a rousing editorial, "Men of Color, to Arms!" urging African Americans to join the struggle, for "Liberty won by white men would lose half its lustre." Since New York was silent on the matter of Black recruitment, Douglass urged men to sign up with the Massachusetts regiments forming outside Boston. The Bureau of Colored Troops was established on May 22, 1863.[5] By the end of the war about 10 percent of all Union soldiers would boast African ancestry. African Canadians defied all British colonial laws to the contrary and hundreds crossed into the United States to enlist. Dr. Martin Delany postponed plans to establish a colony for free people in Africa's Niger Valley and offered his services to the cause. Mary Ann Shadd Cary, who had become a naturalized British subject, left Chatham to become the only female recruiting officer in the Union Army. Her brother Abraham fought, as did young men who had attended school at Buxton, as well as those from Dresden, Amherstburg and the larger communities in London, Hamilton and Toronto. In all about 2,500 African Canadians would join the US Army and Navy.[6]

Cecelia's young husband had a different war. He became one among the handful of Black enlisted men in all-white regiments, although, by a trick of fate, not under his own name. This came about because of a fascinating set of circumstances set off by an illicit romance between Hannah Erickson, protected teenaged daughter of Rochester's wealthiest merchant, Aaron Erickson, and the much older commander of the 14th New York Heavy Artillery Regiment.

Colonel Elisha G. Marshall was a West Point graduate with a very distinguished career. He had previously commanded the 13th New York Volunteer Regiment that was decimated at the Battle of Bull Run and had been wounded at Fredericksburg. The regiment was disbanded in 1863 when the two-year enlistment period ended, and on May 29, 1863, Marshall started recruiting for the 14th New York Heavy Artillery. He was required to entice some 1,800 men into the Union ranks, three and a half times the usual number, because the new unit was intended to defend the all-important harbours at New York and Washington. A bounty of $552 was offered for veterans and $175 for new recruits.[7]

However, enthusiasm had waned as reports of the carnage on Civil War battlefields poured in by telegraph and mail, to be reproduced in the Rochester newspapers. Reports from the Battle of Gettysburg, in which Rochester lost more than fifty men, and other scenes of destruction discouraged men from signing up, despite the fact that if they did so they would receive substantial federal and state bounties, funds for which men who waited to be drafted were not eligible. Instead, resistance to the draft escalated into four days of horrific rioting in New York City, from July 13 to 16. A largely Irish mob burned the Colored Orphanage (fortunately no children were inside) and targeted and victimized Blacks, who were seen as the cause of the war. The homes of known abolitionists were also looted and put to the torch, as was the house of William and Mercy Powell, who had returned to live in the city. As many as five hundred people died.[8]

Undaunted, Major Job C. Hedges pitched a tent on the lawn before Rochester City Hall and he and Colonel Marshall commenced an aggressive recruiting campaign.[9] Recruits were to be paid "One month's pay, $18, in advance, to all who enlist, and $2 premium; Rations, Clothing, Lodging, and Pay begins with enlistment." Since heavy artillery units were meant to be stationed in fortifications designed to defend places of strategic import, the advertisements announced as a further inducement: "No Marching. No Knapsacks to shoulder. The Best Branch of the Military Service."[10]

Meanwhile Colonel Marshall and other officers returning from the front were feted in the dining rooms of Rochester's finest households, including some of the Craig and Erickson families' neighbours on East Avenue. Balls, soirees, fundraising dinners and the like were the order of the day as everyone gathered to celebrate the brave men who were defending the Union from dissolution. At which of these events Elisha Marshall first encountered his future wife is nowhere recorded, but soon love notes began passing through the hands of servants to the upstairs bedroom of pretty young Hannah Erickson. The teenager was equally taken with her much older beau, dazzled by his uniform, his impressive whiskers and his fine military bearing. Just after Hannah's birthday, she ran away with him.

On September 14, 1863, the Rochester *Union and Advertiser* tersely announced their nuptials: "On Sunday, the 13th inst. By the Rev. Mr. Bellamy, Col. E. G. Marshall, U.S.A. to Hannah V. youngest daughter of Aaron Erickson, Esq., all of this city."[11] Hannah was only fifteen years old to her husband's thirty-four.[12] The secret ceremony was performed in Charlotte, Rochester's rather rough-and-tumble harbour at the mouth of the Genesee, teeming with military men and stockpiled materiel, hardly a venue for the wedding of one of Rochester's most eligible young ladies.

The Ericksons were heartbroken by their youngest daughter's elopement. By contrast, when her sister Caroline married New England grocery merchant and banker Gilman H. Perkins, the entire street leading up to the church was lined with well-wishers, and the couple drove to the lavish ceremony in an open carriage decorated with ribbons and flowers. The ball that followed was the talk of the town for months.[13] Colonel Marshall may have been a gallant officer completely smitten with his young bride, but while his family was one of Seneca Falls's best, they hardly moved in the same circles as the Ericksons did in Rochester. Hannah Erickson Marshall was rarely if ever again acknowledged as a member of her own family.[14]

Cecelia Jane Larrison seems to have played a part in the clandestine activity leading up to Elisha and Hannah's elopement. Although a very practical woman, she had a sentimental side that was evident from her own romantic adventures. William too may well have had a role; one envisions him holding the ladder for the lovesick colonel or driving the carriage that carried the couple off to Charlotte to be wed. Whatever the circumstances that embroiled them in Marshall's affairs, William certainly knew the Colonel rather well, considering his own status in life. After a personal request for his services arrived from the Colonel himself, on December 6, 1863, William Henry Larrison joined up for a period of three years. William's enlistment papers describe him as having black hair and skin; five feet, six inches in height; and a farmer by way of occupation. Black men were allowed to serve in white regiments, but only as "undercooks."[15]

The enlisting officer misheard William's surname and instead wrote down the name of a famous general who had been elected to the presidency, William Henry Harrison. Cecelia's husband did not catch the mistake, for although his wife was educated, William still signed his name with an X. "Billy Harrison" repeatedly told comrades that his name was really William H. Larrison, but there was no way to change his enlistment records after the fact.[16] The error would cause Cecelia enduring difficulties.

Cecelia's William mustered in at Rochester on December 31 and moved to the winter quarters set up for Company "H" of the 14th New York Heavy Artillery Regiment. Having cast his net across upstate New York as far as the Adirondacks to fill out the ranks, and having personally convinced one African American undercook that his services were essential if the Union were to win the war, Elisha G. Marshall was commissioned colonel of the 14th New York on January 4, 1864.[17]

According to their friends, the Larrisons were a devoted, affectionate couple who were very much in love.[18] No records document how Cecelia felt about the idea of William's going off to war and leaving her behind, although the hundred-dollar federal enlistment bounty would have been welcome. In any case, the couple soon discovered that only $25 was forthcoming until the time of William's discharge, as well as another $75—$10 in advance, $25 upon the regiment's being established and the rest when he mustered out—from the State of New York. The payment of one month's wages ($13) in advance was supposed to provide for her family in the meantime.[19] They were expected to await the end of the war before the rest would be paid, assuming that Cecelia's youthful husband lived to collect it.

Company "H" was given orders to depart Rochester to take up the defence of New York Harbor. However, Colonel Marshall demonstrated his gratitude to William by seeing to it that instead of serving the troops, he was assigned for at least part of the time to serve as his commanding officer's own cook. Marshall also managed to reward William's earlier assistance in a minor but more concrete way. Despite the fact that there was no mechanism in place for promoting a Black man from undercook to cook, Colonel Marshall did so anyway.

Hannah Erickson, now Mrs. Colonel Elisha G. Marshall, had a fondness for a certain lady's maid she had come to know, even though she was trained in the fine hairdressing styles of an earlier day and more familiar with gowns sported by the belles of Louisville some twenty years before than she was with modern fashion. When Mrs. Erickson accompanied her new husband to what must have been unfamiliarly spartan new quarters at Fort Richmond on Staten Island, Cecelia Jane Larrison went along too, taking her little girls with her.[20] She and William would spend at least the first part of the war together in camp.

Cecelia was now lady's maid to the wife of the regimental commander and entitled to her own salary, which was paid privately by the Marshalls. It was one of poor Hannah's few real luxuries. As the wife of a regimental colonel (he would be brevetted brigadier general by war's end), she had endless status and prestige but lived in a constant state of terror that her husband might be killed or seriously wounded. Too, there were precious few comforts in the military housing she occupied, a far cry from the silks and fine feather pillows to which she had been accustomed as Aaron Erickson's pampered daughter.[21]

Mrs. Marshall expected to stay with her husband through the summer of 1864 until the spring of 1865, which meant that Cecelia and her little girls were able to live with William at least some of the time. One soldier in particular later remembered Cecelia having her elder child with her in the military quarters at Fort Richmond, and took note of how fond of his wife and daughter William seemed to be.[22] The work was very hard, though. Black female servants like Cecelia sometimes accompanied officers' wives very nearly to the front lines. They washed, ironed and packed clothing, brought food and drink as needed, cared for babies and small children, and scrounged what small comforts might be found amidst the exigencies of war. They served as midwives too, for harried military surgeons were ill-suited to the duty and usually otherwise occupied.[23]

Cecelia was able to stay with her husband as long as his unit remained at Fort Richmond. His company was there through April 23, 1864. However, once the theatre of war moved away from New York and its harbour was no longer under threat, General Ulysses S. Grant transferred the 14th New York and other heavy artillery regiments to serve as infantry in the Army of the Potomac. According to a telegram from Grant on April 21, 1864, they were forwarded on to General Ambrose E. Burnside for formation into brigades.[24] Burnside's men, serving under General George Meade, were poised to take Richmond, Virginia, the very heart and soul of the Confederacy, a move President Lincoln believed would end the war.

When Company "H" was sent to Washington in the spring of 1864, Cecelia and her two daughters, Mamie and Sarah, travelled with Mrs. Marshall. Cecelia well remembered the city from her visit there in the winter of 1845, but it was all but unrecognizable, for signs of the conflict were everywhere. The streets were thronged with soldiers. Every nook and cranny was filled with military personnel and stockpiles of materiel. Officers' wives such as Hannah Marshall, along with their servants, were usually put up in boarding houses and hotels, but Washington was bursting at the seams and many ended up as guests in private family homes.[25]

The alleyways and fetid warehouses along the docks were home to tens of thousands of desperate, frightened and often hungry Black people, those from the non-rebel District of Columbia and adjacent Maryland still legally enslaved. Union soldiers brought their own ideas of white supremacy with them into the military. Many considered African Americans the reason why the war was being prolonged and abused them when they could. There was an ongoing problem with supplies to feed the thousands of men, women and children who followed the regular troops. More than forty thousand displaced African Americans were by this time eking out a bare existence in the District of Columbia.[26]

The Posts' old friend Harriet Jacobs, along with two members of the Rochester Ladies' Anti-Slavery Society, were there doing what they could. Jacobs and the women from the Rochester area corresponded with Amy Post, describing the appalling conditions they were trying to alleviate in the contraband camps in and around the nation's capital.[27] Harriet Tubman left her family in Auburn and worked tirelessly throughout the war as a nurse, cook, spy and scout. She was in and out of Washington, for she had the distinction of being the only woman in the entire war to command troops, white or Black, in her raiding efforts in coastal Georgia and the Carolinas.[28]

Cecelia, of course, had once stayed with the Jesups. Ann Heron Jesup was long dead and her husband too had passed on, but Cecelia had made the acquaintance of some of the enslaved Black servants who worked in the presidential mansion and in the homes that lined Lafayette Square north of the White House, so there was a friend or two to greet her when she arrived. There were also several people in town from Toronto. Among the physicians serving the US Colored Troops were three trained in Toronto medical schools: Dr. Alexander T. Augusta was the highest-ranking Black surgeon in the Union Army, while a little boy Cecelia and Benjamin had known from the Coloured Methodist Chapel had grown up to be the first Canadian-born Black doctor, Anderson Ruffin Abbott. There was also one of his old classmates from the Buxton school, Jerome Riley, who worked as a medical assistant. A fourth was someone with whom Cecelia was familiar from her time in Liverpool. William and Mercy Powell's son, Dr. William P. Powell Jr., had trained in British medical schools and now served as a physician in Washington's vastly over-crowded Contraband Hospital.[29]

So Cecelia was familiar with the city and knew people there, but the wartime city was a changed and frightening place. Confederate troops threatened to take the city, and Cecelia feared for the health of her little girls in the face of the rampant disease in contraband and military camps alike. Mrs. Marshall was now pregnant and her husband was sufficiently concerned that he was considering sending her back to Rochester. Cecelia did not wait for her employer's decision but wrote an anxious letter to her husband, explaining the difficult living conditions and the danger to their children she perceived in Washington.[30]

William Larrison was stationed on the battlefields of some of the most horrifying and fatal encounters of the later war years, but he went to great lengths to provide Cecelia with funds to take the children home. Cecelia later wrote of her wartime experience:

When the 14th. Heavy Art. left Rochester, I went to Ft. Richmond on Staten Island and Col. Marshall [was] married to a Miss

Erickson and I went with her. And when the Regt. went to Washington, I went with Miss Erickson there. The Reg't [stayed] but a day at Washington. I got from my husband, an order for some money he had put in Maj. Hedges hands and which Maj. Hedges had sent to his wife, at Elizabethtown N.J. I went then and saw Mrs. Hedges, staid [sic] all night and got the money and went on to Rochester the next morning and remained in Rochester till my husband was discharged in Sept. of the same year.[31]

Elizabeth W. Hedges was the wife of recruiting officer Major Job Hedges, who had signed up William in Rochester. It must have been an interesting encounter, for Mrs. Hedges had been deaf nearly all her life because of a childhood illness. A gracious hostess, she welcomed Cecelia and the two little girls into her home and saw them off to the train in the morning. It was a long and onerous journey on trains that had been commandeered off and on for troop transport. Back in Rochester, Cecelia found accommodation for herself and her children and anxiously waited out the rest of the war.[32]

Cecelia was therefore living in the city when a noteworthy event took place. This was the reunion of the elderly Sojourner Truth with Frederick Douglass. The two venerable and fiery speakers had had a falling out in 1852, but they shared a podium in Rochester in June 1864, where they both quoted Isaiah. The Civil War was a "howling jeremiad," justified to cleanse the nation of the evil that had been slavery, after which Truth believed that America would become a place of beauty, justice and freedom. Sojourner Truth went on to Washington to raise funds and source supplies to help the African American refugees there. A few months later, in October 1864, she had a very pleasant audience with President Lincoln. He treated her with great consideration and signed for her a copy of her book.[33]

Cecelia had come home to a city with a burgeoning war industry in goods and foodstuffs, but one where the escalating price of coal was ruinous for poorer families. Aid organizations were in place to assist soldiers' wives and children, but they foundered on the shoals of increased need coupled with rising costs, and the wives of Black soldiers were always last to receive support. The war news, too, was terrible. Several Rochester regiments were in the thick of the fighting as Union forces battled their way towards Richmond, with appalling casualties.[34] Cecelia could not even correspond with her much-loved William and she had no idea of his condition, although she did know that he had a good friend in Sergeant Palmer, a white man.[35]

Actually, as a cook with the 14th New York Regiment, now assigned as an infantry regiment in the Army of the Potomac, William H. Larrison was in real danger. Cooks and undercooks often ended up in the midst of battle when the lines overran the places where they had set up their equipment, which was very heavy and awkward to move from place to place. Sometimes they were even deployed as soldiers when their units were short of men. Their duties made them responsible for provisioning the men wherever they were located, and it was the cooks who took abuse for the spoiled meat, withered vegetables, maggoty bread and hard biscuit that were often the only fare available. Sharpshooters had their sights trained on cooks, hostlers and others who, like William, provided essential services to the officers and men. There was constant shelling, and disease killed as many men in the Union forces as did the bullets. Cecelia's husband was hospitalized several times during his term of service with undefined illnesses.[36]

However, Colonel Marshall was leading the 14th New York from strength to strength. Transferred to the Provisional Brigade, 1st Division, 9th Corps, Colonel Marshall served as provisional commander through the Battle of the Wilderness (May 5–7, 1864), the battle at North Anna (May 24, 1864) and the horrific Battle of Cold Harbor (June 2–8, 1864), where more than seven thousand men fell within minutes. But General Grant knew that taking Petersburg, Virginia, which straddled the main Southern rail line, would deprive Robert E. Lee of the food and materiel he needed to defend Richmond. They crossed over the James River to take up their position on June 15, 1864.[37]

It was there, at the siege of Petersburg, that William Larrison's luck ran out, and the entire 14th Heavy Artillery's with him. Burnside's men could not break through the Confederate defences, so they dug in. A group of Pennsylvania coalminers convinced the general that they could take the high ground by tunnelling beneath it. The work lasted for weeks under the skeptical eyes of Burnside's officers. On July 30, 1864, the 1st Division, commanded by Colonel Elisha G. Marshall, would be ordered to capture the breastworks along the right side of the crater. They would do so, and sustained terrible losses, only falling back when their ammunition ran out. Then, using some 325 kegs of gunpowder (about 8,000 pounds), Colonel Pleasants and his Pennsylvania coalminers smashed the entire fort to smithereens, and the larger part of the Confederate regiment manning it as well. The result was an enormous crater about 25 feet deep, 150 feet long and 60 feet wide. More than 275 Confederate men and officers lay dead and dying. However, the Union commanders could not capitalize on the opportunity.

The first units to press the advantage the crater presented were supposed to include Pennsylvania's 43rd US Colored Troops (USCT). Black soldiers had distinguished themselves at Fort Wagner, Milliken Bend and other major encounters. Trained for the endeavour and anxious to fight, they were the freshest soldiers in the Union Army at this time. But General George Meade, who initially had not taken the mining endeavour seriously, was anxious for white troops to gain the glory of victory. At the same time, he may have been afraid that if those men were massacred he would be accused of using them as cannon fodder. So instead of well-prepared Black soldiers, his officers drew straws to see whose men would lead the charge into the crater. Brigadier General James Ledlie drew the short straw. His soldiers included the 14th New York Heavy Artillery, commanded by Colonel Marshall. They were ordered to advance without any instructions as to how to proceed, with horrific results. Grant would later lament that "such an opportunity for carrying fortifications I have never seen and do not expect again to have."[38]

The 14th managed to mount the breastworks and held them nearly all day. Wave after wave of soldiers were ordered forward, not around the lip of the depression to take the high ground, but rather into the crater. It quickly filled, and the heat and stench were terrific, new troops scrambling over bodies of the dead and wounded, trying to climb the steep sides. The Black soldiers were sent in only when the situation was hopeless. They too entered the crater. What followed rivalled Fort Pillow as one of the greatest atrocities against African American troops in the entire Civil War. At the Battle of the Crater, Confederate officers ordered that US Colored Troops who surrendered were to be shot.

Lieutenant Freeman Bowley later wrote: "We were the last to reach the Crater by way of the traverse, and the rifles of the Union soldiers were flashing in our faces when we jumped down in there. As I landed inside, I turned for a second to look back, and caught a glimpse of the Confederates bayoneting the wounded men who had just been shot down."[39] John Sergeant Wise, son of the Confederate officer in command at Petersburg and himself a witness to the debacle, provided a damning account, all the more telling since it was filtered through his Southern prejudices regarding the fitness of Blacks as soldiers:

The crater fight was not only one of the bloodiest, but one of the most brutal of the war. It was the first time Lee's army had encountered negroes, and their presence excited in the troops indignant malice such as had characterized no former conflict. To the credit of the blacks be it said that they advanced in better order and pushed forward farther than the whites . . . [but] our men, inflamed to relentless vengeance by their presence, disregarded the rules of warfare which restrained them in battle with their own race, and brained and butchered the blacks until the slaughter was sickening.[40]

Nearly all the USCT soldiers who surrendered were summarily executed by the vengeful Confederates. Of the 14th New York's 400 men, the losses totalled 132, and 1,400 soldiers were captured. Hannah Marshall received a telegram at Rochester from General Ambrose Burnside, stating that her "husband was captured on Saturday when the assault was made upon the Rebel works before Petersburg." Colonel Elisha G. Marshall had been in command of the 2nd Brigade, 1st Division, 9th Army Corps. Major Job Hedges, whose wife had been so kind to Cecelia, was killed leading his battalion against the Confederate breastworks before the regiment entered the crater later that day. He was one of an astonishing 3,826 Union casualties, while the Confederates lost only 1,500 men.[41]

The rest of the 14th New York was reassigned to Major George Randall of Lieutenant-Colonel Gilbert P. Robinson's brigade. But William H. Larrison was already very ill, and he was sick in hospital by the time his regiment took the Weldon Railroad. In that he was fortunate. On August 18 the troops were sent into heavily fortified territory with fire on all sides; 194 soldiers went into battle and some 51 men were wounded, captured or killed. However, by August 21 the railway line was securely in Union hands. With the severing of their supply lines, a blow had been struck from which the Confederacy never really recovered. William rejoined his unit and was present at the Battle of Poplar Grove Church on September 30.

General Lee's forces were stretched impossibly thin. Petersburg and Richmond had already been abandoned. It was the first step on the road to Appomattox. On March 4 Abraham Lincoln was inaugurated for his second term as president of the United States. He visited Richmond on April 3, after Petersburg fell. On April 9, 1865, Robert E. Lee surrendered to General Ulysses S. Grant. Other Confederate generals followed suit, the last being General Stand Waite, who surrendered his Cherokee forces in Oklahoma on June 23, 1865. The Civil War was over.

But the Union victory had already turned to ashes. On April 15, at Ford's Theatre in downtown Washington, a well-known actor ardently loyal to the Confederacy assassinated President Abraham Lincoln. The plot to kill the president had been hatched in Montreal, where fled several of the conspirators after the event. One of the physicians who attended Lincoln's deathbed was Dr. Anderson Ruffin Abbott, now assistant director of the Freedmen's Bureau Hospital. Such was the regard in which Mrs. Lincoln held the Toronto-born physician that she later gave Abbott the shawl that Lincoln had used at his inauguration.[42] Vice-President Andrew Johnson of Tennessee became America's seventeenth president. He proceeded to obstruct efforts to put in place Lincoln's plans for the liberation and enfranchisement of America's four million slaves.

Relieved before Petersburg, William's regiment had defended Fort Steadman against heavy attack in March 1865 and briefly occupied Petersburg. Although the war had ended in April 1865, the 14th New York Heavy Artillery returned to Washington to take up defence of the city. The rank and file of the regiment mustered out at Washington on August 26, 1865. Cecelia's William returned to Rochester on the train with his unit on August 30.

William H. Larrison had spent much of the previous few months in and out of hospital. Carrying heavy loads from camp to camp had caused such a severe rupture (hernia) in his lower abdomen that he could barely stand upright at times. He would never fully recover from the ordeal. Shortly after William made his way back to Rochester, it became apparent that he would be incapacitated for some time. Thousands of demobilized troops were pouring into upstate New York and employment was at a premium, even for the able-bodied among them. It was left to Cecelia, William's ever-resourceful wife, to devise a plan for their future.[43]

CHAPTER 12
Climbing Jacob's Ladder

It is easier to build strong children than to repair broken men.

—Frederick Douglass

MEANWHILE, CECELIA'S STEPSONS HAD grown up. About the same time that she finally decided on her own to move to Rochester, Benjamin's two sons were embarking on new lives as "tonsorial artists," as some of the more florid barbers and hairdressers of their acquaintance styled themselves. Their father's foresight and personal sacrifice had borne fruit. Benjamin Alexander and James Thomas Holmes were now master barbers, ready to become independent businessmen in their own right, with all the risks and rewards that implied.

Just a few months after Cecelia left Toronto for Rochester, James Thomas Holmes, age twenty, completed his apprenticeship and moved back to Canada West. However, he did not return to the house his father had built for him and his brother in Toronto. Rather, he chose to set up his first barbershop in Peterborough, a thriving county town on the Otonabee River, in the Kawartha Lakes district of the province, about 90 miles northeast of Toronto. Very soon his older brother, whom James had left behind in Lowell, would move to the same district. Ben Alexander Holmes would establish himself in Lindsay, an even smaller centre to the west and slightly north of Peterborough, in remote but strikingly beautiful Emily Township. By 1863 Lindsay would be the market town for the new County of Victoria.

How much contact Cecelia had with these two young men, apart from necessary business pertaining to their jointly owned Toronto real estate, is unclear. However, the Rochester connections with African Canada extended far to the north of the shore of Lake Ontario. The Holmes brothers' return to their Canadian homeland provides a remarkable illustration of the intricately intertwined network that existed among the Black activists of upstate New York, the Great Lakes Basin and even the Atlantic seaboard.

If the master barbers' guild in Lowell had picked the locations for the Holmes brothers' first independent professional ventures, they had chosen well. When James Thomas Holmes arrived in Peterborough County, it was booming. The town was named in honour of Peter Robinson, elder brother of Chief Justice John Beverley Robinson, who had managed a major Irish settlement scheme in this part of the province in 1825.[1] A kindly man who was generously supportive of his largely Roman Catholic pioneers, by 1827 he was Commissioner of Crown Lands and Surveyor General of Woods. Under his tenure, settlement terms were lenient, employment opportunities for the impecunious immigrants abundant in road building and other government contract work, and the terms of payment for farmland reasonable. As early as 1830 Robinson had established a policy that Crown-owned land was to be made available to Black settlers on the same terms as to whites.[2]

Blessed with fertile soil, verdant woodland, rich marshes teeming with fish and game, and significant mineral deposits (principally iron ore, lead and good-quality marble), the region also had ample water power for flour, saw and woollen mills. Peterborough was connected by an extensive chain of waterways and by rail to Port Hope and Cobourg on Lake Ontario, with access to the St. Lawrence River to the east and to Lindsay and Beaverton to the west. When James T. Holmes arrived in 1861, Peterborough was a town of about 2,200 residents.

That James Thomas left the United States just months before the Civil War broke out was hardly coincidental. While Cecelia's younger stepson trudged to his new shop through the deep drifts of a Canadian winter, the papers were filled with American news. The election of Abraham Lincoln in November 1860 was salt in the long-festering wounds that divided North and South. Over the course of the winter, state after state seceded. The snows were melting on April 12, 1861, when, thanks to the marvel of the telegraph, the news reached Peterborough on the very day that Confederate troops fired on the Union officers and men holding Fort Sumter in Charleston Bay.

Everyone whom the youthful "Professor Holmes," as he styled himself in some of his advertisements, took to his chair had an opinion about the new Confederate president, Jefferson Davis, and the causes of America's Civil War. Their views were perhaps muted when they commented on the fact that, of all the slave states, only Missouri, Kentucky and Maryland (under some duress) remained in the Union. In October 1861 West Virginia broke away from the Old Dominion, the birthplace of James's father, to become a Union state by 1863.

What had drawn James Thomas Holmes to this outpost of British civilization? There were few African Canadians living on the edge of Canada's vast northern wilderness. For one thing, the Black barbers' informal guild managed how many young journeymen were released into each area. The Toronto market for barbers was likely saturated with the sons and nephews of the city's African Canadian "tonsorial artists" setting up shop, and the Underground Railroad had brought newcomers skilled in such services as well. The Newcastle district, on the other hand, had long cried out for a good barber, as was humorously articulated three years earlier in a newspaper produced by a boys' private academy a few miles north of Peterborough.

Kachewahnoonkah Herald
March 22nd 1858
Et Libras et amicos non plurimos Guevo sel optimos
Dear Mr. Editor

Do you not think it would be possible through the medium of your paper to induce some enterprising man desirous of making a good living to start in the profession of barber and hair cutter. I am sure it would pay. It is really frightful to see the way many of the young men are now going about. They look more like wild men of the woods than civilized beings and if they keep their hair in that state, because they fancy then they have "nobby heads of hair" they are woefully mistaken. I am sure you yourself, Mr. Editor, must coincide with these few remarks. Your own well cropped head setting a fine example. . . Trusting I may soon see a barbers pole protruding itself from some window at the falls.

I remain

Dear Sir

An admirer of short hair[3]

But there was also another factor at play. James had a mentor, a master barber in his own right, who was living in Peterborough, a man his father and stepmother had known well before he moved there. By January 1861 James T. Holmes was boarding in the household of Ralph and Margaret Francis, both forty-seven and of the Baptist faith. They owned and operated a Peterborough "saloon" and lived in a three-storey brick house along with their grandson Ralph F. Johnson, who was three.[4] Census records describe the younger Holmes brother as single, mulatto and Wesleyan Methodist in religion. There were two Roman Catholic Irishwomen living there as well, one age twenty and the other thirty, both employed in the Francis saloon.

Ralph Francis was a very interesting man. He was the grandson of an enslaved Revolutionary War veteran by the name of Jacob Francis. After the conflict Jacob returned to his native New Jersey to marry and then purchase his wife.[5] They raised several children on their Huntingdon County farm, the eldest of whom, John, followed the line of the Erie Canal west in 1835 in search of new opportunities. John married, and he and Julia Francis resided in Rochester's Third Ward, their finances bolstered by a small inheritance after Jacob died in 1836. By the 1840s the family was paying the highest property tax of any African Americans in Rochester, except for Frederick and Anna Douglass. John and Julia educated their children at the school for "coloured" children operated by Reverend Thomas James in the basement of the African Methodist Episcopal Zion church, and set up each of them in either a trade or a business. Ralph trained as a barber and opened his first shop on the main floor of the Rochester House Hotel.[6]

Smart, courageous and angry about the slavery and racial oppression under which African Americans suffered, over the next few years Ralph Francis proved himself a vociferous champion of antislavery and Black civil rights. He took part in local meetings as well as the very contentious convention at Buffalo in 1843, where Presbyterian minister Henry Highland Garnet punctuated his famous speech with the words "Let your motto be resistance!"[7] The Western New York Anti-Slavery Society was founded in 1842 with Ralph and Margaret Francis as members. Francis and his wife were therefore friendly with Amy and Isaac Post, who along with the Stantons and Susan B. Anthony were also members, and with William C. Nell, who was its first secretary. When the Fugitive Slave Law passed in 1850, Ralph Francis along with Frederick Douglass, Harrison Powell and other leading Blacks reorganized the Rochester Vigilance Committee to make it a more efficient form of protection for refugees who managed to get as far as Rochester.[8]

Ralph and Margaret Francis also played a more secret and highly perilous role, for if they were caught, they would lose everything and probably be imprisoned besides. Immediately after the new law was enacted, Ralph Francis closed his barbershop. He and his wife moved to the Lower Falls of the Genesee River to take up management of the Steamboat Hotel. It was located at Kelsey's Landing, on the west bank of the Genesee River. Here the cliffs above the gorge cut by the river rose some two hundred feet. This was the southernmost spot where steamboats were towed upstream; the Genesee River flowed northwards towards Lake Ontario and the Lower Falls blocked their further passage. The hotel was therefore where steamboats leaving for Great Lakes ports such as Toronto and Kingston picked up and deposited passengers.[9]

If Benjamin Pollard Holmes did not know the Francises already because of his connections with Rochester, he would have had occasion to meet them at this time, for Kelsey's Landing was one of the most important Underground Railroad transfer points in the entire Great Lakes Basin.[10] "It is said that the fugitives were taken to the foot of Buell Street [Kelsey's Landing] and put on English steamboats bound for the Queen's dominion. When the ships were three miles out on Lake Ontario, it was said that they would hoist the British flag, a symbol that all on board were beyond the reach of the American slave catchers." It certainly seems that with new federal legislation about to cause a dramatic increase in refugees, Rochester's Underground Railroad operators were creating the infrastructure for a new way to deal with the traffic. It was this system that helped Frederick Douglass pass famous Maryland fugitive William Parker and his party on to Canada, following Pennsylvania's Christiana Riots of September 11, 1851.[11]

The Francis family remained at the Steamboat Hotel for less than two years. Then they crossed the lake themselves, settling in the Canadian town of Port Hope. One suspects they left US soil just a step or two before their arrest by some of the special commissioners appointed to enforce the Fugitive Slave Law. The courageous Margaret Francis and her husband opened the British Restaurant on Queen Street, which is listed in the Port Hope street directory for 1856–57. Ralph and Margaret's daughter, Julia

Ann Francis, married there on March 16, 1857, according to an announcement three days later in the *Tri-City News*.[12] Like her father, Julia's groom, Joshua Johnson, was a barber, and he was the son of another, a man named Chauncey Johnson and his wife, Hannah.[13]

Ralph and Margaret Francis then moved on to Peterborough, some thirty miles to the north. There, according to an 1859 issue of the *Peterborough Examiner*, they took over operation of the North American Hotel. After the great fire of 1861 the same newspaper reports them as proprietors of the newly opened Stewart House. So it would seem that, in moving to Peterborough, James Thomas Holmes was joining an old colleague of his father's in the clandestine work in which both had been engaged. What is more, Ralph Francis had been a Rochester-based barber for many years and his son-in-law in Port Hope also had an apprentice. Both men were thus part of the informal guild of master barbers who managed competition and placed young men in locations where they could prosper at work.

It is interesting to note that even after James Thomas's older brother Ben arrived in the area, the two men did not go into business together. Rather, they established shops in different towns a few miles apart. This was not accidental but rather a well-thought-out plan, based on the population and potential number of customers available in each location. In Peterborough there was already a barber and his son operating a hairdressing shop when James arrived,[14] but given the growing population of both the town and its agricultural hinterland, there was probably sufficient business for another such enterprise, but perhaps not for two.

By 1862 James had a home of his own near his barbershop, which was in Scott's Building on Simcoe Street, where several of Peterborough's larger hotels were to be found. He advertised in the local newspaper and in the Peterborough directories, and by all appearances had a thriving business. Peterborough's mills, breweries and factories were in busy operation and shipping their products south by rail to Cobourg on Lake Ontario and thence to US and European markets. This boded well for James, for all the industry, agricultural marketing and transportation advances meant more businessmen would be coming through Peterborough in need of a shave and haircut.[15]

This was useful, as the young man was considering taking a wife. Just a short distance west of the Peterborough town line lay North Monaghan Township and the farm of William and Ann (Alexander) Johnson. They were an interracial couple who had moved to Peterborough County some years earlier to join Ann's British relatives, several of whom owned local farms. The Johnsons had been married in Toronto at St. James' Church (now Cathedral) in 1839.[16] William, who was West Indian by birth, was both a cook and a farmer. He had started out as a cook on the Lake Ontario steamers and may have been acquainted with Benjamin Pollard and Ann Eliza Holmes when they arrived in Upper Canada. However, by the 1850s the Johnsons were living in a log house on twenty acres just outside Peterborough. Their four daughters, all born in Upper Canada, are listed in the census of 1861 as "mulatto."[17]

James fell in love with the Johnson's eldest daughter, Mary Ann. She was living and working in the household of another Black couple in Peterborough while completing her schooling. By the spring of 1862, the young barber and hairdresser had convinced Mary Ann Johnson to become his bride. She was twenty-two. Although Mary Ann Johnson and her parents, William and Ann Alexander Johnson, attended the Church of England and James was a Wesleyan Methodist, as his father had been before him, they were wed by a local Presbyterian minister. The marriage of Benjamin and Ann Eliza's second son was reported in the *Peterborough Examiner*: "June 19, 1862: At Peterborough on Thurs. 12th inst., James Thomas Holmes to Miss Mary Ann Johnson, both of Peterborough, by the Rev. James Douglass."[18]

Attending the wedding were the Alexander and Redhead families, relations on Mary Ann's mother's side who had emigrated from England in the 1820s and owned land near Peterborough. None of these British immigrants were particularly prosperous; all three families were still living in single-storey log houses while some of their neighbours had constructed frame homes or even brick farmhouses by this time. The Redhead and Alexander farms were literally within walking distance of James T. Holmes's barbershop on Simcoe Street, while the farm on which Mary Ann had grown up was a little farther out of town.[19]

The Johnsons' eldest daughter had married well, for the Holmes barbershop was profitable. From September 1861 to the beginning of 1863, James T. Holmes was actively marketing his hairdressing "saloon" in the *Peterborough Examiner*: "Particular attention paid to children's hair."[20] In business cards placed in later newspapers and also in county directories, James called himself "Professor Holmes," a term sometimes adopted by "first-class" African American barbers, those who appealed to the carriage trade. There he stated that he specialized in ladies' hairdressing; this included not only cutting but styling the hair, and sometimes subtle dyeing, so it was a particularly lucrative aspect of the trade.[21]

Although the Canadian census for 1861 shows only sixty-seven people of African descent in all of Peterborough County, James and his wife were not entirely alone in the town.[22] Nearby lived the family of forty-five-year-old American-born brick-maker John Williams and Jane, his Canadian-born wife. Their son Samuel would be a playmate for the daughter Mary Ann bore her barber husband. James and Mary Ann started their family in January 1863, naming their little girl after Mary Ann's sister Emma.

At least one old acquaintance of the Holmes family's Toronto days moved to Peterborough during this period. William Henderson Edwoods was the eldest son of William Edwoods (sometimes Edwards), who had been a founding member of Washington Christian's Baptist Church on Toronto's Queen Street. His father had passed away in 1862, and the young man came to work for Professor Holmes as a journeyman assistant. This traditional way to help fellow Black barbers migrate and resettle persisted well into the twentieth century. He may have added to the services of the Holmes barbershop certain specialized skills that James Thomas lacked, for his father had not only provided hot and cold baths in his shop but also advertised himself as a perfumer.[23]

James Thomas Holmes needed what assistance William Edwoods could provide, for in 1864 he was forced to take a break from his barbering and hairdressing business. The cause of the hiatus has not been discovered, but he was able to take up his razor again a year later. An 1865 advertisement in the local directory reads: "J.T.H. begs to intimate to the residents of Peterborough, and its vicinity that he still continues in business in the above place, where he is prepared to execute every description of work in his line in the most satisfactory manner."[24] W. H. Edwoods moved on. He married a seventeen-year old girl named Alice Dutton, daughter of William Dutton and Hannah Nash, at Peterborough on July 23, 1867.[25] The Edwoods family left the barbering trade to the Holmes salon in Peterborough and sought a new home in Bowmanville, on Lake Ontario. William is listed in the 1867 directory as a hairdresser with his own salon.[26]

James and Mary Ann had a second child. Rebecca Ann came into the world just as the Civil War ended, in April 1865. However, Cecelia's younger stepson seems to have suffered from either mental illness or a fondness for alcohol, for it was not long after this that Mary Ann took the children and removed herself from their household.[27] She left Canada entirely and went to join her parents. William and Ann Johnson had moved across the lake to Rochester at the end of the Civil War, taking with them their youngest daughter Rebecca. Shortly after her family established itself at Rochester, seventeen-year-old Rebecca Johnson married local barber Augustus Bloxom, a man whose family was originally from Virginia and who had close familial ties in Toronto.[28] Not long after Mary Ann's departure, James T. Holmes closed his Peterborough barbershop and then spent a year in Toronto. However, he soon followed his wife and children to upstate New York.

Ralph and Margaret Francis disappear from both Canadian and American records at this point, but their grandson Ralph Francis (Frank)

Johnson moved first to Cornwall, Canada West (in 1867 this became the province of Ontario), and then departed for the United States. He set up shop in the village of Bath, in Steuben County, New York, about eighty-five miles south of Rochester. Nine years later he moved to Hamilton, in the new Canadian province of Ontario, where he married and raised a family.[29]

Cecelia Jane Larrison and her family had departed from Rochester by the time her stepson's in-laws, Walter and Ann Johnson, moved there. The exact date of death for James T. Holmes is unknown, and he appeared in no official record once he reached New York. He seems to have flown under the radar, as it were, lending further credence to his suspected personal difficulties. The 1873 tax rolls for the City of Toronto show James Thomas Holmes, half-owner of the house at 29 Centre Street, as living in the United States. He died in 1875 and his widow remarried almost immediately. In 1876, his brother began the process of selling the old house on Centre Street that Benjamin Pollard Holmes had built in the last years of his life as an inheritance for his sons.

MEANWHILE, JAMES'S ELDER BROTHER, Ben, had also grown up. The little boy born into slavery in the household of James Fisher Jr. in Richmond, Virginia, listed his birthplace as Upper Canada for the rest of his life.[30]

Despite the outbreak of the American Civil War in April 1861, which had a devastating effect on Lowell's mills because of the embargo on Southern cotton, Ben Alexander did not return to his Canadian home until the following year. Ineligible because of his Black ancestry to enlist in the Union forces, in June 1862 he still had a powerful reason to linger. While his younger brother was courting Mary Ann Johnson in Peterborough, Ben Alexander Holmes was convincing the sweetheart of his schooldays to become his bride. On June 2, 1862, Benjamin Alexander Holmes, age twenty-three, married Lucia A. Holt, who was twenty-one.[31] The wedding was conducted by noted Methodist divine Reverend Lorenzo R. Thayer at Lowell's Central Methodist Episcopal Church.[32] The marriage could not have been performed at all under Massachusetts law only a few short years earlier, for Ben's bride was white.

Lucia had been born in Concord, New Hampshire, on August 21, 1841, to Enoch Holt and the former Hannah Cass, but the family had moved to Lowell and Lucia went to school there. Ben Alexander and his bride left for Canada immediately after their wedding. They had an important event to attend. Transportation must have been very efficient, for ten days after their own wedding, Ben and Lucia were in Peterborough witnessing the marriage of his only brother.[33]

Ben and Lucia Holmes settled about twenty-eight miles from Peterborough, in Lindsay. Lindsay had no Black community at all, although a few enterprising African Canadian farmers were busily clearing bush and planting crops in the surrounding district. According to *Fuller's Directory* for 1865–66, Benjamin A. Holmes was a "hair dresser" located on William Street. The Holmes barbershop occupied a spot near the corner of the main business street, Kent Street, just a block east of the town hall. His skills were badly needed, but how well the local farming population took to the fact that their obviously mixed-race barber had a wife of pure European descent is a matter for conjecture. It is of note that in mid-nineteenth-century Canada West, the only known murder of an African American groom—a barber like Ben and his brother no less—was sparked by his marriage to an Irish girl and happened during his wedding party. That was in the Peterborough–Lindsay area of the province.[34]

Lindsay was about ninety miles northeast of Toronto and had a population of about 1,900. Originally settled in the 1830s where shallow rapids on the Scugog River made an attractive location for a grist mill, it was incorporated in 1857. It was laid out along both sides of the river on the rail line running north from Port Hope. On July 5, 1861, almost a year before Ben and Lucia's arrival, most of downtown Lindsay had burned to the ground. The conflagration wiped out nearly a hundred buildings and rendered four hundred people homeless. Their barbershop, however, does not seem to have been affected, for the fire was halted at William Street. That which had been built of wood was replaced with brick. Soon there were handsome new blocks of stores, hotels and other conveniences lining the town's muddy streets.[35]

As the only local barbering business, Benjamin's establishment was very well patronized. The Victoria County Courthouse was at Lindsay, and on court day he likely shaved not only the judge and both the prosecuting and defence lawyers but the jury, plaintiff and accused as well.[36] Manufacturing was flourishing in Lindsay, in part because of its position on the railroad, and there were grist and carding mills, tanneries, foundries, carriage works, a shoe factory, a commercial dairy, a distillery and at least one brewery. There was also a good deal of transient trade, for Lindsay was the market town for the district and served the needs of a large surrounding agricultural area. Along with flour milling, lumbering was one of the two major "manufactures" of the county in mid-century, with sawn boards being shipped mainly to US markets. The lumber was loaded onto scows at the mills, which were then towed by steamer to Lindsay. There it was put onto rail cars that carried it the forty-three miles to Port Hope, where it was loaded onto lake ships and carried across Lake Ontario.[37]

Ben and Lucia lived above or behind their shop. James and his older brother had plenty of opportunity to visit back and forth, for although there was no direct rail route linking Peterborough with Lindsay, there was regular steamboat traffic. To this day a journey from Peterborough to Lindsay via Bobcaygeon, Sturgeon Lake and the locks at Fenelon Falls is considered one of the most lovely recreational excursions in Ontario.[38] In Ben and James Thomas's day there were First Nations villages bordering Mud Lake, and great forests along the shores of the waterways. There was also a line of stage coaches that ran from Peterborough to Lindsay and on, connecting to both rail and steamboat service to Toronto. The

Holmes brothers could, if they wished, easily reach the city within a day or two to inspect the property they had inherited and catch up with old friends from their schooldays. There is nothing to suggest that they crossed Lake Ontario to visit with their stepmother, however. Ben, and now his wife Lucia, maintained no relationship with Cecelia after her first husband's death.

Two years after their marriage, Lucia Holt Holmes gave birth to the couple's first child. Perhaps she informed her extended family in New England and Nova Scotia by telegraph, for that system of rapid communication had reached Lindsay in 1862. Ben and Lucia's new son came into the world in March 1863 and was christened Walter Benjamin Holmes, his middle name in honour of his paternal grandfather, Benjamin Pollard Holmes. It would be five years before a little brother named Eugene would join Walter in the Lindsay household of Benjamin and Lucia Holmes.

The Civil War must have seemed very distant from Lindsay on the Scugog River and Peterborough on the Otonabee in rural Canada West. Yet the Holmes family had constant reminders. Local newspapers described the progress of the war and regularly reported on Union and Confederate victories. The brothers would have been more interested now than before, since in January 1863 Abraham Lincoln issued the Emancipation Proclamation, which liberated slaves in the rebelling (but not the Union) slave states and called for the enlistment of Black soldiers in Union forces.

While they were in Lowell, the Holmes brothers had likely attended school with or cut the hair of some of the men who volunteered for the Massachusetts regiments. They would have been appalled by the Battle of Fort Wagner, where the officers and men of the 54th Massachusetts Volunteer Regiment fought bravely and well but were slaughtered. That the 54th's white commander, Robert Gould Shaw, scion of a New England abolitionist family, was thrown into the burial pit with his men was reported in the Lindsay and Peterborough papers in the summer of 1863.[39]

Many years later, the *Peterborough Examiner* had this to say about the end of the American Civil War, the influence of which was felt in the furthest reaches of Canada West: "It is interesting to note that on April 17, 1865, the day of Abraham Lincoln's funeral, this little Canadian town closed all its stores and schools, put its flags at half mast, and with two small cannon, owned by a retired British naval officer named Rodden, fired off a memorial salute to the great American."[40]

In the immediate aftermath of war, Irish Americans in 1866 joined in a strange and futile attempt to influence British policy overseas. Ardent Irish nationalists, many of them experienced Civil War veterans, organized themselves into quasi-military units and launched the so-called Fenian Raids all along the border with British North America. One of their songs went: "We are the Fenian Brotherhood, skilled in the arts of war, / And we're going to fight for Ireland, the land we adore, / Many battles we have won, along with the boys in blue, / And we'll go and capture Canada, for we've nothing else to do."[41]

Throughout the conflict along the borders, the two sons of Benjamin Pollard Holmes managed their businesses, cared for their families and watched from afar as the colonies that made up British North America confederated in 1867. The Civil War, followed by the Fenian unrest, had pushed reluctant colonists in Canada West, Canada East, New Brunswick and Nova Scotia to consider joining forces. The enmity between George Brown, the old friend of the fugitive, and Conservative leader John A. Macdonald had been set aside in the common cause. The Fathers of Confederation and their political allies were victorious in leading Canada in its first steps to nationhood, and Macdonald would be knighted for his efforts. On July 1, 1867, church bells rang out across the land to celebrate the founding of the new Dominion of Canada. Canada West was now Ontario, and the national capital was Ottawa.

In November 1868 Lucia Holt Holmes and her husband rejoiced in the birth of their second baby boy. They named him Eugene P. Holmes (the

P probably stood for Pollard). Neither of their children would grow up in Ontario, however. In 1869, less than two years after little Eugene was born, Ben Alexander Holmes and his family decided to sell out and move to the American West. There, they hoped, their interracial marriage would occasion less comment, if not outright hostility, and they could start anew on what had become American's most recent frontier.

CHAPTER 13
Steal Away Home

No State shall make or enforce any law which shall abridge the privileges or immunities of citizens of the United States; nor shall any State deprive any person of life, liberty, or property, without due process of law; nor deny to any person within its jurisdiction the equal protection of the laws.

—Fourteenth Amendment to the US Constitution

WITH HER FAMILY FINALLY together again but rather bleak prospects for the future in Rochester, Cecelia explored a number of possibilities. She could always return to Toronto, for she still owned a home there. However, it might be better to liquidate her one asset to provide for her family's immediate needs. It was in deciding to pursue that option that she put the final nail in the coffin of her relationship with her elder stepson, Ben. She could not sell her house without the agreement of Ben and James Thomas Holmes, as well as release of their dower rights by their wives. She even travelled across the lake to try to convince the two men to consider allowing the land to be formally severed, but she could make no headway, the main opposition coming from Ben and his wife, the former Lucia Holt.

In the end her request was refused outright. After that, Cecelia had sporadic contact with James Thomas on property matters at least, but the final rift with Ben Alexander Holmes was never mended. Benjamin's old friend James Mink had another livery stable right downtown and was helping her collect the rents and pay taxes on the old house that, following a renumbering of the Holmes properties, was now 33 Centre Street, but neither Cecelia nor Mamie would ever live there again. In 1866 James T. Holmes began conducting business on his stepmother's behalf. Whatever his personal difficulties, whether in his mind or with the bottle, he was at least willing to assist Cecelia from time to time.[1]

Cecelia found Toronto very much changed, less by war than by progress, although the Civil War had left its mark on the city in ways that were less tangible than they had been in Rochester. Captain Thomas Dick had made over his block of terraced houses on Front Street into the stunningly elegant Queen's Hotel. During the conflict south of the border, it was home to blue-blooded Kentucky- and Virginia-bred Confederate officers and their wives who had felt forced to leave the United States. With support from Confederate sympathizers, among whom were some of Toronto's oldest and most respectable families, they managed an extensive anti-Unionist espionage operation. Among the conspirators had been Fanny Thruston Ballard's Aunt "Puss" and Uncle Luke Pryor Blackburn, the latter the doctor who launched a germ warfare attack on Union troops by sending boxes of clothing once worn by yellow fever victims. Fortunately the disease could be spread only by mosquitoes, so it was ineffective.[2]

Since nearly all of Captain Dick's staff at the Queen's Hotel were formerly enslaved African Americans, they spied on the spies. Most were now naturalized British subjects and, more important for the purpose, literate. The carefully hatched Southern plots mostly failed, with their content being reported to Canadian officials. City councillors lived in the area, and George Brown and his brother Gordon resided nearby. Both men had supported the Union cause through the pages of the *Globe* all through the years of conflict.

Cecelia renewed her acquaintance with the good captain and also spent time with the families of some of Benjamin's and her dearest friends, including Francis Griffin Simpson and his wife. They had an interesting tale to tell. By 1863 a Union victory was all but assured and President Lincoln had looked to Canada West when planning the coming peace. Wondering how best to help the South's millions of slaves prepare to take up both the rights and responsibilities of American citizenship, he set up the Freedmen's Bureau Inquiry Commission, headed by educator and philanthropist Dr. Samuel Gridley Howe. He came to Canada with two commissioners to examine the conditions of fugitive slaves living there. Among those interviewed was the shoemaker who had befriended Cecelia when she first arrived back from Liverpool, pregnant and alone. Simpson had outlined his opinions on various subjects, including the prejudice that African American immigrants dealt with in Canada and the relevance of liberal politics to Black progress. Other interviewees included the Shadd family; John James Cary, back from his Australian adventure; and Grandison Boyd, who had parlayed his gold into a career as a successful builder and mill owner in Chatham.[3]

After her Toronto sojourn, Cecelia returned to Rochester with a new idea. With no way of raising funds from her Toronto property, she was still entitled to the monthly rental fees. But her husband was unable to find work in Rochester, and in any case he would never again be able to do hard labour. So Cecelia turned her gaze southwards, to the home of her girlhood and the family to whom she had once belonged. Her pride would not allow her to ask for financial support, but she had continued her sporadic correspondence with Fanny. She knew that her husband, A. J. Ballard, had been appointed to an important judicial post by the US government, and that both his and Fanny's families possessed considerable influence. The federal judicial system represented one of the few bulwarks against abuse on which African Americans could rely in the turbulent post-bellum years.

Also, her mother was still alive. Cecelia's long struggle to secure Mary Reynolds's freedom, an effort that had materially contributed to the loss of Benjamin's health and ultimately their marriage, was now a moot point— the six years of her servitude were up. Cecelia was looking forward to seeing her mother and to reacquainting herself with Fanny. She was not, however, anxious to see Fanny's father again. Charles W. Thruston was not a forgiving man.

As the wife of a Union soldier, Cecelia had been legally manumitted, as had her husband, when he enlisted in the service of the United States. Cecelia was also a British subject who had spent many years in what would soon be the Dominion of Canada. Both of them were therefore at least technically free to take their daughters to Kentucky. One short month after William returned to Rochester, Cecelia packed up her family and moved back to Louisville. The Larrisons arrived in September 1865. It had been nineteen years since she last walked its planked sidewalks or looked out over the broad, calm waters of the Ohio. As they crossed over the river into Kentucky, she wondered what she had gotten herself, her two daughters and above all her injured, distressed husband into.

Cecelia had left Louisville in the spring of 1846 at the age of fifteen. She came back to the city almost twenty years later, with children and a husband who, though much loved, would never really be whole again. She found Kentucky changed beyond recognition. Louisville in 1865 was filled with returned servicemen from both armies. Construction crews were busily dismantling the fortifications that had been erected to protect the town from an invasion that never came. The waterfront teemed with steamboats, and a series of rail lines ran across the waterfront and cut diagonal swaths in multiple directions. New factories and warehouses had gone up to serve wartime supply needs, and the city itself had expanded away from the riverfront. Many of the old estates of the Thruston family's friends and relations were now subdivided for housing. Others had been irreparably damaged while serving as army camps, materiel dumps and military compounds, for the Union Army had used Louisville as a command centre for the Ohio Valley.

Cecelia also discovered that she had brought her family into a maelstrom of reorganization and readjustment occasioned by the Southern defeat and the freeing of the state's enslaved workforce. Kentuckians did not take well to the idea that Black Americans would soon become their political equals. Louisville had been occupied by the Northern armies since 1861, causing disruptions in the master–slave relationship that plainly demonstrated to the loyal Unionists that, whatever Lincoln's protestations regarding their state's neutrality, slavery in Kentucky was doomed. More than 25,000 enslaved Kentuckians enlisted, gaining freedom not only for themselves but also for their families. Despite the fact that the Emancipation Proclamation of 1863 excluded neutral Kentucky, neither the military nor the state's enslaved population was willing to accept continuation of the abusive unwaged labour system. Now, in the aftermath of war, Louisville was calm, but the countryside was awash in the blood of Black victims who bore the brunt of Kentucky's anger at potentially losing its human property.[4]

Given the circumstances, Cecelia and William's first step on their arrival in Louisville was to seek out both housing and employment. William was not well physically and perhaps was damaged in spirit as well; he could do no heavy lifting. However, not only did they have two children to care for, they had been so delighted to see one another after the last year of war that another baby was on the way. The competition for jobs was fierce. Louisville with its factories, harbour and railroads attracted hundreds of demobilized soldiers who were desperate for jobs. The city's former slaves were also seeking paying work and were crowded into every available nook and cranny of housing. And because of their persecution in the countryside, thousands more were moving into urban centres.

White patronage could provide essential protection in a society gone mad in the aftermath of war, so in the end it was as much for the sake of her family's protection as it was for friendship that she went to see Fanny Thruston Ballard. Cecelia and Fanny would for the rest of their lives inhabit two entirely separate worlds, and this was never more true than in Cecelia's first years in postwar Louisville; the Black and white cities intersected only rarely, and never in any social sense. But in this Fanny did not fail her, nor did her husband, although no document survives to tell of Cecelia's reunion with the woman whose service she had fled twenty years before. Fanny was nearly forty, a wife and mother. Unfailingly gracious, she would have eased the way for their conversation, indulging in some personal reminiscences interspersed with a pious sentiment or two, for her faith had only grown with age. She also knew where Cecelia's mother was.

Then Fanny would have given Cecelia all the news about her children, Charles Thruston Ballard, now fifteen; Samuel Thruston Ballard, nine; Abigail Churchill Ballard, whom everyone called Abby, eight; and Rogers Clark Thruston Ballard, a boy of seven. The rest of her family had been sadly divided during the years of civil war, but these days they were mending fences. Then there was Cecelia's old friend Sarah, who had been maidservant to Isabella Churchill McCreary. She was a free woman living in Elizabethtown, but pretty, lively Belle had been dead these five years.[5] Fanny and Cecelia been corresponding for years, so it is easy to imagine that what they discussed echoed the topics of their letters to one another, until at last Cecelia was able to bring the conversation around to the issue of employment and ask Fanny to help her find William a job.

Thanks to the Ballard family's influence, Cecelia and her family were cushioned from most of the difficulties facing Louisville's rapidly expanding African American population. On one level she and William could look forward, therefore, to a period of relative prosperity, although Cecelia would never again reach the level of affluence she had experienced as the wife of Benjamin Pollard Holmes of Toronto. Louisville had done very well out of its position as the hub of transport and trade during the war, but the rural parts of the state were reeling from the loss of 65,000 slaves, a majority of whom had lived in the country. Slavery had been the lifeblood of agricultural and livestock profits. There had been plenty of support for the Confederacy in the state too. While Kentucky had remained with the Union, it was one place where men in blue uniforms could look across the battlefield at their own brothers wearing the butternut grey of the Confederacy. The southwest part of the state was so disaffected with Lincoln and Northern policies that it had actually attempted to secede during the war.

While Cecelia was coming home, her Delaware-born husband was moving to an entirely foreign place. She had brought him to a state on the borders of the South, where as a proud Union veteran William Larrison dared not, as a Black man, so much as wear his uniform. There was so much sympathy for the South that it has been said that Kentucky was the only state to secede *after* the Civil War. Such was the backlash against the Thirteenth Amendment to the US Constitution ending slavery that, within a few short years of the war's end, Kentucky seemed for all the world a place where the Lost Cause had not been lost at all.[6]

Memorials to the Confederate dead appeared in the state cemetery at Frankfort and in other cemeteries where Kentucky boys who had died under the banner of Jeff Davis were buried. Decoration Day ceremonies honoured the Southern dead equally if not more than those who had in life worn Union blue. Former Confederate officers were welcomed home with more or less open arms, and the ragged soldiers of the South returned as prodigal sons. The state legislature repealed laws denying former Confederates the vote as early as December 1865. Officers who had led troops against the Union, and even those who spent their war years as spies in Toronto, Montreal and Halifax, entered insurance, law and real estate and rose to high ranks within society and eventually in government.[7]

Reverend Thomas James, whom Cecelia and William knew from Rochester, was everywhere. The US Army had begun recruiting Black soldiers in Kentucky in March 1864. The enslaved came to Louisville to enlist at Camp Taylor, and often their families, fearing retaliation from their owners, came too. Reverend James had managed the camps for the families of Black refugees who flooded into the city during the Civil War. In order to foil slaveholders who came looking for their former property, he devised the strategy of marrying every woman who came into the camp, if she was willing, to a Black soldier. Backed by Union soldiers, he stopped the worst of the abuses against free and enslaved African Americans in the city, acquiring clothing, food and medical attention to meet the overwhelming need. In the last year of the war he saw that all the prisoners remaining in the city's several slave-dealers' pens were liberated. He was still there, negotiating with Army officers, pleading with former slave-owners to free their remaining workers, and trying to alleviate the worst of the suffering.[8]

For Fanny and A. J. Ballard, the loss of the family's nine slaves was a financial blow, but Fanny and her husband had already begun employing German and Irish girls in the house.[9] Fanny had meant what she said in her final letter to Cecelia: she no longer believed in slavery, and the Civil War had confirmed her views on the subject. For the older members of Fanny's family, however, it was a harder transition, if not one with which Cecelia had sympathy.

Samuel Churchill had lent slaves to his daughter Mary Eliza upon her marriage and confirmed Charles W. Thruston's possession of them in his will of 1863. Now all were gone. Feeling unable to continue his agricultural pursuits profitably without slaves, her Uncle Isaac Clark abandoned his extensive farming operations at the old Clark family seat at Mulberry Hill and moved in with his physician brother, William.[10] The inseparable Churchill brothers John and William Henry, Fanny's uncles on her mother's side, abandoned Spring Grove for a mansion on Sixth Street below Broadway, in the newly fashionable district that would, ironically, one day be known as Old Louisville.[11] All very wealthy, it was more the psychological transition than the financial one that was difficult for them. These men had always believed they had a God-given right to own other human beings. Now they learned that they did not.

Charles W. Thruston had inherited human property and continued to purchase, barter, sell and hire slaves throughout the course of his career.[12] Fanny's father had, perhaps paradoxically, also been a staunch Union man, as was her husband. Charles Thruston lived to see the surrender of General

Robert E. Lee's armies at Appomattox, the assassination of President Abraham Lincoln and the beginning of the war's brutal aftermath. He died in his office of a heart attack on November 25, 1865, only eleven days before federal ratification of the Thirteenth Amendment to the US Constitution that emancipated the South's enslaved millions.[13] Fanny, as Charles W. Thruston's only remaining child, inherited his estate.[14] Her careful father left her a life interest in his fortune so that no husband could waste the inheritance she would one day pass on to her children.[15] "Uncle Jack" and his wife, Susan, who had been C. W. Thruston's servants for years, were to remain on in the home of Fanny and A. J. Ballard, with a stipend for their faithful service.[16] Indeed, the Ballards kept several elderly servants as "pensioners upon their good will."

With their new-found wealth, the Ballards commissioned popular architect Henry Whitestone to build a "first class residence . . . which, when completed, will compare favorably with the most expensive houses in the city . . . and it will be finished without regard to expense or labor, and will be a valuable addition to our list of residences."[17]

Renewing her relationship with her former mistress gave Cecelia not only the promise of future employment but also some access to the federal legal power structure in Kentucky. Fanny's husband had long since given up his law practice in order to manage the family's rental properties, as well as the investments of some of Fanny's out-of-state family such as the Jesup-Blair relations who, along with Dr. Croghan's other nieces and nephews, jointly owned Mammoth Cave.[18] However, early on in the war, as an avowed Union man, his brother Bland Ballard had been made a judge of the US District Court, by order of the president. Three months later, A. J. Ballard became clerk of the same federal court in Kentucky, and also a US Commissioner empowered to hear preliminary court cases to decide if they should go on to the federal court. Typically he dealt with matters such as tax evasion, currency counterfeiting or (a particular favourite in Kentucky) operating illegal stills. More serious matters he referred to his brother's court.[19]

The role of the federal courts had taken on new complexity during the Civil War, but that was nothing compared to the postwar circumstances. Opposition to the so-called Reconstruction amendments to the US Constitution in profoundly racist Kentucky would be fierce and implacable. The Thirteenth Amendment (1865) abolished slavery throughout the United States; the Fourteenth, to be ratified in 1868, provided all Americans equal protection under the law; the Fifteenth Amendment, effective in 1870, accorded Americans the right of suffrage without regard to "race, color, or previous condition of servitude." Furious challenges to all three would come before Judge Bland Ballard and his clerk, A. J. Ballard. Another postwar duty was to issue pardons to prominent Kentuckians who had served as Confederate officers. A.J.'s docket book was filled with the names of friends and relatives, business rivals and men he had met—and lost to—across the card table.[20]

It was the final set of cases that took a heavy toll of Fanny's rather sentimental husband. Because Kentucky had sided with the Union there was no "Reconstruction," no occupation by the US Army following the war, and therefore no military protection for the state's beleaguered Black populace. Kentucky's postwar history of assault on its newly freed African American population was among the cruellest in United States history. Since the local courts could not be depended on to prosecute such cases fairly, they were transferred to the United States Court in Kentucky, Judge Bland Ballard presiding. The main culprits were rarely former slaveholders, although many were guilty of illegally retaining people in slavery. While some offered their former slaves wages and protected them from violence, others moved to restrict the movements of African American workers so they couldn't leave the land, refused to allow returning Black soldiers to take away their families, applied corporal punishment at will, and generally continued to treat anyone they could retain in their power as the enslaved people they used to be. These cases too came before Judge Ballard and Commissioner Ballard.

As more and more frightened, grieving people moved into Louisville, Cecelia and her husband learned more about the atrocities. The outright mayhem taking place in rural Kentucky when the Larrison family arrived was largely the work of former farm managers and overseers, along with poor whites. Ruffians took the opportunity to wreak revenge on defenceless African Americans who crossed their path, and in some counties there was a concerted effort to force free Blacks to leave altogether.[21] Rapes; lynchings; burning of houses, livestock and sometimes people; whippings and all manner of atrocities were inflicted by masked "Night Riders" who raged through the countryside on horseback terrorizing the Black population. They even assaulted and abused the few brave white schoolteachers who were there to teach the former slaves of rural Kentucky how to read and write.

Since, under Kentucky law, no Black person could be an independent witness against a white person, all these cases had to come before the Federal Court as well. A. J. Ballard's personal docket book was filled with horrors to rival anything soldiers might see in war.[22] Although Kentucky was not subjected to the more overt effects of "Radical Reconstruction" because it had maintained its loyalty to the Union, the widespread abuses to which the newly manumitted Black population was subjected were so extreme that the district Freedmen's Bureau headquarters was set up in Louisville—in what had been a Union state. Four months after Cecelia arrived with her family, in January 1866, the Tennessee branch of the Bureau of Refugees, Freedmen and Abandoned Lands (the Freedmen's Bureau) was given authority to restore order in Kentucky. Three organizational districts were administered by a very thinly spread cadre of officials backed by US Army troops. A camp for the homeless and distressed was established in Louisville at 18th and Broadway.[23]

The Freedmen's Bureau was important to Cecelia and her family, not because they were among the recently manumitted, but because the services they provided for Black people at Louisville were available to them as well. The Bureau served a variety of functions, including marrying thousands of couples who while enslaved had never been permitted to formalize their unions. The Bureau opened a bank and encouraged newly freed Blacks to begin saving their money against a rainy day (an initiative that would end in disaster). It arranged apprenticeships for Black children and labour contracts for adults to ensure fair treatment, an uphill battle everywhere. Low-interest loans were provided, advice was available on everything from agriculture to labour relations, and in some places the Bureau oversaw land distribution schemes. Chronically underfunded, its work was done without the help of local officials.

But it was the hospitals and schools they maintained that were so necessary to the Larrisons' resettlement in what had been Cecelia's hometown. As African Americans their only access to hospital care was through the Crittenden General Hospital at 14th and Broadway, which had served Union troops during the war. It was now dedicated to the care of African American refugees.[24] What medical attention William Larrison received for his war injuries was provided there. Education for Mamie, now twelve, and her little sister Sarah was also an issue. Public education was unavailable to African American children. Several private academies were established by Louisville's Black churches in the immediate postwar period, but the Larrisons could not afford their fees.[25] The American Missionary Association would help the Bureau fund the new Ely Normal School for the preparation of Black educators, as well as Louisville's first public school for Black students, but it would not be available for three more years.[26]

War Department Order No. 2 empowered the Freedmen's Bureau officials to mediate between state and local law. The Ku Klux Klan was well supported in the state, and lynchings and other outrages were worst where the Black population was highest. After passage of the Civil Rights Act of 1866, Black testimony was permitted in court in the former rebel states, but in Kentucky the courts ignored the order. The crowds of "Regulators" who roved the countryside by night, whipping people and burning homes and schools, threatened white men and even women who dared to speak out against the outrages. Thus a majority of cases that came before Judge Ballard and Commissioner Ballard were attempts by the Freedmen's Bureau to prosecute whites for acts of violence against Blacks.

Judge Ballard had a well-deserved reputation for impartiality, and to his credit, a number of whites served jail time after being convicted of such assaults. He even sentenced white men convicted of murdering Blacks, unheard of in Kentucky, where white supremacy had held sway ever since its founding.[27] Not everyone acquiesced to persecution. Whites did come forward to testify, but they risked being as terrorized (and worse) as the African Americans they tried to assist.[28]

This was the world into which Cecelia and William had brought their two children. And soon they were dealing with an overpowering personal tragedy. Not long after their arrival in Louisville, little Sarah died. She was just three. The Larrisons were utterly devastated. Cecelia and William were in no position to afford a permanent memorial, not even a stone to mark her tiny grave.

But joy had always mingled with sorrow for Cecelia, a fact of her life that helped her move through the most terrible of times. The couple was looking forward to the birth of another child.[29] And this time Cecelia would have her own mother, Mary Reynolds, at her side when she brought her new baby into the world. After two decades apart, and her heroic efforts to set Mary Reynolds free, Cecelia at last had her mother back in her life. Mary, too, was no longer alone and without relatives in Louisville, for Cecelia's little family became hers and would be the support and comfort of her old age.

CHAPTER 14
INTO THE LION'S DEN

Mr President having been delegated by the Colored People of Kentucky to wait upon you and State their grievances and the terrible uncertainty of their future, we beg to do so in as respectful and concise a manner as possible—First then, we would call your attention to the fact that Kentucky is the only Spot within all the bounds of these United States, where the people of color have no rights whatever either in Law or in fact.

Letter to President Lincoln, June 9, 1866[1]

DESPITE THE RECENT LOSS of their child, Cecelia and William had to begin earning a living. They had long since gone through William's wages and the bonus money from his military service, and the couple had no soldier's pension or any other form of income. The rents on Cecelia's Toronto house were for the moment their sole means of support.[2]

Fortunately Fanny Thruston Ballard was related to several of the most venerable Kentucky families, including the Hites, and it was Mrs. Abraham Hite who gave William H. Larrison his first Louisville job. The connections between the Hites and Fanny's Clark relatives had begun before either family migrated from Virginia to become Kentucky pioneers, and now she capitalized on the connection to find employment for Cecelia and William.[3]

Mrs. Hite was an Englishwoman whose husband had been a prominent wholesale merchant of Louisville.[4] She lived near the corner of 1st Street and Broadway, at what had been during Cecelia's early life in Louisville the city's southern limits. As Mrs. Hite's personal coachman, William had relatively light duties and a good deal of healthy fresh air as well. Her daughter, Mary Irwin Barrett, and her family resided with Mrs. Hite; there were several grandchildren, including baby Lewis, so Cecelia's experience as an infant nurse was most welcome. The Larrisons were able to live in, at least until Cecelia's pregnancy became too advanced. The chances of finding not one but two secure positions in Louisville's stunningly competitive employment climate would have been infinitesimally small without Fanny's personal recommendation.

Soon, however, Cecelia's condition prevented her from working. Her husband found rooms for his family on Main Street near Floyd, a few blocks north of his wife's childhood home. Living in the same house was the Ellis family, and Caroline Ellis, a formerly enslaved woman whose husband had fought with the US Colored Troops during the war, would prove a good friend to Cecelia in the years to come.[5] With the advent of the railroads, Louisville had begun to turn its back on the river that had been the city's lifeblood since its founding. Advancing industrialization had come to dominate the waterfront and the older parts of downtown, so merchants and financiers who had once lived near their places of business abandoned the city centre for the clear air and larger gardens of suburban Louisville. Mansions, townhouses and terraces were cut up into flats, and a good deal of infill housing was constructed on what had once been spacious lawns and gardens filled with flowers and shrubs. Housing was at such a premium that even the old slave quarters behind some houses were turned into rental units, many of them occupied by Black families like the Larrisons.

In May 1866 Cecelia gave birth to her baby, a son. Soon after her confinement she sought a new source of income. Since there was no position available where she could take a nursing baby, and remembering her first years as a housewife with children to care for in Toronto, she began to take in fine washing, hand sewing and the specialized ironing needed for silks, ribbons and millinery supplies. This was a supplemental source of income that could be carried out at home; she would not have to seek out someone to care for her infant, at least until he was weaned. She also set herself up to iron linens and uniforms, as well as provide individual laundry services for guests at Louisville's better hotels, with help from her mother.[6]

The district where her family now lived had changed dramatically since Cecelia departed almost exactly twenty years earlier. Streetcars drawn by mules ran on several downtown thoroughfares. There was a railway line to the north, running along Jefferson Street, with the depot on the south side of the street between Brooks and Floyd. Fortifications ringed the city, for Louisville had been threatened by Confederate invasion during the war.[7] The urban boundaries too had expanded. Institutions had been founded, including the Institute for the Blind, a pet project of a Churchill cousin by marriage, James Guthrie, who had directed the Louisville and Nashville (L&N) Railroad during the war. Although the City Marine Hospital stood just south of Fanny and A. J. Ballard's home, none of the city's medical or educational facilities were open to Blacks.

Once her small son was old enough for her to leave him with a neighbour, Cecelia took a job with the widowed Mrs. James Brown Clay. Mrs. Clay had met Cecelia while boarding at the Galt House, after which she rented a home.[8] Cecelia was expected to work a six-and-a-half-day week. Probably not coincidentally, her employer, the former Susan Maria Jacob, had been both a neighbour and a friend of Fanny Thruston Ballard's since childhood.[9] Her husband, James Brown Clay, had been the son of statesman Henry Clay and heir to his Lexington estate, Ashland, which Mrs. Clay sold after the war and freed its enslaved labour force.[10]

Cecelia saw her husband and children each weekend. It was hard to leave her two children, although Mamie was now twelve years old and well able to manage her infant brother. It was also difficult for so affectionate a couple as the Larrisons to be apart. This hardship was shared with neighbours with whom they had recently become quite friendly. Mary and Anthony Bland lived in rooms adjoining their own. Mary was a house servant and Anthony a coachman, and despite a considerable age gap—Mary was but twenty-six and Cecelia ten years her senior—they very much enjoyed one another's company.[11]

After Cecelia had worked for Mrs. Clay for about two years, she found she was expecting another child. Things were looking up financially and the Larrisons moved to Chestnut Street, between Floyd and East Streets, where they welcomed another baby boy into the world in March 1870. Cecelia was forty years old, and pregnancy was now more dangerous than it had been when she was a younger woman. She was attended by the doctor who cared for Fanny's family, Dr. Leachman, who was, along with Fanny and her children, a member of Christ Church. He was a specialist in obstetrical medicine; in the same year that he delivered Cecelia's second son, he invented a new surgical treatment that revolutionized women's medicine of the day.[12]

Within the year, William found them still better housing on Brook Street between Market and Jefferson, in the east end of Louisville's downtown core. Located near the Louisville and Nashville Railroad depot, their lodgings were only blocks from William's workplace. Cecelia always lived within walking distance of the Ballard home.

For Cecelia and William it seemed that joy was never unmixed with sorrow—the baby died after only four months. Soon after, their older boy was taken from them. The son whom William "thought a heap of" was only five years old when he died in 1871.[13] Devastated by grief, the Larrison household had shrunk once more to three, including Mamie, who remained with her mother and stepfather. Cecelia and William would have no more children together.

Then William lost his job. It was a bad time to be out of work. Louisville had emerged from the Civil War relatively undamaged, and the Louisville and Nashville Railroad and a number of newer lines provided the transportation needed to reopen Southern markets served by the city's burgeoning manufacturing operations. However, on a national scale, postwar inflation and rampant investment in railroads, together with economic problems in Europe, would by 1873 start America's first Long Depression.

In 1872 Fanny's husband A. J. gave up his position as clerk of the federal courts in Kentucky and retired to become political editor for the *Louisville Commercial*, an avowedly Republican newspaper. Part of his reasons for this move had to do with his only daughter, Abby. Fanny and A. J. were very concerned about her health. She had gone away to complete her education at Vassar but remained only a single term. They took her north to upstate New York to try Dr. Cordelia Greene's "Castile Water Cure," and then in the winter of 1872 to Florida. But nothing seemed to help.[14]

Since the Democrats were in power, the removal of Fanny's husband from the bench and his intermittent absences from the political scene caused by his family's troubles substantially reduced his ability to assist Cecelia and William. This was a blow, since Cecelia's husband was thinking about applying for the military pension he was due as a wounded war veteran. Still, Ballard had influence in other ways: the *Louisville Commercial* "was for thirty years a champion of racial moderation."[15]

A cascading series of bank failures across the country, beginning with the spectacular crash of Jay Cooke and Company in New York, followed by "Black Thursday" on September 18, 1873, hit industrializing Louisville hard. The Panic of 1873 would last until 1879. Bad as it was for everyone, it was worst for African Americans, most of whom were dependent on their paycheques and lived from day to day, always near the precarious edge of financial ruin.

Kentucky African Americans had already lost their best support and protection with the final closure of the Freedmen's Bureau in 1872.[16] Now the Freedmen's Bureau Savings and Trust Company collapsed, taking with it the hopes and aspirations of thousands of freedmen. Although the

Louisville branch had been one of the most successful in the nation, speculation by new managers brought in when the head office moved from New York to Washington, and investment in railroad stock and highly inflated real estate had put the bank at risk. When the bottom dropped out of the markets in 1874, the Freedmen's Bank could not meet its obligations. At the helm was Cecelia's old Rochester acquaintance Frederick Douglass. Invited to direct the institution at what turned out to be the eleventh hour, he was stunned by how far the bank was overextended. Douglass recommended its closure to Congress, which occurred on June 29, 1874. Thousands of Black families were ruined, for most of them were just beginning to adjust to their new lives as free people. So were African American businesses, social, church and economic associations, and fraternal orders, all of which had invested their members' funds in the Freedmen's Bureau Savings and Trust.[17]

William Larrison, however, was never unemployed for long. A diligent worker with a kindly, cheerful yet respectful demeanour, he was popular with co-workers and earned excellent references from his employers. Too, Fanny and the Ballards were always there in the background, so his family was in a better situation than much of the city's African American population. He worked first for the widow of a pharmacist, Mrs. Wilder, and then as a waiter—which offered the opportunity to earn tips—at the Willard Hotel.[18] The enormous hostelry on Jefferson Street, opposite Courthouse Square, was one of the nicest hotels on the Ohio River. The Willard's creative senior staff managed to maintain its clientele even through the financial panic. However, by the fall of 1874 visitors were finding many of its suites empty and its dining room likewise. Manager W. C. D. Whipps announced in the Louisville *Courier-Journal* that "to suit the times, I have reduced the rates to THREE DOLLARS PER DAY," an advertisement that would continue to run at intervals for three years.[19] Mr. Whipps must have thought a good deal of William Larrison, for he continued his employ, although it is likely that William's wages, like those of tens of thousands of workers across America, were cut to the bone.

The next job Cecelia's husband found was as a coach driver at the Louisville Transfer Company, a position that would also have provided gratuities. Founded in 1861 and incorporated in 1867, the firm mainly provided livery service as well as bringing goods from rail depots and steamboat docks to the city's hotels, homes and businesses. It bore the considerable responsibility of carrying the mail to and from the post office and the railroads. Over the years the Louisville Transfer Company added a local courier service to the several amenities it provided Louisville businesses.[20] In the May 6, 1874, issue of the Louisville *Courier-Journal*, a large advertisement announced the "Louisville Transfer Company's Omnibus Line & Baggage Express," with offices located at the southeast corner of 9th and Green Streets.[21]

But again hard times resulted in labour unrest. Wage cuts, reduced hours and layoffs caused widespread discontent, especially in the railroads. Strike action across the eastern states resulted, and it traversed the Alleghenies to affect the Ohio River railroads in Louisville and Cincinnati.[22] In July 1874 rioting broke out in the streets of Louisville after the Louisville and Nashville and Great Southern Railroads chose midsummer to roll back workers' wages. The first point of attack was the L&N station, almost next door to William and Cecelia's home.

By this time Cecelia was again taking in clothing and linens to wash. Now it was her turn to comfort Fanny, when she and her husband suffered the death of their beloved only daughter, Abby, of tuberculosis. In a vain effort to save her, the Ballards had taken her to Europe.[23] Just twenty and a pretty, lively girl who was the joy of her family, Abby Churchill Ballard died in Menton, on the French Riviera, on April 2, 1874. The Ballards returned to Louisville heartbroken and laid their beloved daughter to rest in the family plot at Cave Hill Cemetery.[24] Fanny was inconsolable for a time, but she went to Europe again with A.J. and other members of the family to try to assuage her grief. Later she would finally put her feelings into action, ordering a special stained glass window from Louis Comfort

Tiffany in her daughter's honour, to be mounted at Christ Church. It was the same Episcopalian church that Cecelia had attended at the side of her young mistress in the long-ago days before her escape to Canada.

Later that same year, Mary Reynolds died. While Fanny had the comfort of her profound belief in a benevolent Creator, Cecelia's church attendance had not long survived the death of her much more religious first husband. She therefore found less solace in times of mourning than Fanny did. Once again in the face of the death of a loved one, the Larrisons were in no position to observe Mary's passing in any tangible way. After a simple service led by one of Louisville's several African American ministers, Mary Reynolds was laid in an unmarked grave and Cecelia went back to work.[25]

Mary had lived all her adult life in Kentucky and had connections in many Louisville households, which must have brought some peace to the bereft Cecelia. She had found her mother, only to lose her again. Although she and William were not members of any religious institution in those years, they roused themselves to take part in activities available through the city's several African American churches. Louisville's African American community was fortunate to have strong leaders in several educated clergymen through these tumultuous years. There had been separate Black Baptist congregations operating with minimal white supervision before the Civil War, an unusual phenomenon in a slave state, and reflective of Louisville's character as a border city that looked to both North and South. African Methodist Churches and other denominations sent missionaries to Kentucky in the immediate aftermath of the war. A series of denominational meetings took place in Louisville and in Lexington, creating a foundation for African American life in Kentucky that would endure for generations.

It was well that the Black community had its own firm foundation. The rising tide of hope that, despite violence and persecution, had buoyed African Americans during the Reconstruction era was by the mid-1870s crashing on the shoals of Kentucky's ultra-conservatism when it came to issues of race.

Kentucky was more influenced by Southern culture and politics than ever before. Although there were Black men in Congress from across the former slave states, no African American politician was elected to the Kentucky state legislature or achieved federal office. In contrast, even men who had led Confederate forces in battle inside the very boundaries of Kentucky now entered politics, took up civil service positions, or became financiers and manufacturers. Former Confederate general Basil Duke helped lay out Cherokee Park, and Bennett H. Young, who had been an officer with General John Hunt Morgan's daring cavalry and later a spy in Canada, was active in public and charitable organizations throughout the city. Both were prominent in Louisville society. Rather surprisingly, Young, who had taken courses at Toronto's Upper Canada College while spying for the Confederacy during the Civil War, took a special interest in "improving" the city's African American community; he sat on the board of directors and made substantial personal donations to the Colored Orphans' Home.[26]

Kentucky also continued to resist all attempts to place Blacks on an equal footing with whites. Cecelia, along with the rest of her family, faced the same oppression as all her Black neighbours. Facilities and services previously open to them were now prohibited on the basis of race, although the lines between Black and white were never as hard and fast in Louisville as they were in other Southern cities. With leadership from the clergy, along with a handful of professional men who had come to the city from other centres, Louisville Blacks now organized to resist efforts to prevent them from taking up at least some of the trappings of citizenship to which they were entitled. A major victory for Black civil rights had already been won through nonviolent protest, ending the segregation of streetcars in Louisville in 1870–71. In fact, one of Judge Bland Ballard's last acts as US District Court judge for Kentucky was to rule against segregation on public transit.[27]

Still, in direct violation of the Civil Rights Act of 1875, theatres and hotels, many public parks and the State Exposition excluded all African

Americans. A good example is the enforcement of separate railroad cars and "whites only" waiting rooms in railroad stations.[28] Meanwhile, in 1877 a general railroad strike spread across the United States, first to Memphis and Nashville. Then it was Louisville's turn. A strike by Black sewer-line workers precipitated a general work stoppage in industry and transportation across the city and beyond. The militia was called out and arms were sent from the state capital of Frankfort. In an irony not lost on observers, the nearly one thousand volunteers were veterans of both the Union and Confederate forces from the recent war. The militia unit was placed under the command of Commonwealth Attorney Basil W. Duke, who was legal counsel for the L&N Railroad.[29] Alongside former Confederates marched men who had worn Union blue, all in an effort to put down the strike and return Louisville—and its highly profitable business and public works operations—to order.[30]

William Larrison was still in the employ of the Louisville Transfer Company at the time, but due to unrest the firm was forced to appeal to the state for financial relief, as reported in the *Chicago Inter-Ocean* of November 1, 1877. That was far too late for the Larrisons. William had already lost his job, and it would be some time before he again found work.

In the midst of the financial turmoil this occasioned, Cecelia's long-lost father arrived in town. In the summer of 1877, an elderly Black man knocked at the back door of the Ballard mansion. Fanny's youngest son, Rogers, took the man into the kitchen. The visitor explained that his name was Adam and that he had worked for Charles W. Thruston many years ago. Rogers offered him a quarter, thinking he would go away, but eventually the man asked to see Miss Fanny. She immediately recognized Adam as Cecelia's father. Even in his eighties, Adam Reynolds still resembled his daughter well enough for Fanny to remember him as the skilled ropemaker who had been sold away a full forty years before. They all sat down at the kitchen table and Adam told his story. After he was sold down the river, he had ended up on a plantation in Arkansas, where, with no hope of returning to his Louisville wife and children, he married again and raised a new family.

Now his wife was dead, so he had worked his passage north on a steamboat, hoping to see Mary and their grown children. Sadly, he had learned that only three years earlier he would have found Mary alive. Since hearing the news, Adam had been living in a Louisville boarding house while he earned money at a local brickyard (at eighty-six!) to pay his return passage to Arkansas. His landlady had absconded with the clothes, the money and all the possessions of her tenants, and ever since he had been sleeping on the floor of her abandoned house, without a blanket and with nothing to eat. Finally, in desperation, he "went to the home of his former master . . . with the faint hopes that some descendant of his old master still lived there and would take compassion on him." Sorry for his misfortune, Fanny Ballard packed a carpet bag with a change of clothing and linen and gave Adam Reynolds enough money to pay his steamboat passage and provide sustenance until he returned to his adult children in Arkansas. They, he assured Fanny, had always been kind to him and would care for him in his time of trouble.

Sadly, there is no record of whether or not Cecelia was ever reunited with her father. However, she certainly would not have been able to help him at all. While Fanny and her husband may well have put some opportunities in Cecelia and William's way, by 1877 straitened finances had forced the Larrisons to move to much cheaper accommodation. They now lived in an alley off Breckinridge Street. Cecelia, who well remembered the alley housing of Washington from both her visits there, must have felt that she had reached a personal nadir. Originally laid out early in the century to provide access to stables and other rear outbuildings for delivery and transportation, the alleys now served the poor of all ethnicities as residential districts.

This was "Smoketown," possibly named for smoke from the stacks of the several area brickyards that employed large numbers of African Americans immediately after the Civil War. Washington Spradling Jr., son of Cecelia's old benefactor from the Underground Railroad era, owned a good deal of real estate in the area. William Larrison was not an old man, but his many years of ill health were wearing on him. His wife was now nearly fifty, although Cecelia was by this time routinely lying about her age.[31]

Cecelia and her family had indeed fallen on hard times, although the alley where they resided was not one of the older, dilapidated ones of the city's downtown core. In the aftermath of Emancipation, domestic workers, including housekeepers, cooks, gardeners and coachmen, lived in alleys of Louisville's better districts in order to be close to their places of employ. Louisville was not yet formally segregated by neighbourhood, and a good many Blacks and whites shared blocks and even houses in the centre of town. In wealthy parts of the city such as where the Larrisons now lived, because of the high cost of housing all but live-in servants resided in the alleyways, while their employers occupied the big houses on the main streets. The developing residential pattern rather disturbingly resembled that of slavery.[32]

Meanwhile, Mamie was employed in a series of domestic positions in Louisville and continued to contribute to the family finances. In the absence of steady employment, her stepfather travelled, taking jobs where he could find them. For a time he worked on the steamboats that still plied the waters between Louisville and Cincinnati, where his old colleague from the war, Wes Wayman, worked as a fireman stoking the engines. It was only in about 1880 that William began working on steamboats regularly.[33]

William also went to the country to work on farms, sometimes for a month or more at a time.[34] While the dangers of the years right after the war had abated, there were still plenty of white ruffians, some of them veterans who would take out their frustrations at their own unemployment on vulnerable men and women crossing their paths.[34] All the time William was away from home, he was at risk. Ku Klux Klan activity had increased exponentially after the withdrawal of federal troops and closure of the Freedmen's Bureau. Lynchings were rarely reported, for it was dangerous for white journalists in rural districts to comment on the violence.

But bloody assaults on Black Kentuckians escalated through the late 1870s, and the next decade saw an epidemic of whippings, hangings, sexual assault and arson, all calculated to keep the people of the country-side cowed and terrorized.

Whenever he went away, Cecelia and Mamie feared that William might never return. And one day he would not.

CHAPTER 15

IN THE BOSOM OF ABRAHAM

Though we have had war, reconstruction and abolition as a nation,
we still linger in the shadow and blight of an extinct institution.
—Frederick Douglass, National Convention of Colored Men,
Louisville, 1883

IN STARK CONTRAST WITH the fearful conditions under which
most of African American Kentucky was living, the Larrisons could see
evidence of Gilded Age America all around them. In December 1879
Louisville saw its largest reception ever when Ulysses S. Grant came to
town. Despite the legislature's being firmly in the camp of the Democrats,
he was adulated at every turn. A delegation of Black Kentuckians addressed
the former president, to which he responded:

I am very much obliged to the colored citizens of Louisville for
their words, and express the hope with them that all the rights of
citizenship may be enjoyed by them as it is guaranteed to them
already by the law and constitutional amendments; and I think the
day is not far distant when, without any embarrassment whatever,
they will, by common consent, enjoy unmolested and freely every
right to judge conscientiously of the suffrages that they want to

exercise wherever they will live, and, in all respect, to be free and equally independent before the law.[1]

While Grant's predictions of racial harmony would prove illusory, Black Americans certainly benefited from increased employment and better living conditions, for Louisville was again booming, in no small part because of its importance as a transportation hub. According to *Frank Leslie's Popular Monthly*, every day 120 railway passenger trains arrived and departed the city's several depots, each representing various rail lines. The old Louisville and Nashville line now connected the city directly with New Orleans to the south and with Pensacola, Florida, to the southeast. Others ran east to Pennsylvania and upstate New York, and still more to Baltimore and the Atlantic coast. There was rail service north through Ohio and west to St. Louis, to Chicago and thence to the great Midwestern cities of Minneapolis and St. Paul, Minnesota, where Cecelia's estranged stepson Ben had settled with his wife, Lucia, and their two sons.

Through the economic turmoil of the 1870s, the Larrisons had been fortunate in having some private income. Cecelia still had the rents from her Toronto property, although inflation and deterioration of the St. John's Ward neighbourhood—well on its way to becoming the slum it would be labelled by the 1890s—had reduced the value of the tenancy. Her younger stepson, James Thomas Holmes, died intestate in 1875. After James's death and the settlement of his estate, Ben Alexander sold the Toronto house (now renumbered as 31 Centre Street) that his father had left his sons in 1859. This required that Cecelia sign away her dower rights to the south half of Lot 7 to clear the way for the transfer, which she did by proxy on June 1, 1876, acting through a Louisville attorney.[2] It was to be the last contact she would have with Ben Alexander Holmes.[3]

The purchaser of Ben's house was shoemaker Francis G. Simpson, who with his wife had been renting the home and now embarked on a major rebuilding of it. Cecelia and Simpson were in correspondence with one another and he became her rental agent. She was tempted to try to dispose of her property again, as she had longed to do at certain points over the past few years. Just then, however, things were again looking up for the Larrisons, so she chose to hold onto her land and the rent monies it provided for a little longer.

By the 1880s the American economy was well on the road to recovery. With a change in management at the Louisville Transfer Company early in 1881, William was hired back on in his old position as coachman. It may well have been he who picked up the great Sarah Bernhardt at one of the city's several train stations and delivered her to the door of the Galt House Hotel. She arrived on February 21, 1881. The Great Bernhardt played in *Frou Frou* that very night to sold-out crowds at Louisville's Macauley's Theatre, just a few blocks west of Fanny and A.J.'s house on Walnut.[4]

That fall seventy men were working out of the Louisville Transfer Company depot at 9th and Green Streets. The company had an assortment of omnibuses, carriages, carts and other conveyances, as well as a "carriage and coupe" kept always at the ready should passenger service be required. The latest in communication tools assisted in the business: according to the *Louisville Courier-Journal* of October 2, 1881, an agent was "constantly at the telephone in the office night and day to receive orders." By May 15, 1882, the *Cincinnati Enquirer* was announcing that the "Louisville Transfer Company . . . is now one of the strongest institutions in the United States."

Since they were far better off than they had been, the Larrisons found a nicer flat at 24 College Street between 1st and 2nd, across from College Street Presbyterian Church. They moved on again within a year, this time to 126 West College Street, where they would remain for the next five years. Cecelia became friendly with Mrs. Mary Dickenson, a woman about fifteen years younger who also made her living washing and ironing.[5] Fortunately there was plenty of domestic work to be had, and Mamie still lived with her mother and stepfather, which was a help to the family finances. It was a nice neighbourhood and this was Cecelia's favourite of their Louisville homes.[6]

The city was growing by leaps and bounds in those years. Competition from Irish and German immigrants, who were particularly attracted to the employment opportunities of the river city, was hard on the African American friends and acquaintances of Cecelia and her family, particularly those who occupied the lowest rungs of the employment ladder.[7] However, Louisville's economic future seemed promising. River traffic was not as important as it once had been, but there were still regular packets to Cincinnati and Pittsburgh and south by way of the Mississippi to Memphis and New Orleans. Iron founding was an important industry, with sewer and oil pipe production a major component; there were also several agricultural equipment manufacturing operations, as well as rolling mills for the production of railroad track, bolts, iron trestles and other heavy equipment. The Bluegrass region was still the heart of agricultural production for the state. There were thirteen large tobacco auction houses in the city, for Louisville was the most important Burley market in the nation; half of all tobacco produced in the American West was passing through its auction rooms yearly. Distilling was also a major source of revenue, as were textiles, particularly from mills producing "Kentucky jeans" for work apparel. Tanneries, leather goods manufacture and shoe production were similarly important, and pork packing, begun in earnest before the Civil War, continued on an expanded scale, with only Cincinnati surpassing Louisville's production.[8]

Although the Larrisons worked very hard, their new-found economic security meant they could join in a variety of interesting entertainments and activities that flourished thanks to the lately buoyant economy. Louisville's postwar elite had moved away from the industrializing downtown. The advent of public transit had made "streetcar suburbs" both fashionable and popular with the families of business and professional men, and Louisville embraced the movement with its southward development. First there was the Louisville Industrial Exhibition, held in a specially constructed facility at 4th and Chestnut in 1872. More than 10,000 visitors daily were reported, and it was all deemed such a success that plans were made for another such fair in 1873. It would continue as an annual event until 1882.[9]

Then came the establishment of the Louisville Jockey Club, which introduced a new form of horseracing to America. It was organized in 1874 and inaugurated a year later by Fanny's cousin Meriwether Lewis Clark Jr., who had spent considerable time in Europe studying how the sport was conducted there. Fanny's husband, A.J., was often called in to judge horse races and was considered an expert on the "sport of kings." Cecelia and her family were as proud as any African Americans in the city on May 17, 1875, when a thoroughbred named Aristides, ridden by African American jockey Oliver Lewis, won the first Kentucky Derby. The racetrack was on land leased from Fanny's uncles John and Henry Churchill at Spring Grove, the old plantation of Fanny's Churchill grandparents, where Cecelia and Fanny had spent so much of their girlhoods. It was now and would ever after be known as Churchill Downs.[10]

There was romance in the air as well. Mamie Larrison was being courted. Her beau was much older but a very good man, ambitious and entrepreneurial, with his own rather upscale used-furniture store. An avowed Republican, as were nearly all Black Kentuckians of the era, Alexander L. Reels was a veteran of the Union Army from Baton Rouge, Louisiana. When he was denied farmland in the redistribution scheme administered by the Freedmen's Bureau after the war, he picked up stakes and moved his family to St. Louis, where he appears in the 1871 city directory listed as a pedlar.[11]

However, the economic prospects were not as auspicious as he had hoped. In 1873 Alexander moved to Louisville with his wife, Elizabeth, and their children.[12] He first encountered William Larrison while Cecelia's husband was still employed as a coachman by the widowed Mrs. Hite.[13] Being about the same age, the two men struck up an acquaintance that both of them enjoyed. With all the changing technology and the switch to central heating, Alexander Reels soon saw an opportunity, so he set himself up as a coal dealer, conducting the business with the help of one employee from his home at 4 Green Street, between 1st and 2nd.[14] His personal life was less successful. By 1880 Alexander's wife had run off to St. Louis with another man; he divorced her, and two children remained behind with their father. He went back to operating a second-hand store and began rebuilding his life. According to the 1880 census, Alexander Reels was forty-four years old,[15] while Mamie was twenty-six. Despite the age difference they began "keeping company," as the saying went.

African Americans like Cecelia and William were concerned that the promises of the Reconstruction era were fast melting away. The Larrisons remembered well the rousing speeches that Frederick Douglass used to give at Rochester's lovely Corinthian Hall. On September 24, 1883, he came to Liederkranz Hall in Louisville to deliver the keynote speech for the National Convention of Colored Men. The event brought together two hundred delegates from states representing more than half the nation. Its purpose was to discuss the conditions and prospects of African Americans and whether or not continued adherence to the Republican Party was warranted, since Abraham Lincoln and the other old champions of the Blacks were dead. Grievances arising from the failure of the Freedmen's Bank due to corruption were aired in a town where the bank had seen perhaps its greatest success and had remained solvent to the end.[16]

The Convention drew attendance from the tiny handful of well-educated community leaders, most of whom had moved to Louisville in the years after the late war. Cecelia had known the Abbotts and Judahs in Toronto, who were of a similar social stratum, as was Dr. Alexander Augusta and his business-minded wife. But her Toronto acquaintances had not had the opportunities available that these newcomers to Louisville did. Many had earned degrees in the universities, colleges and normal schools established for Black Americans in the postwar years, such as Howard

University in Washington, DC, and Virginia State University in Petersburg, within a few miles of that horrific battlefield where William had seen so much carnage.

One important addition to the city's medical services was Dr. Henry Fitzbutler, who arrived in 1872 as Louisville's first Black physician. His grandfather, Levi Foster, had been a Virginia-born fugitive slave with a very successful livery stable business in Amherstburg, on the Canadian side of the Detroit River. The first Black graduate of the University of Michigan's medical school, Fitzbutler was progressive in his views, impatient with Kentucky law and custom that promoted racial discrimination, and an activist by nature. He soon became a local leader. His wife, Sarah, worked with him to establish the Louisville National Medical School to train Black doctors, which would open its doors in 1888. Fitzbutler also published the *Ohio Falls Express*, the principal African American newspaper in Louisville.[17]

These newcomers were educated, cultured and ambitious, and immensely frustrated by the limitations placed on Black achievement in Louisville. Another newcomer was W. H. Gibson, who had come to Louisville from Baltimore to open a Methodist school for free Black children. He became a cashier for the Louisville branch of the Freedmen's Bureau Bank. A very well-educated man and talented in both instrumental and vocal music, he created the Louisville Mozart Society.[18] He was a founder of the United Brothers of Friendship, a fraternal order that spread from Louisville across half the United States. Such people were the mainstay of the Colored Orphans' Home and other institutions created by African Americans who were excluded from Louisville's charitable facilities for the aged, infirm, ill, blind and otherwise disadvantaged.[19]

These families also supported the Republican ticket, and Alexander Reels did as well. However, unlike in most of the South during the Reconstruction years, they were never elected to political office in Kentucky, even when the Republicans were in power, and only a bare handful were accorded local and county positions.[20] This would have little direct impact on the Larrisons—at least until Mamie's new flame came into their lives—although both parties tried alternately to sway and then disassociate themselves from the Black constituency. Kentucky Black men were still able to vote, which was growing rarer in the American South because of gerrymandered districts and newly imposed literacy and other qualifications aimed at keeping African Americans from the ballot box.

The Republicans did not hold the state and had little influence on the lives of people like the Larrisons. Apart from the vagaries of the economy, which directly affected people on the lower economic rungs such as William and Cecelia, the creeping effects of segregation, which was becoming more formalized in these years, were the most direct and obvious effect of Democratic policy. At the Republican rally held on March 2, 1882, at Liederkranz Hall on 3rd Street, so scornfully described by Henry Watterson's staunchly Democratic *Courier-Journal*, were two men well-known to Cecelia. Fanny's husband, A. J. Ballard, was both a strong Republican and the political reporter for the *Louisville Commercial*. Also there was an enthusiastic member of one of the African American Republican clubs, Alexander L. Reels.[21]

Alexander Reels was known to A. J. Ballard. Both were active in the Republican Party, both were regular attendees at rallies, conventions and meetings relevant to party interests, and in the 1880s they lived but three blocks apart. Also, Ballard owned land on Green Street almost adjacent to Reels's shop, and he managed a number of other properties in the immediate vicinity on behalf of his wife's Blair and Jesup cousins. Black Louisville, with few exceptions, was convinced that standing for the Republicans was equivalent to standing for the race. They would, however, not win an election until 1895.[22] Meanwhile, Alexander L. Reels pressed his suit for the hand of Cecelia's hard-working daughter while at the same time the Larrisons were slowly rebuilding their fortunes after their most recent economic crisis.

But no one could predict the havoc that natural disasters can play on a family's circumstances, and for once this was as true for Fanny's family as it was for the more vulnerable Cecelia's. In February 1884 Louisville was inundated by one of the periodic floods it had experienced throughout its history. The entire Ohio Valley was affected. The river was rising three inches an hour on February 6, and hourly reports were coming in from Pittsburgh and Cincinnati that conditions there were worse. Information was passed down the river by both telegraph and the newly available telephone service, and people made what preparations they could in the face of the coming inundation. Flood danger began at twenty-four feet, and the river rose to a full forty-eight feet in hours, floating hundreds of houses off their foundations and destroying wharves and rail yards, factories, hospitals and government offices. By February 9 Beargrass Creek, at the east end of downtown, had overflowed its banks, submerging much of the southeast end of the city. It crested on the fifteenth and by the next day was beginning to subside. The cost to the city, private business and homeowners was incalculable. The flat where the Larrison family lived was completely inundated; Cecelia lost all her precious mementoes, but fortunately she was able to salvage some of the letters from Fanny that she had saved over the years.

But the worst of the disaster fell not on their own heads but on Fanny, her husband and her remaining children. Her oldest son, Charles T. Ballard, had married some years earlier. Then, on January 25, 1883, Fanny and A.J.'s second son, Samuel Thruston Ballard, took as his bride a cheerful and very attractive girl with the unusual name of Sunshine Harris.[23] A little over a year later, Samuel and Sunshine Ballard presented their respective parents with the first of four grandchildren; Mary Harris Ballard, born on April 28, 1884. Nine days after her birth, the *New York Times* reported:

Failures in the West: Ballard & Ballard in Louisville and a Dry Goods Firm in Chicago

The large grain and flour mill of Ballard & Ballard, the largest and best known in the city, failed to-day, with liabilities placed at $160,000, only nominal assets, and uncertain security of the liabilities. It is said that there is fully $100,000 owing to local banks as follows: Western Bank; Falls City Bank, $7,500; Kentucky National Bank, $17,000; Mrs. Sarah Ballard, $10,600. Most of the firm's paper was endorsed by A. J. Ballard, and it is stated in business circles this evening that the security is valueless. The cause of the failure was in the losses to their milling property through the late flood. The failure was precipitated through a suit entered by the Merchants' National Bank of New-York on a note for $10,000.[24]

In 1880 Charles Thruston Ballard, a graduate of Yale's Sheffield Scientific School, and his brother Samuel, whose degree was from Cornell, had established Ballard & Ballard Flour Mills. This was an iconic brand that patented the world-famous Obelisk Flour with its distinctively stylized Egyptian logo, built offices throughout the Midwest with architecture influenced by the tombs of the Nile Valley, and shipped flour to all parts of the globe. The Egyptianizing motif had been the contribution of their brother Rogers Clark Thruston Ballard, who was an engineer and geologist with a Yale education as well, but who also became an officer in the family milling company.

Ballard & Ballard failed because of the widespread flooding of the Ohio River the preceding February. Located on East Broadway, the mills had been flooded by Beargrass Creek and the subsequent bursting of the Ohio River's banks. The waters, rain and accompanying high winds had done extensive damage to their production facilities and destroyed equipment and supplies, as well as stored grain and finished flour products. News of the firm's failure appeared in the *Times* on May 7, 1884. When a follow-up article was printed in the Louisville *Courier-Journal* of May 11, 1884, titled simply "The Ballards," Fanny's mortification must have been complete. A. J. Ballard had signed notes to secure the loans against his own assets, but when the suit was brought forward, it was discovered that his personal finances amounted to between $6,000 and $10,000. He had lost more than $50,000 of his own money in ill-fated silver-mining schemes in Colorado—the security he had provided to his sons' creditors was worthless.

In the ensuing months A. J. Ballard was forced to give up all his personal property, including real estate, stock and his remaining capital.[25] Fanny had to endure a nasty court case that threatened her own large inheritance from her father and grandfather, but Charles W. Thruston had secured his daughter's future well, and in the end she retained her fortune.[26] Her sons refinanced and regrouped, and within a few months Ballard & Ballard was back in business.[27] Despite their financial troubles, perhaps the company's most memorable accomplishment was that it had the distinction of inventing canned biscuit dough, packaged in a tube that when struck against a sharp edge popped open, revealing the dough. The Pillsbury Company would in 1951 purchase Ballard & Ballard and adopt the distinctive cardboard packaging as home to their mascot, the Pillsbury Doughboy.

The bankruptcy and attendant public humiliation hastened Andrew Jackson Ballard's death, which occurred on August 17, 1885. A heavy man, he died of acute dehydration due to dysentery.[28] A. J. Ballard was nearly seventy years old. The Louisville *Courier-Journal* of August 18, 1885, announced that the funeral would be held from the family home at Walnut and Floyd at 4:30 p.m. that day, followed by interment in the family plot at Cave Hill Cemetery. To her everlasting regret, Fanny was visiting North Carolina when her husband entered his final illness. She rushed home as quickly as she could when she learned of the seriousness of his ailment.[29] Perhaps it was of some consolation to the pious Fanny that A. J. Ballard had finally found the faith that had sustained her all these years: he had recently become a member of Christ Episcopal Church.

Fanny's husband died after the 1885 reopening of the great Southern Exposition. This very popular event had first been inaugurated in 1883 by the Louisville Board of Trade to showcase Kentucky's industrial, commercial and agricultural production, and by 1885 it had achieved the status of world's fair.[30] Fanny and A. J. Ballard had even been inspired to show off the produce of their beautiful gardens at the exhibition.[31]

The Exposition was opened by President Chester Arthur on August 1, 1883. On the President's reception committee was the former First Lady of Kentucky, Fanny's Aunt Julia Blackburn, accompanied by her husband, Dr. Luke Pryor Blackburn. The former Confederate spy, who had passed the war years in Toronto and in 1864 made an attempt to infect Union troops with yellow fever through clothing shipped from epidemic victims in Bermuda, had in 1879 been elected governor of Kentucky. He held office until 1883, gaining a reputation in prison and other reform that would earn him (rather ironically, given his wartime efforts) the epitaph the "Good Samaritan."[32] Ulysses S. Grant, in town for the event, said "the exposition will undoubtedly have a great influence in removing whatever sectional feelings may still exist between the people of the South and the people of the North."[33] Illuminated by thousands of Thomas Edison's new incandescent light bulbs, the Exposition of 1885 drew more than a million visitors. There were special days for "coloured" visitors so they wouldn't mingle with the white crowds.[34]

Beneath all the glitter, Cecelia, Mamie and William, along with the rest of the Black community, suffered from the rot of racial prejudice, social and economic exclusion, and outright abuse. The success of the 1871 streetcar desegregation campaign had faded, and public spaces and institutions were almost entirely segregated by the mid-1880s, a legacy of the pernicious creeping progress of racial division, both in custom and in law. Although African and European Americans had traditionally lived within the same neighbourhoods and often in the same households, now whites of any means sold their homes in neighbourhoods into which Blacks had moved. The process was as yet far from complete, though, and there were still many blocks where African American homes and businesses stood side by side with white-owned ones. Schools, the newly founded YMCA for African

Americans, with one branch organized at the Methodist Quinn Chapel in 1886, and other community facilities were concentrated in neighbourhoods with larger Black populations.[35]

Theatres, taverns, guest houses and other venues and services designed for an African American clientele were created. Enterprising men and women responded by opening stores for Black customers, who were now forbidden to enter the ones in which white people shopped. Jobs in the skilled trades, previously the province of talented Blacks, now went to Irish and European immigrants. Although positions as waiters, hotel workers and other direct service positions continued to be dominated by African Americans, most trade unions refused membership to them, and men were increasingly relegated to lower-paying and lower-status labouring jobs. Their wives and daughters continued in positions that uncomfortably reminded them of pre-war slavery: in South-facing Louisville they remained the largest proportion of the household help.

Denied access to benefits and avenues of advancement available to white society, Black American communities looked inward for sustenance and support, largely through the churches that had always sustained them. This was the great period of African American organizing, seeing the rise of multiple national societies.[36] Since most agricultural and industrial fairs excluded Blacks (except those employed there), "Colored Fairs" were held across the state and attracted thousands of people. It was also a time when Blacks engaged in formal sports, despite the pernicious advance of segregation. "Negro League" baseball teams gained popularity in this period.[37] Horses had always mattered in Kentucky, and out of the first twenty-eight Kentucky Derbys run since 1875, fifteen were won by Black jockeys. By 1900, African Americans, however talented, had been all but excluded from racing because of Jim Crow regulations and concerted efforts on the part of white jockeys to have them removed.[38]

The danger that lingered in the countryside and in the rougher districts of Ohio River port towns was an ever-present threat. In January 1883

William again found himself unemployed. He resorted to taking jobs as a cabin boy, or "rouster," on the river steamboats or doing a day or two's field work for local farmers.[39] But this time his luck ran out. Cecelia's husband disappeared.[40]

Everyone who knew the couple bore witness to the love and affection they always showed one another. There was no indication that William Larrison was keeping company with another woman or that he might have deserted his family. Cecelia asked everyone who knew William where he might be and spent every night listening for his step at the door. The Larrisons' friends had their own ideas about what might have befallen her husband, although they were loath to share them with his wife—or widow. There were many "accidents" that could happen aboard a steamboat or while wandering in the country looking for work.

The terror that stalked Black Kentucky, the violence of the times in which they lived and the vicious backlash the war and Emancipation had unleashed against African American Kentucky suggest that William Larrison met a different end.[41] The Ku Klux Klan rode the Kentucky byways, lynch rope at the ready. There were many ways in which a man alone could meet his death.

Cecelia never saw him again.

CHAPTER 16
NOBODY KNOWS THE TROUBLE I'VE SEEN

Success is to be measured not so much by the position that one has reached in life as by the obstacles which he has overcome while trying to succeed.

—Booker T. Washington, 1901

ON APRIL 22, 1888, the Louisville *Courier-Journal* carried the happy announcement that "Mr. A. L. Reels and Miss Mamie A. Lawrence [*sic*] were united in marriage last Tuesday night by the Rev. J. H. Frank." Reverend Frank was the minister of Fifth Street Baptist, by far the largest and best attended of the African American churches in Louisville.[2]

Cecelia was overjoyed. Although her attempts to locate her missing husband distressed her greatly, things were finally looking up again for her dutiful, affectionate daughter. Eighteen years Mamie's senior and closer in age to his new mother-in-law than he was to his bride,[3] Alexander Reels was clearly a man on his way up. He was active in Republican politics, a member of the Grand United Order of Odd Fellows and, as a veteran soldier, eligible for the Louisville branch of the Grand Army of the Republic. He was also a member of the oldest Black Baptist congregation in the city.

Mamie's new husband was bright, personable and ambitious as well. Alexander and his family lived on Green Street at 1st, adjacent to his commercial address, and he employed several African American workers in his profitable second-hand store. This became his principal occupation. Alexander Reels was listed in the business directory as one of only three "colored" merchants under the heading "Second-Hand Stores," out of a total of thirty-one. Green (now Liberty) was one of the city's main business and residential thoroughfares. Trolley lines ran in front and telephone lines crisscrossed above the street.[4]

In 1886 Alexander up-scaled his inventory and became a dealer in used furniture, a considerable step up from a shop that sold second-hand clothing and sundry other items. He now also employed his son, James S. Reels, as clerk.[5] The Reels shop had a few African American neighbours, but this was a racially mixed area. Much of the area was home to Jewish immigrants from Eastern Europe. Alexander Reels's choice of location was strategic: while even poorer whites might be reluctant to purchase furniture at a second-hand store in a predominantly Black district, buying goods in a Jewish neighbourhood was perfectly acceptable, which guaranteed the Reels shop a white clientele. There was a major concentration of German families in the districts to the east and north, and thrifty families would have been clients of both Alexander Reels and his Jewish neighbours.[6]

While Alexander's stock in trade was hardly prestigious, the Reels family was significantly better off than most Black Americans in the city. As a tradesman with his own business, he and his family occupied a level of African American society below that of the professional and university-educated class, but well above the rank and file of labourers and day workers. Louisville's Black community in the 1880s was stratified, although there was mobility between the ranks. The upper class comprised clergymen along with the city's very few dentists, doctors, teachers and lawyers, along with a handful of undertakers and businesspeople.

There were able men in the pulpits of the city's several African American churches, and the city boasted more Black professionals than did most Southern centres of similar size.[7] At this point they were moving their families into comfortable and often luxurious homes west of downtown. These had been sold off by middle-class owners migrating to newly fashionable—and exclusively white—suburban districts such as Cherokee Park and the Highlands, rendered accessible by improved urban transit systems.[8] According to African Methodist Episcopal Zion (AMEZ) minister Alexander Walters, who pastored the 15th Street Church, "Socially the Afro-Americans of Louisville take first rank among the most intellectual and cultured of our land. Many of them own their own homes, and a few have elegant residences. There are a number of business enterprises operated by colored people, such as: contracting, tailoring, shoemaking, with drugstores, insurance companies and undertaking establishments."[9]

Alexander Reels and his children had occupied the next rank of Black society. It was made up of barbers, shopkeepers and people who held positions of responsibility in service to wealthy whites, including butlers, valets and lady's maids in Louisville's finer homes, headwaiters at the better hotels and private clubs, and fashionable seamstresses and tailors. Being in service was no bar to Black society, since nearly everyone had been forced into the lower echelons of the labour market. These men and women were personally ambitious and worked hard not only to achieve upward mobility but also to demonstrate the fitness of Black Americans for fuller participation in civil society. As one contemporary wrote, "Every store owned and controlled by a colored man with success not only helps him, but it in a way lifts up the entire race, and shows that colored men can do other things besides clean houses and drive coal-carts."[10]

By this point in Louisville's history, African American businesspeople and shop proprietors like the Reels, along with the city's tiny professional class, were expanding their horizons to open additional stores, engage in wholesale commerce and invest in real estate. Civil service jobs (with the exception of low-ranking post office jobs) were all but closed to Black men and women in Louisville, particularly with the Republican Party out of power for much of the post-Reconstruction era of the nineteenth century. There were few other avenues for real advancement.[11] Black Republican politicians held federal and state offices in most Southern states during and immediately following Reconstruction, but it would be decades before Kentucky would elect an African American to state or federal office. Since both commerce and large-scale manufacturing were not open to them, it was intelligence and ability along with refinement and ambition that elevated people like the Reels family to leadership positions within their own community. This stratum was active in political protest and community organizing and undertook leading roles in churches and secret societies.[12]

Beneath this layer came those in ordinary domestic service, skilled labourers and craftsmen, and people with jobs as cooks in hotels and private homes, porters, elevator operators, doormen, draymen and the like. With secure employment and relatively stable incomes, these were the mainstays of church and benevolent societies and filled out the ranks of the fraternal orders. Cecelia, along with William and Mamie, had hitherto occupied this economic stratum, their employment rendered more secure by their association with Fanny Thruston Ballard and her family, who saw that they had work even during times of financial hardship.

The vast majority of Louisville's Blacks, however, their numbers swollen by the addition of thousands of rural families seeking safety and employment in the immediate postwar period, undertook menial labouring positions, their day-to-day survival dependent on the whims of white employers and the state of the economy. Such families occupied rickety tenements and the meanest of alley housing, and even former industrial and warehousing facilities along the riverfront. The poorest of the poor, they felt every financial downturn and suffered terribly when the periodic epidemics that plagued late-nineteenth-century American cities swept through their overcrowded quarters.

Cecelia, along with her new in-laws the Reels, was part of an African American life, society and culture that evolved separately from that of European Americans, although their personal aspirations reflected the same late-nineteenth and early-twentieth-century concerns and values. African American newspapers paralleled those of the larger white world and displayed many of the same preoccupations, right down to society pages that reported that such-and-such a lady and her daughter had been away visiting relatives, or that a young couple had announced their engagement.[13] They contained announcements of parties and events that rivalled those of the old Louisvillian white families in their elaborate catering, the fashionable clothing worn by their participants and the elegant furnishings of their surroundings. One of Black Louisville's most prominent men was Albert Hathaway, the personal chauffeur of Fanny and A. J.'s son Charles Thruston Ballard. Co-owner of Ballard & Ballard Flour Mills and, as heir to Kentucky's Clark and Churchill founding families, he was a leading member of Louisville's very class-conscious late-nineteenth-century society. Hathaway and his wife "attended social functions, gave parties, and participated in community projects."[14]

The status to which Mamie's new husband aspired had been amply demonstrated by a party he held for his only daughter, Eulalie, in 1881. Luckily the only surviving copy of the African American Louisville *Bulletin* describes the event. A band was hired for the occasion and "wines and other delicacies of the season were served lavishly." Eulalie Reels was nineteen at the time. Appearing on Saturday, September 24, 1881, the piece sheds much light on the aspirations and social objectives of Louisville's rising business class in the last decades of the nineteenth century:

The Gliding Bell Club.

The party met at Miss Eulalie Reels, on First and Green streets, last Friday, and then proceeded to Mrs. Howard's, on Walnut Street, where they found Prof. John Weet's Band of Music, and a room elegantly furnished for the enjoyment of the same. The ladies were elegantly dressed all in the latest Fourth-avenue styles, and did much in making the gathering both brilliant and agreeable. The club, however, was in no ways sparing as far as means were concerned, as fine wines and other delicacies of the season were served lavishly, and the cups of joy were filled to the very brims.

This party will long be remembered in the society circles of Louisville as one of the most enjoyable entertainments which has been under the auspices of the Gliding Bell Club. The guests present were: Misses Bettie Davies, Mary Dobley, Alice Thompson, S. E. Miller, Mollie Smith, Fannie Hitover, Patsey Johnson, Belle Crane, Lizzie Bennett, Anna Cooper, Anna Smith, Lizzie Johnson, Rosie Allen, Ella French, Jane Cranshaw, Maude Thomas, Sallie Wilhite, Amanda Johnson, Mrs. L. N. Taylor, Mrs. Sallie Johnson, Mrs. Julia Wilkerson, Mrs. Josephine Russell. And of the gentlemen, Messrs. Chas. Williams, N. D. Bennett, Wm. Bennett, J. Mayweather, Wm. Hammond, Jr., H. Hill, Talbot Jordan, Judge Allen, Hay Taylor, Lewis Marshall, J. P. Higgins, Preston Talbot, J. W. Lewis, Jas. Mathews, H. Foster, Geo. Blankenship, Geo. Crane, A. Reals, J. Clarke, Wm. Rankin. A. Payne, dictator; Nath Mathews, assistant dictator; W. R. Perty, secretary.

It was all evocative of upward mobility along with a certain financial success. While most of the people whom Eulalie and her father invited to the Gliding Bell party were in service in rich households, there were also a number of shopkeepers, along with waiters, a restaurant cook and at least one skilled tradesman. After this point, Eulalie disappears from the record, and it's possible that she married and left Louisville. But in the last years of her girlhood, her father had given her a party to remember all her days.

Alexander was therefore attractive as a husband in many ways, not the least of which was his affection for his new mother-in-law. Furthermore, he was both literate and ambitious, with both economic and social accomplishments that William H. Larrison, however amiable and kindly, had never possessed. The family moved to a new address on Preston Street, and while Cecelia shared her daughter and son-in-law's living accommodations, she remained fiercely independent. She was now fifty-eight and suffering some ill health, but her most difficult challenge was that, tragically, she was beginning to lose her eyesight. This meant she could no longer do washing, ironing and the mending of delicate garments for Galt House guests, which had provided a good living in recent years. Instead Cecelia returned to her earlier occupation as a nurse specializing in the care of new babies, living temporarily in a series of elite white homes. This provided her with room and board along with a small wage, but each job ended as the children for whom she was caring grew past infancy.

Cecelia could remember better times. As the wife of steamboat waiter and Underground Railroad operator Benjamin Pollard Holmes, she had once taken her place among Toronto's more respectable Black matrons. Hoping to improve her family's prospects, in November 1887, in anticipation of Mamie's upcoming nuptials, the careful Cecelia had made a truly ill-advised decision. She decided to invest in a commercial venture. The *New York Freeman* of April 10, 1886, had reported that "Mr. A. L. Reels will shortly open an auction and commission house on the west side of First street, between Market and Jefferson streets. This house will be a branch of the main store on the southwest corner of First and Green Streets. Mr. Reels is an enterprising business man and the first one among the race here to enter into this field."

Through all those long years of intermittent hardship, Cecelia had held on to her one piece of real estate. Now she began the lengthy process of selling her Toronto property. The prospective buyer was Francis G. Simpson, the shoemaker who sometimes assisted Cecelia in managing her Toronto property. He was by this time gaining prominence by speaking on behalf of St. John's Ward's increasingly multicultural residents at City Council, and was known as an outspoken advocate of working men of all ethnicities in Liberal political circles. Simpson had already bought—and practically rebuilt from the ground up—the rental home that Benjamin had built as an inheritance for his sons nearly twenty years earlier.[15] It was a complicated process, for Benjamin's heirs were now scattered between upstate New York and Minnesota, and each had a legal claim to the land. The fact that James T. Holmes had died intestate in 1875 held up the sale. On September 18, 1889, Emma and Rebecca Holmes of Rochester, his daughters and only heirs, sold their rights to Lot 7 on the east side of Centre Street for $1,150.[16] Their indentures were written and notarized in Rochester and sent to Toronto. All transactions relating to the severing of Lot 7 were conducted between Louisville and Toronto lawyers and the Minnesota lawyer representing Benjamin Alexander Holmes and his wife, Lucia. The deal with Simpson was at last finalized on October 23, 1889.[17]

As for Mamie, becoming Alexander Reels's wife meant she had improved upon the social position that her mother had once enjoyed in her former Canadian home. A practical nurse of considerable expertise, even in poor economic times Mamie was never out of work. However, men who could afford it preferred their wives to remain at home, and they gave their daughters at least a basic education. Women's income was essential to the household economy of the vast majority of Black Louisvillians, but relieving female family members of their need to go out to work had particular significance for men who, like Alexander, had been enslaved before the war and whose wives had been forced to do the most menial drudgery. Instead, women in Mamie's position joined female clubs and associations, most of which had been founded for benevolent purposes but had already branched out to undertake more political roles. These women's groups were important in organizing resistance to limitations and abuse based on race and gender, agitating for education and against lynching and demanding voting rights for African American women. Their fundraising was essential: Blacks were excluded from nearly all public institutions, from hospitals to nursing homes; the Colored Orphans' Home now had little support except funds raised from within the African American community, largely by women.[18]

Although Cecelia maintained that her husband William had belonged to no church or society in Louisville, she had been involved at least for a time in one of the several female auxiliaries of fraternal orders that proliferated during this period, although its identity has been forgotten.[19] Her daughter Mamie was associated with the Household of Ruth, the female branch of the Grand United Order of Foresters, and possibly also the Sisters of the Mysterious Ten, which was the female branch of Louisville's very popular fraternal order the United Brothers of Friendship.[20] The latter had grown from its Kentucky base to encompass most of the United States; it also had short-lived lodges in Canada as well as in the West Indies and Liberia.[21]

These groups were self-insurance organizations, with burial and health benefit assistance available to the sick and needy, and also important centres of social and intellectual activity.[22] They offered excitement and entertainment too. There were meetings and elaborate ceremonies, annual picnics, band practices, lodge meetings and parades, along with assorted regalia reflective of rising through their ranks. Along with the Black church, these organizations gave creative, forward-thinking people a chance to exercise leadership and organizational skills.[23]

Men like Alexander Reels had to walk a fine line. He was also politically active, a member of the old party of Lincoln, and engaged in organized efforts to resist and ameliorate the effects of racial discrimination. But his prosperity, and now that of Mamie and his mother-in-law Cecelia, depended on white custom as well. The African American press regularly reported efforts designed to resist the insidious effects of the economic, social and residential segregation that thwarted Black people's ambitions and limited the aspirations of their children. Every proposal for improvement in the conditions of the state's African American population passed by the federal government was rejected by Kentucky legislators, including the Civil Rights Act of 1866, which the state Supreme Court declared unconstitutional. Kentucky whites effectively ignored the Civil Rights Act of 1876, which guaranteed equality in public accommodation and transportation and African Americans' right to the due process of law within the court system. Not all whites concurred, however, and this was a struggle in which A. J. Ballard's brother Bland was engaged right up to the time of his death in 1879.

Although Louisville considered itself a progressive place, and this was certainly the case in respect to technological developments—it had adopted electric street lighting almost as soon as it was invented, and by 1889 the first electric streetcars were appearing on city streets—there was profound resistance to change in respect to race relations. Iron-fronted commercial buildings might be going up on the main streets near the river and Louisville was gaining its first "skyscrapers," but the preference of the city's white leadership for maintaining the status quo on the position of African Americans in society, and particularly in government, remained almost unchanged.[24]

But Alexander and his wife Mamie, along with his doting mother-in-law, were hopeful that change could be effected. On a national scale, this was the era of great debate on the "future of the Negro." The failure of Reconstruction was ever more apparent below the Mason-Dixon Line, and the rise of the "redeemed" New South brought with it ever more rigidly enforced Jim Crow–style segregation. This would be codified into law across the South in the last decade of the nineteenth century, prohibiting Black Americans from entering public spaces, eating at restaurants or staying at hotels frequented by whites, and requiring separate facilities for railways, washrooms and schools.[25] This most pernicious legacy of both Southern slavery and pre-war Northern discriminatory practices would endure through the civil rights agitations of the 1950s and '60s. As for Louisville, which prided itself on its "good" race relations, the infrastructure of segregation was more subtly maintained, but it was iron-clad nonetheless. Reconstruction had effectively passed Kentucky by, leaving it a place whose culture, society and economic and political structures remained overwhelmingly white-dominated.[26]

Alexander, Mamie and Cecelia worked diligently, kept a respectable home, saved their money and had great hopes for the future. But their collective upward trajectory was suddenly stymied when Louisville was struck by a massive tornado on March 27, 1890. Known as the "Louisville Cyclone," it lasted a mere five minutes but destroyed 755 houses, took out Union Station and destroyed the Waterworks Tower, along with causing the complete collapse of Falls City Hall with two hundred people inside. The *Chicago Tribune* published a special edition detailing the disaster on March 29, 1890. The brand new Odd Fellows Hall, constructed at great sacrifice by the community to provide African Americans with a space for events, was utterly demolished. While the east end of downtown, where the Reels store and warehouse were located, was not touched by the tornado itself, rebuilding tied up all available investment capital for more than a year.[27] Fortunately, in preparation for his expansion into the auction business, Alexander and his wife had just moved their shop to a less expensive location at 417 Floyd Street, between Green and Walnut, less than two blocks north of the site of Cecelia's childhood home.

Then, in 1893, the United States suffered the worst recession in its history. Alexander's hopes of operating a new commission business were dashed and Cecelia's precious nest egg from her Toronto real estate sale was lost, along with Alexander's own savings. This was the cruellest blow Cecelia had sustained since William went missing years before. Mamie went back to nursing while Alexander tried to recoup the family's financial losses. Unable to afford the membership fees, Cecelia dropped out of the women's association whose events she had attended with her friend Caroline.[28] Cecelia continued to share the home of her daughter and son-in-law, but with her eyesight so compromised, she was by this time barely eking out a living.[29]

Profoundly concerned about her own and her family's financial stability, Cecelia applied for the military pension due her as the wife of a Union Army veteran. Ever resourceful, she may have been inspired to take this step when the annual National Encampment of the Grand Army of the Republic came to town. This enormous event filled every hotel room in the city in September 1895. The Grand Army was an integrated veterans' group that had been founded after the Civil War. Although it foundered in the 1870s, it was revived in the next decade and was important in protecting the voting rights of Black veterans, as well as helping to arrange pensions for veterans' widows and children who were in need, both African American and white. The organization rotated its gatherings between cities; this was the first time the encampment had been held south of the Mason-Dixon Line, in part because of concerns about how the Black veterans who were regular attendees would be treated there.[30] Alexander Reels was a veteran and was very likely involved, and at any rate it would have been impossible to avoid the throngs of old soldiers, who had once fought one another wearing Union blue and Confederate grey, as they marched through the streets and shared stories over campfires in the surrounding woodlands and parks.

The process of registering for a pension seemed straightforward enough, the more so because Cecelia could read well and wrote a fluid, legible hand, so she was not intimidated by forms and bureaucracy, as some of her less literate friends might have been. Among them were widows, such as Caroline Ellis, who were already receiving pensions for their husband's wartime service, so the process of making the application probably seemed simple enough at first glance.[31] However, acquiring William's Civil War pension became progressively more complicated even as it became more urgent.

Cecelia had little help in putting together her first application. Although the widowed Fanny Thruston Ballard and her many friends and relations continued to be a potential source of assistance in employment and legal matters, Fanny now spent much of her time travelling between her many relations.[32] She passed summers at a series of resorts and then left Louisville in the winter of 1895 with her son Samuel Thruston Ballard and his wife, Sunshine, for an extended European vacation. But Fanny's always fragile respiratory system finally failed her. On April 26, 1896, Louisville's

Courier-Journal reported that Mrs. Fanny T. Ballard was ill with pneumonia in Vienna; four days later, Cecelia's former mistress died. Her heartbroken sons brought her body home, and the funeral took place on June 7 at Fanny's beloved Christ Church, which had become a cathedral only two years before. She was laid to rest at Cave Hill Cemetery beside her husband, her daughter Abby and her little boy Bland, about whose loss she had written to Cecelia so long ago.[33]

Her last will and testament raises the question of how close Fanny's relationship with her former maid had been in recent years. On the verge of blindness, Cecelia was being forced to seek employment in a series of less and less affluent Louisville households. The very wealthy Fanny could have easily ensured Cecelia's comfort for the rest of her days, but she left her only $100, along with a shawl made of black cashmere to remember her old mistress by. The note attached to her will says the bequest was to Cecelia "who was my maid in slavery days."[34] Although this was the equivalent of nearly a year's salary for a domestic servant at the time, it was hardly enough to preserve the aging, ailing woman from the ravages of poverty.

With Fanny gone, Cecelia reapplied her energies to acquiring the military pension that was due to her. In 1898 she engaged a Washington agent named John Raum, an Illinois-born lawyer who was the son of the Commissioner of Pensions and specialized in negotiating Union Army pensions with the federal government.[35] Her initial application denied, she continued to pursue the matter, and a long series of correspondence ensued between Cecelia, her representatives and the Pension Bureau, which was located in the nation's capital. It was all enormously frustrating.

One major obstacle was the fact that William's service records were all in the name of Harrison. Major Hedge's misspelling of his surname on William's enlistment papers on December 6, 1863, had come back to haunt her. Another was that Cecelia had no actual proof of her husband's death. Pension officials suspected that William had simply abandoned his wife for another woman. Despite all her protestations that William was a good and faithful husband, there was no way to prove that either. Poor Cecelia's claim had two strikes against it from a bureaucratic point of view.

In investigating her new claim, government agents sought out individuals who had known William during his term of military service. They interviewed his and Cecelia's friends in Louisville, and all of them testified to the strength of the couple's marriage.[36] Sophia Alexander, so good a friend that she said she and Cecelia were like sisters, swore out an affidavit saying that "He seemed like a sober industrious man, was always studying for a living. I never seen him in no way out of the way. His relations with his wife were pleasant. They seemed to get along well together and to be fond of one another." The interviewer then asked if Mrs. Alexander believed Cecelia had taken up with another man after William's disappearance.

> No, she never got any divorce from him. She never would [do] that. She always said, "I wonder what become of Wm.?" She has never married nor, assumed marriage relations with any man, since Wm. Larsen [Larrison] went away. I never saw a man about her house. She has been an honest, hard working woman and has no property and no income or, means of support—only what she works for. She generally washes for rich people, good families that had money.[37]

Cecelia was also required to swear that she had not become someone else's wife after William's departure, with or without benefit of clergy.

The pension officials went to great lengths to refuse her the benefits due her as the legal wife of a presumably deceased veteran. They even went so far as to inquire if Cecelia was actually a widow at the time she wed William Henry Larrison. In response she forwarded to Washington her only copy of her marriage certificate, signed at Rochester in 1862 by Reverend Coit. The matter was, however, settled by Francis Griffin Simpson of Toronto; he confirmed that she had been living with her first husband at the time of

Benjamin's death in 1859.[38] So many of the people she had known in Toronto were dead—William Hickman, Wilson Ruffin Abbot, James Mink, Benjamin Gross, all long passed—that only the much younger Francis Simpson, whom she had met on her return from Liverpool in 1854, was still alive to testify to her marriage there and to the death of her first husband, Benjamin.

Curiously, Francis Simpson's affidavit makes no mention of Cecelia's stepsons or their children. Yet he had purchased his home from Ben after James Thomas died and knew both men well. Ben Alexander Holmes had passed by this time, leaving two sons, both medical men with excellent incomes. James Thomas Holmes and his wife, Mary Ann, had left two daughters, Emma, now thirty-three, and Rebecca Ann, thirty-one, who were living in upstate New York. Cecelia was certainly aware of their whereabouts, for the women had to sign away their rights to Lot 7 on Centre Street to clear the way for sale of Cecelia's land in 1889. Clearly the rift between Cecelia and her stepsons' families had only widened over the years.

On May 6, 1898, Mamie A. Reels made her deposition to the Special Examiner for the US Treasury Board in Louisville. As was becoming a habit with both Mamie and her mother, she chose to shave a few years off her age, suggesting that she had been five rather than eleven when she and her family arrived in Kentucky after the Civil War. Mamie also claimed that she had no recollection of her life before the Larrison family moved to Louisville from Rochester, and that she did not remember a time when her mother and stepfather, William Henry Larrison, were not already living together as a couple.[39]

The wheels of Washington officialdom ground slowly. Cecelia again turned to the family to which she had once belonged for help in navigating the shoals of bureaucracy. Always the closest of the boys to his mother, Fanny's youngest, Rogers, had lived for many years in his mother's home. He had even, at his mother's request, taken Fanny's Thruston surname in

1884. He never married. Fanny seems to have asked Rogers to take a hand in Cecelia's affairs should she ever need help of any kind, although he was clearly not pleased about doing so. He went about matters dutifully, but with a certain contempt for the elderly woman's manifest need. It was all very unpleasant for Cecelia.[40]

Now known as Rogers Clark Ballard Thruston, he was a meticulous record keeper. He was also an elite white Southerner who had grown up in the household of his proslavery grandfather Charles W. Thruston, so Cecelia was not above appealing to his prejudices when she visited him to ask for assistance. When he asked her to explain her defection from his mother's service all those years ago at Niagara Falls, she answered ingenuously that local Blacks "jest took me away." This fed into the common slaveholding mythology of the pre-war years that African Americans were actually happy in their chains, and that it was the blandishments of abolitionists that "enticed" the enslaved to run away, rather than their own overwhelming hunger for liberty.[41]

Describing Cecelia after a visit she made to him at her "old home," he writes: "she is now old and decrepit, blind in one eye and with a cataract on the other."[42] He also explains how his mother's letters to her former maid came into his possession: Cecelia was too proud to ask for a handout and so offered to sell him some of their correspondence. He paid five dollars, adding five cents for streetcar fare to see her home. However, Thruston spoils the impression of kindness with his next words, saying he will have to purchase any remaining letters, but that "it makes little difference for she will call for more money anyhow. She is the last of the old negro slaves to return to her old mistress for aid and support in her declining years . . . My parents did it for the rest of their old slaves, so I suppose I can do it for old Cecelia."[43] If that was his intention, he could well have provided her with more than he apparently did, for she suffered very much from want in old age.

On her next visit, Cecelia attended R. C. Ballard Thruston at his office. The beautiful home that A. J. Ballard had built for his wife and their children in 1867 had been sold. Those high-ceilinged, finely furnished rooms now housed the Detention Home of the Juvenile Court, with separate accommodation for Black and white children.[44] This time, perhaps alarmed by Cecelia's physical condition, Thruston provided more substantial assistance, for he referred Cecelia to no less a personage than William Lindsay, the US senator from Kentucky.

Senator Lindsay was a seemingly odd choice of champion. Republican William McKinley was president, while the Kentucky senator was a Democrat and a former Confederate officer. Although the Republicans held an overwhelming majority in both houses of government, since Lindsay was representative of her home state he was actually in the best possible position to provide Cecelia with the help she needed. On September 22, 1899, Cecelia addressed a letter to the senator. She implored Lindsay to intervene, have her case reopened and "adjudicate it upon the proof filed" in earlier petitions.[45]

In her letter Cecelia refers to depositions by two Union Army veterans, Chauncey Webster and Charles A. Van Horne, who served with William in the 14th New York Heavy Artillery. Van Horne had a particularly clear memory of William Larrison:

> I remember a colored man in the company by the name of Wm. Harrison, or Larrison. I understood that his name was in the rolls as Harrison, but I heard him say during the service that his name was not Harrison, but that it was Larrison. I can't recall that I heard him say why his name was put down as Harrison, though I often heard him say that his name was Larrison and not Harrison. He was generally spoken of as "Billy". He was one of the cooks for the company. I can't recall the name of the other cook, who was also a colored man, but he was commonly called "Hank". I can't recall his last name.[46]

Cecelia also filed her husband's discharge papers and reasonably pointed out that she would not have them in her possession if she were not in truth his widow.

In these years Cecelia continued to live off and on with Mamie and Alexander, but with her typical independence she undertook a series of live-in domestic positions in order to support herself. Serving as a baby nurse did not require the clear vision and close work that fine laundry and mending did, and which her failing sight no longer permitted her to do.[47]

Meanwhile she met periodically with Fanny's youngest son. Thruston always mentions Cecelia with a degree of condescension. By all accounts he was a fine man, a pillar of Louisville society and generous in his support of charitable and cultural causes. He had also become an historian of considerable note, which might have helped him understand more fully the strictures under which African Americans lived in this post–Reconstruction era world, but having never been poor himself, he was unable to sympathize with Cecelia's plight. Too, as a true son of the South, R. C. Ballard Thruston could not empathize with the problems facing an elderly and ailing Black woman who had once, a great many years earlier, been his mother's slave. Mistaking her age at the time of her escape to Canada, after one meeting with Cecelia he wrote: "Cecelia ran off when she was only 20 years old, and that over fifty years ago. I fail to see any legal or moral claim on the family for support but Mother seemed to recognize some such obligation, or entertained some such desire for she left Cecelia a legacy."[48]

Although he did refer her to Senator Lindsay, very little money changed hands between Fanny's youngest son and the woman who had once served his family so faithfully. Cecelia sent the first of four letters addressed to Thruston on March 31, 1898. Written in a careful, precise hand, it requested a loan of $4.40 to pay for an eye specialist, as the Pension Board required a medical certificate testifying to the poor condition of Cecelia's eyesight. The letter concludes: "if you would be kind enough to let me have that amount if I get my Pension it will be returned to you."[49]

He responded positively, recording in his ledger for April 1898: "Donations re: Dr. T. A. Bullington on [blank] of Cecelia J. Larrison (colored), $4.50." One may judge the degree of both his personal wealth and his charity towards poor Cecelia by another note on the same page: "Donations re: 1/3 of $3,250.00 paid for Westminster Peal of 4 bells placed by my brothers and me in Christ Church Cathedral, Louisville, Ky., in memory of my parents, $1,083.33."[50] The April 10, 1898, edition of the Louisville *Courier-Journal* announced the service of dedication for the bells. Bishop Dudley, who officiated, said that he hoped they might ring out "a solace to the sick and a grace for the dying, and that those who rang the bells might be inspired with a devout spirit."[51] One can well imagine the thoughts on hearing this of an old African American woman who slipped into one of the back pews to pay her last respects to the woman she had known and loved since she herself was a baby.

Cecelia's second letter to Thruston, of February 14, 1899, updated him on the progress of her application and asked for a little money to purchase coal for heating purposes, as she had slipped on some ice and "hurt my self very bad and I am not able to do any thing. I have not got my pension yet but I will pay you back as soon as I get it." The third note she sent him contained truly tragic news. It describes Cecelia's "distress about the death of my son-in-law this morning at 2 o'clock" and went on to ask: "Will you please let me have a few dollars . . . as I would like to get me a little something to norish me. He has been sick 4 months in bed."

Although it is unlikely they were actually without food, the family's situation was bad enough. Alexander L. Reels died on September 12, 1899. Mamie and her mother had given up their jobs to nurse him after he suffered a massive stroke at the age of sixty-three. While Alexander's son James, who worked for a coal dealer, did his best to assist, he had his own family to provide for. Mamie's strong, protective and very ambitious husband was reduced to bedridden helplessness. He was treated by one of Louisville's few Black physicians, Dr. Stone.[52] Remembering that he was always working towards the finer things in life, his widow and the mother-in-law to whom he had always been so kind spent their last dollar on giving him a respectable funeral. Alexander was laid to rest by African American undertaker William Watson, whose horses and carriages were so beautiful that they were routinely rented by Louisville's white undertakers.[53]

The death of Alexander L. Reels had a catastrophic effect on the lives of his widow and his increasingly frail mother-in-law. Months of ill health had ruined Alexander's business, and with it, the family finances. Without the rents from her Toronto property that had always sustained Cecelia and her family through lean times, the issue of her Union Army widow's pension gained new urgency. There was nothing left to sell. What little Cecelia had retained from her earlier, much more comfortable life had been lost in the 1884 flood at their College Street address. She had not even a photograph of William, the husband she had adored and whom everyone remembered as a "loving and kind and a quiet man" who was extremely fond of his wife.[54]

The last surviving note from Cecelia Jane Larrison to Fanny's youngest son was written a few days after Alexander's funeral. On September 27, 1899, she asked that Thruston directly address Colonel Evans at the Pension Bureau, confirming "my condition in poverty and blindness . . . I have just forwarded on two affidavits calling up my claim again." This last plea for assistance must have fallen on more sympathetic ears. Later that autumn, Cecelia's attorney in Washington informed her that her pension benefits were forthcoming. She received the first payment on October 11, 1899.

By this time American race relations had reached their lowest ebb since the end of the Civil War. Frederick Douglass had died in 1895, and a year later the US Supreme Court rang the death knell for the aspirations of millions of Black Americans in their ongoing determination to finally be accepted—and respected—as American citizens. For millions, *Plessy v. Ferguson* extinguished the expectations that a better day was coming, engendered by Abraham Lincoln's Emancipation Proclamation in 1863. Just as Judge Roger Taney's Dred Scott decision had denied African

Americans citizenship in 1857, the courts in 1896 decided that the Fourteenth Amendment, which provided for equal protection under the law, did not guarantee all Americans the same access to facilities and institutions. Those whose ancestors had been carried from Africa to American shores were entitled only to accommodations that were "separate but equal" to those available to their white contemporaries. Black Americans were well aware that *separate* would never mean *equal*.

Interestingly, the dissenting opinion against legalizing segregation at the federal level was delivered by a Kentuckian. Republican Supreme Court justice John Marshall Harlan wrote that the American Constitution "neither knows nor tolerates classes among citizens. In respect of civil rights, all citizens are equal before the law. The humblest is the peer of the most powerful. The law regards man as man, and takes no account of his surroundings or of his color when his civil rights as guaranteed by the supreme law of the land are involved."[55]

Although Cecelia could not know it, this new legislation further inflamed the gaping wound that existed between Black and white America. It was one that would not begin to be healed until the peaceful agitation of Reverend Martin Luther King Jr.—and all the valiant people who marched with him—helped bring the Civil Rights Act into being in 1964. She would not be there to see it.

CHAPTER 17
I'll Fly Away

Those are the same stars, and that is the same moon,
that look down upon your brothers and sisters,
and which they see as they look up to them,
though they are ever so far away from us, and each other.

—Sojourner Truth[1]

WILLIAM'S MILITARY PENSION WOULD help make the last decade of her life less onerous, although the monthly twelve-dollar stipend to which Cecelia was entitled did not go far. The prideful and upright Cecelia would have been loath to see it that way, but the industrious Mamie became her mother's prop during her declining years. She continued to go out to work as a nurse, sharing rooms with the aging Cecelia in a series of tenements. Finally they sold off their last bits of furniture and china and moved into a boarding house at 829 West Broadway.[2] Far to the west of downtown, this was now part of an almost entirely Black district. In Louisville, residential segregation had come into practice long before it was codified in law.[3] With Fanny dead, there was no longer any need for Cecelia to reside within walking distance of the old Ballard home at Walnut and Floyd.

Cecelia Larrison had been sixty-eight when Alexander Reels passed away. Her eyesight failing, she developed kidney trouble as well. After

October 1906 she found she could no longer go out to work. This strong and resilient little woman was being laid low at last by a combination of blindness and age. There was a worldwide recession as well, further straining the two women's finances, and in 1908 Mamie had to stop working to nurse her mother through her last, lingering illness. They were reduced to living on Cecelia's pension, and perhaps some assistance from James Reels and from the fraternal orders to which Mamie and Alexander Reels had belonged during his lifetime, Cecelia's own memberships having all lapsed when she "got infinancial," as Mrs. Ellis put it. The days of skating parties enjoyed by the Reels children and notices in the society columns of Louisville's Black newspapers were but a distant memory.

But the deeply loving bond that existed between Cecelia and her only surviving child remained undiminished through all the joys and sorrows she and her daughter had experienced together. On June 4, 1909, Cecelia Jane Larrison died of acute nephritis, or kidney failure. In a letter that her physician, Dr. W. T. Hayes, provided to support Mamie's claim to the Pension Bureau in Washington, he said that in all his years of practice he had never seen a daughter more solicitous of her mother's welfare or more willing to sacrifice herself to her care.[4]

The Louisville *Courier-Journal* of June 7, 1909, carried Cecelia's obituary: "LARRISON: Entered into eternal life, Cecelia Jane Larrison, beloved mother of Mrs. Mamie Reels, at her residence 829 West Broadway, after a lingering illness. Funeral will take place this afternoon from Quinn Chapel, 9th and Walnut streets, at 2 p.m. Friends of the family are invited to attend without further notice." The ceremony was conducted by Reverend J. C. Anderson of the Quinn AME Chapel.[5] The minister had served at St. James Church, St. Paul, Minnesota, until September 1900. Since Walter and Eugene Holmes had occasionally attended while at university there, one wonders if Anderson ever made the connection between the two families and let Cecelia know how well Benjamin's grandsons were doing. Those two young men did not, however, seek any connection with Cecelia, the elderly soul responsible for so much of their father's and uncle's early upbringing in Toronto.

Cecelia Jane Larrison, née Reynolds, was interred at Eastern Cemetery in a plot that the faithful Mamie had purchased for her. Cecelia finally found a resting place in her home soil, and she lies there yet, though no monument was ever placed in her memory. This very special woman was seventy-eight when she died. Typically for those who followed the paths of the Underground Railroad out of the slave South, the most tangible legacy left behind by Cecelia Jane Reynolds and the two good men she married was their children. Brought up under the proverbial paw of the British lion, they flowered into adults who were fully prepared to take their place in a civil society that recognized both their humanity and their right to self-determination. These hopes were not to be realized in their day, nor even in our own. But despite ongoing social and economic exclusion based on race, heirs to the freedom-seekers have continued to agitate for the rights promised long ago in those brilliant, optimistic words set down by America's Founding Fathers when they drafted the Declaration of Independence.

Mamie and her half-brothers, Ben and James Holmes, had grown up armed with the best tools their parents and the African American expatriate community of antebellum Toronto could provide. Each navigated the barriers that white society erected against their progress in his or her own fashion. Despite the excellence of his training in Lowell and the support of the barbers' guild, James Thomas had been broken by the struggle, although his two daughters went on to live long and fruitful lives. Brother Ben and his white wife, Lucia, finally found a place in their adopted Minnesota home, where honour and good works counted for more in the eyes of their neighbours than their interracial marriage did. As for Walter and Eugene Holmes, the two grandsons Cecelia's first husband did not live to see, they went on to surmount every obstacle in their paths, the elder in particular enjoying a stellar career in quite an unlikely place.

Mamie continued her struggles on her mother's behalf, even after Cecelia's death. The Pension Bureau was by then attached to the US

Treasury Department, and it held up the reimbursement due for the burial of a veteran's widow on a minor technicality: undertaker T. H. Hankin's funeral home had recorded a different date for Cecelia's passing than did Dr. Hayes on her death certificate.[6] Eventually Mamie received a reduced stipend of $12.40, and the file on William Henry Larrison and his much-loved wife Cecelia was closed forever.[7]

What Mamie Reels did afterwards is truly inspiring—she simply spread her wings and flew. At the age of fifty-eight, Mamie showed herself fully the equal of her venturesome mother by following what was called a generation earlier the "Exodusters."[8] Post–Civil War America had seen the migration of hundreds of thousands of newly enfranchised Black Americans to the nation's expanding frontier. Pushed by racial persecution, the rise of sharecropping in place of outright slavery in much of the South, and the indignities of Jim Crow–style segregation, they were attracted by the availability of land and new opportunity in the far western reaches of the continent. They packed up families, furniture and often livestock to begin the long trek, first to Kansas, then to Oklahoma and finally to Nebraska and beyond. Among the thousands of optimistic migrants was Mamie Reels.

Leaving Louisville three years after her mother's passing, Mamie settled in Guthrie, about thirty miles north of Oklahoma City. This rapidly growing town, not yet three decades old, had begun as a tent city and the epicentre of the April 1889 land boom that opened Oklahoma to incoming settlers. Mamie had again found herself a man who loved her, and there, as the bells rang in the New Year on December 31, 1912, she became the wife of Civil War veteran Newson Alexander.[9] He was a homeowner and self-employed businessman who was already a familiar figure in the town; according to the *Oklahoma Guide* of January 2, 1913, "Mr. Alexander, the paper hanger, took unto himself a better half last Tuesday night."

Mamie may have moved west specifically to join her new husband. Newson Alexander belonged to the Grand Army of the Republic (GAR), the same Union Army veterans' association that her first husband, Alexander Reels, and also her long-lost stepfather, William, were eligible to join. Not only had the GAR held its grand Encampment at Louisville in 1895, her first husband had also been active in the Grand United Order of Odd Fellows. As the wife of a veteran, Mamie had therefore been eligible to join its women's auxiliary, the Household of Ruth, which was popular in both Louisville and Guthrie, Oklahoma. State-based chapters of the various fraternal orders came together with great fanfare in annual Grand Lodges, opportunities for people like Newson and Mamie to become acquainted with members resident in far-flung parts of the United States.

There were other opportunities for them to have met as well. Louisville church groups and women's associations regularly met with their counterparts in other states, and the Sisters of the Mysterious Ten in particular had branches in both Louisville and Guthrie.[10] Local and regional African American organizing was on the cusp of the development of national societies. The Niagara Movement had begun at the very spot where Cecelia took her first frightening, exhilarating steps towards freedom. Under the leadership of W. E. B. Du Bois in 1905, the group's first meeting had to be held on the Canadian side of the border for safety's sake. This had grown by 1909 into the first incarnation of the National Association for the Advancement of Colored People (NAACP). Women's societies were moving forward at a similar pace, and within the next few years activists such as Mary Church Terrell, who in 1896 had planted the first seeds of the National Council of Colored Women, would also see the foundation of the highly influential National Council of Negro Women, with offices in Washington and chapters across the United States.

Mamie's groom had been born in Tennessee. Newson, along with his mother and siblings, was free.[11] The Alexanders migrated to South Alton, Madison County, Illinois, in 1872. Part of what archaeologist and Underground Railroad historian Cheryl LaRoche calls the "geography of resistance," this region had seen major Underground Railroad activity before the Civil War. It was home to Lyman Trumbull, who chaired the Senate Judiciary Committee in his close friend Abraham Lincoln's administration and drafted the Thirteenth Amendment to the American Constitution. The region attracted many Southern Blacks after the conflict ended; they purchased farms, built churches and schools and formed their own small but flourishing communities.[12]

When Mamie married Newson Alexander, she gained adult siblings who considered her part of the family in ways that Ben and James Thomas Holmes never had, and with whom she and her husband were in regular contact. Newson's sister Margiana was the wife of Civil War veteran William P. Winn, who had served in Company D of the 18th US Colored Troops. They had moved to Monticello, in Platt County, Illinois, where William had his own barbershop.[13] Newson's youngest sister, Sarah Jane, married Edward Comley; in 1910 they moved to Faribault, Minnesota, and there raised their children, Pleasant and Clarence Comley.[14] Both Ben Alexander Holmes and his wife Lucia were dead by that time, and it is doubtful that anyone would have made the connection between their family and the now-deceased Cecelia and her stepchildren in any case.

In common with thousands of Southern Blacks who sought new beginnings west of the Mississippi after the Civil War, Newson had first set his sights on Kansas, which despite its bloody beginnings as a state had become a destination for African Americans migrating out of the South.[15] By 1880 nearly forty thousand African Americans had made their home there, including intrepid migrants educated in the fine grammar school that Reverend William King had established in Buxton, Canada West—and some from Grey and Simcoe Counties, north and west of Toronto as well—for there were African Canadians inspired by the vision of the American West who chose Kansas as their postwar home, while some went to Nebraska.

Dissatisfied with his prospects in Kansas, Newson moved on to Oklahoma and settled in Guthrie in 1889. It was a rough-and-ready place in those days. The Kansas, Illinois, Indiana and other western papers were filled with news of clashes between early squatters, whose land rights were not protected when the land boom began, and occasionally with the disenfranchised Native Americans, for this was former "Indian territory." However, for people like Mamie and Newson Alexander and some fifty thousand other would-be pioneers, Oklahoma promised both free agricultural land and a chance to start again in a place where the possibility of political equality and freedom from white domination beckoned.

On April 15, 1889, the *Daily Register* of Rockford, Illinois, reported: "some fifty or more families of negroes have left Fort Smith, Ark[ansas], for the vicinity of Guthrie, Oklahoma, where they and numerous other colored people will establish a colony." They did not know what they were heading for, but they knew they were leaving behind the grinding poverty, racial violence and political exclusion that characterized the "New South." This was the period when the Democratic Party reasserted itself, and state after Southern state gerrymandered voting districts, formulating impossibly difficult citizenship tests, demanding proof of literacy and imposing "grandfather clauses" (the profoundly racist origin of the modern expression) requiring that each new voter prove that his grandfather had also enjoyed the franchise.

The failure of the Republican Party and long-time Democratic domination of the "solid South" left Black Americans without either protection or political leverage. As the African American paper the Atlanta *Independent* noted on July 7, 1906, "We have nothing left us for civic and moral development except our secret orders. We have been successfully eliminated from the politics of the South and we have nothing left to help us develop a useful and helpful citizenship except the church and secret societies."

White-owned papers countered with warnings of a Black land rush in Oklahoma and a "Plot to make it a Negro State."[16] Indeed there were dreams in that direction, for anything seemed possible in these wide western lands. Incoming African Americans founded thirty-two all-Black towns. One was

Langston, Oklahoma, which had its own town council and newspaper. Schools and colleges were established there for Black youth who were looking to take up opportunities denied them in the post-Reconstruction South.

In moving to Oklahoma, Mamie had thereby entered a kind of a promised land for African America. By 1892 Guthrie's population of ten thousand was about one-third Black and included several city officials: a justice of the peace, a member of the school board, a city councillor and two police officers. There was a Black attorney, several physicians and many shop owners. Her husband, unlike most of the town's African American residents, had already given up on the old party of Lincoln. In the wake of Reconstruction, the Republicans had proven themselves less and less willing to promote the rights of African Americans. Newson Alexander became a Democrat and ran for municipal office, as reported by the *Guthrie Daily Leader* of March 31, 1894:

The Democracy, always progressive, and recognizing the number and influence of the colored population of this city, honored N. M. Alexander by conferring on him the nomination from the Fifth Ward. Mr. Alexander is a gentleman of high character, and believes that the ultimate destiny of the negro is linked with that of the Democratic party. He has studied closely political ethics, and arrived at this conclusion from deduction, and not from fancy. He is a man of property, and has the highest respect for all who know him, regardless of color.

Unfortunately Newson was not elected and the Republicans continued to stack the school board of a city where education, under the influence of powerful men in political office, would soon be entirely segregated.[17] By 1912, when Mamie arrived, Oklahoma's racial climate had already deteriorated. A majority of African Americans remained Republicans, producing "indignation meetings" on the part of white settlers, who had migrated there mainly from the Southern states, bringing their racial attitudes with them. They would eventually impose the strictest segregation on the state's Black settlers. Oklahoma instituted Jim Crow laws that required railroads to provide separate cars and accommodations in stations for Blacks and whites. The "grandfather clause" was added to the state constitution to disenfranchise men who had previously been registered to vote.[18] But African Americans continued to push forward their agenda of self-help and self-improvement in hopes of a better day. The *Oklahoma Guide* shows that Mamie's new husband donated one dollar to the Excelsior Club in 1909. Literate himself, he was giving of his meagre earnings to an African American women's organization that had in 1908 begun a lending library "for the race" in Guthrie City.[19]

The evolving racial prejudice and ever-present threat of violence sent hundreds of Blacks in search of yet another place to live. Advertising by the Canadian government lured African American farmers with the promise of free land in the western provinces of Saskatchewan, Manitoba and Alberta. After several hundred Oklahoma Black families crossed the border, white Canadians complained to federal authorities. The welcome once afforded Cecelia and Benjamin Holmes as passengers on the Underground Railroad had given way in Mamie's middle age to practical if not legal rejection of Black social and political aspirations on the part of white Canada. The venerable Imperial Order of the Daughters of the Empire petitioned Ottawa to halt further African American immigration, citing the hoary racist chestnut that white women on isolated prairie farms might become prey to the sexual aggression of Black men. Canada sent agents to Oklahoma to persuade preachers and community leaders to counsel would-be emigrants against coming to so unhospitable a land as Canada was proving itself to be.[20]

Himself too old to fight, Newson Alexander and his wife, Mamie, saw the sons of their friends enthusiastically volunteer for service when the First World War broke out. Their patriotism was proven by mass enlistment—more than five thousand African Oklahomans served in the US forces.

However, their return four years later was accompanied by increased European immigration. Such heightened competition for jobs was always a spark to the tinder of American racial unrest. Into this powder keg Kentucky filmmaker D. W. Griffith tossed his monument to the myth of white superiority, *The Birth of a Nation*, in 1915. This encomium to the Ku Klux Klan packed cinemas across the American West, enhancing the secret society's attractions for new recruits and legitimizing mob attacks on innocent Blacks, who were all too often subjected to torturous deaths as lynchings became public spectacles.

At the same time, fears of "Bolshevik infiltration," aroused by the rise of Communism in Russia and the subsequent imprisonment and execution of Tsar Nicholas and his family, heightened nativist sentiments and lent another weapon to the white supremacist arsenal. Organizations such as the NAACP were suspected of Communist infiltration and were nearly helpless in the face of the overwhelming tide of anti-Black sentiment. In the *New York Times* of October 5, 1919, an article appeared with the following title: "FOR ACTION ON RACE RIOT PERIL: Radical Propaganda Among Negroes Growing, and Increase of Mob Violence Set Out in Senate Brief for Federal Inquiry" and subheadings such as "The War's Responsibility," "Reds Inflaming Blacks" and "Industrial Clashes."[21] Even more overtly, the *Times* on October 19 published a follow-up article: "Reds Are Working Among Negroes."

Mamie and her husband watched in horror as the Ku Klux Klan gained members, arousing a marked increase in racial persecution in Oklahoma.[22] There was also labour unrest. Oklahoma's white paperhangers and painters were members of the Painter's Union, which went on strike in February 1920.[23] Wallpaper and paint companies held firm for a time and then began to employ African Americans skilled in the trades, one of whom was Mamie's husband, Newson, to break the back of the union. Inevitably, violence followed. What was dubbed by Black poet and NAACP agent James Weldon Johnson the "Red Summer" of 1919 culminated in the 1921

Tulsa Riots, which saw the destruction of more than a thousand homes and businesses and upwards of three hundred deaths—the true numbers have never been ascertained.[24]

But by that time the Alexanders had already fled Oklahoma for the relative safety of Kansas City, Missouri. It was one of the more stable metropolises of the American Midwest.[25] The Black population of Kansas City was 30,893 out of about 225,000 people overall, and there were almost 20,000 more people living in adjacent counties. Mamie and her husband moved into the African American commercial and residential district centred on 18th Street at Vine and set up housekeeping in a home owned by Sarah Fields. She was the widow of Harrison Fields, a cousin of Newson Alexander, also from Illinois.

The extended Fields-Alexander family lived at 1812 Charlotte Street in a small frame shotgun house with a porch that ran the width of the home. Handily, since Newson Alexander was a self-employed paperhanger, just to the north along 18th Street were two shops advertising paint and wallpaper. These provided him with both referrals to potential customers and the material needs for his vocation. Newson had always made a good living, and Mamie was listed in the census for 1920 as a housewife; unlike the vast majority of Black women in the city, and in keeping with her previous status as a Louisville housewife, she did not go out to work.[26]

Despite the ongoing pernicious fact of racial discrimination and a profoundly corrupt local political scene, this was in some ways a wonderful place to live in those years. The period immediately following the Great War was one of real prosperity and growth for Kansas City's African American population. Mamie's aging husband was one of many skilled African Americans employed in the local building trades. They lived in what was known as the Church Hill neighbourhood, where during the first decades of the twentieth century more than 90 percent of the population was Black. The community's two major churches, the Allen AME (1866) and Second Baptist (1865), occupied opposite corners at 10th and Charlotte, just a few blocks from Mamie's new home, and the Lincoln School, founded in 1867, was the first for African American children and a magnet for their families. This was a fully developed all-Black neighbourhood, with places of entertainment, restaurants, boarding houses, saloons and movie theatres, providing its residents with opportunities prohibited to them by the whites-only rules in so many establishments outside the district.[27] The area boasted the Black-owned Security and Investment Association, begun in 1922; the first African American–owned automobile dealership, started in 1923 in the Roberts Building at 1826–30 Vine Street; and the first dry cleaning establishment owned by a Black man in the entire United States, located at 1814 Vine Street.[28]

These were the days of the Harlem Renaissance, and both artistic and industrial endeavours highlighted the talents and creativity of the "New Negro" under leadership provided by such men as W. E. B. Du Bois and Marcus Garvey, the Jamaican founder of the United Negro Improvement Association. In Kansas City the era saw the establishment of the Paseo YMCA and of the influential newspaper published by Chester Arthur Franklin, *The Call*.[29] As part of this flourishing community Mamie and her husband had the opportunity to hear readings by the great Black poet Langston Hughes, who dominated the literary scene, and to view the works of artist Aaron Douglass (originally of Topeka, Kansas), who was a major local cultural figure.[30]

Mamie's years in Kansas City saw a real flowering of African American music, too, exemplified in the unmistakable "Kansas City sound" of jazz music played by big bands in the district's places of entertainment. Prohibition began in 1920, but rampant political corruption meant that Kansas City became known as a "wide-open" city where prosecution for liquor sales and consumption was not an issue.[31] Ragtime, popularized by Scott Joplin, had been the rage in the many clubs at the east end of 12th Street. Jazz brought both money and fame to Black performers, and more than 120 nightclubs and dancehalls were in operation, mainly in the 18th and Vine area, where the Alexanders made their home.

Fraternal orders were the mainstay of Black society there, so Mamie and her husband may well have been among the attendees at the 38th Grand Lodge held in their new hometown by the Grand United Order of Odd Fellows (GUOOF), jointly with the Household of Ruth, in the summer of 1921. According to the *Kansas City Advocate* of July 21, "Odd Fellows and Household of Ruth Were Given the City This Week." Accompanied by church services, ceremonies were held at the Sumner High School. Other activities included "contest drills" between the GUOOF, the Knights of Pythias, the Knights of Labor and other fraternal orders active in the area; a picnic attended by all the groups, hosted by the Household of Ruth at Heathwood Park; and performances by church choirs and their soloists and by bands associated with the various orders. The July 29, 1921, edition of the *Topeka* (Kansas) *Plaindealer*, another African American paper, mentions that an accomplishment of the past year was the creation of a burial fund for members of the Household of Ruth.[32]

The Alexanders could also enjoy sporting events. The great American pastime of baseball was fully segregated, leading to the rise of African American teams. Some early players had travelled with the All Nations barnstorming team in the period immediately before the First World War, while others had played for the 25th Infantry Wreckers while stationed at Fort Huachuca while in the service. This was the heyday of Black baseball, and Kansas City dominated the Negro National League established in 1920.[33]

Newson and Mamie Alexander left Kansas City after the death of their landlady in 1922. They moved in with Newson's relatives in Carrollton, Illinois. His health was failing, and Mamie lost her second husband on March 6, 1927, at the age of seventy-nine. Newson M. Alexander was buried in the Carrolton City Cemetery three days later.[34]

The widowed Mamie was homesick for her Kentucky home and the friends she had known there, so she moved back to Louisville. Her only remaining family there was her stepson by her first marriage, James S. Reels, who had a good job as a porter and doorman at the German-owned Ewald

Iron Company, 231 West Main Street.[35] At seventy-three years old, Cecelia's daughter again found herself a position in domestic service, this time as a housekeeper. Mamie also renewed her membership in the Household of Ruth, her eligibility assured as the widow of not one but two members of the Grand United Order of Odd Fellows.

Mamie Alexander is listed in the 1927 directory for Louisville as a domestic servant living at 547 South 11th Street, and in 1928 at the same address but this time as a cook. By then Mamie was spending her off-hours at 1619 West Chestnut Street, boarding in the home of a woman she had known in her earlier years in the city. Bertha Hastings was a fellow nurse and an active member of the Household of Ruth. It was there, cared for by friends who loved her, that Cecelia's only surviving daughter endured a lingering and sadly painful death from breast cancer. She passed away on March 16, 1928, and was laid to rest in a plot owned by the Household of Ruth, her burial paid for by insurance she had purchased through her membership over the years.[36]

By the time Mamie died in Kentucky, her two stepbrothers, Ben Alexander and James Thomas Holmes, had already passed away. After the breakup of his marriage, James T. Holmes had closed his Peterborough barbershop in about 1866 and gone to Toronto, where he looked after his stepmother's property for a year or two. He soon followed his wife and children to upstate New York. Cecelia's younger stepson must have died in about 1875, for in that year Mary Ann (Johnson) Holmes remarried. Her second, much younger, husband was William H. Coleman, also from Virginia. He had worked as a farmhand for a white family in West Bloomfield, New York, about twenty-five miles south of Rochester. At the time of their marriage, Coleman already owned a home in Rochester's Ward 2. It was right downtown and in a predominantly white district west of the Genesee River. He was twenty-four and his bride, the former Mrs. Mary Ann Holmes, was thirty-three.

Mary Ann's new husband had a good position as a porter at the Osburn House hotel. He became stepfather to Emma and Rebecca Holmes, who were eleven and nine, and the Colemans set up housekeeping in the frame house they shared with Mary Ann's youngest sister and her husband, Rebecca and Augustus Bloxom.[37] The widowed Ann Johnson, Mary Ann and Rebecca's mother, also lived with the family (interestingly, the British-born Mrs. Johnson was the only person in the household who could not read or write). The family was part of the tight-knit Rochester Black community that Cecelia and her husband William had known before the Civil War. Of the people she had once known, Amy Post was still in Rochester and continuing to agitate for civil and suffrage rights, especially for women,[38] but the Douglass family had departed for Washington, DC, after a terrible fire burned all their papers and most of their household goods.

Emma and her sister were very fond of their stepfather and adopted his surname; as adults they were known as Emma and Annie Coleman. Their mother passed away in 1882 at the age of forty-three and was laid to rest in Mount Hope Cemetery. In 1890 Emma, twenty-seven, was working as a domestic servant, while Rebecca (Annie) at twenty-five was a cook. By 1892 the sisters, who were very close, had moved from Rochester to Syracuse, New York.[39]

In 1899 Emma Coleman, then thirty-six, became the wife of Stephen Lewis Watkins. Born in New York State, he had relations on both sides of the US–Canadian border. Emma and her husband lived in Jordan Village, Onondaga County. It was a very small place just west of Syracuse, and they were the only Black family there. Their home was mortgaged, but they did own it, and Stephen Watkins worked as a farm labourer. Through the Watkins connection Emma and her sister became part of an extended Black community that resided in Auburn, Syracuse, Rochester, Canandaigua, Buffalo and many of the smaller places in between. The district had a long and proud abolitionist and reforming past, and routes of the Underground Railroad had run through its churches, basements and barns for nearly half a century.[40]

Benjamin's granddaughters would have known Harriet Tubman, for she and several family members whom she had rescued from Maryland slavery

21. Ad for the barbershop of Cecelia's younger stepson, James Thomas Holmes, in downtown Peterborough, Canada West (now Ontario). *Fuller's Counties of Peterborough & Victoria Directory, for 1865 & 1866.*

22. Home of John Craig and his son-in-law, Rochester's wealthiest businessman, Daniel W. Powers, where Cecelia was employed while in Rochester, later headquarters of the Boy Scouts of America.

23. Ad for the barbershop of Cecelia's elder stepson, Benjamin Alexander Holmes, in Lindsay, Canada West. He and his family moved to Faribault, Minnesota, in 1865. *Fuller's Counties of Peterborough & Victoria Directory, for 1865 & 1866.*

24. Ambrotype of the great African American abolitionist and newspaper publisher Frederick Douglass in 1856, as Cecelia knew him at Rochester, New York.

25. Wilson and Ellen Abbott's son, Anderson Ruffin Abbott, was the first Canadian-born Black doctor. He served as a surgeon for the United States Colored Troops and was in Washington, DC, while Cecelia was there during the Civil War. Dr. Abbott attended President Lincoln on his deathbed and was given the shawl the president had worn to his inauguration as a gift from Mary Todd Lincoln.

Jany 17. Mr. Henry Larrison, from Newark Co. Del. went to Wilmington, on fot. on Sat. 12th inst. Sent forward by Thos. Garrett. Was married a month ago, but his master promising to sell him, & by avarice giving him permission to go to Wilmington, he improved y' oppy., which he long wished for, to escape.

26. Handwritten record by Underground Railroad stationmaster and newspaper publisher Sidney Howard Gay, describing the escape of Cecelia's second husband, William Henry Larrison, from his New Castle County, Delaware, owners.

27. African American undercook at City Point, Virginia. The heavy equipment William Larrison was forced to carry, first as an undercook and later as a cook for the 14th New York Heavy Artillery Regiment, left him partially disabled, a major factor in Cecelia's decision to move her family to Louisville in 1865.

28. Cecelia's former mistress and long-time correspondent, Fanny Thruston Ballard.

29. Fanny's husband, Andrew Jackson Ballard, clerk of the US District Court in Kentucky.

30. Rogers Clark Ballard Thruston, Fanny's youngest son, who assisted Cecelia in her old age. The portrait was painted by Jules Aviat in 1906, when Cecelia was in regular contact with Thruston.

31. The Thruston home on Walnut Street, at Floyd, where Cecelia visited Fanny, was built on the site of Cecelia's childhood home in slavery. It was designed in 1866 by noted architect Henry Whitestone and was considered a showpiece.

32. Green Street (now Liberty), near Alexander and Mamie Reels's home and second-hand furniture shop. The busy corner with trams and electrical power lines above was part of a largely Jewish district just a few blocks north of Fanny and A. J. Ballard's Walnut Street home.

34. Cecelia worked caring for infants and small children after her sight began to fail. Some of the spirit of this kindly and courageous woman comes through in images such as this of African American nursemaids caring for white children.

Mr. A. L. Reels will shortly open an auction and commission house on the west side of First street, between Market and Jefferson streets. This house will be a branch of the main store on the southwest corner of First and Green streets. Mr. Reels is an enterprising business man and the first one among the race here to enter into this field. THE FREEMAN correspond-

33. Mamie's husband, Alexander Reels, was an excellent businessman. The following announcement appeared in the New York *Freeman* of April 10, 1886. It was this plan that encouraged Cecelia to sell her Toronto property and invest in the business of her future son-in-law.

LARRISON—Entered into eternal life, Cecilia Jane Larrison, beloved mother of Mrs. Mamie Reels, at her residence, 829 West Broadway, after a lingering illness.

Funeral will take place this afternoon from Quinn's chapel, Ninth and Walnut streets, at 2 p. m. Friends of the family are invited to attend without further notice. —

35. The funeral of Cecelia Jane Larrison took place at Louisville's historic Quinn Chapel, with Reverend J. C. Anderson performing the service. Louisville *Courier-Journal*, June 7, 1909.

36. Dr. Walter B. Holmes, Ada, Minnesota. This is the only known image of any member of Cecelia's family. Dr. Holmes was the first Black doctor to graduate from the University of Minnesota Medical School, and the Medical Officer of Health for Norman County, Minnesota.

37. Guthrie had a very large Black community, including J. W. Matthews, whose shop is pictured here. One of the men standing in front may have been Mamie's second husband, Newson Alexander, a Civil War veteran.

38. Cecelia's eldest stepson, Ben Alexander Holmes (1839–1896), and his European American wife, Lucia Holt Holmes (1841–1901), were buried far from their original Lindsay, Ontario, home. They lie in Maple Lawn Cemetery, at Faribault, Minnesota. Why both death dates are incorrect on their tombstones remains a mystery.

39. Below is the only known image of Benjamin and Cecelia's home on Centre Street; it shows later additions made during its ownership by shoemaker and community spokesman Francis G. Simpson. The University Avenue Armouries in the foreground (demolished in 1963) were constructed in 1891 and opened in 1894.

Residence of Cecelia and Benjamin Holmes

AERIAL VIEW OF EXCAVATED FOUNDATION
CECELIA AND BENJAMIN HOLMES RESIDENCE

40. Cecelia lived with her new husband, Benjamin, in this Centre Street home between 1846 and 1859, when he passed away. It provided rental income until she sold it in 1889 to Francis G. Simpson.

41. Black porcelain doll head belonging to the child of one of Cecelia and Benjamin's Centre Street neighbours. It was found on property owned by Black barber Edward Jones.

42. African American minstrel figurine recovered from a lot owned by barber Edward Jones.

43. This plate decorated with a scene of Eliza crossing the ice, from *Uncle Tom's Cabin*, was found in a privy next to Cecelia's Centre Street property.

made their home in nearby Auburn. After serving throughout the Civil War as a nurse, scout and spy, she had returned to upstate New York, where she married, late in life, another Union Army veteran named Nelson Davis. Some twenty-two years her junior, Davis had been wounded and did not expect to live long. He wanted Harriet, denied financial recognition for her military service by the same draconian bureaucrats who had made it so difficult for Cecelia to receive her due, to have his pension. To everyone's surprise he lived for many years and the marriage was a happy one. She lost none of her zeal for helping others as she grew older. Harriet Tubman spent her later life working for the cause of women's suffrage and opened a home for aged and infirm Black women who had no other place to go.[41]

After Emma's marriage, Rebecca "Annie" Coleman boarded with the family of Frank and Adeline Bailey in Ward 16 of Syracuse.[42] Frank Bailey was a music teacher whose father was of West Indian origin. Rebecca was working as a domestic, likely for white employers. Ten years later she went to live with her sister's family in Jordan Village, for Emma was very ill and needed the loving nursing that only her sister could provide. Emma Watkins died in 1911 and was buried in Maple Grove Cemetery there. Rebecca Ann went back to Rochester, where she continued in service almost until her own death in December 1945. She was laid to rest in Mount Hope Cemetery. Neither of Benjamin's two granddaughters bore children, but Stephen Lewis Watkins moved out to Ohio after his wife's death to join a daughter from his first marriage there, and her descendants honour his memory.

Of all the children raised in the households headed by Cecelia and her two husbands, it was Benjamin's older son, Ben Alexander Holmes, and his family who finally attained the lofty goals their parents had set for them. In 1865 Ben and Lucia left Lindsay for a new home in Faribault, in southeast Minnesota.[43] They were in search of a place where their interracial family could be free of the countless insults, snubs and more overt threats to which such families were subjected in the smaller towns of the Canadian countryside.[44]

The couple and their two little boys travelled from Canada West to Minnesota to join Lucia's older sister, Mariam. She married George H. French in Lowell, Massachusetts, in 1847 and had moved out to Sumner, Iowa, about 165 miles southeast of Faribault, by 1860.[45] The Holmes and French families were soon joined by several others of Lucia Holt Holmes's relations from Massachusetts, New Hampshire and Nova Scotia, who spread out, taking advantage of the inexpensive farmland and wide-open spaces offered by the American Midwest. Benjamin and Lucia Holmes took their young family to Faribault, in Rice County. The town was in need of a barber, and Ben Alexander Holmes, a light-skinned Black man with supportive white in-laws, foresaw a brighter future in the newly minted Minnesota prairie town than he had found in Canada West.

The interrelated Holmes and Holt families were part of a much larger migration out of North America's eastern seaboard to take up lands vacated by the tragic "removal" of most of Minnesota's Native American population, a process considered complete in 1863. Already living in southeast Minnesota Territory near the Wisconsin border was Lucia's older sister, whose husband was a Nova Scotian. She and her family had abandoned the spectacular wind-swept Fundy Shore for life on a Minnesota farm.[46]

African Americans had been in the old Northwest since the time of the fur trade. Beginning in the 1820s, more followed the Erie Canal and then continued on to the limits of the frontier, trying to find a place where the blight of racism might not follow. A handful of Black Southerners lived there too, including fugitive slaves with relatives in Ontario. They invested in land, started newspapers and developed a series of protest and resistance organizations designed to combat racism and ameliorate the conditions for African Americans there. During the Civil War, a conflict in which 24,000 Minnesotans fought, including 100 free Blacks, officers among them sent "contraband" freed slaves to fill in the ranks of agricultural labourers, with their wives along to become household servants. The Homestead Act of

1868 guaranteed that lands would be made available to Union Army veterans and previously enslaved African Americans, but few became farmers. Sadly, they discovered that the territory's white American pioneers had brought their prejudices with them.

Instead Blacks settled in Minnesota's cities and towns; predictably, a substantial number were highly skilled barbers who established shops. The less skilled did heavy labour on the docks, drove wagons and carriages or went into service. At resorts on Lake Minnetonka, people who had been enslaved in the South became waiters, housemen, cooks and chambermaids or caddied on the golf course. Talented musicians among them entertained the well-heeled guests in hotel dining rooms and local dancehalls.[47]

Upon their first arrival, the Holmeses had discovered a thriving Black community in the state capital of St. Paul and in the Mississippi River port town of Minneapolis, despite the fact that the 1870 census reported only 759 African Americans in the territory. African American newspapers and churches and a healthy infrastructure of mutual support, with fraternal orders and benevolent societies, provided a welcome. Racial discrimination was already rearing its ugly head, though, for Black children were prevented from attending most public schools, and their parents from active participation in Minnesota social and political life.[48]

Fortunately Ben and Lucia's experience in Faribault was quite different. Named for a French Canadian fur-trading family, the prairie city had no Black population at all when the Holmes family arrived. A milling and market town at the confluence of the Cannon and Straight Rivers, it was an unusually cultured place. Home to three state institutions—the School for the Blind, the School for the Deaf and the School for the Feeble-Minded—and with substantial postwar immigration from both New England and Maritime Canada, the district soon became known as the "Athens of the West." As early as 1856 one observer wrote: "Society is forming out of all classes, nations and tongues. The [mixed bloods are a] wealthy . . . and influential class . . . Canadian and Parisian French are our taylors [*sic*] and dry goods clerks. Irish as well as Americans are our shoe makers . . . New England Yankees are our aristocrats."[49]

Ben provided a much-needed service to the frontier town. There was no competition at all when he opened Faribault's first barbershop.[50] With the proceeds from their Canadian properties he and Lucia built a fine home. He and his wife, along with their two young sons, moved relatively easily into Faribault's small social realm. Received with open arms by the same very progressive bishop who was responsible for attracting the state institutions to the town, Ben and his little family joined the congregation at Faribault's Episcopalian cathedral. Their children attended Sunday School and were admitted to the local schools. Ben himself became a lifelong member of the Brotherhood of St. Andrew, an otherwise entirely white organization. Ben and Lucia took their faith to heart. When the issue of barbershops operating on Sundays aroused the ire of Sabbatarians, Ben stood against his fellow Black tonsorial specialists in opposing Sunday openings.[51]

But the Holmes family occupied a middle position between Minnesota's Black and white worlds. Ben and Lucia were anxious to ensure that their sons had access to the resources and society of African Americans living at or near the state capital. By virtue of the town's railroad links to St. Paul and Minneapolis, only fifty miles to the north, Ben and his sons were able to participate in the state's largest Black community. He became an active member of the Order of Good Templars, which, typically, served simultaneously as a fraternal order, event organizer and burial society. His name appeared occasionally in the pages of the *Western Appeal*, the flourishing African American newspaper based in St. Paul that would soon open offices in Minneapolis, Louisville, St. Louis and Chicago. According to the September 3, 1887, issue, he had been appointed to a committee responsible for developing programming for a "Colored People's Day" to be held on September 22 at the Minnesota State Exhibition; the article's celebratory tone barely masked the journalist's indignation that Blacks would be welcome at the fair only on that special day.

Cecelia's elder stepson also joined African American organizations that arose in the Jim Crow years to combat segregation and resist the racial violence that terrorized Black Americans, even in those far northwestern reaches of the nation. Renamed the *Appeal*, on May 1 and 9, 1891, the newspaper's pages noted that Mr. B. F. Holmes [*sic*] was representing Faribault in plans to establish a "state Afro-American League of Minnesota Convention" to be held in Minneapolis on May 27.[52] The League predated the Niagara Movement and the NAACP. Founded by attorney Frederick McGhee, it received wide support among Black Minnesotans, who in their earlier lives had acquired first-hand experience of prejudice and the viciousness it could engender. This was succeeded by the National Afro-American Council, which held meetings in 1902 in St. Paul, Minnesota, with Booker T. Washington and Ida B. Wells-Barnett among the attendees.[53]

Lucia and Ben's two fine sons had very successful careers that fully bore out their parents' wisdom in moving their family to Minnesota. Eugene P. Holmes became the first Black dentist (1893) and Walter Benjamin Holmes the first Black doctor (1894) to graduate from the University of Minnesota. Both had a scientific bent. First Walter moved to Minneapolis, where he became assistant secretary of the Minneapolis Chamber of Commerce and in 1887 earned his bachelor of science degree. He worked as a hydraulic engineer until 1891, but, always desirous of a medical career, he began studies at the University of Minnesota's new medical school. Walter edited the university magazine, *Ariel*, from 1891 to 1893; joined the Epilson chapter of the Nu Sigma Nu fraternity, an association he would value throughout his life; and participated fully in university life.[54] His skin colour apparently no bar to his popularity with both professors and fellow students, in 1894 Walter B. Holmes graduated at the head of his class of thirty-two with a cum laude degree as doctor of medicine.[55]

Walter's younger brother, Eugene, opened a dental office in Minneapolis and shared a flat with his older brother until he married.[56] Evidence of Eugene Holmes's acceptance by white society by virtue of his professional status, the designation "colored" did not appear in city directories beside his name. He had an excellent practice on Nicollet Avenue. He married twice, both times to women of European ancestry. His first marriage ended in divorce in 1899, after which he took to wife a French-Canadian woman originally from Roberval, Quebec.[57] After his second marriage Eugene built a house at 3100–39th Avenue South, Minneapolis, in 1913.[58] In the eyes of the census-taker who visited the property in 1920, both he and his wife Annie were as white as all the rest of the neighbouring families.

Neither of Ben and Lucia's sons garnered as much as a mention on the part of Minnesota's African American press, unlike their father. Indeed, they lived very much in the white world, although Eugene was for a time a member of the Knights of Pythias of North and South America, Europe, Asia, and Africa, the African American branch of the order. As lifelong Republicans, however, it is likely that both of Ben's sons joined their father when he attended the June 1892 convention in Minneapolis. More than a thousand Blacks came to protest lynching and the imposition of Jim Crow legislation. An eloquent African American former congressman from Virginia named John Mercer Langston was present, as was Frederick Douglass. The elderly Black statesman was travelling through the Midwest supporting suffrage efforts led by his old friend Susan B. Anthony. Black delegates demanded that the Republican Party pass a resolution condemning lynch law, and do all in its power to "wipe the foul blot from the escutcheon of the nation." Their entreaties fell on deaf ears.[59]

Cecelia's first husband Benjamin did not have long-lived descendants. In 1896 his older son, Ben Alexander, died at the age of fifty-eight and was buried in Faribault's Maple Lawn Cemetery. Interestingly, his obituary repeated the protective fiction that his father and mother had devised so long ago when, diverted from their original destination of Liberia, they came to live in Canada. Although he was actually born in Virginia in 1838, Ben's obituary in the Faribault *Republican* of September 16, 1896, presented his biography as follows:

Died in this city on Friday forenoon last, Sept. 11. He had been in poor health for about two years. Mr. Holmes was born in Toronto, of colored parentage, in 1839. His early life was passed in Lowell, Mass., and he married Miss Lucia A. Holt, of Concord, N. H. He came to Minnesota and settled in Faribault in 1869, opening a barber's shop. He has since been a continuous resident of our city, and through his industry, integrity, and exemplification of many Christian virtues, won the respect and esteem of all who knew him. He was past grand deputy of the I.O.G.T. [International Order of Good Templars], officer and one of the most active members of the Brotherhood of St. Andrew. It was mainly owing to his active efforts that the law directing the Sunday closing of barber shops was enacted. Mr. Holmes is survived by his wife and two sons, viz: W. B. Holmes, MD and E. P. Holmes, dental surgeon, of Minneapolis. The funeral was held in the cathedral on Sunday afternoon at two p. m. and was largely attended. The services were conducted by Rev. Slattery. The pall bearers were T. H. Loyhed, J. B. Wickham, J. C. N. Cottrell, William Milligan, F. A. Davis and J. W. Parshall. The interment was in Maple Lawn Cemetery. There were present at the funeral from other places Dr. W. B. Holmes, E. P. Holmes and wife, and Miss Gertrude Eustis, of Minneapolis, Mrs. George H. French, of Sumner, sister of Mrs. Holmes, and Mrs. Whitson, of Owatonna.

Ben Alexander Holmes did not leave a will, and probate continued for nearly nine years. At issue were two lots he owned in the east end of town,[60] today a comfortable residential district near a branch of Minnesota's world-famous Mayo Clinic. Benjamin's widow, Lucia Holt Holmes, the high-school sweetheart with whom he had fallen in love so many years ago in Lowell, also died at the age of sixty. Her obituary appeared in the *Rice County Journal* of August 21, 1901:

Died Tuesday evening, Aug. 13, after several months' illness with
a cancer. The funeral was held Thursday from the cathedral and
the remains laid at rest in Maple Lawn. She was born in Concord,
New Hampshire, in 1841, and came to Faribault with her husband, the late B. A. Holmes, in 1869. She is survived by two sons,
Drs. E. P. and W. B. Holmes.

Ben and Lucia's younger son, Dr. Eugene B. Holmes, lived another
twenty-three years, dying in Minneapolis on March 24, 1924. He was buried beside his parents. His widow, Annie, was thirty-nine; she continued in
their home until she eventually remarried.

But Benjamin's eldest grandson, Walter Benjamin Holmes—his middle
name honouring both his father and his grandfather—enjoyed a career that
was nothing short of stellar. As a man of visibly African ancestry with considerable talents and a slightly reserved bearing, he took the extraordinary
move of migrating to the extreme northwest corner of the state after his
graduation from medical school. In 1897 Walter opened a practice in
Minnesota's Red River Valley. Physicians were scarce in that part of the
state, and he was soon appointed medical officer of health for Norman
County and made his home in the village of Ada.

Like his brother and his father before him, Walter wed a woman of
European ancestry. On April 20, 1906, he married the widowed Valborg
S. Norby, a native of Christiana, Sweden.[61] The intimate family ceremony
took place at the home of her brother in La Cross, Wisconsin, with the
apparent approval of her many relations in the area. Walter and Valborg's
interracial marriage, still illegal in a great many parts of the United States,
occasioned no overt public comment in the sparsely settled part of rural
Minnesota where they returned to live. After the wedding Dr. Holmes
resumed his practice in Norman County, while his bride raised the three
sons from her previous marriage and became a leader in charitable and
particularly Red Cross organizations in the area.

Reasons for the local acceptance of their union likely included Walter's respected professional status coupled with the wealth his bride brought with her to the marriage. Her first husband, Joris C. Norby, had been a very prosperous farmer and lumberman who also had a half-interest in a flour mill and in telegraph operations in northern Minnesota.[62] Valborg inherited a fine farm and substantial investments that ensured the family a level of comfort unusual even among the better-off of their overwhelmingly white neighbours. Of Walter's three stepsons, all volunteered for military service in the First World War, the eldest, Erling, after graduating from the University of Minnesota law school in 1915.

Walter B. Holmes went from strength to strength. He served on the board of the Red River Valley Medical Association and was a full member of the American Medical Association. He also qualified as a pharmacist, was a member of the State Pharmaceutical Association and was appointed physician and surgeon of the Great Northern Railroad in 1907. He was on the local branch of the National Defense Committee during the First World War and in 1917 was appointed examining physician for the US Army's draft board. In one of the inevitable ironies that arose because of discriminatory policies, this dark-complected man was charged with assessing the fitness of white men for duty in a military system that prohibited African Americans from fighting, except in rigidly segregated units.[63] After the war he continued to be active in his fraternity and was a committed and enthusiastic member of the Royal Arch, the Zuriah Lodge of the Masons, an otherwise all-white lodge.

The authors of a local history published in 1918 say of the physician:

> Doctor Holmes is possessed of many pronounced natural attributes, and brings to his labors in any direction a virile personality. While firm in his convictions, he is none the less tolerant of the opinions of others, and is held in high regard in and about the county and outside of it. He is an extensive reader and student,

well versed in world history and is accounted one of the foremost scholars in the county. He has written many articles on sanitary science and the prevention of disease, especially in schools, and which have been published in the local press and copied into many papers in the larger centers.[64]

But for all his personal prominence in northern Minnesota, Walter B. Holmes was more than aware of the rising racial violence of the early twentieth century. On June 15, 1920, in Duluth—a port city on Lake Superior where Dr. Holmes and his white wife often holidayed—three Black men were brutally lynched by a ravening mob out to avenge the alleged rape of a white girl. The charge was eventually proven false, but the men were dead and no one was ever convicted of their murders. The Duluth lynchings remain a blot on the racial history of Minnesota to this day.

After twenty-one years of happily married life, Dr. Holmes lost his wife on March 28, 1927. She was laid to rest in the cemetery at Ada, Minnesota, near the grave of her first husband. Walter B. Holmes, now retired and spending his days gardening and reading his beloved poetry, passed some of this time writing erudite, beautifully crafted letters to his stepsons and their families. Filled with verse, both quotes from the great poets and Shakespeare and original compositions, along with Biblical references, moral tales and aphorisms, they are the outpourings of the heart and mind of a brilliant, cultured man. Benjamin Pollard Holmes would have been proud to know that his eldest grandson had surpassed anything he could have dreamed in terms of erudition and the respect of his family, his community and his professional associates.[65]

Walter survived his wife by just three years, dying on October 27, 1930, at the age of sixty-seven. He was buried beside his mother, father and brother in Faribault. Sadly, there was a good deal of undignified squabbling over his estate, with his mother Lucia's several Holt relations and their children attempting to wrestle Walter's considerable wealth from the stepsons to whom he had left it. However, the matter was eventually settled in their favour.

Dr. Holmes had no children of his own, but the boys he raised grew into fine men. After being called to the bar, Erling Norby settled in Great Falls, Montana, and served as a flying instructor in the First World War. After the war he moved to Marysfield, California, where in 1926 he was elected district attorney.[66] Frithjof, the second boy (called Fritz), followed his brother to Great Falls and embarked on a successful career in real estate. The youngest, Joris Christian Norby, saw heavy fighting as a marine in France and was wounded several times. After his discharge Joris settled in Caspar, Wyoming, and then moved on to Corpus Christi, Texas, where he started a construction company.[67]

IN EXAMINING THE FASCINATING lives led by their offspring, it is clear that the legacy left behind by Cecelia Jane Reynolds and her two husbands, Benjamin Pollard Holmes and William Henry Larrison, was much greater than the sum of its parts. They were proud, daring people, and despite the troubles of the afflicted James Thomas, led productive lives. Ben took an active role in protesting and resisting all efforts to blight the lives of himself, his family and his community. His sons far exceeded the boundaries with which segregation and other forms of racial prejudice might have circumscribed their attainments.

But look at the astonishing heritage they shared. Ben and James Thomas had freedom-seekers for parents and for a stepmother, who went on to devote their lives and what resources they had to helping others make their way on the Underground Railroad. No one will ever know how many people owed their liberty to brave souls like Benjamin Pollard Holmes who engineered their crossing into Canada, or how many rejoiced in the warm reception they met because of women like Cecelia. These remarkable people contributed from their small savings to the multiple causes that sought both to challenge the American slave system and to help those who fled its bonds. And they also took weary refugees into their own homes to offer the food and clothing and warmth and *welcome* they needed to recover from their fear-filled journey.

Cecelia Jane Reynolds gave birth to four children and lost three of them in childhood. She worked hard for her family, sometimes enduring desperate hardship, to give Benjamin's two boys and her own Mamie the very best life she could. That loving woman crossed an ocean and lost her marriage trying to save her mother from bondage. She died long years after Fanny, whom she had loved as a child and whose lifelong affection for her, however unequal their stations in life, had been both real and enduring. It is a measure of her trust in the woman who had once owned her body that in time of extreme need, she had chosen to follow her heart and "steal away home."

Neither Cecelia nor the men she loved left descendants to carry knowledge of their personal courage and sacrifice forward to the present day. Their spirit lives on, though, in all the people who know that someone was there to greet their ancestors at the last stop on the Freedom Road. Because of what they believed and their stunning accomplishments, we are in a very real way all heirs to Cecelia's bravery, and to the sacrifices that she and her family made for the sake of liberty.

This book was written so we can all pay tribute to strong, incredibly resourceful women like Cecelia Jane Reynolds and to valiant, committed men like Benjamin Pollard Holmes and William Henry Larrison. They broke the chains that bound them and set out in search of a Promised Land. *Steal Away Home* is their story too.

EPILOGUE

FOR A LONG TIME I thought Cecelia's story ended there, with the death of faithful Mamie and the passing of Benjamin's two sons and their children. None left descendants to carry on her tale of trials and of triumph, or to recount stories of the two good men Cecelia loved and lost along the way. But I was wrong.

The magic that is archaeology takes us back in time. Today we can reach out and touch artifacts evocative of Cecelia's daily experiences as a fugitive slave, wife, mother and, between 1846 and 1860, resident of Toronto's vital, energetic and politically aware African American expatriate community. Archaeologists are painstakingly piecing together the fragments of her world, and with it clues to the lives of the hundreds of freedom-seekers who found refuge in what is now Ontario in the years before the American Civil War.

For me, history is always about individual people, and it is about place. I have travelled to nearly all the cities that Cecelia and her two husbands knew, following her youthful footsteps through Louisville, Washington and the natural wonder of magnificent Mammoth Cave. After combing the street directories, I have been to each of the addresses where she lived in Toronto and Rochester. Tracing her family's Civil War experience led me from the New York harbour defences at Staten Island's Fort Richmond to Petersburg, where the Battle of the Crater site is today a national park. In Louisville I stood on the pavement in front of each of her homes, though not one of the flats and cottages she occupied there has survived the ravages of time.

I have found each location redolent of her experience. The Cataract House may be long gone, but the roaring of the great Falls at Niagara echoes the feelings of hope and despair, regret and excitement of her long-planned escape. The landing place on the Canadian side rings with her incandescent joy when she stood on free soil for the first time. Benjamin's modest Toronto home was torn down more than half a century ago, but the streets he and Cecelia knew in old St. John's Ward are still there, though lined now with looming office towers and paved over with asphalt and concrete.

This is a love story too, about many different kinds of love. In Rochester the exquisite classical lines of the Erickson house, now the Genesee Valley Club, still grace broad and beautiful East Avenue. When I stand in those lofty and opulent rooms, I see not their modern furnishings but rather Cecelia slipping up the servant's stair, bearing billets-doux for young Hannah from her dashing colonel. There was great love too in the elegant Louisville home that A. J. Ballard built for his Fanny. It has now gone to dust, but the bells that Fanny's sons donated in their parents' memory still call the Louisville faithful to worship at Christ Church Cathedral every Sunday morning.

But even that pales in comparison to the unbreakable bond that existed between Cecelia's enslaved parents. I cannot fathom the depth of affection that drove Adam Reynolds—at eighty-six years of age!—to work his steamboat passage north from Arkansas in a vain quest to be reunited with Mary, the bride of his young manhood, from whom he had been sold away a half-century before.

All these spaces speak to me too of the crushing burden on soul and body that was the American slave system. They also ring with the joy, courage, sheer hard work and incredible ingenuity that brought Cecelia and tens of thousands of people like her out of slavery into the light of freedom. The new families they raised, once they had achieved the liberty they so avidly sought, the homes they built, the churches and benevolent and fraternal societies they founded, and the community service they performed were all a triumph over the soul-destroying exploitation of their bodies they had suffered in bondage.

And once they reached freedom they never allowed the memories of the loved ones they had been forced to leave behind fade. Cecelia, along with her dignified, perceptive Benjamin and most of their friends and acquaintances on both sides of the border, worked to help others achieve the same liberty. They risked their own freedom to help those travelling the pathways to free soil, all the while saving their earnings in hopes of buying beloved family members out of slavery.

Nothing I had done or felt or experienced over the course of my work on the life and times of Cecelia Jane Reynolds prepared me for the emotions that swamped me when I stood in the backyard of the little house she once shared with Benjamin and his sons on Toronto's Centre Street. This was the very place where she used to stand, the soil itself redolent of that small, courageous, indomitable woman.

Many physical changes have taken place in Cecelia's old neighbourhood over the intervening decades. The city armouries were built behind Osgoode Hall in 1891, taking out the entire city block below Cecelia's old home on Lot 7.[1] The red sandstone bulk of old Toronto City Hall, constructed in 1899—the largest civic building in North America in its day—still dominates the northeast corner of Queen and Bay Streets. The northern end of Cecelia's street was expropriated in the first decade of the twentieth century to build Toronto General Hospital, and blocks below it along Queen were torn down in the 1960s to make way for the curving modernist towers of Toronto's "New" City Hall. And soon there will be a modern courthouse there, and the layers of soil that hold clues to the everyday lives that people like Cecelia and Benjamin, Ben and James Thomas, and the always faithful Mamie led in that place so long ago will be torn away.

By some astonishing coincidence, the remnants of Cecelia's house, the homes of several of the Holmes family's neighbours and friends, and even the church they attended were part of a massive archaeological dig that took place in downtown Toronto in the summer of 2015. The largest urban excavation in North America at the time, the dig brought to light evidence of what had once been Toronto's most densely packed nineteenth-century neighbourhood.

Occupied by successive waves of immigrants, the last rundown, decrepit houses and small factories there had been demolished in 1961 to make way for a parking lot. And there, safely sealed beneath the pavement, awaited the single most important multicultural history site left in downtown Toronto. In the course of their work the archaeologists exposed the foundations of the small frame building with a brick façade that was Cecelia's first home in freedom. They measured and mapped the structural changes that a succession of African Canadian, Irish, Jewish, Italian and Chinese residents on that one small house lot had wrought over time. They sifted through tens of thousands of artifacts uncovered at this and adjacent properties. They pieced together the puzzle of Cecelia's and her successors' past.

Thanks to their efforts, there is now tangible evidence of the long series of tenants who occupied the Holmes property, both during Cecelia's own tenure and following its 1889 purchase by the ambitious Francis Griffin Simpson. He and his family lived in the house Benjamin had built as a rental property and legacy for his boys, and he bought Cecelia's former home as an income property. Simpson retained the backyard for his own use, building a workshop against the rear fence and caching dozens of half-made and damaged shoes in a hole he dug in what had once been Cecelia's vegetable garden, while his son lived in her old house.

While the Simpsons lived there, and in the years after, the narrow streets and mostly frame houses of old St. John's Ward attracted tens of thousands of immigrants. The fugitive slaves of Cecelia's day had by the 1880s given way to a flood of Jews fleeing the pogroms of Tsarist Russia. As their African American predecessors had done before them, they started anew and opened shops, constructed workspaces and tenements in their backyards, and operated small factories. The first Jewish charities in the city started there, their maternal health centre today represented by Mount Sinai Hospital's state-of-the-art facilities on University Avenue—the former College Avenue where Cecelia used to walk with Benjamin's little boys of an evening.

As the district's Jewish residents gradually accumulated enough capital to make their homes elsewhere, the aging houses of "The Ward" welcomed Italian and Eastern European families fleeing the depredations of war. But lack of public services coupled with extreme poverty and the predilection of Toronto's well-to-do to seek out their more illicit pleasures there conspired to give St. John's Ward a notoriety that few of its hardworking immigrant residents deserved. Eventually these families left as well, clearing the way for Chinese immigration, and Torontonians of my own age remember these few blocks as the city's colourful, fragrant, exotic Chinatown.

All these layers of intersecting history have masked the less monumental but profoundly evocative personal histories of those hopeful, industrious African American families who once made their homes in old St. John's Ward. But archaeology is a very precise pursuit. Its devotion to exposing the minutest detail of data left behind in the soil is both single-minded and absolute.

In 2015, a dozen jeans-clad young people wearing hard hats and work boots spent long months toiling at the site on which today is Centre Avenue. They peeled away the pavement and then, using sharpened hand trowels, removed layer after layer of soil and debris. The more public jewel in the crown of the 2015 archaeological excavation was the site of the British Methodist Episcopal Church, whose property backed onto those of Cecelia's northern neighbours. In the basement hall of its less elaborate frame predecessor Cecelia Jane Reynolds had learned to read, and her younger stepson was baptized in its chancel. A lifetime later, in 1859, Benjamin's funeral cortege wound its slow way from its front steps to the Toronto Necropolis Cemetery. His unmarked grave is shaded by a huge oak tree in this peaceful garden of the dead on the shores of the Don River.

The simple handmade pews and rough plank floors that once echoed with the footsteps of Samuel Ringgold Ward, Frederick Douglass and Samuel J. May were eventually found inadequate for its congregation's needs. The church, rebuilt in brick and right to the property line, would survive until the 1980s, for the final three decades of its life hosting a Chinese congregation. In the 1950s its elders removed the spires and refaced the entire front, but out of respect for the building's unique heritage, they preserved the stone block bearing its dedication. It was set carefully into the threshold of the basement, so everyone coming for Sunday School or Bible study could thus acknowledge their faith centre's African Canadian progenitors.

There were dozens of intersecting buildings, houses, sheds and factories on the adjacent lots, all now subject to the same scrutiny. Because of its special importance to my studies, the little house in which Benjamin Pollard Holmes and his wife Cecelia once lived was left as the last area of this vast, complicated site to be excavated in the fall of 2015.

In its final incarnation, Cecelia's house on Centre Street had become a very-low-rent boarding house, the proliferation of broken liquor bottles discovered by the archaeological team mute testimony to the character of its most recent occupants. The archaeologists sorted through fine layers of dirt laid down when owners named Wong, Fong and Lim lived there, working ever backwards through years of residency by the Silverstein, Sachs, Siegle, Deltman, Glazier and Greenbaum families. Then came a complex series of traces left in the soil by residents from the British Isles, George Skene and Cecelia's tenants Henry Loan and the widowed Eliza Bannon. Then the debris of an African Canadian family, her good friend Francis Griffin Simpson and his son.

At long last the bottom levels were reached. Excavation had by this time exposed the foundations and then the basement floor, filled with debris left behind by Cecelia and Benjamin's children and by themselves. The archaeologists dug out a series of trash pits and the still-odoriferous vault of the

Holmes family's "necessary house." Finally, just as the snow began to fall, the original levels of the Holmes family occupation there—and the veritable treasure trove of household goods they contained—were exposed.

The very deepest layers of Lot 7 on the east side of Centre Street contained an intricately laid pattern of artifacts. These testify to the rather wonderful quality of life that Benjamin had provided for his little family. Their house itself may have been modest, but those sheltered by its walls lived well. There was a good deal of beautiful china and glassware found at the site, and one cannot help but envision Cecelia entertaining the church ladies in her small, tidy parlour. She poured tea from a majolica teapot into gilt-edged white porcelain cups, stirring in the milk she bought at Willis Addison's grocery store with silver-plated spoons. Cakes she had made in the small kitchen addition at the rear of her home were set out on a lovely cobalt-blue glass plate, and the ladies ate them from pretty blue-sprigged china plates that imitated Wedgwood's best moulded jasperware.

Cecelia must have envied her neighbours their brown transfer-printed bowl bearing the scene from *Uncle Tom's Cabin* of Eliza crossing the ice. The wealth of artifacts found on adjacent lots defies the modern view of St. John's Ward as an irretrievably impoverished place to live. Although most of the residents worked with their hands, their household furnishings included porcelain tea sets, pressed glass tumblers, framed prints and fancy hardware for the doors and windows. Lace curtains hung from brass rods at their windows, and their children attended school in spotless pinafores and shiny black boots whose buttons were found scattered throughout the yards of these cottage homes.

While her mother served tea, Cecelia's daughter Mamie played quietly with a china doll. Its cloth body has long since disappeared, but a diminutive china leg was found buried at the deepest levels of the backyard. The leg was white, but the little girl of African Canadian barber Edward Jones, a few doors up the street, had a doll whose shiny black porcelain head reflected her own African heritage. Archaeologists also discovered a Black minstrel figurine, evidence of the continuing popularity of demeaning "Jim Crow" performances, despite the best efforts of Wilson Ruffin Abbott and his contemporaries to have them banned by Toronto City Council.

Cecelia shushed her boisterous stepsons as they arrived home from school, telling them to put away the slates and slate pencils with which they did their lessons before going out into the street to play jacks with the neighbourhood boys. When the abstemious Benjamin arrived from his latest voyage on the Lake Ontario steamboats, he shook his head at the men he encountered in the alleyway playing dice and gambling over a domi-noes game. Perhaps he and Cecelia took the children into the garden to enjoy a bit of air before dinner. There beneath the sod lay the skeleton of the family's much-loved dog, carefully interred in a long-forgotten cere-mony presided over by Benjamin's boys.[2]

After the evening meal, Cecelia might sit down to write yet another letter to her old mistress in faraway Louisville. Quarters would surely be cramped if her mother Mary's purchase could be arranged and the older woman came to live with them, as was Cecelia's fondest dream. Sitting at the well-scrubbed kitchen table, she painstakingly formed her letters. Her steel-nibbed pen has long rusted away, but the bowl of the stoneware ink-well into which she dipped it survives, part of a rather elaborate writing set recovered from a refuse pit at the rear of her yard.

The clamouring voices I hear when I stand on the site of Cecelia's Toronto home speak in Yiddish and Polish, Romanian and Sicilian, Cantonese and Mandarin. But the first people here spoke in the soft accents of the Southern homes they had fled in search of freedom. And thousands of them found it too, here in these small houses lining the narrow, muddy streets of Toronto's first immigrant-reception neighbourhood.

As I write these words, ardent preservationists are demanding that the discoveries made at what has come to be called the BME Church Site be memorialized in a tangible way at the new Ontario Courthouse. I have lent my own voice to theirs. Otherwise, this unique, profoundly moving, unimaginably important piece of our collective past will disappear forever.

To me, the terminus of the Underground Railroad will always be that little house on Centre Street, and Cecelia will always be that intrepid fifteen-year-old girl poised on the brink of Niagara Falls, waiting to make those first fateful steps that would take her forever out of the darkness of bondage. Once she crossed over the river and reached that other shining shore, she indeed used her freedom well. The two good men she married adored their children and sacrificed everything for them. Their memory cannot end with their deaths.

Cecelia and her companions on the Freedom Road were ancestors to generations of brave African Canadians. They have fought in every one of this nation's wars, and despite the persistent, pernicious racism they continue to face, their knowledge, achievement and creativity have always been crucial to the building of Canada.

The freedom-seekers cry out to be remembered.

ACKNOWLEDGEMENTS

Steal Away Home is the result of more than eight years of research, so there are literally dozens of people to thank. I have visited nearly every place that Cecelia is known to have lived or worked over the course of her life, so it seems most appropriate to acknowledge by location the help of all the incredibly generous historians, librarians, archivists, descendants, editors and others who gave of their knowledge and their time to help make this book possible. Their assistance has been invaluable, and the responsibility for any errors or misunderstandings that appear in these pages is mine alone.

In Kentucky, as always, my thanks to friends and colleagues who have helped me come to understand the history and context of Cecelia's life. The staff at the Filson Historical Society have been wonderful, particularly James Holmberg, my first and best friend there, who kindly read over the Louisville parts of my manuscript, and former librarian Pen Bogert, who discovered Cecelia's gravesite and gave unstintingly of his own research findings. The Filson provided a much-needed research fellowship, and I am grateful for all the discoveries that made possible. I miss the late J. Blaine Hudson, Dean of Humanities at the University of Louisville, whose friendship and formidable scholarship regarding slavery, the Underground Railroad and race relations in Louisville contributed to making *Steal Away Home* a better book.

I am grateful to Don Ball and Marcia E. Hemmings, my perennial Louisville hosts, who have patiently helped me work through the meaning of my discoveries uncounted times over the years; to the ever-helpful Jim Pritchard, now retired from the Kentucky State Archives at Frankfort; to all the staff of the Louisville Public Library, the Jefferson County Archives and the Kentucky State Archives at Frankfort who assisted with the project; and to my dear friend and companion in all things historical, Anne Butler of Kentucky State University. Anne, I am so sorry you did not live to see this volume completed, and I love you always.

For Cecelia's life in Rochester, I was blessed to receive help from the staff of the Rochester Public Library and also at the Rare Books and Special Collections at the University of Rochester. My friend and colleague Judith Wellman toured with me the places Cecelia had been and shared her scholarly knowledge of the Underground Railroad in upstate New York, as did Charles Lenhart, whose study of abolitionism there is seminal to my work. Daniel Broyld, now of Central Connecticut State University, gave me permission to consult his ground-breaking doctoral research long before the publication of his own book, which I very much appreciate.

Turning to my hometown of Toronto, the focus of much of my Underground Railroad–era research, I find it almost impossible to single out all the individuals who were most important to the completion of *Steal Away Home*. First among them is Guylaine Petrin, who conducted hundreds of hours of in-depth research into Cecelia's life and times and also reviewed the entire manuscript for errors and omissions. Thank you, Guylaine!

I owe more than I can express to our small cadre of historians who share with one another their findings in Toronto Black history. My friends and sisters Afua Cooper, Adrienne Shadd, Hilary Dawson and Natasha Henry—I am so grateful to be one of you. Heather Ioannou, thanks for telling me the story of Grandison Boyd; and Matthew Furrow, I appreciate your letting me use your transcripts of the Samuel Gridley Howe interviews. Gary Moriarity, you have always been there for me and I love you. I miss Donald Nethery and his incisive historical insights more than I can say. Former Eatons company archivist Judith McErvel was reading my draft manuscript for me when she passed away in April; I will never forget her affection and the many years of our friendship.

None of this could have been accomplished without the help of the dedicated staff of the Baldwin Room, Toronto Public Library, and especially Mary-Rae Shantz, Bill Hamade and Alan Walker; the Archives of Ontario, particularly Tim Sanford; and retired archivist Karen Teeple and all my old friends at the City of Toronto Archives. Journalist John Lorinc discovered the news about the archaeology at the British Methodist Episcopal Church site, and the wonderful Jane MacNamara of the Toronto branch of the Ontario Genealogical Society reviewed the Toronto sections of *Steal Away Home* for me. Thank you!

I can't express enough gratitude to Holly Martelle, the archaeologist who excavated the site of Cecelia's Toronto home, who has been unfailingly generous in providing me with early and open access to her findings. She too checked over relevant sections of the manuscript and offered photographs and maps of the site findings, so everyone who reads *Steal Away Home* can see how we know what we know.

To scholars and community historians further afield in Canada whose knowledge and historical understanding inform this book, I offer heartfelt thanks: James St. George Walker of the University of Waterloo, who is my teacher, my mentor and my friend; Stephanie Bangarth, whose unfailing support and friendship I treasure; the incomparable Bryan and Shannon Prince and everyone in Buxton, the home of my heart; and especially Alice and Duane Newby, not lost but gone before, and their beautiful, accomplished daughters Quinn and Blair, who brought me into their deeply loving family when they learned I had none.

The details of Benjamin Pollard Holmes's early life in Virginia were especially difficult to uncover, and I am grateful to Frances Pollard, Vice President for Research Services, who has always been there for me at the Virginia Historical Society. The staff members of the Library of Virginia have always been unfailingly helpful, and I owe a special debt of thanks to historians Marie Tyler-McGraw and Jane Ailes, who helped me sort out the fateful voyage of the *Saluda*. Another special person whom I've never actually met is family historian Carolyn Gutermuth, who provided information about James T. Fisher and his family in Richmond; I only wish I could have included more here. Mary Virginia Currie of the McGraw-Page Library, Randolph-Macon College, Ashland, Virginia, helped with the details of Benjamin's early religious life.

Lee Artman of the Central Rappahannock Heritage Center was helpful, and I am indebted to Page McLemore and the delightful folks at the King and Queen Courthouse Tavern Museum. They did hours of work both with and for me and also introduced me to Sally Walker, who, with the kind permission of property owner Helen Longest, took us out into the fields of Goshen to see the graves of Alexander and Betsey Fleet. Betty Newsome, it was very kind of you to send the pictures of Thomas Claiborne Hoomes's gravestone found at Melrose Plantation. As for Reverend Brown and Nannie Taylor, who invited us to visit New Mount Zion Church and the remarkable J. C. Graves Museum they created there to illuminate the early African American history of King and Queen County, Virginia—well, they moved both me and my husband, Norm, to tears.

I visited some fascinating places I would never otherwise have seen on my journey to find Cecelia and her family. Thanks to Julia Clebsch and Melissa Axeman of the US National Park Service, I spent a wonderful week in their home at Fort Wadsworth on Staten Island. The staff of the Staten Island Historical Society was very helpful too. I was delighted to discover information at both the main branch of the New York Public Library and the Schomberg Collection as well as in the New York branch of the National Archives and Record Administration.

As for William H. Larrison's eventful life, I explored an entirely new set of Canadian connections with Petersburg, Virginia, thanks to my dear friend and colleague Martha Williams and retired archivist for Virginia

State University, Lucius Edwards. Don Papson and Tom Calarco were most generous in sending me their scans of Sidney Howard Gay's diary entry regarding William H. Larrison's flight to freedom, as well as the letter from Frederick Douglass to Gay about arranging to purchase Grandison Boyd's freedom.[1]

Minnesota has a rich history that has always intrigued me, never more so than the northwestern corner of the state that we visited last summer in the footsteps of Dr. Walter B. Holmes. We are grateful to Solveig Kitchell of the Norman County Historical and Genealogical Society for the assistance she gave, especially when we arrived so late in the day. The descendants of Dr. Holmes's stepsons, Barbara Cosens and Karen Schoenig, shared his precious letters, and Connie Ferris took a special trip to Faribault to photograph the family graves.

Other historical societies, archives and organizations where I visited and received wonderful assistance from staff include the Historical Society of Washington, DC, the National Archives and Records Administration, the Library of Congress, the Blair House and St. John's Church on Lafayette Square. I spent a very productive week at the Huntington Library in San Marino, California, and had an excellent visit in the Duke University Archives Special Collections, thanks to Jane Moss of the Department of Canadian Studies, John Thompson of the History Department, and the John Hope Franklin Center. The Historical Society of Pennsylvania and the American Philological Society were the sites of several return visits. In Lowell, Massachusetts, I would like to thank incredibly knowledgeable archivist Martha Mayo, now retired, who spent years studying local African American history.

To my dear friends of many years, Chris Koch and his partner, James Gitau, thanks so much for the hospitality, driving me around and the wonderful dinners while I visited the National Archives and Records Administration branch outside Atlanta to read A. J. Ballard's court docket books for post–Civil War Kentucky. Veta Smith Tucker of Grand Valley

State University in Grand Rapids, Michigan, has spent many hours discussing African Canadian and African American transnationalism with me, and also fact-checked this manuscript. I thank her for her friendship.

Funding, fellowships and visiting professorships have provided the support essential to completion of this volume. The Canada Council for the Arts has been generous in providing writers' grants, for which I am forever grateful. My year at Yale University's Gilder Lehrman Center for the Study of Slavery, Resistance and the Underground Railroad as Canadian Bicentennial Visiting Professor was fabulous. Thanks to David Blight, Nancy Ruther, David Spatz and Melissa McGrath for making our time in New Haven so special and so enlightening. Judy and Steve Alderman, we treasure your friendship.

The Harriet Tubman Institute at York University, Toronto, was my professional home for a good many years, and I am deeply appreciative of former director Paul Lovejoy, current director Michele Johnson and all the staff and students I worked with there. Marcel Martel, Chair of History at York, helped in every way possible and I am grateful to him and to the entire faculty for their support. To Chairs Paul Doerr and Gillian Poulter, History and Classics Department, Stephen Henderson of the Planter Studies Centre, the Research and Graduate Studies Department, and Claudine Bonner in Sociology, I can't thank you and everyone else at Acadia University enough. My three years as a Harrison McCain Visiting Professor made completing this book possible; I thank each and every one of you.

I have the very best publisher and editor any writer could ask for. Iris Tupholme, senior vice-president and executive publisher at HarperCollins Publishers Ltd, I am more grateful than I can say for your brilliant insights and for understanding why Cecelia's story is so very important. Thank you for your patience and for always being there, Iris. Likewise I am indebted to Doug Richmond, now an editor at House of Anansi Press, who did much to help shape this volume, and to the wonderful Laura Dosky, who has juggled an incredible amount of detail and has always been so supportive. Thank you to Gillian Watts (copyeditor and indexer), Patricia Macdonald (proofer) and

Mary Rostad (mapmaker). My utmost appreciation to managing editorial director Noelle Zitzer and senior production editor Maria Golikova. They have been nothing short of heroic in their efforts to make *Steal Away Home* the very best book it can be. I am very thankful to be working with the talented and enthusiastic marketing and sales team at HarperCollins: Colleen Simpson, Lauren Morocco, Catherine Knowles, Michael Guy-Haddock and Cory Beatty. Patrick Crean, I am so glad you're there too, and thank you for your friendship, always.

Michael Levine, Chairman of the Westwood Agency in Toronto, is the most enthusiastic and energetic agent I could ever find. Thank you, Iris, for introducing us—you were right! Michael is perfect for me and we're doing a host of exciting projects together. I am grateful to Denise Bukowski for her excellent early advice and for presenting the concept of *Steal Away Home* to HarperCollins in 2007. John Silbersack of Trident Media in New York offered his generous support through the midlife of the manuscript, for which I thank him.

Finally there are the people who make my life complete and who make my research and writing possible. Norm's children, Jason and wife Karina with children Max and Sawyer, Graham, Sara and James have grown up with Cecelia, and I'm sure they are very glad that *Steal Away Home* is finally going to press. My husband, Norm Frost, travels with me, puts up with me, forgives me over and over again for neglecting my living family in favour of people long dead, reads everything I write, and loves me all the time. I couldn't do it without you, Norm.

NOTES

Introduction

1. Although extensive records survive for the families of Thruston, Ballard, Clark and Churchill in the Filson Historical Society, Fanny Thruston Ballard's papers were partly destroyed in a fire at her son's Glenview home in 1906. Rogers C. B. Thruston, who was an assiduous collector and preserver of historical information, lost many of his own records (along with those of his mother) then, as he was at the time residing in his brother Charles T. Ballard's home.

Chapter 1: Way Down in Egypt Land

1. Austin Steward, *Twenty-Two Years a Slave, and Forty Years a Freeman, Embracing a Correspondence of Several Years, While President of Wilberforce Colony, London, Canada West* (Rochester, NY: William Alling, 1857), 304–5.
2. Mary Eliza Churchill was born April 14, 1804, and married Charles W. Thruston on May 27, 1824. She died February 9, 1842. Charles William Thruston (1796–1865), a Louisville attorney, merchant and manufacturer also served in the state legislature. He was the son of Charles Mynn Thruston (1738–1812) and Frances Eleanor Clark (1773–1825), sister of General George Rogers Clark and the explorer Captain William Clark. She was the widow of Captain James O'Fallon when she married Thruston, and Charles had two half-brothers who were brought up in St. Louis, John and Benjamin O'Fallon, with whom he was very close and much of the detail regarding his business dealings comes from his correspondence with Col. John O'Fallon. For the Churchill genealogy, see "Armistead Churchill and His Descendants," *William and Mary Quarterly* 10, no. 1 (July 1901): 39–44. Charles Timothy Todhunter, *The Churchill Family Genealogy*, 2 vols., vol. 2 (Utica, KY: McDowell Publishing, 1988): 555–87. For the Thrustons see "The Thruston Family of Virginia," *William and Mary Quarterly* 25, no. 3 (January 1917), 192–98; Kathleen Jennings, *Louisville First Families: A Series of Genealogical Sketches* (Louisville, Ky: Standard Printing, 1920), 59–68, 113–124.
3. Cecelia Larrison's death record (Jefferson County Death Records, June 5, 1909) and "Mortuary Record for Week Ending June 10, 1909," Louisville Cemetery, both give her birthplace as Virginia. The record is confusing, and somewhat inaccurate. Her age as given at death is incorrect; she is listed as being sixty-three years old, which would have meant she was born in 1846, the year of her escape to Canada. She was actually seventy-eight and had been reporting her age as significantly younger on official documents for some years.
4. "Bill of Sale, Wm. Cotton, Mary & Child $400," October 4, 1831, Charles W. Thruston Papers, Filson Historical Society, Louisville, KY. William Cotton was a slave dealer who had a slave pen at New Orleans, but he summered in Kentucky, purchasing slaves for the Southern trade. He was an associate of the notorious dealer Rice Carter Ballard (1800–1860), who traded slaves from Richmond, Virginia, between the east coast and New Orleans, as well as up the Mississippi and Ohio Valleys in the 1820s and '30s. Will of William Cotton, Series 4, Folder 407, Rice C. Ballard Papers, University of North Carolina Special Collections: Manuscripts Division, Coll. No. 04850. See also Tomoko Yagyu, "Slave Traders and Planters in the Expanding South: Entrepreneurial Strategies, Business Networks, and Western Migration in

the Atlantic World, 1787–1859" (PhD diss., University of North Carolina at Chapel Hill, 2006), 87–88, 258; Walter Johnson, *Soul by Soul: Life Inside the Antebellum Slave Market* (Boston: Harvard University Press, 1999), 48, 53, 56–57, 61; and Martha H. Swain, Elizabeth Anne Payne and Marjorie Julian Spruill, eds., *Mississippi Women: Their Histories, Their Lives,* vol. 2 (Athens: University of Georgia Press, 2010), 33. There was a brisk trade into Kentucky of slaves born in Virginia, whence most of the elite families and their "servants" had migrated. Although state regulations intermittently forbade importing slaves for the purpose of selling them, the limits of the laws were continually tested.

5. Adam Reynolds was Cecelia's biological father. Evidence comes from a fascinating account by Fanny's youngest son, describing his mother's relationship with her runaway maid. Rogers Clark Ballard Thruston commented that Fanny recognized Adam even in old age because of the *strong family resemblance between him and Cecelia*; Rogers Clark Ballard Thruston, "Memoir Regarding Cecelia Jane Reynolds," 1899, Ballard Family Papers, Filson Historical Society, Louisville, KY [hereafter RCB Thruston Memoir, 1899]. According to the census Thruston owned around 32 slaves in 1830 before he purchased Mary Reynolds and Cecelia Reynolds.

6. Adam's original owners may have been members of the Reynolds family that maintained an important rope-manufacturing business throughout the Revolution at Yorktown, as noted in the *Virginia Gazette* of January 31, 1777. Some migrated to Kentucky, bringing slaves with them, and the *Louisville Directory* for 1832 lists four Reynolds households. There is no bill extant for Adam's purchase. Perhaps he came down to Charles W. Thruston from his mother's or father's family or had belonged to Mary Eliza's family, the Churchills. His surname suggests that his origins were elsewhere; how enslaved African Americans chose their surnames is complicated and merits further study, but it seems that most used the name of their first owner after they arrived from Africa, retaining it through sales and other transfers of their ownership. Surnames came down through both male and female lines because so many were involved in "abroad" marriages, where members of the couple belonged to different slaveholders. As a psychological dehumanizing ploy, slaveholders did not employ surnames for their slaves, at best assigning to all of them the surname of their owner. However, enslaved men and women used surnames among themselves. Owners were quite aware of this, as witnessed by the many advertisements for fugitive slaves that included such words as "My slave Caesar, calls himself George Smith." Cecelia's use of the Reynolds surname was recognized by the Thrustons. John Boles, *Black Southerners* (Lexington: University Press of Kentucky, 1984), 43; Eugene D. Genovese, *Roll, Jordan, Roll: The World the Slaves Made* (New York: Pantheon Books, 1974), 443ff; Herbert Gutman, *The Black Family in Slavery and Freedom, 1750–1925* (New York: Vintage, 1976), 185–256; Mechal Sobel, *The World They Made Together: Black and White Values in Eighteenth-Century Virginia* (Princeton, NJ: Princeton University Press, 1987), 154–164.

7. E. P. Christie who founded the entertainment group the Christie Minstrels, claimed that he based his blackface music routines on the singing of the men he supervised in a New Orleans ropewalk. Jacqui Malone, *Steppin' on the Blues: The Visible Rhythms of African American Dance* (Champagne-Urbana: University of Illinois Press, 1992), 52.

8. For instance, letters dated March 15 and April 23, 1821, between Thomas Buckner and Charles W. Thruston detail Thruston's attempt to sell one of the men belonging to Buckner. Buckner Family Papers, Filson Historical Society, Louisville, KY.

9. The proximity of the two factory buildings to the Thrustons' home is not surprising for the era.

Louisville was a typical "walking city" of the early Industrial Revolution, lacking public transportation and without neighbourhood segregation of business, industry and residential districts. While this juxtaposition of industry and luxury homes seems surprising to modern sensibilities, it made excellent sense in Charles W. Thruston's day, particularly since he operated his establishment with slave labour. Louisville slaveholders were careful to provide regular oversight, in part because the riverfront offered so many opportunities for slaves to escape.

10. James F. Hopkins, *A History of the Hemp Industry in Kentucky* (Lexington: University of Kentucky, 1951), 143–44.

11. Louisville *Journal*, December 21, 28 and 30, 1831, and on into January 1832. Hiring out one's slaves was frowned upon everywhere because it broke down the traditional mechanisms of control between slaves and their owners. However, it was a common way for slaveholding families to capitalize on their investment in human property. Christmas week was the normal hiring time. Contracts with their owners would be struck for a period of one year, including wages, and often stipulating medical care, the taxes the owner would otherwise pay on each enslaved individual, one or two suits of clothing (winter and summer), shoes, perhaps a blanket or two, and of course their room and board. J. Blaine Hudson, "Slavery in Early Louisville and Jefferson County, Kentucky, 1780–1812," *Filson Club Historical Quarterly* 73, no. 2 (July 1999): 249–83, and "References to Slavery in the Public Records of Early Louisville and Jefferson County, Kentucky, 1780–1812," *Filson Club Historical Quarterly* 73, no. 3 (October 1999): 325–54; Hanford Dozier Stafford, "Slavery in a Border City: Louisville, 1790–1860" (PhD diss., University of Kentucky, 1982); Mary Lawrence O'Brien, "Slavery in Louisville During the Antebellum Period, 1820–1860: A Study of the Effects of Urbanization on the Institution of Slavery as It Existed in Louisville, Kentucky" (MA thesis, University of Louisville, 1979), 40–57; Marion B. Lucas, *A History of Blacks in Kentucky*, vol. 1, *From Slavery to Segregation, 1760–1891* (Frankfort: Kentucky Historical Society, 1992), ch. 5; Richard C. Wade, *Slavery in the Cities: The South, 1820–1860* (London: Oxford University Press, 1964), 38–54; and Clement Eaton, "Slave Hiring in the Upper South: A Step Toward Freedom," *Mississippi Valley Historical Review* 46, no. 4 (March 1960): 663–78.

12. A letter from Charles to his half-brother John O'Fallon in St. Louis reads: "Our house is nearly completed it will be convenient, comfortable and neat. I am at this time very much engaged with my ropewalk—my business is considerably enlarged, so much that I have been compelled to employ a foreman [Adam Reynolds?] he is a very accomplished workman. I am now turning out nearly $100 worth of work daily." Charles W. Thruston to John O'Fallon, October 8, 1827, Thruston Papers, Filson Historical Society. There survive in Charles W. Thruston's papers at the historical society a large number of receipts for slaves both hired and purchased by Charles, and occasionally by his cousin Alfred. For the dissolution of their partnership see Deed of Sale, Alfred Thruston to Charles W. Thruston, December 4, 1833, Thruston Papers, Filson Historical Society. Alfred Thruston had taken a job as first cashier at the Bank of Louisville. Adam Reynolds is not mentioned in the sale; he may have belonged outright to Thruston or his wife and was thus not part of the property owned in partnership with his cousin.

13. O'Brien, "Slavery in Louisville," 18–22; Jay Stottman, staff archaeologist, Kentucky Archaeological Survey, "Consumer Market Access in Louisville's 19th-Century Commercial District" (unpublished report, 2004); and "Draft Report: Excavations at the Commonwealth Convention Center Site, Louisville, 2004"; Stafford, "Slavery in a Border City, 22–24; Wade, *Slavery in the Cities*, 55–79, 111–13.

14. Marie Jenkins Schwartz, *Born in Bondage: Growing Up Enslaved in the Antebellum South* (Cambridge, MA: Harvard University Press, 2000), 118–20.

15. H. W. Hawes is listed as a rope-maker in the 1832 *Louisville Directory*, so he was familiar with the business. However, after a protracted legal battle with Thruston, he filed for bankruptcy on August 8, 1842; Case File 0524, RG 21, U.S. District Courts, Bankruptcy Case Files, Kentucky State Archives. For a discussion of the sale and slave prices, see C. W. Thruston to John O'Fallon, April 25, 1836, and January 26, 1838, Thruston Papers, Filson Historical Society.

16. George H. Yater, *Two Hundred Years at the Falls of the Ohio: A History of Louisville and Jefferson County* (Louisville: Filson Club, 1987), 51; Hopkins, *History of the Hemp Industry*, 135–56. The resulting lawsuit lasted for many years; "Agreement of Release," Henry W. Hawes to A. J. Ballard (Fanny's husband) and Samuel Churchill Thruston (her brother), September 29, 1849, Thruston Papers, Filson Historical Society. By this document Hawes returned the ropewalk, equipment and land to Charles W. Thruston, his son-in-law and son acting as his agents in the matter. *Stockton v. Ford*, 52 US 11 How. 232 (1850), http://supreme.justia.com/us/52/232/case.html.

17. For the interstate trade, see Robert Gudmestad, *A Troublesome Commerce: The Transformation of the Interstate Slave Trade* (Baton Rouge: Louisiana State University Press, 2003); Steven Deyle, *Carry Me Back: The Domestic Slave Trade in American Life* (New York: Oxford University Press, 2005); Michael Tadman, *Speculators and Slaves: Masters, Traders, and Slaves in the Old South* (Madison: University of Wisconsin Press, 1989); and the classic works: Frederic Bancroft, *Slave Trading in the Old South* (Chapel Hill: University of South Carolina Press, 1931), and Thomas D. Clark, "The Slave Trade between Kentucky and the Cotton Kingdom," *Mississippi Valley Historical Review* 21, no. 3 (December 1934): 331–42. Asher says that after the sale of the rope-walk, Charles W. Thruston had twelve remaining slaves and a net worth for tax purposes of $35,025; Brad Asher, *Fanny and Cecelia: The Remarkable Friendship Between an Escaped Slave and Her Former Mistress* (Lexington: University of Kentucky, 2011), 32.

18. Fanny Thruston Ballard to Cecelia Jane Holmes, March 11, 1852, Ballard Family Papers, Filson Historical Society: "Your brother Edward, Papa still owns . . . he is now in his sixteenth year."

19. Fanny Thruston was given a superior education, particularly for a girl of her class and times. She was taught first by Henry A. Griswold, son of a prominent Episcopal bishop. He was not only a "bibliophile, geologist and mathematician, but he was familiar with the literature of many cultures, being fluent in Greek, Latin, French, Spanish, Italian and German." See Louisville *Courier-Journal*, March 6, 1923, for his biography. For the bills for Fanny's education, see H. A. Griswold to Charles W. Thruston, February 9, 1836, Thruston Papers, Filson Historical Society. The next year Fanny attended the Young Ladies' Seminary on Third Street between Green and Market. Fanny went on to Prather Grove Seminary, a very advanced educational institute, to study languages and literature, natural philosophy and history, along with mathematics, penmanship and bookkeeping. Fanny's cousin Caroline O'Fallon was also there, her tuition supplied by Fanny's father; M. C. Farnsworth to Charles W. Thruston, December 18, 1837, Thruston Papers, Filson Historical Society. The following term's bill includes voice and piano lessons; M. C. Farnsworth to Charles W. Thruston, February 26, 1838, Thruston Papers, Filson Historical Society. An advertisement is in the Louisville *Journal* of February 25, 1839. Caroline O'Fallon was a childhood friend and long-time correspondent of Julia Dent, who married Ulysses S. Grant; John Y. Simon, ed., *The Papers of Ulysses S. Grant*, vol. 28, *November 1, 1876–September 30, 1878* (Carbondale: University of Southern Illinois Press, 2005), 318.

20. Wilma King, *Stolen Childhood: Slave Youth in Nineteenth-Century America*, 2nd ed. (Bloomington: University of Indiana Press, 2011), ch. 3.

21. Benjamin Drew, *A North-Side View of Slavery: The Refugee; or, The Narratives of Fugitive Slaves in Canada. Related by Themselves, with an Account of the History and Condition of the Colored Population of Upper Canada* (Boston: John P. Jewett, 1856), 152. From the safety of Canada, Alfred T. Jones described his 1833 escape from Madison County, Kentucky: "I learned that my master was negotiating with another party to sell me for $400. Upon this, I wrote for myself a pass—it was not spelled correctly, but nobody there supposed that a slave could write at all." That Cecelia could not write is demonstrated by the fact that she signed her first marriage lines with an X. Marriage Registers of St. James Cathedral, November 19, 1846: "Banns, Benjamin Pollard Holmes, and Cecelia James Reynolds, both of the City of Toronto."

22. Isabella Beeton, *The Book of Household Management* (London: S. O. Beeton, 1861), 976.

23. Samuel Churchill Thruston, who was Fanny's only remaining brother, received a manservant of his own at the same time. Asher, *Fanny and Cecelia*, 18.

24. Charles's father, Charles Mynn Thruston, was not yet twelve when he accompanied his father, the "Fighting Preacher," onto the battlefields of the Revolutionary War; Gates Phillips Thruston, *A Sketch of the Ancestry of the Thruston-Phillips Families; with Some Records of the Dickinson, Houston, January Ancestry, and Allied Family Connections* (Nashville, TN: Thruston, 1909), 14–15.

25. "The Thruston Family," in Jennings, *Louisville's First Families*, 113–24.

26. Colonel William Oldham (1753–1791) distinguished himself at Brandywine and the Battle of Monmouth before moving to Kentucky in 1779. He lost his life commanding Kentucky militia forces at St. Clair's Defeat, November 4, 1791. His daughter, Abigail Penelope Pope Oldham (1789–1854), was brought up along with her brothers Richard Oldham and John Pope Oldham in the household of her stepfather, Henry Churchill (1768–1842), and married his younger brother Samuel Churchill (1779–1863) when she was fourteen.

27. Samuel Churchill served as a state senator in 1814–19 and in the Kentucky Legislature beginning in 1830. See "The Churchill Family" in Jennings, *Louisville's First Families*, 59–68.

28. Cecelia's circumstances were similar to those of Kate Billingsby of Hopkinsville, Kentucky. "Aunt Kate as she is generally called is a small black negro and in going into her home you will find it furnished in lovely antique furniture in a disreputable state of repair. She met me with a dignity and grace that would be a credit to any one of the white race to copy, illiterate though she may be. Her culture and training goes back to the old Buckner family, at one time one of the most cultured families in Christian County . . . being a maid when old enough, to one of Frank Buckner's daughters." *Kentucky Slave Narratives: A Folk History of Slavery in Kentucky from Interviews with Former Slaves* (Bedford, MA: Applewood, 2006), 60.

29. Dr. John Croghan (1790–1849) was one of several children of Charles W. Thruston's aunt Lucy Clark Croghan (1765–1838) and her husband William (1752–1822), who lived at Locust Grove on Louisville's eastern outskirts. He was trained at William and Mary University and the University of Pennsylvania medical school. Dr. Croghan bought 2,000 acres along the Green River near Bowling Green, including Mammoth Cave, in part to experiment with curing consumptives by having them live in the cool, dry air of the caves, which held a steady year-round temperature of 59° Fahrenheit. Remains of the stone huts the doctor built for his tubercular patients are still evident near the cave entrance. However, the cure was a failure and John Croghan himself succumbed to the disease. He returned to Louisville in 1846 and rented out the Mammoth Cave operation until his own death from tuberculosis in 1849.

30. Cecelia may have renewed her acquaintance with Stephen Bishop when Dr. Croghan brought him to Locust Grove in winter of 1841–42. There Bishop produced a map of Mammoth Cave's more than 300 miles of passages, a phenomenal piece of cartography that would remain the authoritative chart of the caves for almost a century. See "Map of the Explored Parts of the Mammoth Cave of Ky., by Stephen Bishop, one of the Guides," in Alexander Clark Bullitt, *Rambles in Mammoth Cave During the Year 1844* (Louisville: Morton and Griswold, 1845). Bishop also fell in love with Dr. Croghan's pretty housemaid, Charlotte. His owner rewarded Bishop by allowing Charlotte to move to Mammoth Cave with her new husband and become a housekeeper at the Mammoth Cave Hotel. His former owner Franklin Gorin, who began developing the cave for tourism, admired him, writing after Bishop's death: "Stephen was a self-educated man. He had a fine genius, a great fund of wit and humor, some little knowledge of Latin and Greek, and much knowledge of geology, but his great talent was knowledge of man." W. Stump Forwood, *Historical and Descriptive Narrative of the Mammoth Cave of Kentucky* (Philadelphia: Lippincott, 1870), 26.

31. Fanny's first letter to Cecelia in Toronto mentions her: "Isabelle Churchill married a merchant of St. Louis; and Sarah your old friend still lives with Belle in St. Louis." Fanny Thruston Ballard to Cecelia Jane Holmes, March 11, 1852, Ballard Family Papers, Filson Historical Society.

32. Ann Heron Croghan Jesup (1797–1846), daughter of Lucy Clark Croghan and William Croghan, was born at Locust Grove. She married Thomas Sidney Jesup, a Virginian career military officer who fought in Upper Canada in the War of 1812. President James Monroe appointed Colonel Jesup Quartermaster General of the United States Army on May 8, 1818. He also served in Florida, where there was controversy over his capture of Chief Osceola. He was away for a good deal of their marriage, and his wife and several children often stayed with her brother, Dr. John Croghan, at Locust Grove for extended periods. There survive many letters between Dr. Croghan and the Jesups attesting to a warm relationship, and Charles W. Thruston conducted the general's business relating to his Kentucky lands, and those that Ann had inherited from her parents' estate, on their behalf. Fanny and Cecelia would have visited Locust Grove on many occasions, staying overnight while Ann and her children were in residence. Fanny was the same age as Mary Jesup, who was to become the wife of James Blair. See Croghan Letters to General Jesup, 1842–46, Locust Grove; Gwynne Tuell Potts and Samuel W. Thomas, *George Rogers Clark, Military Leader of the Pioneer West, and Locust Grove, the Croghan Homestead Honoring Him* (Louisville: Historic Locust Grove, 2006); Clifford L. Kieffer, *Maligned General: The Biography of Thomas Sidney Jesup* (San Rafael, CA: Presidio, 1979). The pertinent Thomas Sidney Jesup Papers are in the Library of Congress, MSS27789, and there are several other collections pertaining to this important family at Princeton University (Blair Papers) and also at the Library of Congress, the Huntington Library at San Marino, California (Blair Family Papers), and the Washington Historical Society (Blair-Janin Papers).

33. James Blair was the second son of Francis Blair, a Virginia journalist and publisher educated in Kentucky. Francis Preston Blair (1791–1876) and his wife, Eliza Violet Gist (1794–1877), had three sons, Montgomery (1813–1883), James (1819–1852) and Francis Preston Jr. (1821–1875). William Ernest Smith, *The Francis Preston Blair Family in Politics*, 2 vols. (New York: Da Capo Press, 1969); Virginia Jean Laas, *Love and Power in the Nineteenth Century: The Marriage of Violet Blair* (Fayetteville, AR: University of Arkansas Press, 1998); and *Wartime Washington: The Civil War Letters of Elizabeth Blair Lee* (Urbana and Chicago: University of Illinois Press, 1991). Naval officer James Blair earned a fortune providing pilot services and operating steamboats on the

Sacramento River during the California gold rush; he died of a ruptured aorta in 1852, leaving Mary a widow with three small children, and she never remarried. As publisher of both the *Washington Globe* and the *Congressional Globe,* Francis Preston Blair Sr. had been in the White House inner circle as a member of Jackson's "Kitchen Cabinet." However, his opposition to the extension of slavery made him an opponent of the Mexican War; his star waned under the administration of President James K. Polk. The Blairs were Washington high society; their home is preserved as elegant guest quarters for visitors to the White House. Silver Springs, Maryland, is named after the family's summer home.

34. Henry Griswold Jesup, *Edward Jessup of West Farms, Westchester Co., New York, and His Descendants* (Cambridge: Jesup, 1887), 148–49.

35. Edward Hawkins Sisson, *America the Great* (e-book, 2014), 1300; E. J. Applewhite, *Washington Itself: An Informal Guide,* 2nd ed. (Lantham, MD: Madison, 1993); Richard F. Grimmett, *St. John's Church, Lafayette Square: The History and Heritage of the Church* (Minneapolis, MN: Hillcrest, 2009), 152–53. See also Rachel A. Shelden, *Washington Brotherhood: Politics, Social Life, and the Coming of the Civil War* (Chapel Hill: University of North Carolina Press, 2003), 53.

36. Amy S. Greenberg, *A Wicked War: Polk, Clay, Lincoln, and the 1846 U.S. Invasion of Mexico* (New York: Vintage, 2013), 74.

37. Interestingly, the artist Eastman Johnson later lived with his politician father just a few doors east of the Jesup home. The district was a fashionable one known, according to historian John Davis, as "the Ridge." In 1859, having returned from study in Europe, Johnson painted his famous *Negro Life at the South,* which depicts the enslaved socializing in an alley located one block west of the Jesup house. It shows a rear yard area attached to a tavern that was right next door to the Johnson home. While the image is idealized (no privies or laundry tubs are in evidence), with a banjo player providing music for a boy dancing and a courting couple, it also provides real insight into the living conditions of urban slaves. The quarters at the rear display rough wood and peeling paint, while the grounds are littered with trash. The variations in skin tone of the figures presented, including a light-skinned girl preparing vegetables and a baby held by a much darker-skinned woman on the roof of the rickety structure, offers a subtle critique of the sexual oppression of enslaved Black women by white men. See John Davis, "Eastman Johnson's *Negro Life at the South* and Urban Slavery in Washington D.C.," *Art Bulletin* 80, no. 1 (March 1998): 67–91. The painting was shown first at the National Academy of Design in 1859, clearly identified as a Washington scene, but it soon acquired an alternative title, *My Old Kentucky Home,* which confused generations of journalists and some art historians (Davis, 69). Davis makes the point that Eastman Johnson's sister, Harriet, married Reverend Joseph May, who was the son of abolitionist and Unitarian minister Samuel J. May and a nephew of Bronson and Abby (May) Alcott (hence Louisa May Alcott's middle name). However, John Fairfield, who was the political patron of Johnson's father in Washington, consistently voted with the proslavery South in opposition to the wishes of his constituency. The racial unrest referred to here was the Snow Riot; see Jefferson Morley, in *Snow Storm in August: The Struggle for American Freedom and Washington's Race Riot of 1835* (New York: Anchor Books, 2011), describes the riots in which one casualty was the fashionable oyster house on Pennsylvania Avenue owned by freedman Beverley Randolph Snow. It was burned to the ground and Snow fled to Toronto.

38. Indeed, a notorious "slave jail" was located behind an otherwise unremarkable house on G Street, just blocks from the Jesup home.

39. An early example was Jesse Torrey, whose shock was so great that he penned an important anti-slavery tract following his 1815 visit; Jesse Torrey, *A Portraiture of Domestic Slavery in the United States* (Philadelphia: Torrey, 1817), cited in Davis, "Eastman Johnson's *Negro Life*," 71.

40. Quoted in Davis, "Eastman Johnson's *Negro Life*," 73. The rule against presentation of such petitions was repealed, largely through the efforts of former president John Quincy Adams, in 1844; he argued that the gag rule violated the right of petition guaranteed by the US Constitution. For an extensive discussion, see Jeffrey A. Jenkins, "The Gag Rule, Congressional Politics, and the Growth of Anti-slavery Popular Politics" (PhD diss., Northwestern University, 2005).

CHAPTER 2: THAT BRIGHT AND SHINING LAND

1. Steward, *Twenty-Two Years a Slave*, 303–4.

2. J. Blaine Hudson, *Fugitive Slaves and the Underground Railroad in the Kentucky Borderland* (Jefferson, NC: McFarland, 2002), ch. 4 and 5. This and Hudson's *Encyclopedia of the Underground Railroad* (Jefferson, NC: McFarland, 2006) discuss the mechanisms developed to facilitate slave escape. Both books contain multiple references to the Underground Railroad between Kentucky and the towns and cities in the Great Lakes Basin, and to the links between the Niagara and Detroit River borderlands and the Upper South. The late J. Blaine Hudson, who was an expert on Underground Railroad activities among African Americans at Louisville, suggested to me that it was free Black barber Washington Spradling, who assisted at least thirty-three former slaves in purchasing their freedom, who engineered Cecelia's escape. He was literate and had a shop just a short walk from the Thrustons' Walnut Street home. J. Blaine Hudson, personal communication, 2008.

3. Many years later, Booker T. Washington wrote of his childhood on a Virginia farm: "I have never been able to understand how the slaves throughout the South, completely ignorant as were the masses so far as books or newspapers were concerned, were able to keep themselves so accurately and completely informed about the great National questions that were agitating the country . . . they kept themselves informed of events by what was termed the 'grape-vine' telegraph." Booker T. Washington, *Up from Slavery: An Autobiography* (Garden City, NJ: Doubleday, 1900), 8, accessed June 10, 2016, http://docsouth.unc.edu/fpn/washington/washing.html. The song was sung to the tune of "Oh Susannah," and was printed in the *Liberator* of December 10, 1852.

4. J. W. Erick and Coleman Daniel were the two partners. Erick is elusive but Daniel (1791–1863) was born in Caroline County, Virginia, and was probably associated with the Clark family prior to moving to Kentucky. He was a merchant and city politician, representing Ward 2 in Louisville's municipal government in the first decades of the nineteenth century.

5. "$300 Reward. Ran Away from the Subscribers, living in Louisville, on the 19th of November last, a negro man named ANDREW JONES . . . " *Indiana Democrat*, February 12, 1831. A plasterer by trade, about forty years old and five feet, ten inches or so tall, he had lost nearly all his teeth but had "a pleasant countenance when spoken to, and [was] plausible and intelligent." Andrew's wife, Maria, was also described: "28 or 29 years of age, is large, likely and well-made . . . usually talks loud and distinctly, and had, when she left, a thick coat of hair." It is interesting to note that the advertisement accords a surname to Andrew Jones. Slaveholders were well aware that their slaves had last names, but generally recorded them only in cases such as advertisements, or occasionally in wills, where it was necessary to ensure that the self-identification was recognized.

6. Two decades later an agricultural census shows Andrew and Maria Jones living on Lot 3, Concession 4, of Sandwich East. They owned a hundred-acre farm with thirty acres under cultivation and a seventy-acre woodlot, and four more children had been born to them. Census of Canada West, 1851, Sandwich East, Essex County; Agricultural Census of Canada West, 1851, Sandwich East, Essex County.

7. Lauren E. LaFauci, "Taking the (Southern) Waters: Science, Slavery, and Nationalism at the Virginia Springs," *Anthropology & Medicine* 18, no. 1 (2011): 7–22; Audrea McDowell, "The Pursuit of Health and Happiness at the Paroquet Springs in Kentucky, 1838 to 1888," *Filson Club Historical Quarterly* 69, no. 4 (October 1995): 390–420. On November 23, 1838, C. W. Thruston had a financial interest in at least one such resort. He advanced $500 for "improvement of the Shepherdsville Springs and Paroquet Tract of land in Bullitt County," secured by a mortgage on the property. C. W. Thruston Papers, Folder 15, Filson Historical Society, Louisville, KY.

8. Lucy Delaney, whose sister Nancy escaped to Canada via Niagara Falls in similar circumstances, explains that Nancy was advised by her mother, who had a friend in Toronto, to flee while she was so close to the border. (The fact that she knew the friend's location is interesting in itself, for it supports the contention that there was two-way communication between the largest city in Canada West and Louisville.) The young woman waited until her owners were away for the day seeing the sights. She carefully locked up her owners' trunk, left the key where it might be found, and used the distraction of a local festival to make her way to the ferry and safely across into Canada. Nancy told her sister, "A servant in the hotel gave me all necessary information and even assisted me in getting away"; Lucy A. Delaney (Lucy Ann), *From the Darkness Cometh the Light; or, Struggles for Freedom* (St. Louis, MO: J. T. Smith, 1891), 16–17.

9. Until 1841, New York law permitted visiting slaveholders to retain their human property for up to nine months, the better to support the commercial enterprises of tourist resorts such as Saratoga Springs and Niagara Falls; Paul Finkelman, "Slaves in Transit and the Antebellum Crisis," in *Historic U.S. Court Cases: An Encyclopedia*, vol. 2, ed. John W. Johnson, 2nd ed. (New York: Routledge, 2001), 608–10.

10. Although the Cataract House burned to the ground in 1945, fifty-three of the hotel's ledgers, many of them from the antebellum years, were preserved in a fireproof safe; Cataract House Register, May 1, 1844–September 12, 1847, Niagara Falls Public Library, Niagara Falls, NY. Cecelia's escape was arranged in advance; for how else would Benjamin Holmes have known to go to the Cataract House before the Thruston party's arrival?

11. It was both dangerous and inconvenient for Benjamin to book a room at Niagara Falls. Because of the current below the waterfall, steamboats could penetrate the Niagara River only as far as Lewiston on the US shore and Queenston on the Canadian. After that, passengers took a short railway ride to complete the journey to the Falls. Also, as a Black man Benjamin faced discrimination at the hotel. Unlike the white guests who signed in before and after him, there is no room number beside Benjamin's name. Guests of African descent may have been accommodated in segregated dormitories apart from the white visitors, as was the case at Saratoga Springs, a popular resort in upstate New York that also catered to Southern guests. Jon Sterngass, "African American Workers and Southern Visitors at Antebellum Saratoga Springs," *American Nineteenth Century History* 2, no. 2 (2001): 35–59. See also Edgar McManus, *A History of Negro Slavery in New York* (Syracuse, NY: Syracuse University Press, 1966), 141–79.

12. The Cataract House was an important way station on the route to Canada. Its Southern guests were quite correct in suspecting the African American staff of conspiring to help their "servants"

escape. They also hid freedom-seekers who arrived at the border independently, passing them on to Canada in a well-coordinated operation that began as early as 1840. Nearly every waiter employed at the Cataract was African American or African Canadian, and at least one lived in Toronto with his family in the off-season. Working at the Cataract House in 1850 was Moseby Hubbard (listed as Moses in the 1850 US census). He continued his seasonal employment at the Falls through at least 1875. His story is well documented, for his son, William Peyton Hubbard, became Toronto's first (and last) Black deputy mayor. Bill Bradberry, "A Better Glimpse into Cataract House's Past," *Niagara Gazette*, February 5, 2013. For Hubbard, see US State Census, 1865, Niagara Falls, "Cataract Hotel"; Stephen L. Hubbard, *Against All Odds: The Story of William Peyton Hubbard, Black Leader and Municipal Reformer* (Toronto: Dundurn, 1987); and Catherine Slaney, *Family Secrets: Crossing the Colour Line* (Toronto: Dundurn, 2003), 207.

13. Born in Scotland, Thomas Dick (1809–1874) came to Upper Canada in 1833. Although Benjamin P. Holmes usually worked the Niagara route on the *Transit*, operated by Captain Hugh Richardson, it had been damaged in an accident the month before. Despite their very different backgrounds, Captain Dick and Benjamin developed a special relationship, and the good captain would in later years witness Benjamin's will. Captain Dick was suspected of assisting fugitives on their way across the lake to Canada, and Richardson openly admitted his involvement. His personal antislavery sentiments were demonstrated years later, when Richardson was on the Toronto committee formed to protest the proposed rendition of fugitive slave John Anderson to the United States on a charge of murder. See "Canada," *British and Foreign Anti-slavery Reporter*, 3rd ser., 9, no. 2 (February 1, 1860): 27; "Thomas Dick," K. R. Macpherson, *Dictionary of Canadian Biography*, accessed October 5, 2016, http://www.biographi.ca/en/bio/dick_thomas_10E.html.

14. Samuel Thruston's brash nature was manifest in his early exploits, including fighting a duel on June 21, 1842 at the age of fifteen against a thirteen-year-old opponent over "an affair of the heart," as reported in the Boston *Traveler* of July 5, 1842, quoting an article in the *Louisville Sun*.

15. Many years later, the famous Black composer Nathaniel Dett, who played the piano at the Cataract Hotel as a young man, described the parlour as he remembered it just after the turn of the twentieth century; R. Nathaniel Dett, "From Bell Stand to Throne Room: A Remarkable Autobiographical Interview with the Eminently Successful American Negro Composer," *Black Perspective in Music* 1, no. 1 (Spring 1973): 76.

16. Fanny had an acquaintance there already. Solon Whitney co-owned the Cataract House with his two brothers-in-law, and his wife, Frances, helped him manage the hotel. The former Frances Drake (1822–1883) had been brought up in Kentucky and moved in the same social circles as the Thrustons. Her father was Samuel H. Drake, the first manager of the Louisville Hotel, in which Charles W. Thruston and several of Fanny's relations had a financial interest. A. Vaudricourt, *A Guide to the Falls of Niagara* (New York: Burgess, Stringer, 1846), 10; Judith Wellman, "Solon and Frances Whitney House," in *Survey of Sites Relating to the Underground Railroad, Abolitionism, and African American Life in Niagara Falls and Surrounding Area, 1820–1880* (New York Historical Research Associates, April 2012), 133–36; http://www.niagarafallsundergroundrailroad.org/index.php/sites/56-10-solon-whitney-home; Judith Wellman, "Site of the Home of Peter A. Porter, Elizabeth Porter, and Josephine Porter," in *Survey of Sites*, 1–7, accessed June 14, 2014, http://www.niagarafallsundergroundrailroad.org/assets/Uploads/11-Site-of-the-Home-of-Peter-A-Elizabeth-and-Josephine-Porter.pdf; Samuel H. Drake, "The American Hotel," in *The Craftsman*, vol. 2, 1829–30 (Rochester, NY: E.J. Roberts, 1830), 139; "Louisville Hotel," *Pittsburgh Gazette*, November 25, 1833; Obituary of Samuel H. Drake, *Albany Daily Advertiser*, October 7, 1836.

17. Quoted in William R. Irwin, *The New Niagara: Tourism, Technology, and the Landscape of Niagara Falls* (University Park: Pennsylvania State University Press, 1996), 22–23.

18. Michael Power and Nancy Butler, *Slavery and Freedom in Niagara* (Niagara-on-the-Lake, ON: Niagara Historical Society, 1993), 56–57.

19. Examples of First Nations souvenirs brought home from the Falls can be found in the collections of the Missouri State Museum. See also S. DeVeaux, *The Falls of Niagara; or, Tourist's Guide to This Wonder of Nature* (Buffalo, NY: William B. Hayden, 1839), 163.

20. "It was the custom of wealthy planters from the South to visit Niagara Falls each season and bring with them from one to three body servants. Some of these servants were quite gaily dressed"; "Site of the Cataract House," 11, accessed October 12, 2014, http://www.niagarafallsundergroundrailroad. org/documents/02_Site%20of%20the%20 Cataract%20House.pdf.

21. Miss Leslie, "Niagara," *Godey's Lady's Book* (December 1845): 230–38.

22. *Niagara Falls Gazette*, August 5, 1856. One of the most prolific Underground Railroad conductors in the whole region, at Lockport Emancipation Day celebrations in 1859, John Morrison was presented with a gold-headed cane as a "mark of respect from his associates." See Michelle Anne Kratts, "Bringing Lost Souls Home: John Morrison, a Hero of Niagara," accessed May 12, 2016, http://myoakwoodcemetery.com/kratts-korner/2013/3/26/bringing-lost-souls-home-john-morrison-a-hero-of-niagara.html; and Judith Wellman, "Niagara Falls Underground Railroad Heritage Area Management Plan, Appendix C," in *Survey of Sites*, accessed May 15, 2016, http:// www.niagarafallsundergroundrailroad.org/assets/Uploads/NF-HAMP-Report-Appendix-C-1. pdf. An abolitionist visitor wrote that Morrison ferried several fugitives across the river during her own stay; Robert Clemens Smedley, *History of the Underground Railroad in Chester and the Neighboring Counties of Pennsylvania* (Lancaster, PA: John A. Hibstand, 1883), 281–82.

23. Ann Everitt, "Diary of a Trip to Canada and the USA," entry for June 4, [184–], Mickle Family Papers, Special Collections, Guelph University Library. This is from the transcription by Jane Ward, with corrections by Cynthia Kerman. Frederick Law Olmsted had travelled thousands of miles "without finding elsewhere the same quality of forest beauty which was once abundant about the falls, and which is still to be observed in those parts of Goat Island where the original growth of trees and shrubs had not been disturbed"; J. B. Harrison, "Movement for the Redemption of Niagara," *New Princeton Review* (1886): 233–45.

24. Exactly this sequence of events occurred in the case of a woman known only as Jane, who was left behind at the Cataract by her owners while they visited the battlefields on the other side of the river. She fled by way of the ferry and was harboured in Canada in the home of a "respectable coloured man." Although her location was discovered, she declined to come to the door to meet her former owner; as he stood in front of the house she conversed with him from the safety of an upper window. All his blandishments and threats made no impression, so he commenced to curse abolitionists, British law and the Queen under whose protection Jane was sheltering. This was too much for the patriotism of the gathering crowd, one of whom replied: "Say that again and I'll knock your teeth down your throat." The slaveholder slunk away, and Jane was free. "An Interesting Incident," *Frederick Douglass' Paper*, June 26, 1851.

25. Among the Thrustons' older relatives and friends were several who had built military reputations on their exploits on the Niagara frontier. Jesup was wounded at Chippewa. See Kieffer, *Maligned General*, ch. 2. Charles's first cousin George Croghan was the "Hero of Sandusky." At the tender age of twenty-three, he defended Fort Stephenson against nearly overwhelming odds when it had been given up for lost; Alan Taylor, *The Civil War of 1812: American Citizens, British Subjects,*

Irish Rebels and Indian Allies (New York: Vintage Books, 2010), 242; H. Z. Williams, compl. *History of Sandusky County, Ohio* (Cleveland: H. Z. Williams & Bro. 1882), 101–8.

26. "The 'Maid of the Mist,' a Steam Boat to ply across the Niagara River immediately below the Cataract, launched Saturday last, and is expected to commence her trip on the 1st of June"; "Niagara Falls Steam Ferry Boat," *Albany Evening Journal*, May 28, 1846. See also "Niagara Falls," *Vermont Phoenix* (Brattleboro), March 5, 1846.

27. J. D. Tivoli, *A Guide to the Falls of Niagara* (New York: Burgess, Stringer, 1846), 10–11.

28. Francis Lieber, *Letters to a Gentleman in Germany: Written after a Trip from Philadelphia to Niagara* (Philadelphia: Cary, Lea and Blanchard, 1834), 335.

29. Reverend William Troy, *Hair-Breadth Escape from Slavery to Freedom* (Manchester: W. Bremner, 1861), viii.

30. RCB Thruston Memoir, 1899.

Chapter 3: Chilly Waters in the Jordan

1. Hiram Wilson to William Goodell, "Friend of Man," copied to *The Emancipator*, September 10, 1840. The "coloured friend" was Grandison Boyd. Reverend Hiram Wilson (1803–1864) was a dedicated missionary to Canada's fugitive-slave population, a former Lane Rebel and a graduate of Oberlin College. He was first sent to Canada in 1836 by evangelist Charles Grandison Finney and the next year he solicited funding from the American Anti-Slavery Society to move to Toronto. In 1842 he joined with Kentucky freedom-seeker Josiah Henson to found the British-American Institute, the first integrated manual labour school in Canada, at the Dawn Settlement (now Dresden, Ontario). Wilson was a regular correspondent with abolitionists and the antislavery press in the United States. See "Rev. Hiram Wilson of St. Catharines," *St. Catharines Journal*, November 4, 1852; "Death of Hiram Wilson," *Liberator*, May 13, 1864, 79; J. Brent Morris, *Oberlin, Hotbed of Abolitionism: College, Community, and the Fight for Freedom and Equality in Antebellum America* (Chapel Hill: University of North Carolina Press, 2014), 83–87; William H. Pease and Jane H. Pease, "Henson, Josiah," *Dictionary of Canadian Biography*, vol. 11, accessed January 13, 2016, http://www.biographi.ca/009004-119.01-e.php?BioId=39700.

2. Robin W. Winks, *The Blacks in Canada*, 2nd ed. (Montreal: McGill-Queen's University Press, 1997), 96; William Renwick Riddell, "The Slave in Upper Canada," *Journal of Negro History* (October 1919): 372–86; and, most recently, Adrienne Shadd, "Chloe Cooley and the 1793 Act to Limit Slavery in Upper Canada" (unpublished report to Ontario Heritage Trust, 2007), and historical plaque, accessed May 12, 2016, http://www.heritagetrust.on.ca/CorporateSite/media/oht/PDFs/Chloe-Cooley-ENG.pdf.

3. *An Act to Prevent the Further Introduction of Slaves and to Limit the Term of Contracts for Servitude*, Statutes of Upper Canada, 3 George III, cap. 7, 1793; *An Act for the Abolition of Slavery Throughout the British Colonies; for Promoting the Industry of the Manumitted Slaves; and for Compensating the Persons Hitherto Entitled to the Services of Such Slaves*, 3 & 4 Will. IV, c. 73, 1833 (effective August 1, 1834).

4. The ship cleared port on August 3, 1840; *Spectator* (New York), August 10, 1840.

5. "Emancipation Declaration of Alexander Fleet of King & Queen County Va., at Richmond, Va., July 18, 1840," and "Emancipation Declaration of James T. Fisher Jr., Richmond, Va., July 30, 1840"; Hiram Wilson (Toronto) to Joshua Leavitt (New York), August 28, 1840; *The Emancipator*, September 10, 1840.

6. Carey C. Hall, "King and Queen County Courthouse," in *Old Houses of King and Queen County*, ed. Virginia D. Cox and Willie T. Weathers (King and Queen County Historical Society, 1973), 91. Early records were lost in a courthouse fire in 1828, but the new courthouse was burnt to the ground, along with most of the village structures, on March 10, 1864, in retaliation for an ambush on Union troops that involved local soldiers and militia. Robert Pollard Jr. rebuilt the house and courthouse. See Barbara Beigun Kaplan, *Land and Heritage in the Virginia Tidewater: A History of King and Queen County* (Richmond: Kaplan, 1993), 82–83; Elizabeth H. Hutchinson, "King and Queen County Courthouse," *Bulletin of the King and Queen County Historical Society of Virginia* [hereafter KQCHS] 8 (January 1969): 1–2.

7. Robert Pollard Sr. (1763–1835) trained as a clerk and in 1792 succeeded Richard Tunstall Jr. at the King and Queen County Court; Hall, "King and Queen County Courthouse," 91. In 1794 Robert Pollard married Elizabeth Harwood. They had four children: Maria; Priscilla; Elizabeth (Betsey), born on June 6, 1800; and Robert, born in 1804; "Harwoods of King & Queen," *William & Mary Quarterly* 10, no. 3 (January 1902): 198–99. Betsey's birth date is recorded in the Hoomes family Bible, in the collections of the Virginia Historical Society, Mss6:4, H7655:3 and on a sampler she embroidered that survives in the collection of the King and Queen Courthouse Tavern Museum. The relationship with Katie is inferred from letters that Benjamin and his mother published in the Richmond papers after his escape. There was no adult white woman, but two boys and a girl were living in the Pollard household at that time, along with eight slaves; US Census, 1810, Virginia, King and Queen County. The earlier ownership history of Catharine or Katie (Hoomes) Holmes cannot be certainly reconstructed from surviving evidence. See note 11 below for the Hoomes family connection.

8. Alexander's father, William (1757–1833)—or "Captain Billy," as he was commonly known—had served in the Revolution and voted for ratification of the US Constitution at the convention of 1788; VHS, "Records of the Fleet Family," vol. 2, 76. Captain Billy Fleet purchased Goshen, in King and Queen County, Virginia, in 1800 and divided two thousand acres with his sons. Dr. Christopher B. Fleet (1796–1845) constructed Fleetwood across the road from his father's house, and Alexander Fleet built Melville next to it. *Virginia Colonial Abstracts*, vol. 2, 478. Goshen and Melville still stand on either side of the road leading from Tappahannock to Richmond, about four miles east of St. Stephen's Church; *Virginia Genealogical Society Quarterly Bulletin* 2, no. 1 (January 1964): 9. See also Diane Longest, "Goshen," in KQCHS 67 (July 1989): 4.

9. William Cathcart, ed., *Baptist Encyclopedia: A Dictionary of . . . the Baptist Denomination in All Lands*, rev. ed. (Philadelphia: L. H. Everts, 1881), 793. Rather surprisingly, after the Civil War Alexander Fleet opened a small school in his house, and subsequently one for free African American children, which he financed personally.

10. Major Thomas Claiborne Hoomes was born in King and Queen County on June 16, 1781, and died there on February 6, 1821, leaving Betsey Pollard Hoomes a very young widow. The dates come from his tombstone, discovered by Elizabeth Burnette Newsome in a field on her property in 2002, and included here thanks to her. Betty E. B. Newsome, personal communication, July 2012; Beverley Fleet, *King and Queen County* (Baltimore, MD: Genealogical Publishing, 1961), 88. Betsey's remarriage took place in about 1829, for the 1830 tax records show Alexander Fleet as responsible for 287 acres of land from Thomas Claiborne Hoomes's personal estate. The dates for Christopher and Alexander and the rest of the Fleet family come directly from stones in the Goshen cemetery.

11. Letter of Alexander Fleet, Section 8, Bagby Papers, Virginia Historical Society. Robert Pollard Sr. and Thomas Claiborne Hoomes were both descended from George Hoomes of Bowling

Green, who died in 1733 in Caroline County. George's grandson Joseph married Priscilla Hoomes, and one of their two sons was William Pollard (1726–1781) of Buckeye. He was a close friend of neighbour Patrick Henry. William's sister Frances married George Rogers of Caroline County, and was therefore the aunt of George Rogers Clark and William Clark of Kentucky and great-aunt of Charles Thruston, Fanny Thruston's father. The family intermarried with many well-known Virginia and later Kentucky families. Fanny Thruston Ballard's mother was also a member of this family through the Churchills, so Benjamin Pollard Holmes was actually a relative of Fanny Thruston on both her mother's and father's sides. See *Old Homes of Hanover County* (Hanover, VA: Hanover County Historical Society, 1983), 63; and Mary Pollard Clarke, "The Will of Joseph Pollard of King & Queen County, Virginia," *William and Mary Quarterly*, 2nd ser., 2, no. 3 (July 1922): 162–66.

12. Thomas R. Gray, *Confessions of Nat Turner* (Baltimore, MD: Thomas R. Gray, 1831), accessed June 9, 2016, http://docsouth.unc.edu/neh/turner/turner.html.

13. James T. Fisher Jr. (1803–1868) was related to Alexander Fleet by marriage. The Richmond *Commercial Compiler* notes that his brother, Dr. Christopher Brown [it should be Bennett] Fleet, was married on September 28, 1820, to Mary Ann McKim, "only daughter of the late Mr. Andrew McKim of this city." Mary Ann was a first cousin to Elizabeth McKim Fisher, James's first wife, who died in 1833. Andrew McKim had been in partnership with his brother Robert, Elizabeth's father, until his death late in 1805. See Beverley Fleet, *King and Queen County* (Baltimore, MD: Genealogical Publishing, 1961), 88. Mary Ann died October 23, 1828, and was buried at Goshen; death notice, *Richmond Enquirer*, November 11, 1828.

14. At this time the Fishers' home was one of only three between 23rd and 24th Streets on the south side of East Franklin Avenue. The Sanborne fire insurance map for 1865 shows the block as much more densely populated, but the only building that straddles Lots 53 and 54 the Fisher home was described in the tax rolls as a handsome flat-fronted Georgian with two dormers and a little porch on the left (east) front. The map also shows a two-storey brick building behind marked "Servants." There are no houses standing there today, although a historic photo in the collections of the Library of Virginia shows a boarded-up home of this description slated for demolition in the mid-twentieth century. See Tax Rolls for Richmond, Virginia, Jefferson Ward, 1839, for the alphabetical listing of James Fisher's annual property tax; and also Samuel Mordechai, *Richmond in Bye Gone Days, Being Reminiscences of an Old Citizen* (Richmond, VA: George M. West, 1856), 330.

15. David R. Goldfield, *Urban Growth in the Age of Sectionalism: Virginia, 1847–1861* (Baton Rouge: Louisiana State University Press, 1977), 133ff; Jack Trammell, *The Richmond Slave Trade: The Economic Backbone of the Old Dominion* (Charleston, SC: History Press, 2012), 59–62; Midori Takagi, *Rearing Wolves to Our Own Destruction: Slavery in Richmond, Virginia, 1782–1865* (Charlottesville: University Press of Virginia, 1990), 78–79. See also Kimberly Merkel Chen and Hannah W. Collins, "The Slave Trade as a Commercial Enterprise in Richmond, Virginia," MPS 127-6196, National Register of Historic Places, July 25, 2006 (rev. April 9, 2007), Virginia Department of Historic Resources, Richmond, VA.

16. *Minutes and Proceedings of the First Annual Convention of the People of Colour* (Philadelphia: Committee of Arrangements, 1831), accessed July 29, 2016, http://www.blackpast.org/aah/national-negro-convention-movement-1831-1864#sthash.JYTJBSlH.dpuf; David Walker, *Walker's Appeal, in Four Articles; Together with a Preamble, to the Coloured Citizens of the World*, 3rd ed. (Boston: D. Walker, 1830). William Lloyd Garrison who had previously been a printer

for Benjamin Lundy's *Genius of Universal Emancipation*, started the *Liberator* on January 1, 1831, publishing a letter "To the Public" that stated his commitment to what came to be called "immediatism" (as opposed to espousing the gradual manumission of American slaves over time), including these words: "I am in earnest—I will not equivocate—I will not excuse—I will not retreat a single inch—AND I WILL BE HEARD."

17. Clement Eaton, "Slave Hiring in the Upper South: A Step Toward Freedom," *Mississippi Valley Historical Review* 46, no. 4 (March 1960): 663–78.

18. Such transactions usually took place during Christmas week. See for example, the bond of Francis K. Conn to Charles C. Johnson, both of Richmond, VA, January 29, 1824: a slave hiring contract requiring that he furnish "Godfrey," whom he had hired, with "a suit of comfortable linsey clothes, one pair of shoes & stockings, two shirts and two pairs of pantaloons of tow linen as he may want them during the year." He goes on to promise to pay, "on or before the 25th day of January 1825," fifty dollars to Johnson for the hire and "to pay the tax on said boy." VHS Mss2, C7624, a1, accessed July 26, 2012, ttp://vhs4.vahistorical.org/vhsimages/manuscripts/Mss2/Mss2.C7624a1_front.jpg.

19. Richmond tax records for these years show that Fisher maintained an office for his company in the rear yard of his home. Since Benjamin later intended to set himself up in the tobacco trade in Liberia, I am assuming he learned the business at his Richmond employer's side. The Fisher house stood on the southwest edge of the hillside, overlooking the James River and Shockoe Bottom, where slavedealers had their pens.

20. Several free Black families moved to Toronto in the years following the Nat Turner Rebellion, and Benjamin had likely encountered at least some of them while living in Richmond. The Carters, Waddells, Hickmans and Gallegos all had active members in Richmond's free Black community when Benjamin was there. The intermarried clan of Pattersons, Dunlops and Rosses came from Fredericksburg, but several members worked intermittently in Richmond.

21. Marie Tyler-McGraw, *In Bondage and Freedom: Antebellum Black Life in Richmond, Virginia* (Richmond, VA: Valentine Museum, 1988), and *At the Falls: Richmond, Virginia and Its People* (Richmond, VA: Valentine Museum, 1994), especially ch. 4.

22. On earning one's own money by "overwork" and on the question of self-purchase, see John Saillant, ed., *Afro-Virginian History and Culture* (New York: Routledge, 1999), 85; and J. Blaine Hudson, *Fugitive Slaves and the Underground Railroad in the Kentucky Borderland* (Jefferson, NC: McFarland, 2002), 139–41. There are examples in Benjamin Drew, *The Refugee: Narratives of Fugitive Slaves in Canada* (1856; reprint, Toronto: Dundurn, 2008).

23. Ellinor, twenty-one, and her baby girl, Ann Eliza, had originally belonged to Elizabeth's father, Robert McKim, and his wife, Elizabeth Montgomery, formerly of Loudon County. Robert McKim was a noted maker of Windsor-style chairs, including those gracing the Virginia capital building. In 1820 Ellinor and little Ann Eliza were sold to Robert's spinster sister-in-law, Jane (or Jeanette) Montgomery. Robert knew he was dying, and as he had suffered a major reversal in his business, he wanted to shelter them and his other valuable possessions from creditors. See Giles Cromwell, "Andrew and Robert McKim: Early Windsor Chair Makers," *Journal of Early Southern Decorative Arts* 6, no. 1 (May 1980): 1–20. The deed of sale for Ellinor reads in part, "[I] do grant, bargain and sell unto the said J Montgomery the following Negro slaves: Ellinor a woman of about twenty one years old, and her female child called Ann Eliza about nine months old, and William, or Billy, a lad of about nineteen years old . . . [A considerable amount of furniture and other household items is then carefully listed.] . . . But it is hereby agreed and expressly stipulated between the parties that

the condition of this bill of sale is and shall be that the said McKim is allowed and authorized to retain the use of the said slaves, furniture and to have possession of the same until the first day of January in the year 1823"; Deed of Sale, Robert McKim to Jeanette McKim (October 13, 1820), Richmond City Circuit Court, Deed Book 18, 69. I am indebted to Carolyn Gutermuth for sharing with me this important document detailing Ann Eliza's early history.

24. The reluctance is inferred from Alexander Fleet's issues with fugitive slaves. Should he force Benjamin to return to Melville, the young man would be dissatisfied with being so far from his wife and any children she would bear him, and might run away to be near them.

25. F. Johnston, *Memorials of Old Virginia Clerks* (Lynchburg, VA: J. P. Bell, 1888), 233–34. Because of courthouse fires, Robert Pollard Senior's will does not survive. That the will contained instructions to manumit Benjamin comes from letters he and his mother both wrote, the contents of which was published in the *Richmond Dispatch* after his 1840 escape. Katie Holmes lived in the household of Robert Pollard Jr.; Robert was widowed, and the two elderly souls were the only occupants of the house, with the exception of a maid. The 1870 census describes Catharine Holmes, aged 78, as Black and a "domestic servant"; US Census, 1870, King and Queen County, VA. They would die within a month of each other in 1878. Benjamin's white half-sister, Betsey (Pollard) (Hoomes) Fleet, died June 26, 1841, and was buried in Goshen Cemetery. Her husband remarried and passed away in 1877. He was interred between his first and second wives, but, unusually, Betsey's grave faces in the opposite direction to those of Alexander and Martha Ann (Hill Butler) Fleet.

26. "I learn of Mr. Holmes that his father, who was his master, died some years since and left him free, as he was told, but his assumed master, Alexander Fleet, of King and Queen co., who had hired him out at Richmond for 9 years and received his wages, emancipated him on the condition that he would go to Liberia"; Hiram Wilson to William Goodell, *The Emancipator*, September 10, 1840.

27. David O. Whitten, "Slave Buying in 1835 Virginia as Revealed by Letters of a Louisiana Negro Sugar Planter," *Louisiana History: Journal of the Louisiana Historical Association* 1, no. 3 (Summer 1970): 231–44; F. Johnson, ed., *Memorials of Old Virginia Clerks* (Lynchburg: J. P. Bell, 1888), 231–33.

28. This was according to the principle of *partus sequitur ventrem* adopted by Virginia in 1662 to deal with the issue of which slaveholder would own the offspring if the parents were owned by two different people. "The child follows the condition of the mother" became pervasive in American slave law. Thomas D. Morris, *Southern Slavery and the Law, 1619–1860* (Chapel Hill: University of North Carolina Press, 2004), 43–49. The point was forcibly brought home when James Fisher Jr. experienced some reversals of fortune in 1837, owing to the US-wide banking crisis brought on in part by President Andrew Jackson's withdrawal of support for the Bank of the United States. This is reflected in Fisher's need to sell off his factory property in Shockoe Bottom. The company rallied and Fisher moved his very large operation further west, to 12th Street near Cary. This was sold when he retired, along with furnishings and equipment; see advertisement "By John R. D. Payne," *Richmond Whig*, December 31, 1852. The timing of the sale is significant. Fisher would normally have conducted slave hiring for his operation during Christmas week. There would only have been slaves he owned on the premises in late December; the ones he had hired for the previous year had gone back to their owners by that time.

29. Marie Tyler-McGraw, *An African Republic: Black and White Virginians in the Making of Liberia* (Chapel Hill: University of North Carolina Press, 2014), 12. According to the excellent

dissertation by Alex Lovit, "'The Bounds of Habitation': The Geography of the American Colonization Society, 1816–1860" (PhD diss., University of Michigan, 2011), 41, "From 1820 to 1840, 85 percent of slaveowners who emancipated their slaves for Liberian colonization were of Upper South origin, and though the practice of Liberian manumission became somewhat more common in the Lower South over time, by the 1850s, 75 percent of colonizationist manumitters still were Upper South natives." He cites as his authority Eric Burin, *Slavery and the Peculiar Solution: A History of the American Colonization Society* (Gainesville: University Press of Florida, 2005), 36, 46.

30. "Speech of the Hon. Henry Clay, before the American Colonization Society: In the Hall of the House of Representatives, January 20, 1827" (Washington, DC: Columbian Office, 1827), 11–12. Clay had articled at Richmond but chose Kentucky as his home. He negotiated the bill that resulted in the 1820 Missouri Compromise. He was a former Speaker of the House and, with John C. Calhoun and Daniel Webster of Massachusetts, one of the great triumvirate of antebellum American politics. He was a slaveholder himself, although Clay always maintained that he opposed the institution. He was active in the American Colonization Society for many years.

31. Marie Tyler-McGraw, "Richmond Free Blacks and African Colonization," *Journal of American Studies* 21 (1987): 207–24; Tyler-McGraw, *African Republic*.

32. Hiram Wilson to Joshua Leavitt, *The Emancipator*; reprinted in *The Colored American*, September 19, 1840.

33. Katie Hoomes is referring to the slaves of Dr. Aylett Hawes, an Edinburgh-trained physician and planter in Rappahannock and King William Counties. In his will he freed all 110 of his slaves and provided substantial funding for their emigration and settlement in Liberia. They were conveyed by the ACS to a new settlement some sixty miles south of the capital, Monrovia, at Bassa Cove with the assistance of the Pennsylvania branch of the ACS; they landed in the late fall, 1834. However, angry slave traders incited an attack by local tribes on June 10, 1835, which killed nearly one-fifth of the settlers. Monrovia settlers retaliated and, after about six months of warfare, re-established the Bassa Cove settlement. See Burin, *Slavery and the Peculiar Solution*, 86–87. However, some of the Hawes emigrants prospered, as did Reverend A. P. Davis, who wrote to the ACS on October 11, 1849, praising the colony. See also Sarah H. Hale, *Liberia; or, Mr. Peyton's Experiments* (New York: Harper & Brothers, 1853), 251–53. The fullest and most recent account is in Mary Tyler-McGraw, "Aylett Hawes and William Grimes: Utopian Emancipator and Freedom Seeker," *Virginia Emigrants to Liberia*, Virginia Center for Digital History, University of Virginia, accessed June 14, 2014, http://www.vcdh.virginia.edu/liberia/index.php?page=Stories&section=Hawes%20and%20Grimes.

34. Hiram Wilson to Joshua Leavitt, *The Emancipator*; reprinted in *The Colored American*, September 19, 1840.

35. Cummins describes Benjamin P. Holmes, with his wife and child, as of "good character" and "young and active" on the list "Applicants for Emigration to Liberia" in 1840. The whole family "went out August 1840," according to the same source. C. Cummins to Samuel Wilkerson, July 8, 1840, American Colonization Society Papers, Incoming Correspondence, Reel 34, A78, pt. 1, Library of Congress.

36. The manumission documents were published in their entirety in Hiram Wilson (Toronto) to Joshua Leavitt (New York), August 28, 1840; *The Emancipator*, September 10, 1840.

37. The advertisements informed would-be settlers that "emigrants who are able to provide for their own wants, should furnish themselves with mattresses, bed-clothes, two suits of wearing apparel,

cooking utensils &c; and if mechanics, the tools of their trade; if farmers, hoes, spades, axes, augers, saws, &c." It went on to assure them that "only two deaths occurred in the two expeditions of 1839," and that "Emigrants will find their farm lots surveyed, and cabins ready for their reception on their arrival." *African Repository and Colonial Journal* 16, no. 10 (May 15, 1840): 1.

38. It is possible that his employer had availed himself of Benjamin's literacy skills in record-keeping or accounting. Census documents show that James Fisher Jr., like most other tobacco manufacturers, had a strong preference for having young men and boys as his workforce. Midori Takagi maintains that after 1840, only males were employed in the tobacco industry; Takagi, *Rearing Wolves*, 26.

39. H. S. Tanner, "A New Map of Virginia, with Its Canals, Roads and Distances, from Place to Place along the Stage and Steamboat Routes" (Philadelphia: H. S. Tanner, 1833), Harvard Digital Resources, accessed July 22, 2012, http://vc.lib.harvard.edu/vc/deliver/~maps/012018947.

40. This was Scottish-born John McPhail, a Norfolk Presbyterian elder; Philip J. Staudenraus, *The African Colonization Movement, 1816–1865* (New York: Columbia University Press, 1961), 109–10.

41. See, for instance, the *Baltimore Sun*, August 10, 1840.

42. Joseph A. Boromé, Jacob C. White, Robert B. Ayres and J. M. McKim, "The Vigilant Committee of Philadelphia," *Pennsylvania Magazine of History and Biography*, 92: 3 (July 1968), 326n17. See also Alan Ballard, *One More Day's Journey: The Story of a Family and a People* (Bloomington, IN: iUniverse, 2011), 32–37. This was the only integrated antislavery group in the city; Levit, "Bounds of Habitation," 84.

The people who boarded the *Saluda* very likely included Robert and Harriet Purvis. Robert Purvis (1810–1898) would become the first Black member of the Pennsylvania Anti-Slavery Society in 1842, serving from 1845 to 1850 as its president. See Margaret Hope Bacon, "Robert Purvis: President of the Underground Railroad," *Pennsylvania Legacies* 5, no. 2 (November 2005), 15, accessed July 21, 2012, www.hsp.org/files/legaciespurvis.pdf; and *But One Race: The Life of Robert Purvis* (Albany: State University of New York, 2007). Harriet Forten Purvis (1810–1875) and her husband operated an Underground Railroad station in their home. Purvis was active in abolitionist circles from 1830, when he helped launch *The Liberator*; he assisted in formation of the American Anti-Slavery Society in 1833 and the Pennsylvania Anti-Slavery Society in 1837. He went to Britain to promote American antislavery and to combat the influence of ACS agents; see Boromé et al., "Vigilant Committee," 321.

The Minute Book of the Vigilant Committee of Philadelphia, in the collections of the Pennsylvania Historical Society, for the period between May 31, 1839, and July 25, 1844, curiously makes no reference at all to the *Saluda* incident. Although the Minutes of the Philadelphia Female Anti-Slavery Society survive in the Pennsylvania Historical Society collections, there is no mention of it, nor is the Holmes family listed as recipients of funding from either the women's organization or the Vigilant Committee. However, many records were burnt by Robert Purvis after Congress passed the draconian new Fugitive Slave Law in 1850, lest he or his wife be prosecuted.

43. *Thirty-First Annual Report of the American Colonization Society* (Washington, DC: ACS, 1848), 50; Robert B. Davidson (Philadelphia) to Franklin Knight (Washington, DC), August 16, 1840, Incoming Correspondence, Domestic Letters, ACS Collection, Library of Congress [hereafter LC], 518. The local ACS agent blamed the Vigilant Committee: "The Abolitionists are endeavoring to get up a prejudice here against the *Saluda*, saying 'she is not safe,' that 'she is a floating coffin' . . . they seduced away the emigrants"; O. K. Canfield (Burlington, NJ) to Franklin Knight (Washington, DC), August 16, 1840, Incoming Correspondence, Domestic Letters, ACS

Collection, LC, 533–35. I am indebted to historian Jane Ailes for the mortality statistics regarding the settlers who went on the *Saluda's* early voyage; personal communication, January 29, 2012

44. This was not first time that potential Liberian settlers had jumped ship at Philadelphia. On January 8, 1840, Benjamin Coates wrote to Judge Wilkinson, the Buffalo businessman who had taken on (without salary) the herculean task of righting the foundering financial affairs of the ACS, to report that free Black emigrants who arrived at Norfolk with more than $6,000 from Georgia to invest in Liberian enterprises "have been so wonderfully beset, abused and insulted, by our black abolitionists that they are anxious to be off as soon as possible." Some had in fact left before the *Saluda* sailed from Norfolk the previous January; see John McPhail (Norfolk) to Samuel Wilkinson (Washington, DC), January 11, 1840, regarding the defection of Peter and Lewis, both of Alexandria.

45. The story of Benjamin Pollard Holmes is extremely well documented. When he and his wife arrived in Toronto with their baby, Benjamin told Reverend Hiram Wilson his tale, and Wilson used it as means of discrediting the American Colonization Society. He published several articles in the antislavery press, including the manumission papers of both Benjamin and Ann Eliza Holmes. The travails of the *Saluda* were widely published in the contemporary press and there is a good deal about it in the papers of the ACS. Finally, James T. Fisher, using a pseudonym, wrote to the Richmond newspapers complaining that the ACS had never informed him that Ann Eliza and her baby were not in Liberia, but rather in Toronto. Moreover, he implied that the ACS never intended to reimburse their fares or the cost of their six months' supplies, even though they had "lost" three people owned by him and the Fleet family. He cited a letter that could only have been sent by Benjamin himself, describing the conditions of the young man's escape with his family. Finally there is the letter that Catharine Hoomes sent to her son warning him of what had happened to other emigrants to Liberia; it was also published in full.

46. It was known as Lot Street at the time, but for the sake of modern readers it is here rendered as the more recognizable Queen Street.

47. The houses were on the south side of Richmond Street, between Victoria and Church Streets; Tax Records for St. Andrew's Ward, City of Toronto Diffusion Material, D 318, Reel 6131, Archives of Ontario. As Grandison Boyd was Burnham's agent, he also collected Benjamin's rent of $15 per year. Boyd married Mary Ann (Patterson) Ross at the British Wesleyan Church on November 18, 1834, in the presence of her brother-in-law George Ross; Home District Marriage Register, 1831–40, vol. 10.

48. Michael L. Nicholls, "Strangers Setting among Us: The Sources and Challenge of the Urban Free Black Population of Early Virginia," *Virginia Magazine of History and Biography*, 1st ser., 108, no. 2 (2000): 155–79.

49. Mrs. Boyd, the former Mary Ann Patterson, had been twice married. Her first husband, whose estate settlement took years to finalize, was Corbin Lane Ross. His brother was George Woodford Ross and the two of them owned land on Queen Street near Spadina Avenue (where the Horseshoe Tavern stands today) as well as property in Virginia. Correspondence survives in Fredericksburg attesting to the intimacy and durability of their family connections with those who remained behind in the Old Dominion. The Rosses were intermarried with the DeBaptistes in Fredericksburg and thus were close kin to George DeBaptiste, one of two leading figures in the Detroit River Underground Railroad. See, for instance, *Wilkins v. Gordon & Wife*, in *Cases Decided in the Supreme Court of Appeals of Virginia* (Richmond, VA: Department of Purchase and Supply, 1842), 547–58; and Guylaine Petrin, "Migrations from Virginia to Toronto" (presentation, Tubman

Seminar Series, York University, January 21, 2013). Mary Ann Boyd inherited land in Virginia from her first husband, and her brother-in-law George Woodford Ross owned a number of Toronto properties. He lived on a successful farm on Toronto's western outskirts; see "Grant from Maria Willcocks, to Geo W. Ross in consideration of L315 for East ½ of Lot 10 on Plan D10," deed no. 10918, May 28, 1834 (registered July 10, 1834), microfilm 19-043, Toronto Land Registry Office. See Erin Brubacher, "The Ross Family," *Report for Heritage Mississauga*, 2006.

50. "Our Coloured Citizens: Interviews with Some of Them on Important Subjects," *Globe* (Toronto), February 5, 1886, 6.

51. "Effects of Equal Freedom on the Colored People," *The Philanthropist* (Cincinnati, OH), March 10, 1837, 1.

52. "There are a good many different societies among the colored people here. There is what is called the 'St. John's Society,' and an Odd Fellows' Society, and a Masonic Institution, also. The St. John's Society has both male and female members. The object of the Society is to take care of each other, to provide money for those who are sick who belong to the Society, bury the dead decently, and if there are any in need, they assist them. We do not go to the white people hardly at all for charity. We take care of ourselves." Interview with Alfred Butler, Samuel Gridley Howe Papers, Freedmen's Inquiry Bureau, File 10: Canadian Testimony, 310.

53. The Underground Railroad was a highly illegal system of fugitive slave assistance, most of the details of which remain mysterious to this day. Very little is known about the mechanisms of slave escape, south of the Mason-Dixon Line particularly, although in the North Frederick Douglass would one day complain that it might as well be called the "upper ground railroad" for the amount of information published about it in newspapers and discussed in abolitionist circles. An efficient "grapevine telegraph" extended great distances and transmitted information about "passengers" on their way up the line to "conductors" in far distant places; this mechanism was acknowledged at the time but its workings are not documented. See Frederick Douglass, *Narrative of the Life of Frederick Douglass* (Boston: Anti-Slavery Office, 1845), 101. For a recent discussion, see Sergio A. Lussana, *My Brother Slaves: Friendship, Masculinity, and Resistance in the Antebellum South* (Lexington: University Press of Kentucky, 2016), especially ch. 5. The classic work debunking mythology surrounding the Underground Railroad and the traditional focus on white as opposed to Black conductors and heroes is Larry Gara, *The Liberty Line: The Legend of the Underground Railroad* (Lexington: University of Kentucky Press, 1961), although since then there has been a vast amount published on the topic that emphasizes Black agency.

54. Black families living in Ancaster petitioned the lieutenant-governor for protection as early as 1828, after one man was kidnapped and carried South for sale. See William Renwick Riddell, "A Petition," *Journal of Negro History* 15 (1930): 115–16.

55. George Brown purchased a large piece of land in the southwest part of the province where the village of Bothwell would be founded. His long support of abolition and local Black causes, coupled with his implacable hostility to the American institution of slavery, won him the support of the usually very conservative African Canadians, who helped secure his seat as a reforming "Clear Grit" politician by bloc voting, an early manifestation of what became the Liberal Party of Canada.

56. One authority for the *Transit's* western port is none other than Charles Dickens, who travelled on the boat from Queenston to Toronto after his sojourn at the Falls; Charles Dickens, *American Notes for General Circulation* (London: Chapman and Hall, 1843), 777.

57. Hiram Wilson wrote to *The Philanthropist* of March 10, 1837: "These slanders were copied, and for some time were quite current in Canada; they excited much suspicion among the citizens, and

were extremely prejudicial to the interests of the new-comers."

58. James Silk Buckingham, *Canada, Nova Scotia, New Brunswick and the Other British Provinces in North America* (London: Fisher, Son & Co., 1842), 6

59. Richard H. Bonnycastle, *The Canadas in 1841*, vol. 1 (London: H. Colburn, 1842), 132–36.

60. Speech by Reverend Samuel Ringgold Ward, Freemasons' Hall, London, England, 1856, quoting Captain Hugh Richardson, in C. Peter Ripley, ed., *The Black Abolitionist Papers*, vol. 2, *Canada, 1830–1865* (Chapel Hill: University of North Carolina Press, 1986), 158–59. See also Samuel Ringgold Ward, *Autobiography of a Fugitive Negro* (London: John Snow, 1855), 158.

61. "The land was purchased from John Cawthra and James Leslie of Toronto for the sum of £25 on July 7, 1838, by W. R. Abbott and others who founded Coloured Wesleyan Methodist Church of Toronto"; Frederick Armstrong, *Toronto: A City in the Making* (Toronto: Dundurn, 1988), 78. Adolphus Judah was married to Jane Toyer, Ellen Toyer Abbott's sister, whom Wilson Abbott had purchased along with another sister, Mary, out of Maryland slavery; Catherine Slaney, *Family Secrets: Crossing the Colour Line* (Toronto: Dundurn, 2004), 25, 40. The property record for the church reads: "George Wilkinson, Wilson R. Abbott, Thomas G. Bruckner, Matthew B. Truss, and Joseph P. Turner, trustees, by the name of the trustees of the Coloured Wesleyan Methodist Church in Canada, for a chapel and burying ground in the city of Toronto."

62. He was in Toronto by September 18, 1835, according to his naturalization documents (dated 1843) and lived on King Street; Upper Canada Naturalization Registers, 1828–50, RG 5, B 47, vol. 1, accessed March 10, 2015, http://data2.collectionscanada.gc.ca/e/e120/e002993432.jpg.

63. "Description of Emancipation Day celebrations and parade in Toronto by Jehu Jones, black Lutheran clergyman who attended Aug. 1, 1839, celebrations," in Ripley, *Black Abolitionist Papers*, vol. 2, 82–83.

64. *St. Catharines Journal*, April 27, 1842.

65. "Grant from Grandison Boyd, Tobacconist, to Francis Nicholls, for W ½ Lot 11, Plan D10. William Osborne witnessed," deed no. 20303, November 3, 1842 (registered November 7, 1842), microfilm 19-051, Toronto Land Registry Office. William Osborne was a white land agent with close friendships among Black Torontonians.

66. Allen P. Stouffer, *The Light of Nature and the Law of God: Antislavery in Ontario, 1833–1877* (Baton Rouge: Louisiana State University Press, 1992), 68–70. There were other reasons for leaving Toronto. Hiram Wilson was roundly criticized by Peter Gallego in a series of letters to *National Anti-Slavery Standard* in New York, complaining that the missionary was painting African Canadians in a less than flattering light in his fundraising drives, although Wilson had strong defenders who also wrote to the paper. The damage was considerable. Wilson lost control of his Canada Mission to the fugitive slaves to three prominent white Rochester businessmen and left Toronto.

67. Roland M. Baumann, *Constructing Black Education at Oberlin College: A Documentary History* (Athens: Ohio University Press, 2010), ch. 2. Elijah B. Dunlop attended the African American convention at Buffalo in 1843 where Reverend Henry Highland Garnet advocated violent overthrow of the slave regime; Henry Highland Garnet, "An Address to the Slaves of the United States of America," in *Afro-American History: Primary Sources*, ed. Thomas R. Frazier (New York: Harcourt, Brace & World, 1970): 113–19. Frederick Douglass also attended and took the Garrisonian view, although his perspective on pacifism and political engagement would soon change. Elijah B. Dunlop and his cousins moved to Oberlin in 1844 to study at the integrated college there; "Catalogue and Record of Colored Students, Oberlin College, 1835–1862." The

Pattersons went to Rochester and opened a successful barbershop. Dunlop became a representative for Black interests in his adopted home of St. Catharines after his return.

68. "Extensive Forgery in This City," *Toronto Colonist* and *Toronto Examiner,* reprinted in the *New York Evening Post,* May 30, 1841, 1.

69. The 1842 Cane map, with details of buildings, shows no construction on the first and second blocks of Centre Street north of Osgoode Hall; James Cane, "Topographical Plan of the City and Liberties of Toronto in the Province of Canada," 1842, T1842/4Mlrg, Toronto Public Library. The Holmes house was on Lot 7, but the numbers were recalibrated several times over the years, and the same house had a number of different street addresses. Benjamin P. Holmes first appears as a freeholder on Centre Street in the tax assessment rolls of Toronto in April 1845.

70. The burial register for the York General Burying Ground, Toronto, reads: "Holms, Hannah, w/o Benjamin Holms, born US, buried 16 April 1845, 44 yr. Consumption" (record no. 2155). Her remains were transferred to the Toronto Necropolis in 1855.

Chapter 4: The Land of Promise

1. Quoted in Joseph Sturge, "Report on Free Labour, Presented to the General Anti-Slavery Convention," in *Analysis of a Report of a Committee of the House of Commons, on the Extinction of Slavery* (London: Society for the Abolition of Slavery Throughout the British Dominions, 1833), 5.

2. "Minutes of the Executive Council of Upper Canada, March 21, 1793," in E. A. Cruikshank, *The Correspondence of Lieut. Governor John Graves Simcoe: With Allied Documents Relating to His Administration of the Government of Upper Canada,* vol. 1 (Toronto: Champlain Society, 1923), 204.

3. Major works on Black Canadian history are few. The only really sweeping analysis comes from Robin W. Winks, *The Blacks in Canada: A History,* 2nd ed. (Montreal: McGill-Queen's University Press, 2005). James St. George Walker, *A History of the Blacks in Canada: Study Guide for Teachers and Students* (Ottawa: Minister of State for Multiculturalism, 1980), now long out of print, and Walker's more recent "African Canadians," in Paul R. Magocsi, ed., *Encyclopedia of Canada's Peoples* (Toronto: University of Toronto Press, 1999) are both authoritative, while for the Underground Railroad, complete with many rare images, see Daniel G. Hill, *The Freedom-Seekers: Blacks in Early Canada* (Agincourt, ON: Book Society of Canada, 1981). Focusing on settlement and the rise of African Canadian agricultural colonies is an excellent book by Donald George Simpson, *Under the North Star: Black Communities in Upper Canada before Confederation* (Trenton, NJ: African World Press, 2005).

4. The Toronto *Globe,* September 10, 1844, states that the population in 1826 was only 1,719; at the time of incorporation in 1834, it was 9,654—it had quadrupled in a decade. For an admiring description, see "Toronto," *Illustrated London News,* January 30, 1847, accessed December 18, 2015, https://personal.uwaterloo.ca/marj/genealogy/voyages/toronto.html.

5. *Brown's Toronto City and Home District Directory, 1846–7* (Toronto: George Brown, 1846), 22.

6. James Taylor, *Narrative of a Voyage to, and Travels in, Upper Canada: With Accounts of the Customs, Character, and Dialect of the Country: Also, Remarks on Emigration, Agriculture, &c.* (Hull, UK: J. Nicholson, 1846), 32–33; Frederick H. Armstrong, *A City in the Making: Progress, People and Perils in Victorian Toronto* (Toronto: Dundurn Press, 1988), 209–10. Captains Thomas Dick and Andrew Herron bought the *Chief Justice Robinson* in 1850; Henry Scadding, *Toronto of Old* (Toronto: Adam, Stevenson, 1873), 376–77.

7. *Brown's Directory*, 28.

8. Judge John Pope Oldham was the brother of Abigail Churchill, Fanny and Samuel Thruston's grandmother. Thornton had belonged to his wife's sister, Susan Talbot Brown. He fled Louisville in 1831 with Oldham's son, William, in hot pursuit. The story of Thornton and Lucie Blackburn is told in my *I've Got a Home in Glory Land; A Lost Tale of the Underground Railroad* (New York: Farrar Straus & Giroux and Toronto: Thomas Allen, 2007).

9. Election records at the City of Toronto Archives note that the Mansion House Hotel on Richmond Street was used as the polling station in the St. James Ward municipal elections in January 1847 and in 1848. There are also multiple notations in the municipal accounts that James Mink was paid by the city to transport convicts from the Toronto jail to the one at Kingston. *Brown's Directory*; Richard Neilson, "George Mink: A Black Businessman in Early Kingston," *Historic Kingston* 46 (1998): 111–21.

10. *Brown's Directory*, 7.

11. J. Armstrong, ed., *Rowsell's City of Toronto and County of York Directory for 1850–1* (Toronto: Henry Rowsell, 1850), lxxvii. See also the very moving eulogy for Washington Christian contained in the front the Amherstburg Baptist Association ledger at the Baptist Church Archives, McMaster University, Hamilton, Ontario.

12. W. H. Pearson, *Recollections and Records of Toronto of Old* (Toronto: William Briggs, 1914), 300–302; Eric Arthur, *Toronto: No Mean City* (Toronto: University of Toronto Press, 1978), 86, ill. 4.25. The church was built in 1844 as a British Wesleyan congregation separate from the earlier Methodist church on Adelaide; Thomas Edward Champion, ed., *The Methodist Churches of Toronto* (Toronto: G. Rose & Sons, 1899).

13. Arthur, *No Mean City*, 46. A year later these buildings would temporarily serve as an insane asylum.

14. Census of Upper Canada, 1842, Toronto, St. David's Ward. Cary was a trustee for the Baptist church at Queen and Victoria and rented his first Toronto home from Mary Ann Boyd's brother-in-law, George Woodford Ross. Quoted in "Our Coloured Citizens: Interviews with Some of Them on Important Subjects," Newton Cary said he had arrived in the city on July 11, 1832, and had his first barbershop on King, opposite the cathedral; *Globe* (Toronto), February 5, 1886.

15. *Provincial Freeman*, August 5, 1854; Daniel Hill, "Negroes in Toronto, 1793–1865," *Ontario History* 55, no. 2 (1963): 73–91.

16. Armstrong, *Rowsell's Directory*, lxxvi; William Kilbourne, *The Firebrand: William Lyon Mackenzie and the Rebellion in Upper Canada* (Toronto: Dundurn, 2008), 29; Hilary Dawson, "From Immigrant to Establisment: A Black Family's Journey," *Ontario History* 99, no.1 (Spring 2007): 31–43.

17. Pearson, *Recollections and Records*, 42.

18. Ibid., 313.

19. Thomas Smallwood, *A Narrative of Thomas Smallwood, (Coloured Man:) . . . Together with an Account of the Underground Railroad* (Toronto: James Stephens, 1851), 43, Samuel J. May Antislavery Collections, Cornell University, accessed July 31, 2012, http://ebooks.library.cornell. edu/cgi/t/text/pageviewer-idx?c=mayantislavery;cc=mayantislavery;q1=toronto;rgn=full%20 text;view=image;seq=1;idno=20869801;didno=20869801. He corresponded with the *Albany Weekly Patriot* newspaper in 1843–44 under the assumed name "Samuel Weller," telling stories of the abuse of individual slaves and naming names of slaveholders who were guilty thereof; Smallwood, 55–56; 61ff.

20. Commonly known as the Act of Union 1840 (3 & 4 Victoria, c. 35). For the census, see Peter

Gallego, "Report and State of the Colored People Living in Toronto," Governor General's Office, Miscellaneous Records, Upper Canada 1835–1841, RG 7, G 14, vol. 5, 2193–2202, microfilm H-1178, Sydenham Papers, Library and Archives Canada. Gallego then left the city, so the report was presented to the governor general of Canada, Lord Sydenham, by his friend and fellow abolitionist Edouard de Ste.-Remy.

21. The tax rolls for St. George's Ward, 1835, show William Hickman in the shop occupied by Jarrad Banks in the 1834 directory. The first reference to William Hickman appears in the *Christian Guardian*, June 17, 1838. He was one of several men present at a meeting on January 13, 1838, at the home of white abolitionist William Osborne, to discuss immigration of fugitive slaves and the British emancipation proclamation and to protest the murder of white abolitionist publisher Elijah P. Lovejoy in Alton, Illinois. Betsey Hickman, the former Elizabeth Dunlop, was a near relation of Elijah B. Dunlop, although the exact connection cannot be determined from available sources.

22. Hiram and Hannah Wilson's Toronto home is not listed in any street directory. A visiting African American Lutheran minister, Reverend Jehu Jones, was entertained in the missionary's Elizabeth Street home when he attended Emancipation Day celebrations on August 1, 1839; Jehu Jones to Charles B. Ray, August 8, 1839, in Ripley, *Black Abolitionist Papers*, vol. 2, 76–83. However, they fell on hard times, for Wilson was no money manager. An article in the January 10, 1857, issue of the *Provincial Freeman* reads: "J. C. Brown of Chatham tells us that Hiram Wilson lived five years in his house at Toronto, and that he was exceedingly poor at first . . . why J. C. Brown and Hiram Wilson lived as neighbours under the same roof for five years."

23. Ripley, *Black Abolitionist Papers*, vol. 2, 73–74. J. C. Brown (1796–186?) had visited Texas in the 1820s at the request of Benjamin Lundy to explore the possibility of Black colonization. Lundy, who later visited Canadian Black settlements, was the abolitionist publisher of the *Genius of Universal Emancipation*, where William Lloyd Garrison began his career in both journalism and antislavery. Brown returned to the United States at his wife's urging but was captured at Louisville and accused of "stealing slaves" from their owners. Escaping when a white supporter posted bond, he returned with his family to Toronto. In 1849 he moved to Chatham, where he assumed an important leadership role in local affairs as well as those of the Dawn Settlement and the British-American Institute.

24. Armstrong, *Rowsell's Directory*, 68, shows Adolphus Judah living next to the Abbott home at the corner of Albert and Teraulay, in 1850.

25. Pearson, *Recollections and Records*, 13. Like James Mink and Willis Addison, Philips was a pewholder in the Richmond Street Methodist Church, despite being listed as a labourer and sometimes as a whitewasher in the city directories.

26. Toronto Tax Assessment Records, St. Patrick's Ward, 1845, Archives of Ontario.

27. Murray W. Nicholson, "Peasants in an Urban Society: The Irish Catholics in Victorian Toronto," in *Gathering Place: People and Neighbourhoods of Toronto, 1834–1945*, ed. Robert F. Harney (Toronto: Multicultural History Society of Ontario, 1985): 47–74; Barrie Dyster, "Captain Bob and the Noble Ward: Neighbourhood and Provincial Politics in Nineteenth-Century Toronto," in *Forging a Consensus: Historical Essays on Toronto*, ed. V. L. Russell (Toronto: Toronto Sesquicentennial Board, 1984): 87–115.

28. J. F. Johnson, ed., *Proceedings of the General Anti-slavery Convention called by the Committee of the British and Foreign Anti-slavery Society and Held in London from Tuesday, June 13th, to Tuesday, June 20th, 1843* (London: John Snow, 1843), 285–87.

CHAPTER 5: UNDER THE PAW OF THE BRITISH LION

1. James Taylor, *Narrative of a Voyage to, and Travels in, Upper Canada: With Accounts of the Customs, Character, and Dialect of the Country: Also, Remarks on Emigration, Agriculture, &c.* (Hull, UK: J. Nicholson, 1846), 18–19.

2. Couples marrying in the Anglican and Roman Catholic Churches could request that banns be posted for each of three weeks prior to the ceremony, in case anyone knew if one or the other of the couple was already married, for instance.

3. "Benjamin Pollard Holmes, widower, and Cecelia Jane Reynolds, spinster, both of the city of Toronto," November 19, 1846, Marriage Registers of St. James Anglican Church/Cathedral, York (Toronto), 1800–1896, reprinted in John Ross Robertson, *Landmarks of Toronto*, vol. 3 (Toronto: John Ross Robertson, 1898), 395ff. Cecelia signed the register with an X. She had not yet learned to write so much as her own name.

4. Ripley, *Black Abolitionist Papers*, vol. 2, 81n7. There was no official Church of England position on slavery, what with so much of its income having come from slaveholding in the West Indies and to its sister Episcopalian churches in the South. For a discussion of what this meant in British North America, see Allen P. Stouffer, *The Light of Nature and the Law of God: Antislavery in Ontario, 1833–1877* (Baton Rouge: Louisiana State University Press, 1992), 144–49.

   A considerable number of Black Toronto residents for whom there is a marital record were married by Reverend Grasett in this period. Henry J. Grasett (1808–1882) was born in Gibraltar and brought up in Quebec City. Educated at Cambridge, he was ordained and became a deacon in Quebec before moving to Toronto. For more than forty years he would serve as curate to the Reverend John Strachan, who became the first bishop of York in 1839. Both Bishop Strachan and Reverend Grasett are buried beneath the altar of St. James' Cathedral. He long served as secretary of the Society for Civilizing and Converting the Indians[!] and Propagating the Gospel among the Destitute Settlers in Upper Canada and was a frequent speaker at Toronto's annual Emancipation Day ceremonies. See H. E. Turner, "Henry James Grasett," in *Dictionary of Canadian Biography*, vol. 11, accessed August 2, 2012, http://www.biographi.ca/009004-119.01-e.php?id_nbr=5554; William James Darnley Waddilove, *The Stewart Missions: A Series of Letters and Journals, Calculated to Exhibit to British Christians, the Spiritual Destitution of the Emigrants Settled in the Remote Parts of Upper Canada* (London: J. Hatchard & Son, 1838), 225.

5. Ministers of the Baptist, Methodist and other dissenting faiths were legally permitted to perform marriages starting in 1831, but the clergyman had to have taken the oath to the Queen and become naturalized. For a civil service the couple needed both a licence to wed and to post a bond witnessed by two guarantors, a simple condition to meet, so many Blacks in Toronto were married at St. James. Some African Canadian couples chose to marry in the British Wesleyan Chapel, but it was only intermittently served by a regular preacher. Many Protestant ministers in Canada were American-born; posted only temporarily to Canada West, they were reluctant to become naturalized British subjects. An exception is found in the Court of Quarter-Session for York County, vol. 11, 1840–42, 290. On April 8, 1842, Reverend Alexander Hemsley of the African Episcopal Methodist Church took the oath of allegiance and received the necessary certificates to authorize him to solemnize matrimony. He was a fugitive slave who had fled Maryland in 1818, settling in New Jersey. When state laws passed in 1836 threatened him and his family, he moved to St. Catharines, Upper Canada, and pastored AME congregations there until the late 1840s. See Ripley, *Black Abolitionist Papers*, vol. 2, 260n.

6. According to Smallwood, in 1847 Dunlop was an agent for the "Anti-Slavery Societies of Canada West," most likely the Black-led British American Anti-Slavery Society, as the Anti-Slavery Society of Canada was not founded until 1851; Thomas Smallwood, *A Narrative of Thomas Smallwood, (Coloured Man:)... Together with an Account of the Underground Railroad* (Toronto: James Stephens, 1851), 43, Samuel J. May Antislavery Collections, Cornell University, accessed July 31, 2012, http:// ebooks.library.cornell.edu/cgi/t/text/pageviewer-idx?c=mayantislavery;cc=mayantislavery; q1=toronto;rgn=full%20text;view=image;seq=1;idno=20869801;didno=20869801, 57. See also "Minutes of the National Convention of Colored Citizens Held at Buffalo 15–19 August 1843," in Howard H. Bell, *Minutes and Proceedings of the National Negro Conventions, 1830–1864* (New York: Arno Press, 1969); Oberlin College Special Collections, Subgroup IV: Alumni Records, Series 3, Office of the Secretary, RG 5 (compiled 1972). There was some sort of dispute within the British American Anti-Slavery Society of Canada, however, for Dunlop and W. H. Day were both very publicly dismissed on December 1, 1847. The statement of ostracism was published by Charles Freeman on April 28, 1848, in the *North Star*, Frederick Douglass's Rochester-based paper.
7. The Holmeses and Mullins were near neighbours, and Francis served in one of Toronto's hotel dining rooms or upscale restaurants, just as Benjamin did himself when the lakes were closed to navigation in the winter months. According to the 1846–47 Toronto directory, Mullin lived with his wife, Rachel, at 13 Elizabeth Street, just two blocks from Benjamin's Macaulaytown home. According to Guylaine Petrin, his 1844 naturalization papers show that he had been in the province since 1837. He served in the 1st Company of the 2nd Provincial Battalion to help defend the province against American supporters of William Lyon Mackenzie, who formed "hunting lodges" and after the 1837 rebellion attacked the borders at Niagara and Detroit; Francis Mullin served from November 1838 to March 1839. The Mullins moved to Chippewa, on the Niagara frontier, in 1851 but returned to Toronto in 1861 and spent the rest of their lives there. The Mullin family was Baptist and their son, named Washington Christian Mullin in honour of Elder Christian, was a streetcar conductor. They had descendants still living in the twentieth century. They appear as "Papist" in the Gallego census, but that might be a misreading of the original, since they are generally listed as Baptist.
8. Elizabeth Jane Errington, *Wives and Mothers, Schoolmistresses and Scullery Maids: Working Women in Upper Canada, 1790–1840* (Montreal: McGill-Queen's University Press, 1995), 136–84.
9. The issue was a rivalry between Richardson's ships and those of the Royal Mail Line, whose proprietor was Donald Bethune. In trying to undercut one another, they both went bankrupt. However, Richardson was an honourable and much admired figure in the city who had been mentored in his early career by Chief Justice John Beverley Robinson, and he rose like a phoenix from the ashes. See Frederick Armstrong, *A City in the Making: The Growth of Victorian Toronto* (Toronto: Dundurn, 1987), 209–10.
10. This aspect of her character is inferred from her refusal to ask for funds from Fanny Thruston Ballard when Cecelia was almost entirely destitute in her later life. Also, her autobiography in the US Pension Bureau file in relation to her second husband's Civil War service shows Cecelia to have been fiercely independent and proud of her ability to make her own way in the world.
11. Eric Arthur, *Toronto: No Mean City* (Toronto: University of Toronto Press, 1978), 87, ill. 4.46.
12. This was a subject of some comment in 1863 when the Freedmen's Bureau Inquiry Commission interviewed formerly enslaved Americans living in Canada West.
13. *Brown's Toronto City and Home District Directory, 1846–7* (Toronto: George Brown, 1846), 7, 11, 19; W.H. Smith, *Smith's Canadian Gazetteer* (Toronto: H.W. Rowsell, 1946), 38, 193–96;

Guylaine Petrin, "Migrations from Virginia to Toronto" (presentation, Tubman Seminar Series, York University, January 21, 2013).

14. Frederick H. Armstrong and Ronald J. Stagg, "Mackenzie, William Lyon," *Dictionary of Canadian Biography*, vol. 9, accessed May 15, 2016, http://www.biographi.ca/en/bio/mackenzie_william_lyon_9E.html.

15. Frederick Douglass (1818–1895) was born enslaved in Talbot County, Maryland, on the state's eastern shore. Separated from his family at an early age, he fled slavery in September 1838, reaching New York by way of Philadelphia. He married Anna Murray, a free Black woman, and moved to New Bedford, where he became a member of the African Methodist Episcopal Zion Church and eventually a Sunday School leader and licensed preacher. He subscribed to the *Liberator*, which impressed him deeply, as did the first speech he heard William Lloyd Garrison deliver. In 1840, with the encouragement of Reverend Thomas James, formerly of Rochester, New York, Douglass gave his first antislavery lecture, his eloquence so impressing Garrison and others that he was chosen to deliver a series of abolitionist lectures across the northern United States on behalf of the American Anti-Slavery Society, starting in 1841. Douglass spent from 1845 to 1847 on an extended lecture tour of Britain and Ireland, where he spoke out against both slavery and the tenets of the American Colonization Society.

Frederick Douglass took his family to Rochester in 1847 to begin the *North Star*, a move bitterly opposed by Garrison, although the men remained friends for a time. He eventually became convinced that a more overtly political form of resistance would be needed to convince the United States to end the South's peculiar institution; he famously broke with Garrison over his belief that the South could be convinced to give up slavery by moral suasion alone. Douglass eventually rejected Garrison's contention that the Constitution was a proslavery document. He was a proponent of education and self-determination and was drawn to the political resistance espoused by Liberty Party founders, including New York State abolitionist and philanthropist Gerrit Smith. A close friend of Elizabeth Cady Stanton and the Anthony family, he was present at the Seneca Falls women's rights convention. The masthead of the *North Star* read: "Right is of no Sex—Truth is of no Color—God is the Father of us all, and we are all brethren." In 1851 the paper merged with Gerrit Smith's *Liberty Party Paper* to become *Frederick Douglass' Paper*. On July 5, 1852, at Rochester's Corinthian Hall, Douglass delivered his famous speech, "What to the Slave Is the 4th of July?"

He was personally abstemious and profoundly spiritual, although often critical of what he perceived as hypocritical religiosity. Douglass initially opposed the outmigration of refugee Blacks to Canada West because he felt antislavery could best be furthered by people who remained in the United States, but he still operated a very active Underground Railroad station at Rochester with the help of Anna and his friend, the tailor Jacob Morris. His own freedom was purchased by British friends after another speaking tour, because of fears that the most prominent spokesman of Black America might be returned to slavery under the Fugitive Slave Law of 1850.

The first version of his autobiography, *Narrative of the Life of Frederick Douglass* (Boston: Anti-Slavery Office, 1845), was a bestseller. It was quickly followed by *My Bondage and My Freedom* (New York: Miller, Orton & Mulligan, 1855). In later years he would publish *The Life and Times of Frederick Douglass* (London: Christian Age Office, 1882), which was revised ten years later (Boston: DeWolf & Fiske, 1892).

16. *Brown's Toronto City and Home District Directory, 1846–7* (Toronto: George Brown, 1846), 724.

17. Perhaps Benjamin's little boys helped as well. Fellow Kentuckian Josiah Henson's twelve-year-old son Tom had taught him to read and write. Now at the faraway Dawn Settlement, Henson would in 1849 publish his autobiography. Cecelia wrote a good hand, a skill she would retain even in old age, and she displayed a facility with language well beyond that of mere literacy.

18. *Recollections and Records of Toronto of Old*, 44.

19. Barrie Dyster, "Captain Bob and the Noble Ward: Neighbourhood and Provincial Politics in Nineteenth-Century Toronto," in *Forging a Consensus: Historical Essays on Toronto*, ed. V. L. Russell (Toronto: Toronto Sesquicentennial Board, 1984): 87–115.

20. John M. Tinsley (1783–1892) was the grandson of a Revolutionary War–era Irish immigrant, one of whose sons married a free Black woman. With Elisha Edmunds, later a Toronto barber, he had been a member of the "Richmond Blues" who searched out Nat Turner in the Great Dismal Swamp and returned him to stand trial in 1831. Tinsley and his wife, Douglass, had for some years explored the possibility of moving to Canada West before they arrived in 1843 with their sons, married daughter and son-in-law. Their first venture, a grocery, failed when Tinsley's wife suddenly died. Her bereaved husband built a pair of attached houses for his family and started his own construction company. The other house was occupied by Tinsley's daughter Elizabeth and her husband, William Custalo, a shoemaker. William Custalo's ancestors had been freed very early: a James and a William appeared in the "List of Free Negroes" in the Richmond, Virginia, tax rolls as early as 1799; John and Douglass Tinsley, who moved to Henrico County in 1814, also appeared on the list in that year, and John's sister, Polly Tinsley, in 1816; "List of Free Negroes," 1799, Richmond City (Virginia) Personal Property Tax List, 1787–1819, microfilm nos. 363–64, Library of Virginia.

    The Tinsley homes were on present-day Dundas Street near the southwest corner with Bay Street. According to the 1840 US Census, Tinsley lived two doors from George Cary in Cincinnati. He continued to have interests in Ohio: John J. Cary and J. M. Tinsley signed the resolutions of an anti-colonization meeting in Cincinnati published in the *Philanthropist* of March 15, 1843. John Meriwether Tinsley had the distinction of being the only Black person with a biography in Charles Pelham Mulvany, *History of Toronto and County of York, Ontario*, vol. 2 (Toronto, C. Blackett Robinson, 1855), 162–63. Tinsley's mixed ancestry is not mentioned. This fascinating old man lived to be 109 years old, dying on October 5, 1892. His passing elicited long obituaries in Toronto papers and even garnered mention in "Telegraphic Brevities," *New York Times*, October 7, 1892. His funeral was attended by some of Toronto's most prominent citizens, including John Ross Robertson of the Toronto *Telegram* and several aldermen.

21. *Minutes of the National Convention of Colored Citizens Held at Buffalo, August 15–19, 1843* (New York: Piercy & Read, 1843), accessed July 20, 2016, http://coloredconventions.org/items/show/278.

22. Although the requirements changed, depending, for one thing, on how much money people brought with them to invest, William Hickman Sr. applied for naturalization after less than two years in the country and was refused, although he had, as he pointed out in his petition, brought with him enough funds not only to purchase a house but also to start a business. See "Petition of William Hickman," Civil Secretary's Correspondence, Upper Canada Sundries, vol. 14, May 1834, RG 5, A1, Library and Archives Canada [hereafter LAC].

23. "Petition of Benjamin Holmes," County of York Naturalization Registers, 1828–50, vol. 8, 1847, 1, in RG 5, B47, LAC. He had actually met the residency requirement by July 1, 1847, according to his listing in the register.

24. The Toronto *Globe* of January 8, 1848, stated that W. R. Abbott was odds-on favourite for the Alderman's seat, "as he is a large owner of property in the ward, and altogether better suited for

the office." His opponents and the eventual winners were W. R. Campbell and Robert Britton Denison; *Colonist* (Toronto), January 14, 1848.

25. Benjamin Pollard Holmes had taken the precaution of listing Benjamin Alexander's birthplace as Canada in all official records, to avoid issues regarding his legal status—still that of slave until 1865. It is entirely possible that "little Ben" had no idea he was born in Virginia, for he maintained all his life that he was a native of Toronto.

26. The Wilmot Proviso was proposed to prevent slavery from being instituted in lands acquired from Mexico. A discussion of its implications appeared in the *Signal of Liberty*, February 20, 1847, and a host of other abolitionist newspapers.

27. Montreal newspapers commented on the effect the increase in numbers was having on local white populations, in an article dated October 31, 1850: "It is estimated that nearly one thousand have reached Canada since the commencement of the agitation, many of whom have passed into the interior, where they intend abiding. There appears to be less sympathy shown for them than formerly, and many seem actually to want the *necessaries of life*." Quoted in the *Maryland Colonization Journal*, 6, No. 2, May 1852, 186.

28. Samuel Ringgold Ward, "Canadian Negro Hate," *Voice of the Fugitive*, October 21, 1852.

29. For a fuller discussion of George Brown and his family's antislavery activities, see Smardz Frost, *I've Got a Home in Glory Land*, 285–88; Fred Landon, "The Anti-Slavery Society of Canada," *Journal of Negro History* 4, no. 1 (January 1919): 33–40; Stouffer, *Light of Nature*, 106–10; Hill, *The Freedom-Seekers*, 106, 220n15.

30. Thomas Dick had built in 1843 a row of elegant red brick homes along the north side of Front Street, east of Teraulay (Bay) Street, which he rented to the Presbyterian Knox College until it could acquire its own building. These later became Toronto's famous Queen's Hotel, on the same site as today's grand old lady, the Fairmont Royal York. See K. R. Macpherson, "Dick, Thomas," *Dictionary of Canadian Biography*, vol. 10, 231, http://www.biographi.ca/en/bio/dick_thomas_10E.html.

31. The Elgin Association was founded in Toronto on June 7, 1850, and remained a joint stock subscription company to support the nine-thousand-acre settlement until after the Civil War. All the stockholders recovered their investments; George R. Ure, *Handbook of Toronto* (Toronto: Lovell & Gibson, 1858), 168–69. A good overall source on the Buxton settlement is Sharon A. Roger Hepburn, *Crossing the Border: A Free Black Community in Canada* (Champaign-Urbana: University of Illinois Press, 2007). See also W. H. Pease and J. H. Pease, *Black Utopia: Negro Communal Experiments in America* (Madison: Historical Society of Wisconsin, 1963); J. H. Silverman, *Unwelcome Guests: Canada West's Response to American Fugitive Slaves, 1800–1865* (Millwood, NY: Associated Faculty Press, 1985); and Victor Ullman, *Look to the North Star: A Life of William King* (Boston: Beacon, 1969).

32. Within two years the local white school had closed, as nearly all the children in the area were attending the Buxton school because of the superior education it offered. Hepburn, *Crossing the Border*, 159.

33. US Census, 1850, Monroe County, New York, Rochester City. The Pattersons also appear as barbers in the 1851 Rochester city directories. According to Guylaine Petrin, their mother, Lydia Dunlop Patterson, is buried with Grandison Boyd and his wife in the Toronto Necropolis.

34. Victoria Sandwick Smith, "Rochester's Frederick Douglass," pt. 1, *Rochester History* 67, no. 3 (Summer 2005): 3–28; "Rochester's Frederick Douglass," pt. 2, *Rochester History* 67, no. 4 (Fall 2005): 3–30.

35. The Fugitive Slave Act was part of a group of laws passed on September 18, 1850, that included provisions for ending the slave trade in the national capital, bringing in California as a free state, and allowing concessions relating to slavery in the new Texas territories. Its formal name was *An Act to Amend, and Supplementary to, the Act Entitled "An Act respecting Fugitives from Justice, and Persons escaping from the Service of their Masters," Approved February Twelfth, One Thousand Seven Hundred and Ninety-Three*, and was signed into law by President Millard Fillmore.

36. The commissioners were paid seven dollars for each person they turned over to be returned to slavery, and five dollars should they adjudge a man, woman or child to be genuinely free.

37. *Constitution and Bye-laws of the Anti-Slavery Society of Canada* (Toronto: George Brown, 1851); Fred Landon, "The Anti-Slavery Society of Canada," *Journal of Negro History* 4, no. 1 (1919): 33–40; and "Abolitionist Interest in Upper Canada," *Ontario History* 44, no. 4 (1952): 165–77; Ian Pemberton, "The Anti-Slavery Society of Canada" (PhD diss., University of Toronto, 1967); Stouffer, *Light of Nature*; Robin W. Winks, "A Sacred Animosity: Abolitionism in Canada," in *The Antislavery Vanguard: New Essays on the Abolitionists*, ed. Martin B. Duberman (Princeton, NJ: Princeton University Press, 1965): 301–42.

38. Henry Bibb (1815–1854) was the son of a Kentucky slave, James Bibb. He fled in December 1837, leaving his wife and child, but returned for them the following summer. Recaptured, he escaped again, and after another attempt was forced to flee from New Orleans. A resourceful, very intelligent man, he finally made his way to Detroit, where he became a noted lecturer on the antislavery circuit. He met Mary Miles (1820–1877), a free Black woman from Rhode Island, through his abolitionist activities and they married in June 1848. When the Fugitive Slave Law threatened Henry's freedom, they moved to Sandwich, Canada West, where his wife opened a school for Black children. Henry Bibb, who had acquired basic literacy in slavery and improved his education in Detroit, wrote the autobiographical *Narrative of the Life and Adventures of Henry Bibb, an American Slave* in 1849. The couple started up the *Voice of the Fugitive*, the first African Canadian abolitionist newspaper, on January 1, 1851; it continued publication until his early death in 1854. Such was the respect with which he was held in Detroit, the joint Emancipation Day ceremonies that year became a waterborne funeral. The authoritative work on Henry and Mary Bibb has been done by Afua Cooper: "'The Voice of the Fugitive': A Transnational Abolitionist Organ," in *A Fluid Frontier: Slavery, Resistance and the Underground Railroad in the Detroit River Borderlands*, ed. Karolyn Smardz Frost and Veta Smith Tucker (Detroit, MI: Wayne State University Press, 2016): 129–49; "'Doing Battle in Freedom's Cause': Henry Bibb, Abolitionism, Race Uplift and Black Manhood, 1842–1854 (PhD diss., University of Toronto, 2000); "The Search for Mary Bibb, Black Woman Teacher in Nineteenth-Century Canada West," *Ontario History* 83, no. 1 (1991): 39–54; "Black Women and Work in Nineteenth-Century Canada West: Black Woman Teacher Mary Bibb," in *We're Rooted Here and They Can't Pull Us Up: Essays in African Canadian Women's History*, ed. Peggy Bristow (Toronto: University of Toronto Press, 1999): 143–70. Also see Jason Silverman, "'We Shall Be Heard!': The Development of the Fugitive Slave Press in Canada," *Canadian Historical Review* 65, no. 1 (1984): 54–69; and Ripley, *Black Abolitionist Papers*, vol. 2, 110n, 192n.

39. Ure, *Handbook of Toronto*, 168.

40. For Harney's occupation, see J. Armstrong, ed., *Rowsell's City of Toronto and County of York Directory for 1850–1* (Toronto: Henry Rowsell, 1850), 56.

41. *Globe* (Toronto), April 1 and April 3, 1851; "Another Anti-Slavery Meeting Last Night," *North Star*, April 10, 1851; Hilary Russell, "Frederick Douglass in Canada," *CRM Magazine* 4 (1998): 24; Ure, *Handbook of Toronto*, 165–66.

42. Douglass, *Life and Times*, 288–89. William Parker, who led the defence against the slaveholders, wrote his own account, "The Freedman's Story," in *Atlantic Monthly* 17 (February 1866): 152–66; (March 1866): 276–95.

43. *Liberator*, October 4, 1850, cited in Frederick Landon, "Negro Migration to Canada after the Passing of the Fugitive Slave Act," *Journal of Negro History* 5, no. 1 (January 1920), 25.

44. Armstrong, *Rowsell's Directory*, xxxv, 36.

45. "FOR NIAGARA AND LEWISTON.—The steamer *Chief Justice Robinson* leaves Toronto for Niagara and Lewiston, daily, (Sundays excepted) at half-past 7 o'clock A. M.,—Returning, leaves Lewiston at 1 o'clock P. M."; ibid., xxxv.

46. Francis Lewis, *The Toronto Directory and Street Guide* (Toronto: H. & W. Rowsell, 1843), 109. For Hockley's fortuitous rescue, see "Daring Attempt and Successful Escape of a Slave: Another Bold Stroke for Freedom," *National Anti-Slavery Standard*, August 20, 1853.

47. Ripley, *Black Abolitionist Papers*, vol. 2, 158n.

48. For the pharmacy, see his advertisement in the *Provincial Freeman*, April 14, 1855, for "Alexander T. Augusta's Central Medical Hall," one door south of Elm on Yonge Street. It also sold dyestuffs, an important commodity in a city where all but the elite had to make their own clothes and the poorest had to purchase used ones. Mrs. Augusta's fine ladies' haberdashery is described in Dalyce Newby, *Anderson Ruffin Abbott: First Afro-Canadian Doctor* (Markham, ON: Fitzhenry & Whiteside, 1998), 78.

49. Samuel Ringgold Ward wrote in the *Provincial Freeman* of March 25, 1854: "On their arrival in Toronto, and other places along the Canadian frontier, that is along a boundary of some five hundred miles, they are usually destitute of everything. The Anti-Slavery Society of Canada and a Ladies Society of Toronto provide these refugees with food, clothing, tools or whatever they require until they may procure employment for themselves."

50. The 1850 city directory counted 1,617 women in domestic service and only 263 men. Judge William Campbell employed a "coloured girl" as a housemaid, and Black cooks, butlers and coachmen were considered status symbols into the early part of the twentieth century.

51. William Still (1821–1901) began working for the Society in 1844 as a janitor and soon became secretary of the Pennsylvania Anti-Slavery Society and ran a very busy Underground Railroad station at Philadelphia. He kept careful records, including accounts of the people who passed through on their way north. His book is a goldmine of information about freedom-seekers and includes letters from some in Toronto. In a letter from John Henry Hill, October 4, 1853, Hill, a runaway, tells his benefactor that he will be going to work for "a man named Tinsley, who is a master workman in this city . . . everybody advises me to work for Mr. Tinsley, as there is more steadiness to him"; William Still, *The Underground Railroad* (Philadelphia: Porter and Coates, 1872), 192–93.

52. In 1849, accused of malfeasance in the case of the foundering British-American Institute, Wilson moved to St. Catharines, Canada West, where he and his second wife devoted their lives to receiving and educating African American refugees from bondage. Their numbers increased dramatically after passage of the 1850 Fugitive Slave Law by the US Congress. They worked personally with Harriet Tubman in assisting newcomers, with financial support from the American Missionary Association. Owen Thomas, "Harriet Ross [TUBMAN]," *Dictionary of Canadian Biography*, accessed November 2, 2016, http://www.biographi.ca/en/bio/ross_harriet_14E.html.

53. "Proceedings of the North American Convention," *Voice of the Fugitive*, September 24, 1851, in Ripley, *Black Abolitionist Papers*, vol. 2, 149–69.

54. *Voice of the Fugitive*, October 22, 1851, in ibid., 170–76.

55. Mary Ann Shadd (1823–1893) was descended from a German Revolutionary War–era mercenary. Wounded, he married the free Black woman who had nursed him back to health. His grandson Abraham Doras Shadd and his wife, Harriet, moved from Wilmington, Delaware, to West Chester, Pennsylvania, to educate their children in Quaker schools. Shadd, who had a successful shoemaking business, was a brilliant man who served as secretary for the first Black National Convention, held at Philadelphia in 1830, and he and Harriet ran a very efficient Underground Railroad station out of their home. Mary Ann authored *Hints for Colored People of the North* in 1849, and after moving to Canada wrote an immigrants' guide for African Americans titled *Notes on Canada West* in 1852. In 1853 Mary Ann started the *Provincial Freeman*, which she published from Windsor, Toronto and finally Chatham. She had a series of male editors—in reluctant deference to gender conventions—and was a provocative and outspoken lecturer. She married Toronto-based barber Thomas F. Cary in 1856, although she ran her newspaper from Chatham and rarely lived with him. They had two children and Thomas died in 1860. Mary Bibb, widowed in 1853, married Isaac N. Cary and thus became Mary Ann Shadd Cary's sister-in-law; they loathed one another. During the Civil War Mary Ann was the Union Army's only female recruiting officer. She moved to Washington, where she taught and studied law at Howard University; she was not admitted to the bar because of her sex. See Jane Rhodes, *Mary Ann Shadd Cary: The Black Press and Protest in the Nineteenth Century* (Bloomington: Indiana University Press, 1998); Ripley, *Black Abolitionist Papers*, vol. 2, 110n, 192n.

56. The prospectus of the Canadian Mill and Mercantile Association was published in *Voice of the Fugitive*, May 6, 1852. William King was a shareholder, as was George Brown, and John M. Tinsley was president. See Smardz Frost, *I've Got a Home in Glory Land*, 302–5.

57. There were six Michigan delegates: C. C. Foote, J. W. Brooke, R. Banks, J. H. Powers, A. Dorrick and E. P. Benham.

58. Charles Foote (1811–1891) was an Oberlin College graduate (1840) and a New Englander by birth. Based in Detroit, the clergyman supported the Liberty Party, formed in 1840 during the great abolitionist schism, to seek a political solution for slavery. Libereta L. Green, *The Beacon Tree: A Tale of the Underground Railroad, Utica, Michigan* (Mt. Clemens, MI: Macomb County Historical Society, 1976), cited in "Seymour Finney Hotel and Barn," Charles H. Wright Museum of African American History, accessed September 15, 2015, http://ugrr.mmaps.magian.com/media/Pdf/Seymour_Finney_Hotel_and_Barn_3.pdf.

59. Daniel G. Hill, *Negroes in Toronto: A Sociological Study of a Minority Group* (PhD diss., University of Toronto, 1960), 369. Hiram Wilson left Toronto in 1843 after a particularly nasty set of exchanges in the *Colored American* between Peter Gallego and some of Wilson's defenders, on this very topic. In the summer of 1851, Foote conducted a lecture tour through New England and New York State. His exaggerated claims of destitution raised a good deal of money, but African Canadians insisted that they provided all the help incoming refugees required. See "Puce River Black Community," Ontario Heritage Trust, August 2007, accessed May 24, 2013, http://www.heritagetrust.on.ca/CMSImages/34/3479a022-cc44-4415-99a0-a24365e1c9ce.pdf; Cooper, "Doing Battle in Freedom's Cause," 243. Charles Foote went on to become pastor of the First Christian Church of New York City.

60. Sending used clothing, schoolbooks and other items to a US address helped avoid the often ruinous customs duties that hampered the attempts of missionaries such as Hiram Wilson and were the subject of regular complaint in the antislavery press. Reverend Charles Foote probably knew helpful officers at the border.

CHAPTER 6: GOT MY LETTER

1. There is no additional postmark on the envelope, so this letter was not forwarded on through the postal service, but there was much intercourse between the Detroit River region and the colonial capital at Toronto, and he could easily have found a traveller to carry it. Fanny's youngest son, Rogers Clark Ballard Thruston, was meticulous in his records and noted the address and any other distinguishing information before discarding the envelope. He notes that it was sent "care of Rev. C.C. Foote, C.W." Fanny Thruston Ballard to Cecelia Jane Holmes, March 11, 1852, Ballard Papers, Filson Historical Society.

2. Fanny seems to have found nothing odd in her former maid's planning a healthful European vacation, or that Cecelia and her husband had accumulated sufficient wherewithal to contemplate one. Slaveholders gave lip service to the idea that their servants were utterly incapable of managing without them, but the reality of dealing with individuals and human beings on a day-to-day basis belied such notions. The work of the South was done by enslaved hands. African American skill, ingenuity, creativity and industry were everywhere in evidence.

3. Charles Thruston Ballard (1850–1918) studied at General William H. Russell's military school in New Haven, Connecticut, and then entered Yale University in 1867, where he was a member of Xeta Thi. He founded Ballard & Ballard Flour Mills with his brother, Samuel T. Ballard, in 1850. Class Secretaries Bureau, Yale University Sheffield Scientific School, *Biographical Record: Classes from Eighteen Hundred and Sixty-Eight to Eighteen Hundred and Seventy-Two of the Sheffield Scientific School* (New Haven: Yale University, 1910), 99–100.

4. Bland Ballard lived only from October 29, 1851, to August 15, 1852.

5. Andrew Jackson Ballard (1815–1885) was the son of a pioneer soldier, Bland Ballard, and Susan Cox Ballard, both from pioneer families of early Kentucky. He was a graduate of Transylvania University in Lexington and practised law in Louisville, starting in 1837. In 1843–44, he represented Louisville in the state legislature but refused the nomination for a second term.

6. What Fanny did not say and Cecelia did not learn until years later was that Charles did not trust Fanny's new husband. In fact, when the engagement was announced, he enlisted several of her powerful Churchill relatives to convince her of Ballard's unsuitability as a husband. Though A. J. Ballard came from good pioneer stock and was an attorney and former state representative, he was far from wealthy. He had also earned the nickname "Black Jack" for his gambling and drinking habits. However, Fanny had a will of steel that belied her fragile appearance. After wavering momentarily in the face of family criticism, she went ahead with the wedding at her parish home, Christ Church, on April 27, 1848. Her father, served by an enslaved couple named Jack and Susan whom he had owned for years, set up housekeeping in the brick "office" he had built earlier on a corner of the property as a business and personal retreat.

   Andrew Jackson Ballard represented Louisville in the state legislature for 1842, as had Fanny's father in 1824, 1834 and 1844, but he declined further involvement in politics in favour of his law practice. After his marriage he managed investments, mainly Kentucky properties belonging to Thruston and Clark family members living in St. Louis, Washington and other places; most were inheritances from the Croghan and Clark estates. He also owned rental properties, some given to him by Fanny's father and others that he had purchased. Fears for his financial solvency were well founded, but Ballard adored his "little wife" and for the most part the marriage was a very happy one. For their financial troubles, see *Mercantile Bank of New York v. Ballard's Assignees*, 83 Kentucky 48L, September 1885, in "Cases of the Court of Appeals in Kentucky," *American State Reports Containing the Cases of General Value and*

Authority . . . Decided in the Courts of Last Resorts in Several States, vol. 4, ed. A. C. Freemen et al. (San Francisco: Bancroft-Whitney, 1889), 160–67.

7. Scrofula was a nasty form of tuberculosis that affected the neck and jaw.

8. Samuel Churchill Thruston (1825–1854) married Kate Keller of Louisville on September 17, 1850. See William Harris Miller, *History and Genealogies of the Families of Miller, Woods, Harris, Wallace, Maupin, Oldham, Kavanaugh, and Brown* (Kentucky: W. H. Miller, 1907), 595.

9. Dr. Bernard Gaines Farrar (1785–1849) in 1820 took as his second wife Fanny's aunt Ann Clark Thruston (Charles W. Thruston's only full sister) in 1820. His first wife was a daughter of William Christy, a fur trader and founder of St. Louis, by whom he had several children. Farrar served as a soldier and surgeon in the War of 1812 and was a member of the first territorial legislature of Missouri. He made a fortune in medicine and the apothecary business and subsequently purchased vast tracts of real estate north of St. Louis. Hyde Park owes its origins to his estate. Walter B. Stevens, *St. Louis: The Fourth City, 1764–1911*, vol. 2 (St. Louis: S. J. Clarke, 1811), 475ff; "The Farrar Family, Continued," *Virginia Magazine of History and Biography* 10, no. 2 (October 1902), 206–7.

10. Abigail Prather Churchill Clark (1818–1852) was Mary Eliza Churchill Thruston's next youngest sister and Fanny's aunt. She married Fanny's cousin on her father's side on January 9, 1834, and moved with him to St. Louis; this was Meriwether Lewis Clark, son of William Clark of Lewis and Clark fame. After his wife's death, Lewis sent his children to live with their Churchill relatives. One of the children was Meriwether Lewis Clark Jr., who after being raised by Fanny's uncles John and Henry Churchill, founded Churchill Downs racetrack on the old Spring Grove estate. Todhunter, *Churchill Genealogy*, vol. 2, 642–57.

11. Samuel C. Thruston was unsuccessful in his business ventures and tried to make a go of farming. He owed substantial sums at the time of his death, but the farm on the Salt River belonged to his father, Charles, who had given him only a life interest in the property. Thruston Senior specifically protected the land from his son's creditors, devising it to his daughter, Fanny, and her children. The estate was administered by her husband, A. J. Ballard, and her uncle, John R. Churchill. It was assigned by Fanny to her sons, who successfully defended it against a suit by the Mercantile Bank of New York against Sam Thruston's estate. See *Mercantile Bank of New York v. Ballard's Assignees*, 160–67.

12. The prominent and very wealthy brothers John (1791–1865) and Benjamin O'Fallon (1793–1842) were Charles and Ann Thruston's half-brothers by their mother Fanny Clark's first marriage; they had been brought up by their uncles George Rogers Clark and William Clark. See James J. Holmberg, *Dear Brother: Letters of William Clark to Jonathan Clark* (New Haven, CT: Yale University Press, 2003), 37n13; "RG," *My Military History Research Interests* (blog), accessed March 28, 2011, http://mymilitaryhistory.blogspot.com/2009/05/rifle-regiments-officer-sketches.html.

The Clarks and O'Fallons were noted for harsh treatment of their slaves, and Fanny Clark O'Fallon's second husband, Charles M. Thruston (Fanny Thruston Ballard's grandfather) "was in all likelihood a severe master"—indeed, he was murdered by his manservant. See William E. Foley, ed., *Wilderness Journey: The Life of William Clark* (Columbia: University of Missouri Press: 2004), 45–46. The previous year William Clark had reported that "Thruston has three Negroes back he has lost 6 Negroes this year"; William Clark to Jonathan Clark, June 8, 1799, Draper Mss., 2L50, in ibid., 291n7. After her husband was murdered, Fanny Thruston's grandmother married for a third time, this time to her cousin Dennis Fitzhugh. She eventually joined her brothers and the sons of her first marriage in St. Louis. William Clark was also callous in his treatment of slaves, even of the faithful York, who had accompanied him on his journeys with Meriwether Lewis on behalf of President Jefferson. He routinely resorted to whippings as punishment and did not give him his longed-for freedom until sometime after 1815; ibid., 167–69.

13. Isabelle "Belle" Penelope Pope Churchill (1829–1861) married Atreus Joshua McCreary in 1834 at the age of sixteen, at the home of her parents. Her husband owned a store in Hardinsburg, Breckinridge County, Kentucky, before moving to Missouri to join his mother's family in the mercantile business. He owned a warehouse and an important store at St. Louis. Belle was another of Fanny's Churchill aunts, despite her being three years Fanny's junior. She died during the Civil War, during which her husband became a Confederate general. It appears that Cecelia had a special friend in Belle McCreery's maid, Sarah; this may be "Sarah Churchill, mulatto, age 55" in Census of the United States, 1870, Elizabethtown, Hardin County, Kentucky.

14. Thomas James Churchill (1824–1905) was married to Anne Maria "Annie" Sevier. He was the fourth youngest brother of the family, and though less than two years her senior, he was Fanny's uncle. Charles Thruston Churchill was born January 10, 1826, in Spring Grove and died March 20, 1865, in Elizabethtown, Hardin County, Kentucky. He was another of Fanny's uncles, born the same year she was, and a special friend and regular correspondent of her brother Samuel Churchill Thruston. Charles married Susan Churchill Payne, his first cousin, at Louisville on March 21, 1850, and lived in Hardin County. Abigail Oldham Churchill, Fanny's grandmother, had inherited a large quantity of land from the estate of her father, the pioneer and soldier William Oldham, who was killed at St. Clair's Defeat on November 4, 1791.

15. Julia Maria Preston Pope Churchill (1833–1937) was Fanny's mother's youngest sister and very close to her niece. She later married physician Luke Pryor Blackburn (1816–1887) as his second wife and spent the Civil War years in Toronto, where her husband was a spy for the Confederacy. He was later elected governor of Kentucky. Nancy Disher Baird, *Luke Pryor Blackburn: Physician, Governor, Reformer* (Lexington: University Press of Kentucky, 1979); Andrew McIllwaine Bell, *Mosquito Soldiers: Malaria, Yellow Fever, and the Course of the American Civil War* (Baton Rouge: Louisiana State University Press, 2010); Lowell H. Harrison, "Luke Pryor Blackburn," in John E. Kleber, ed., *The Kentucky Encyclopedia* (Lexington: University Press of Kentucky, 1992), 84.

16. Ten years Julia's senior, Emily Anne Churchill (1822–1914) married Hampden Zane of Wheeling, Virginia (later West Virginia) on March 31, 1842. Her eldest daughter, Abigail Churchill Zane, born February 9, 1843, died of tuberculosis on July 3, 1860. On December 27, 1866, at St. James' Cathedral in Toronto, Emily Zane's second daughter, Mary Eliza (1844–1917), married George R. R. Cockburn (1833–1912), an Edinburgh-born educator who came to Canada in 1858, first as president of the Toronto Model School and then as principal of Upper Canada College. He went on to a successful career as a (very) conservative member of Parliament, from 1887 to 1896. They had three children: George R. R. Cockburn Jr. died in infancy. Hampden Zane Cockburn (1867–1913) graduated from Upper Canada College and fought in the Boer War; he was the first to win one of only five Victoria Crosses awarded to Canadians for valour. He died on a ranch in Saskatchewan after a fall from a horse, without having married. Emily St. Aubert Cockburn (1871–1943) became the wife of Sir Thomas Tait (1864–1940), vice-president of the Canadian Pacific Railway, and resided in Montreal. They had one daughter, Winifred (born 1892), a socialite who in 1920 and 1921 was one of Canada's first national champions in pairs figure skating. Marion Spence, Upper Canada College Archives, personal communication; Richard B. Howard, *Upper Canada College, 1829–1979*:

Colborne's Legacy (Toronto: Macmillan, 1979), 437–38; "Death of Lady Tait," *Ottawa Citizen*, August 9, 1942.

17. John Pope Oldham (1785–1858) was the son of Kentucky pioneers William Oldham and Penelope Pope. After William Oldham's death at St. Clair's Defeat in 1791, Penelope remarried. Her second husband was Henry Churchill, of one of Louisville's most illustrious founding families. John, his brother Richard and his sister Abigail were brought up in the Churchill household, a large estate known as Spring Grove, on the outskirts of Louisville. At the age of fourteen Abigail Churchill married her stepfather's youngest brother, Samuel Churchill. The marriage produced sixteen living children, the eldest of whom was Mary Eliza Churchill, Fanny Thruston's mother. John Pope Oldham married Malinda Talbot and had two sons and two daughters. Clayton Talbot Oldham, named for his maternal grandfather, was the young man sent to Detroit to claim Thornton Blackburn.

18. John Bullock was the only son of the Oldhams' daughter, Susan, who married William Fontaine Bullock. After his mother died, John Bullock was brought up in the household of his grandparents, John Pope and Malinda Oldham. He became the postmaster for Wheeling, West Virginia.

19. Thornton Blackburn actually belonged to the sister of Aunt Malinda, Oldham's wife, but John Pope Oldham was superintendent of the estate that Susan Brown's deceased husband had left and therefore was responsible for trying to retrieve the man after he escaped in 1831. The Blackburn story is told in my book *I've Got a Home in Glory Land: A Lost Tale of the Underground Railroad* (New York: Farrar Straus Giroux and Toronto: Thomas Allen, 2007).

20. John Ross Robertson, *Landmarks of Toronto*, vol. 2 (Toronto: John Ross Robertson, 1898), 881, 884; Henry Scadding, *Toronto of Old* (Toronto: Adam, Stevenson, 1873), 575; Maurice D. Smith, *Steamboats on the Lakes* (Toronto: James Lorimer, 2005), 27.

21. Samuel Ringgold Ward, "Letters from Canada," no. III, *North Star*, February 12, 1852.

22. Rhodes, *Mary Ann Shadd Cary* (Bloomington: Indiana University Press, 1998), especially ch. 3 and 4. The first issue of the *Provincial Freeman* appeared in Windsor on March 24, 1853, while Cecelia and her family were out of the country.

23. Frederick Douglass, *The Life and Times of Frederick Douglass* (Hartford, CT: Park Publishing, 1881), 284.

24. Elijah Barnett Dunlop (1816–1898) was born in Richmond, Virginia, and came to Toronto in the 1830s. After his time at Dawn and later Oberlin College, he moved to St. Catharines and married Elizabeth Wheaton of Drummondville (now part of Niagara Falls, Ontario) on October 30, 1848. The ceremony was performed by T. B. Fuller, according to the Niagara District Vital Records. He was thirty-six when he arrived in Australia; "Dunlop, E. B., 36 Dec. 1852, Madison," fiche 005 002, Public Record Office, Australia. He seems to have been quite successful as a goldminer, moving around a bit. His name is listed in the incorporation notice for the Morning Star Amalgamated Quartz Mining Company published in the Victoria *Gazette* in 1864. At the time Dunlop was living in Blue Mountain and owned seven shares of the mine. The *Argus* (Ballarat) of March 21, 1863, shows Dunlop living in Indigo and serving as a school trustee at Columbia Reef, alongside several white men, presumably on an equal footing. The same paper of April 19, 1897, mentions E. B. Dunlop as prominent in the local Mechanics' Institute (a forerunner of the modern public library system) at Bendigo. His later life was less promising: he died after a stay in the Bendigo Benevolent Asylum in 1898. He was buried on September 20, 1898, in the White Hills Cemetery, Bendigo (grave 13615, section unknown).

25. Elijah B. Dunlop, Madison Passenger List, December 1852, Inward Shipping Records, Public Record Office of Victoria, Melbourne PROV, VPRS 7667. The four Toronto Black men were listed one after the other in the ship's list. No passenger list bearing the name of Zachariah Dunlop Patterson has been discovered, but he was in Australia by 1854, was mentioned in several newspaper articles working as a barber there, and spent the rest of his life in the southern hemisphere.

26. Eulogy of James D. Tinsley by Samuel Ringgold Ward, *Provincial Freeman*, August 5, 1854; "The ship's list of the *Epaminondas*, under Captain Condy, from the port of New York for Port Philip, Australia," State Records of South Australia, Archives Services. At the end of the two columns of lists are five men marked "(coloured)": J. D. Tinsley, J. H. Tinsley, Francis Russell(?), Squire Nelson and Richard Williams; the latter two are known to have come from Hamilton, Canada West.

27. The ship was reportedly "one of the finest and fastest out of the port of New York, having spacious cabins fitted up with every attention to comfort, and even luxury." Travellers could purchase their tickets from W. H. Fellows, Wellington Street, as noted in the Toronto *Globe* of July 29, 1852. According to Lloyd's Register, the *Epaminondas* was built at Quebec in 1850. Sheathed in yellow metal to the waterline (to prevent barnacles from attaching themselves and to retard rot), 117 feet long and three-masted, it was built for the firm of Granger and Company, which registered the ship at Belfast (its port of survey was Liverpool). It had a passenger capacity of 250 but sometimes carried nearly twice that number of anxious emigrants, as attested by a report of its arrival on December 24, 1853, after a voyage of some 119 days, published in the *South Australian Government Gazette* of June 19, 1854.

28. Frederick Douglass to Sidney Howard Gay, June 12, 1852, Sidney Howard Gay Papers, Rare Book and Manuscript Library, Columbia University, New York.

29. About twenty-five years old, George Browne had a wife, originally from Pennsylvania, named Mary. The Browns (their name now spelled without the terminal *e*) rented another house on Centre Street in subsequent years, and George is listed as a carter in the 1856 city directory. There was a second George Brown, a cook, who was forty-two years old and had a wife named Elizabeth. They are also listed on Centre Street in the contemporary directories. In the absence of an 1851 census for Toronto (since lost), it is not possible to tell which of the two George Brown(e)s rented the Centre Street house of Benjamin and Cecelia Holmes. (To complicate matters, there was a third man of the same name, single and also a cook, who lived in a shanty with several other Black men in Etobicoke, about nine miles west of the city proper, in 1851.)

30. Massachusetts had struggled with the issue of school integration, but it was instituted very early in such towns as Salem, despite the fact that Blacks encountered strong resistance in Boston for many years. The existence of a course of barbering instruction in Lowell is suggested by a number of factors, including the large number of Black barbers in the town and surrounding area with youthful apprentices living in their households and working in their shops, and the fact that both James Thomas and Benjamin Alexander Holmes were fully trained barbers who opened their own shops when they returned to Canada in 1860 and 1862, respectively. See "Jeremiah B. Sanderson to William C. Nell, June 19, 1842," in C. Peter Ripley, ed., *Black Abolitionist Papers*, vol. 3, *The United States, 1830–1846* (Chapel Hill: University of North Carolina Press, 1991), 385–88. Sanderson spent the summer of 1842 in Lowell in the barbershop of his "foster brother," fellow Black activist Horatio W. Foster.

31. The son of Samuel and Elizabeth (Rebecca) Turner, originally of Milford, Delaware, he was brought up in Philadelphia, where he lived with his parents at 53 Currant Alley, in one of the very poorest parts of the city. Turner moved to Toronto in 1835 and was naturalized in 1843;

Upper Canada Naturalization Registers, 1828–50, RG 5, B47, vol. 7. On the same page of the register appears prominent Black abolitionist Newton Cary, as well as Charles Philip Anderson, David Hollins, Francis Russell, Thomas Johnston and Henry Miller (later a minister at Owen Sound). Only Joseph P. Turner, Newton Cary, David Hollins and Francis Russell signed their own names. Turner was a close associate of the city's Black elite. In addition to the Abbotts—probably the wealthiest African American transplants living in Canada West—other Black church leaders included saw manufacturer Thomas Smallwood, a former Underground Railroad operator whose published memoirs shed much light on the system of fugitive-slave assistance in Washington, DC, and Matthew Truss, who came to Toronto from Augusta County, Virginia, before 1833. His story was similar to Benjamin's: Matthew was supposed to receive his freedom on the death of his owner. Instead he was allowed to purchase himself and his wife on the condition they immigrate to Liberia, but they found Canada more attractive and went there instead. See Roger Lane, *William Dorsey's Philadelphia and Ours: On the Past and Future of the Black City in America* (New York: Oxford University Press, 1991), 295. Turner's mother died at the age of 104 on March 18, 1865, and was buried from her Current Alley address. Turner went on to minister to the Charles Street AME church in Boston and wrote regularly for the *Christian Recorder* until his death in October 1863. See David N. Johnson, *Sketches of Lynn or the Change of Fifty Years* (Lynn, MA: Thos. P. Nichols, 1880), 438; *Lynn City Directory*, 1858, accessed June 22, 2013, http://www.lynnhistory.com/Directories/1858/Pg16.html.

32. Reverend Joseph Peniel Turner (1805–1863) was very active in the New England AME Church, travelling widely and attending church meetings. He was the first minister at the new AME Church at Lynn, Massachusetts, in 1857. See Johnson, *Sketches of Lynn*, 438. See also "Plymouth Church, Mass.," *Christian Recorder*, February 1, 1862; "From the East," February 21, 1863; and "From the East," March 28, 1863. His death was announced in the October 24, 1863, edition of the same paper.

33. This would explain why their names do not appear on any passenger register but those of their friends and contemporaries who travelled to Australia do.

34. Basil Lubbock, *The Colonial Clippers*, 2nd ed. (Glasgow: James Brown and Son, 1921), 5–8.

CHAPTER 7: GO DOWN MOSES

1. Douglas W. Bristol Jr., "Regional Identity, Black Barbers and the African American Tradition of Entrepreneurialism," *Southern Quarterly* 43, no. 2 (Winter 2006), 76.

2. There are multiple histories of Lowell, Massachusetts, an early one consulted for the purposes of this volume being Henry W. Coburn, *History of Lowell and Its Peoples* (New York: Lewis Historical Publishing, 1920); see ch. 6, note 31.

3. Insights into the apprenticeship and training of young African Americans headed towards such careers are provided by the very detailed diary of William Johnson, a master barber who taught a series of young men the trade in Natchez, on the Mississippi River, and the documentation provided by Cyprian Clamorgan in his valuable volume *The Colored Aristocracy of St. Louis*. See Bristol, "Regional Identity," 73–94, and his more recent volume, *Knights of the Razor: Black Barbers in Slavery and Freedom* (Baltimore, MD: Johns Hopkins University Press, 2010), 45–55; and Cyprian Clamorgan, *The Colored Aristocracy of St. Louis*, ed. Julie Winch (Columbia: University of Missouri Press, 1999), 49. Another important source is Quincy T. Mills, *Cutting along the Color Line: Black Barbershops and Barbers in America* (Philadelphia: University of Pennsylvania Press, 2003).

4. Clamorgan, *Colored Aristocracy*.

5. Douglas Bristol Jr., "From Outposts to Enclaves: A Social History of Black Barbers from 1750 to 1915," *Enterprise and Society* 5, no. 4 (December 2004): 594–606. As for the prohibition against Sunday shaves, see the diary of Ann Everitt, Mickle Family Collection, Special Collections, University of Guelph.

6. Mills, *Cutting Along the Color Line*, 56–58; Ted Delaney and Phillip Wayne Rhodes, *Free Blacks of Lynchburg, Virginia, 1805–1865* (Lynchburg, VA: Warwick House, 2001), 41–42.

7. Barry Malone, "We Cut Heads: The Black Barbershop as a Public Sphere," paper presented to the Association for the Study of African American Life and History (ASALH), Pittsburgh, PA, September 28, 2004, accessed May 15, 2015, http://allacademic.com/meta/p116566_index.htm. For a comprehensive history of the role of African Americans in barbering, see Mills, *Cutting Along the Color Line*, ch. 1.

8. See, for instance, the long descriptive obituary of barber Richard Jackson, "Death of 'Dick' Jackson," *Toronto World*, June 3, 1885.

9. Eric Baldwin, "Religion and the American Industrial City: Protestant Culture and Social Transformation in Lowell, Massachusetts, 1824–1890" (PhD diss., Boston University, 2009), 144.

10. Gray Fitzsimons, "Walking Tour of Downtown Lowell: A Dozen Sites Associated with Anti-slavery in the Spindle City, 1830–1860" (unpublished paper, May 2011), accessed May 22, 2013, libweb.uml.edu/clh/Exhibit/AntislaveryTour.pdf. However, by the 1850s, when the Holmes family arrived, the Lowell "system" was deteriorating. Technological advances meant labour needs were outstripping the old source of supply; there were immigrants now in the mills, which also employed growing numbers of men, but they were all white. The manufacturers employed no African Americans and nearly all the Black families in Lowell were involved in hairdressing.

11. James Oliver Horton, "Generations of Protest: Black Families and Social Reform in Ante-bellum Boston," *New England Quarterly* 49, no. 2 (June 1976): 242–56.

12. Cecelia's elder stepson, Ben Alexander, most likely was inducted into Prince Hall Freemasonry during his time at Lowell. He continued his involvement for the rest of his life.

13. Baldwin, "Religion and the American Industrial City," 9–13. Some scholars have observed that the emphasis on morality in Lowell was little more than enlightened self-interest on the part of mill owners. See John W. Cox and Dennis Shirley, "Corporate Funding of Public Schools in Antebellum Massachusetts: The Waltham Exception," *Massachusetts Historical Review* 13 (2011): 53–54. Lowell's founder seems to have been genuinely committed to the reforms implemented first at Waltham and then at Lowell, but those who took his place are considered by many historians to have been much more interested in increasing profits than in the intellectual or moral qualities of their workers. See Seth Luther, *An Address to the Workingmen of New England* (Boston, 1832), 18, 28; and Howard M. Gitelman, *Workingmen of Waltham: Mobility in American Urban Industrial Development, 1850–1890* (Baltimore, MD: Johns Hopkins University Press, 1974), 4–5, cited in Cox and Shirley, "Corporate Funding," 53–54.

14. Connell O'Donovan, "Descendants of Mingo and Dinah: From West Africa to Colonial Massachusetts," chronology based on research by Martha Mayo, Lowell Historical Archives, accessed June 4, 2014, http://people.ucsc.edu/~odonovan/Walker_Family_Chronology.html.

15. Cox and Shirley, "Corporate Funding," 47–49, 58–59; Brian C. Mitchell, "Good Citizens at the Least Cost per Pound: The History of the Development of Public Education in Antebellum Lowell, 1825–1855," in *The Continuing Revolution: A History of Lowell, Massachusetts*, ed. Robert Wieble (Lowell, MA: Lowell Historical Society, 1991): 118–23. Caroline Van Vronker is reputed

to be the first Black high school graduate at a publicly funded school in the United States. But if the school system was colour-blind in respect of its students, it was not when it came to hiring teachers. Caroline was the daughter of a "genteel and accomplished" local barber, Henry Van Vronker. Although she graduated as a teacher with excellent qualifications, she was denied employment in her field. Teachers of colour in Lowell were prevented from supervising the education of white students for many years; Martha Mayo, personal communication, June 2013.

16. The young Virginian had been living quite openly in Lowell since his 1844 arrival, advertising his "Hair-Cutting, Curling and Champooing Saloon [sic]" with "Cologne, oils, razors, etc., constantly on hand" in the 1851 city directory; George Adams, *The Lowell Directory: Containing the City Record, 1851* (Lowell, MA: Oliver March, 1851), 35. Walker Lewis had a shop in the Washington House, and he also boarded Nathaniel Booth.

17. Fitzsimons, "Walking Tour," 10; Adams, *Lowell Directory*, 24, 30, 79, 106. There are sixteen "Hairdressers" listed in the directory, including the partnership of Walker Lewis and Peter B. Lew at 12 Merrimack Street, "a few doors east of Central Str."; their advertisement appears on page 35. Both Walker's and Peter's houses were "at Centralville." Horatio W. Foster, at 65 Center Street, was listed as a "wig and hair-oil manufacturer" with a home on Chapel Street (208, in the commercial section of the directory). Charles E. LaMasure was a hairdresser living at Mrs. E. Black's boarding house, 82 Central Street (28,112). Another was Edwin Moore, whose shop was at 18 Merrimack and his home on Fayette (134). Ezekiel White made hair restorative and lived on Sumner, at the corner of Davis (191). William F. Brooks advertised his shop on the ground floor of the Mechanics' Institute, "near the Merrimack House" (35); he lived on "Kirk Street Avenue" and employed Edward B. Lewis, whose house was on Maiden Lane (116). Samuel L. Lewis operated his hairdressing business out of his home at 234 Merrimack; John L. Lewis, who boarded there, was also a hairdresser (116). Daniel Barth's shop, where Nathaniel Booth worked as a free man, was located at no. 3, the American Block.

18. His religious convictions may have been a concern, however, as Walker Lewis had converted to the Church of the Latter-day Saints and risen to the rank of elder. The *Lowell Advertiser* of November 9, 1852, mentions that when the Holmes family arrived, Walker Lewis was on an extended journey to the "Valley of the Great Salt Lake" to consult with Mormon elders; cited in O'Donovan, "Descendants of Mingo and Dinah." Lewis's son had married a white woman in Boston, which caused such consternation that Brigham Young was quoted as saying that had the interracial couple not lived in Boston among so many "Gentiles," he would have had them murdered. Disappointed and dismayed by his treatment at the hands of the Mormon church, Walker Lewis returned to Lowell in November 1852 and reopened his shop. He died in 1856 at the age of fifty-eight, before Benjamin's sons ended their time at Lowell, so they must have finished their training elsewhere; City of Lowell death register, 1856, no. 635. Thanks to Martha Mayo for permitting me to use her excellent chronology of the Walker-Lewis family.

19. John Levy led a fascinating life. Born in Nevis, he sailed for England as a youth and was caught up in the War of 1812. On his way home he stopped in Boston, where he married Walker Lewis's sister and trained as a barber. Throughout his long career he also traded foodstuffs and other goods back and forth to the West Indies. In 1826 the extended Lewis family, including John Levy and his wife, migrated to Lowell. He then set up hairdressing businesses in both Lawrence, Massachusetts, where he had the first and only barbershop, and Lowell. He later abandoned his wife and moved to Albany, Rochester and then Geneseo, New York. He was proud to state that he always had a copy of the *Liberator* in his shop. At the end of his life, in 1870, he returned to

Lawrence, living with his daughter and writing his memoirs. See John Levy, *Life and Adventures of John Levy* (Lawrence, MA: Robert Bower, 1871).

20. Wilbur H. Siebert, "The Underground Railroad in Massachusetts," *Proceedings of the American Antiquarian Society* (April 1935), 49–50.

21. O'Donovan, "Descendants of Mingo and Dinah."

22. James O. Horton and Lois E. Horton, *Black Bostonians: Family Life and Community Struggle in the Antebellum North* (Teaneck, NJ: Holmes and Meier, 2000), 88; Dorothy P. Wesley and Constance P. Uzelac, eds., *William Cooper Nell: Selected Writings,1832–1874* (Baltimore, MD: Black Classic Press, 2002), 6–7; William Cooper Nell, *The Colored Patriots of the American Revolution* (Robert F. Wallcut, 1855), 325; Mayo, Walker-Lewis family chronology.

23. Horton and Horton, *Black Bostonians*, 96. For Thomas Walker, see Horton, "Generations of Protest," 253. Lewis's family was from Barre, Massachusetts, where his parents, Peter Lewis and Minor Walker, were married December 5, 1792; Massachusetts, Town and Vital Records, 1620–1988 (online database), Ancestry.com, 2011; original data from Town and City Clerks of Massachusetts, *Massachusetts Vital and Town Records* (Provo, UT: Holbrook Research Institute [Jay and Delene Holbrook]).

24. The brothers arrived in Lowell in 1852, after the 1850 census, and at least James had left before the next census was taken in 1860. However, Benjamin A. Holmes's obituary specifically names Lowell, Massachusetts, as the place where he received his education; *Faribault* (Minnesota) *Republican*, September 16, 1896.

25. Bristol, "Regional Identity," 76.

26. An important source on barber training and the treatment of apprentices in the households of master barbers is the diary of William Johnson of Natchez, who had learned his trade as a slave and, once freed, was a respected and valued hairdresser, shaver and stylist. He was a controversial figure because of his personal aspirations to enter the planter class and own slaves. Johnson's home was designated a historic site by the National Park Service in 2005. For a fascinating analysis of Johnson see Edwin Adams Davis and William Ransome Hogan, *William Johnson's Natchez: The Ante-Bellum Diary of a Free Negro* (Baton Rouge: Louisiana State University Press, 1968).

27. Another possibility is that they booked passage under false names, a simple matter in the days before passports became the norm. Sailing under their own names out of either Boston or New York, both of which had regular traffic with Southern ports, might have seemed too dangerous to Cecelia and Benjamin. Both were fugitive slaves, despite being naturalized British subjects, and sailing from America's eastern seaboard left them vulnerable to recapture.

28. David W. Bartlett, *London by Day and Night; or, Men and Things in the Great Metropolis* (New York: Hurst, 1852), 11.

29. Ward, *Autobiography*, 291. On proslavery Americans in Liverpool, see William P. Powell to William Lloyd Garrison, 1854?, Maria Chapman Weston Papers, Boston Public Library, accessed January 17, 2015, https://bpl.bibliocommons.com/item/show/4531897075_letter_to_dear_mr_may.

30. Herman Melville, *Redburn: His First Voyage, Being the Sailor-Boy Confessions and Reminiscences of the Son-of-a-Gentleman, in the Merchant Service* (1849; Chicago: Northwestern University Press, 1969), 202. While this is fiction, it reflects Melville's memories of Liverpool during his time at sea.

31. Ward, *Autobiography*, 220–21.

32. Vanessa D. Dickerson, *Dark Victorians* (Urbana: University of Illinois Press, 2008), 60–61.

33. William Pentecost Powell Sr. (1807–1879) was a grandson of Elizabeth Barjova, who was the cook for the Continental Congress. His enslaved father was Edward Powell, who was freed with New York's abolition act in 1827, and his mother was a free woman. His wife, Mercy O. Haskins, was Native American. The politically savvy Powell had the benefit of a superior education. While in New Bedford, he addressed the Massachusetts legislature in 1837 on the issue of racial discrimination and fought for the integration of schools.

    William Powell was a founder of the American Anti-Slavery Society and secretary of the Manhattan Anti-Slavery Society, and he wrote frequently to the *Liberator* (Boston), the *Voice of the Fugitive* (Sandwich, Canada West) and the *National Anti-Slavery Standard* (Boston and Philadelphia), the official organ of the American Anti-Slavery Society, on subjects ranging from identification of all slavery in the United States as "Negro Slavery" to the need for education of Black youth to citing specific fugitive-slave rendition cases and denouncing the Fugitive Slave Law of 1850 for facilitating the return of slaves to their former owners. He chaired meetings of a vigilance committee known as the Committee of Thirteen, as noted in the *National Anti-Slavery Standard*, October 13, 1851.

    Powell and his wife arrived in England on December 12, 1850, and opened the Coloured Seamen's Mission in Liverpool, which they operated until 1861. They then returned to the United States and reopened their New York boarding house and mission for sailors; some 2,000 Black sailors operated out of New York, and more than 3,800 had been hosted by the Powells since 1840, according to the *Sabbath Recorder*, June 1, 1848. See William Powell to William Lloyd Garrison, July 18, 1863, in Donald Yacovone, ed., *Freedom's Journey: African American Voices of the Civil War* (Chicago: Lawrence Hill, 2004), 72–75, and Yacovone's introductory paragraphs on Powell, 75; William Lloyd Garrison, *The Letters of William Lloyd Garrison*, vol. 4, *From Disunionism to the Brink of War: 1850–1860*, ed. Louis Ruchames (Cambridge, MA: Belknap Press, 1976), 42n1; W. Jeffrey Bolster, *Black Jacks: African American Seamen in the Age of Sail* (Cambridge, MA: Harvard University Press, 1998), 206; Black Abolitionist Archive, University of Detroit, Mercy, accessed October 5, 2013.

34. Philip S. Foner, *History of Black Americans*, vol. 2, *From the Emergence of the Cotton Kingdom to the Eve of the Compromise of 1850* (Westport: Greenwood Press, 1983), 242.

35. Powell's ancestry, worth and reason for departing were published in an article titled "The Shame of America," *Frederick Douglass' Paper*, July 31, 1851. He travelled with a glowing letter of reference to William Rathbone, a Liverpool merchant and reformer who had been the city's mayor during the Irish famine years. See William Lloyd Garrison to William Rathbone Esq., October 1, 1850, in *Letters of William Lloyd Garrison*, 40–43.

36. In Liverpool, as elsewhere, Black guests were more readily hosted by those whose own ancestry was African. While well-to-do African American and Canadian visitors were handsomely accommodated in white-operated hotels and guest houses, those who could not afford their rates found housing where they could. Britain was no more free of racism than elsewhere, and Liverpool had been a centre of the slave trade and the trade in slave-produced goods for generations.

37. William Lloyd Garrison's two-week stay in Liverpool was, as he reported in the July 20, 1853, edition of the *Liberator*, "rendered more agreeable by the kindness of our mutual friend, Wm. P. Powell, Esq., formerly of New York." Powell also continued his work on behalf of the antislavery cause. In 1857 he wrote from his home at 123 Field Street, Everton (a suburb of Liverpool), to Maria Weston Chapman in Boston. A six-page list accompanied boxes of goods for the Boston bazaar donated by the Liverpool Ladies' Anti-Slavery Society, complete with suggested prices and

the names of their donors (his wife was clearly a member, for several of the items were made by "Mrs. Powell"). William P. Powell to Maria Weston Chapman, October 30, 1857, Maria Weston Chapman Correspondence (1835–85), Boston Public Library.

38. For instance, the famous fugitive George Marshall stayed with the Powells on his way back from Australia. As he intended to settle in Syracuse, New York, Garrison sent on a letter of reference for Marshall written by William Powell, to Reverend Samuel J. May, who was the Unitarian minister and Underground Railroad station operator there; William Lloyd Garrison to Samuel J. May, October 26, 1855, *Letters of William Lloyd Garrison*, 349–50.

39. His letter was quoted in the *Standard* on August 6, 1853. His eldest son, William Pentecost Powell Jr. (1834–1919), pursued his medical studies in London, returning to the United States to become one of only thirteen African American surgeons in the Union Army during the Civil War. He worked at the Contraband Hospital in Washington from 1863 on, and then in various parts of the country, including San Francisco, where he lost his medical certificate in an earthquake. Towards the end of his life he returned to England. A photograph of Dr. Powell was recently discovered in his military pension application file; see Jill L. Newmark, "Face to Face with History," *Prologue*, 41, no. 3 (Fall 2009), accessed July 30, 2016, http://www.archives.gov/publications/prologue/2009/fall/face.html.

40. Jeffrey Green, "Black Women in Britain 1850–1897," accessed June 30, 2015, http://www.jeffreygreen.co.uk/093-black-women-in-britain-1850-1897.

41. E. Daniel Potts and Annette Potts, "The Negro and the Australian Gold Rushes, 1852–1857," *Pacific Historical Review* 37, no. 4 (November 1968): 381–99. See also E. Daniel Potts and Annette Potts, *Young America and Australian Gold: Americans and the Gold Rush of the 1850s* (St. Lucia: University of Queensland Press, 1974).

42. The information about the Patterson barbershop is from an account of a murder that the brothers witnessed, published in the *Ballarat Star*, September 18, 1858. The court proceedings were recounted in considerable detail in "County Court of Bourke: Patterson v. Travers," Melbourne *Argus*, June 21, 1854. The incident had taken place on March 17, 1854. Americans had access to Australian papers and followed news of their friends overseas. On October 7, 1854, William C. Nell wrote in a letter to a friend, the white Quaker abolitionist Amy Post, in Rochester: "J. H. Putnam sends me an Australian paper containing an account of (Rochester) Patterson's ejection from a Saloon at the bidding of some Americans—Patterson received £50 damages"; Wesley and Uzelac, *William Cooper Nell*, 292–93. This was Joseph Hall Putnam, a Boston schoolteacher and hairdresser; he was the husband of Caroline, one of Black abolitionist lecturer Charles Lenox Remond's five sisters. When Putnam died, William Nell wrote to the *Liberator* on January 28, 1859: "to the antislavery cause he gave an intelligent and unwavering support, being one of those model Colored Americans, whose theory is hatred of oppression and whose practice coincides therewith"; Dorothy Burnett Porter, "The Remonds of Salem, Massachusetts: A Nineteenth-Century Family Revisited," *Proceedings of the American Antiquarian Society* 95 (1985): 292.

43. Eventually J. J. Cary returned to Toronto and opened a barbershop on King Street with the profits of his Australian sojourn; Potts and Potts, "The Negro and the Australian Gold Rushes," 387. Cary was interviewed in Toronto by Samuel Ward Howe in 1863.

44. Henry Hickman (1831–1872) married Fannie Freeland and had fourteen children in Australia. His partnership with Zachariah D. Patterson in Ballarat was dissolved on October 13, 1856, with Patterson apparently at fault; *Ballarat Star*, October 14, 1856. While Patterson signed the documents of dissolution, Hickman could only make an X. He had come from Virginia with his

parents in 1832, when there was as yet no public school available in the Town of York. Hickman was eventually forced into bankruptcy, as reported in the *Ballarat Star* between January 26 and March 28, 1858. He moved his family to Bendigo, where he died on July 28, 1872, in the hospital at Sandhurst. His death record states that he was a hairdresser, aged forty-five, and that he had suffered for three months of a "disease of the brain"; Schedule B, Deaths in the District of Sandhurst in the Colony of Australia, July 1872.

Both the Patterson brothers remained in Australia. They too abandoned prospecting in favour of the barbering trade. James Dunlop Patterson married in Australia and had several children, but his brother Zachariah, who sometimes had difficulty with both business practice and social conventions, had an illegitimate son whose mother sued for support. He moved to New Zealand in 1862, where his financial difficulties repeated themselves, and he eventually died there. The New Zealand connection is attested by a list of bankrupts that includes the name Zachariah Dunlop Patterson in the *Otago Daily Times*, December 7, 1864.

45. Meanwhile Elijah B. Dunlop abandoned his Canadian family, living a rather itinerant life moving from place to place in the goldfields. His wife is listed in the St. Catharines, Canada West, directory for 1865 as "Dunlop, Mrs. Elizabeth (widow Elijah), seamstress." Dunlop's early success in the goldfields did not continue; he died just before the turn of the twentieth century in an Australian poorhouse at the age of eighty-one.

46. More than 300,000 subsidized passengers emigrated between 1850 and 1855 alone.

47. For instance, Professor William G. Allen, who travelled to England to lecture on antislavery in 1853, wrote to the US antislavery papers on June 20, 1853: "Our passage from America to England was a pleasant one, barring the melancholy accident—the loss of four sailors at sea—of which you already know; and our stay of two weeks in Liverpool was rendered more than agreeable by the kindness of our mutual friend, William P. Powell, Esq., formerly of New York"; *Frederick Douglass' Paper*, August 5, 1853, reprinted from the *Liberator*. Allen was the first Black professor at a white American college; see Richard Blackett, "William Allen: A Forgotten Professor," *Civil War History* 26, no. 1 (March 1980): 39–52.

48. He left on April 8, 1853.

49. Lois Brown, "African American Responses to *Uncle Tom's Cabin*," paper delivered at "*Uncle Tom's Cabin* in the Web of Culture," conference sponsored by the National Endowment for the Humanities, Harriet Beecher Stowe Center, Hartford, CT, 2007, accessed January 11, 2015, http://utc.iath.virginia.edu/interpret/exhibits/brown/brown.html. While in Great Britain, William Wells Brown wrote *Three Years in Europe* and *Clotel, or the President's Daughter* (1853), which was the first African American novel. He had attended the Buffalo Black National Convention in 1843 along with Elijah B. Dunlop, Ralph Francis and Harrison Powell, who lived in Rochester and would serve as a witness when Cecelia remarried there in 1862. He also authored a travel book while he was in England, a sojourn that influenced his literary career for the rest of his life. Brown did not stay at the Powells' but rather at Brown's Temperance Hotel, Clayton Square.

50. Nancy Koester, *Harriet Beecher Stowe: A Spiritual Life* (Grand Rapids, MI: William B. Eerdmans, 2014), 176–77.

51. Julia Chybowski, "The 'Black Swan' in England: Abolition and the Reception of Elizabeth Taylor Greenfield," *American Music Research Center Journal* 14 (2006): 8–25; William Wells Brown, *Three Years in Europe* (London: Charles Gilpin, 1852), 8–9.

CHAPTER 8: DON'T BE WEARY, TRAVELLER

1. Only one other Benjamin Holmes is known for that era, but he was a prominent white man, a justice of the peace in Sydney who always styled himself "Benjamin Holmes, Esq." It seems unlikely that the unclaimed letters at the Adelaide post office would be intended for a person so prominent and whose location was well known.

2. There is no passenger list bearing Cecelia's name for any ship travelling to a North American port during the appropriate period, but given that she was at least six months pregnant when she boarded, it is difficult to believe that she again worked her passage. It is doubtful that she would have taken a stewardess position, which required carrying heavy hot-water cans for passenger bathing and coal hods to heat cabin stoves. As a respectable "widow" she may have been considered a suitable choice for personal servant or children's nurse; a number of her specialized employment positions after her British sojourn did entail working with children. While there survives no crew list bearing her name, several passengers between October 1853 and March 1854 were accompanied by children's nurses. It is unlikely that she would have travelled alone by way of Boston. Although Benjamin was a naturalized British subject he was not with her, and whether or not slave-catchers in an American port would have made the distinction was a risk she would not have run. According to the *Novascotian, Acadian Recorder* and *Evening Reporter*, among the vessels landing at Halifax directly from Liverpool during this period were the *America*, the *Niagara*, the *Canada* and the *Europa*. "Halifax, Nova Scotia, Ship Arrivals and Departures, 1851–1872," Immigrant Ships Trancribers Guild, accessed July 31, 2016, http://immigrantships. net/halifaxlists/halifaxarr_depart1853.html.

3. John Henry Tinsley married an Englishwoman from Norfolk, Julia Ann Lammas, on August 5, 1873. The marriage register lists James as a hairdresser, aged forty-one, and his bride as a thirty-one-year-old dressmaker; "Schedule D: Marriages Solemnized in the County of Bourke, 1873." She died at thirty-eight, on June 6, 1876; "Schedule B: Deaths in the District of Carleton in the Colony of Australia, 1876." On June 30, 1890, an article in honour of John M. Tinsley's 107th(!) birthday in the Toronto *Globe* mentioned that he had descendants in Australia, so the Toronto and Australian branches had evidently stayed in touch.

4. "James D. Tinsley . . . was with me in London, in February last, having arrived from Australia, in the *Great Britain.* He was to have taken the Cunard steamer for Boston, (thence to Canada,) on the 25th of February; but he waited till the 1st of March, and took the *City of Glasgow,* which, alas! has not since been heard from"; Samuel Ringgold Ward, letter to *Provincial Freeman,* July 8, 1854.

5. According to Ward, Tinsley had returned from Australia in mid-February, landing at Liverpool on the steamer *Great Britain,* armed with a series of letters of introduction of which he and his friend Ward availed themselves. Acquired during his sojourn in Australia, they provided entrée to "some of the first literary and scientific gentlemen of London; to the Secretary of the Young Men's Christian Association of the British Metropolis." They came "from the Secretary of a kindred Society in Melbourne; from the pastor of the Baptist Church in Melbourne; and from the Superintendent and Teachers of the Melbourne Baptist Sabbath School, in which Mr. T., was an honoured, useful and beloved teacher—though there was not a black or coloured person in the school." The latter was particularly a subject of comment on the part of Reverend Ward, who was very dark-skinned and had experienced, along with his family, some of the worst "Negro hate"—as he termed it—that Canada had to offer.

6. Mary "Mamie" Holmes's exact date of birth was not recorded; the 1900 US Census for Louisville, Kentucky, shows her as having been born in March 1858, which is incorrect by four years. Mamie

and her mother before her were both fairly cavalier about their ages, usually shaving off a few years and sometimes entire decades. However, her birthday date would have been fairly common knowledge, so the month is likely correct.

7. Tax Assessment Rolls, City of Toronto, St. John's Ward, 1854. In the records of 1855 and 1856, the latter dated April 30 of that year, Cecelia was acknowledged as both freeholder and landlord for Lot 7, the land Benjamin had purchased in 1844. She continued to use the term "widow" in all public documents through April 1856.

8. The transfer from James Lukin Robinson and his wife, Emily, took place on March 12, 1854; Abstract Index for Plan 147, County of York Land Registry Office, RG 61–64, GSU 197293, Archives of Ontario.

9. Bruce West, *Toronto* (New York: Doubleday, 1967), 159; "Canadian Cholera Epidemic of 1854," in *Encyclopedia of Plague and Pestilence: From Ancient Times to the Present*, ed. George C. Kohn, 3rd ed. (New York: Facts on File, 2008), 58–59.

10. *Brown's Toronto General Directory* (Toronto: W. R. Brown, 1856), ix–x.

11. Ibid., xx.

12. John James Cary was listed in the *North Star* of June 13, 1850, as the Toronto agent for *Frederick Douglass' Paper*.

13. *Brown's Directory*, ix–xv.

14. It is unknown how many Black Americans came to the city in this decade. The manuscript census for 1851 for the cities of Toronto, Montreal and Halifax is lost. Only by examining city directories and the tax assessment rolls for this period can one begin to gain a sense of their numbers.

15. The loss of the manuscript census for 1851 Toronto is indeed unfortunate, as it is impossible to trace which free Black families came to Canadian cities in the immediate aftermath of the Fugitive Slave Law and which had arrived in the 1840s. However, the rather sudden blossoming of so many new organizations and fraternal orders in the 1850s suggests that the bulk of the migration happened then. There was also by the mid-1850s a distinct change in the tone of political discourse: those who had heeded David Walker's *Appeal* and espoused the militant Reverend Henry Highland Garnet's call to action now migrated to the capital of Canada West convinced of the need for active opposition to slavery and slaveholding advocates, both in and outside Congress.

16. "For the Freeman," *Provincial Freeman*, August 19, 1854.

17. Ripley, *Black Abolitionist Papers*, vol. 2, 378n5, 380n2, 448n4, 485n8. The paper moved to Chatham in 1855. See also Abbott Papers, Baldwin Room, Toronto Reference Library; Mary Ann Shadd Cary Papers, Archives of Ontario; Moreland-Springharn Collection, Howard University; Armistead Collection, Tulane University, Louisiana. The Alvin McCurdy Collection in the Archives of Ontario also contains Toronto material, as do the Daniel G. Hill Papers at both the Archives of Ontario and Library and Archives Canada, including images and documents used to write *The Freedom-Seekers*.

18. In June 1854, the Rochester Ladies' Anti-Slavery Society announced that it would dispose of unsold Irish and English donations to the antislavery cause at a bazaar held in Toronto, in conjunction with the Anti-Slavery Society of Canada annual meeting. See *Frederick Douglass' Paper*, June 2, 1854, which also carried a letter from "our excellent friend" Agnes Willis, the wife of Reverend Michael Willis, president. She was a regular correspondent of Douglass's Rochester paper. The bazaar was held on June 21, annoying Mary Ann Shadd, who felt the money should come to her paper.

19. An activist and outspoken advocate for Black rights, William Watkins and his equally accomplished son, William J. Watkins, corresponded with abolitionists ranging from Garrison and the Tappan brothers to Frederick Douglass and the Boston-based Charles Lenox Remond and William C. Nell. The paper also had a regular "Colored Correspondent." See, for instance, "Canadian Items," *Frederick Douglass' Paper*, April 21, 1854, and one of a series of notes "From Our Canadian Correspondent" in the May 5, 1854, edition, signed "A Colored Canadian."

20. See also "A Colored Baltimorean," in Ripley, *Black Abolitionist Papers*, vol. 3, 96n6; Ripley, *Black Abolitionist Papers*, vol. 2, *Canada*, 444n2; Bettye J. Gardner, "William Watkins: Antebellum Black Teacher and Anti-Slavery Writer," *Negro History Bulletin* 39 (September/October 1976): 623–25. On his lecturing from his Rochester base, see "Wm. Watkins' Labors," *Weekly Anglo-African*, June 30, 1860. Watkins was quoted about the causes of the Civil War in the Toronto *Globe*, July 12, 1861.

21. Northup's memoir of his terrible experiences was widely available across the continent; Solomon Northup, *Twelve Years a Slave: Narrative of Solomon Northup, a Citizen of New York Kidnapped in Washington City in 1841, and Rescued in 1853* (Auburn, NY: Derby & Miller, 1853).

22. Toronto Normal School Register, XIII Session, 1855, City of Toronto Archives; Hilary Dawson, "Alfred M. Lafferty, MA, 1839–1912: An Early Black Graduate of the University of Toronto," *Ontario Black History News* 20 (1998), 5–6; County Marriage Register, Kent County, Ontario, vol. 36 (1858–1869), July 3, 1862. Marriage of Emeline Shadd, 27, to Henry L. Simpson.

23. Heather M. Butts, "Alexander Thomas Augusta: Physician, Teacher and Human Rights Activist," *Journal of the National Medical Association* 97, no. 1 (January 2005): 106–9; Ripley, *Black Abolitionist Papers*, vol. 2, *Canada*, 378n5, 380n2, 448n4.

24. Fanny Thruston Ballard to Cecelia Jane Holmes, August 2, 1855, Ballard Family Papers, Filson Historical Society, Louisville, KY.

25. Samuel Churchill Thruston was unsuccessful in his business ventures and had tried to make a go of farming. He owed substantial sums at the time of his death but the farm on the Salt River belonged to his father, Charles W. Thruston. See chapter 6, note 8, and Abraham Clark Freeman, ed., *The American State Reports: Containing the Cases of General Value and Authority*, vol. 4 (San Francisco: Bancroft-Whitely, 1889), 160–67.

26. See Louisville *Daily Courier*, April 8, 1854, for the announcement of Samuel C. Thruston's funeral, to take place at the home of A. J. Ballard on Walnut Street that very day.

27. John Croghan died in 1849 and left the resort to his nieces and nephews in a complicated arrangement of guardianship that would endure until the last of them died. His will dictated that the Bishops were to have their freedom in 1856 and be sent to Liberia, but instead they apparently used the funds to purchase land near Mammoth Cave. Stephen was already dying. He too had contracted tuberculosis, probably from contact with patients who were part of Dr. Croghan's failed experiment and with his owner. Stephen Bishop died in the summer of 1857 and is buried in the Mammoth Cave cemetery. The federal government began acquiring land in 1928 to make Mammoth Cave into a national park; Katie Algeo, "Mammoth Cave and the Making of Place," *Southeastern Geographer* 44, no. 1 (2004): 27–47.

28. Fanny's husband, A. J. Ballard, owned nine slaves, including three children under ten, according to a slave census taken by the federal government in 1850. He hired out several men to work on steamboats. Two of his slaves, one of them a ten-year-old girl, had run away. On April 12, 1851, he sued the owners of the steamboat *Bunker Hill* for the loss of his slave Jerry. On January 14, 1854, he sold a young man named Phil to his father-in-law, Charles W. Thruston, who remained

an unreconstructed slave owner. Fanny herself seems to have been trying to divest her home at least of enslaved labour; by 1860 there were only two household servants listed, both of them of German origin. US Census, Louisville, Kentucky: Slave Census, 1850; Nominal Census, 1860. See also Petition of A. J. Ballard to the Chancery Court of Louisville, Kentucky, 12 April, 1851, Circuit Court, Case Files, *A.J. Ballard v. Silas F. Millar, Peter Felone and Mrs. Job Whipple*, box/ drawer 2-119, document/case 7583, PAR 20785106, Kentucky Department for Libraries and Archives, Frankfort, Kentucky; cited in Loren Schweninger, ed., *The Southern Debate over Slavery*, vol. 2, *Petitions to Southern County Courts, 1775–1865* (Champaign-Urbana: University of Illinois Press, 2007), 270–72.

29. In American slave law, the "condition of the child follows the condition of the mother." Kentucky was originally a colony of Virginia, and Virginia had rationalized hereditary slavery in the late seventeenth century: "all children born in this country shall be held bond or free only according to the condition of the mother"; Act XII, *Laws of Virginia*, December 1662, in W. W. Hening, ed., *Hening's Statutes at Large*, vol. 2 (Virginia, 1823), 170, accessed July 31, 2016, https:// memory.loc.gov/ammem/awhhtml/awlaw3/notes.html#i38.

30. The 1846 Wilmot proposal to ban slavery in territories acquired during the Mexican War had failed, sparking the establishment of the short-lived Free Soil party. The wealthy philanthropist and abolitionist Gerrit Smith, who lived in Peterborough in upstate New York, bankrolled anti-slavery efforts and had been a founder of the Liberty League, insisting that women's suffrage be included in its platform. By this time the Liberty Party was all but dead and some of its adherents would join the Free-Soilers in the new Republican Party in 1854. Smith had given away thousands of acres of land he inherited in upstate New York to African Americans so they could meet the property requirements for voting. He was elected to the US House of Representatives in 1852. He resigned his seat two years later in disgust over the willingness of Northern politicians to bow to Southern interests. Edward J. Renehan, *The Secret Six: The True Tale of the Men Who Conspired with John Brown* (New York: Crown, 1995); Judith Wellman, *The Road to Seneca Falls* (Urbana: University of Illinois Press, 2004), especially ch. 7.

31. William Lloyd Garrison, "No Compromise with the Evil of Slavery" (1854), in *Civil Rights and Conflict in the United States: Selected Speeches*, Lit2Go, accessed February 9, 2016, http:// etc.usf.edu/lit2go/185/civil-rights-and-conflict-in-the-united-states-selected-speeches/5061/ no-compromise-with-the-evil-of-slavery-speech-1854/.

32. There are dozens of articles and books about John Brown. Examples include W. E. B. DuBois's classic *John Brown* (Philadelphia: G. W. Jacobs, 1909); David S. Reynolds's remarkable biography *John Brown, Abolitionist: The Man Who Killed Slavery, Sparked the Civil War, and Seeded Civil Rights* (New York: Vintage, 2005); Louis DeCaro's several works, including *Fire from the Midst of You: A Religious Life of John Brown* (New York: New York University Press, 2002); and the classic by Stephen B. Oates, *To Purge This Land with Blood: A Biography of John Brown* (New York: Harper Row, 1972).

33. Abraham Lincoln, "Speech at Peoria, Illinois," in *Collected Works of Abraham Lincoln*, vol. 2, ed. Roy P. Basler (New Brunswick, NJ: Rutgers University Press, 1953), 248–83.

34. The deed was not actually assigned until March 14, 1854, although Benjamin purchased Centre Street Lot 7 in 1844. He may have owed money against the purchase price of £100—a considerable amount—but the owner, James Lukin Robinson, did not receive his own formal deeds to the St. John's Ward lands from his father, John Beverley Robinson, until 1852. Since J. L. Robinson was running for office in 1854, awarding formal deeds would ensure that people on his several

lots met the property qualification for voting. Guylaine Petrin, personal communication, 2012. See Abstract Index for Plan 147, County of York Land Registry Office, instruments 43724 and 53113, GSU 197293, RG 61–64, Archives of Ontario.

35. *Brown's Directory*, viii.

36. There is no record of the tenant's identity. The 1855–56 directory gives Benjamin P. Holmes as the householder on Centre Street, probably copying from earlier records, and there is no name given on the tax rolls. However, this is the only year in which Cecelia J. Holmes is listed as freeholder of the property but not also as tenant. Tax Assessment Rolls for St. John's Ward, City of Toronto, Centre Street, 1856, City of Toronto Archives.

37. F. R. Berchem, *Opportunity Road: Yonge Street, 1860–1939* (Toronto: Natural Heritage Books, 1996), 60.

38. Fanny Thruston Ballard to Cecelia Jane Holmes, January 16, 1857, Ballard Family Papers, Filson Historical Society.

39. People of African descent were so routinely part of ships' crews that there were special British maritime laws and policies in place to protect them in American ports of call. See Thomas Twiss, *The Law of Nations: On the Rights and Duties of Nations in Time of Peace* (Oxford: Oxford University Press, 1861), 229–31.

40. The Negro Seamen's Act of 1822 was passed in South Carolina following the Denmark Vesey plot, which had threatened Charleston, and was twice amended; Edlie Wong, *Neither Fugitive nor Free: Atlantic Slavery, Freedom Suits, and the Legal Culture of Travel* (New York: New York University Press, 2009), 183–85. Other ports, including New Orleans and Mobile, routinely jailed Black sailors of any nationality. There were repeated protests against the practice, including some emanating from meetings held at William Powell's New York boarding house, before his migration to England.

41. An "old-time" steamboat steward's duties are detailed in Jessup Whitehead, *The Steward's Handbook and Guide to Party Catering* (Chicago: John Anderson, 1889), 4–6, accessed December 10, 2015, https://books.google.ca/books?id=cJBCAQAAIAAJ. While his book pertains to American steamers, the duties were much the same. Steward was an envied position, and by the 1850s it paid nearly as well as the job of first mate.

42. W. Jeffrey Bolster, *Black Jacks: African American Seamen in the Age of Sail* (Cambridge, MA: Harvard University Press, 1998), 168; *Helpful Hints for Steamboat Passengers* (1855), collections of the State Historical Society of Iowa, reproduced by Explorations in Iowa History Project, Malcolm Price Laboratory School, University of Northern Iowa, 2003, accessed Nov. 12, 2013, https://www.uni.edu/iowahist/Frontier_Life/Steamboat_Hints/Steamboat_Hints2.htm.

43. A packet ship ran a regularly scheduled route between ports, while ships like the *Black Eagle* took work as they found it, most often doled out by ships' brokers. Brokers operated out of every port; they arranged for transhipment of cargoes as well as complements of emigrants destined for the southern hemisphere, a proportion of whose passages were subsidized by the British government. These were known as "assisted immigrants" in the ship's lists.

44. There were several ships called the *Black Eagle* but the very large one that plied Australian waters is most likely the vessel on which Benjamin Pollard Holmes was employed. It was built on the "North American principle," that is, of softwood except for the oaken ribs. The article describing the *Black Eagle* appeared in the *Courier* of Hobart, Tasmania, dated May 2, 1854, quoting the Liverpool *Mercury*. According to the register of British ships in the National Archives of Australia, the *Black Eagle* was constructed in 1852.

45. "Emigrant Ships to Australia and New Zealand in 1854–1856: Appendix No. 10, Victoria, Return of Ships and Emigrants Dispatched by Public Funds to Victoria, in 1854, 1855, and up to the 31st March 1856," *British Parliamentary Papers*, 1856, vol. 24 [2089], 393, accessed May 18, 2013, http://www.theshipslist.com/ships/australia/aust1850s.shtml. I am indebted to the work of very generous genealogists for this information; see TheShipsList-L Archives, RootsWeb, accessed May 18, 2013, http://archiver.rootsweb.ancestry.com/th/read/TheShipsList/2007-02/1172506623.

46. Ibid.

47. The January 26, 1855, edition of the Liverpool *Mercury* shows the *Black Eagle* in port at Melbourne, Australia. On January 30, 1855, the same paper announced that it had cleared port, bound for Callao, Peru.

48. *Belfast News Letter*, April 15, 1856. The fullest account of the case is given in "Hints to Quack Doctors," *Medical Times and Gazette* 12 (January 5–June 28, 1856), 428. The article is dated April 26, 1856.

49. Oddly, the tax assessment rolls for that year give his age as thirty-one. Benjamin Holmes is listed as freeholder of Lot 7 on the east side of Centre Street, with the property valued at £24. Benjamin had a tenant named Alfred August, a carpenter, aged twenty-seven.

50. On September 12, 1856, Benjamin and Cecelia mortgaged Lot 7 in order to build a second, rental house on the property. "Mortgage, Canada Permanent Building & Saving Co., to Benjamin Holmes and his wife Cecelia Jane Holmes, Sept. 12, 1856," Deed 63844, County of York Land Registry Office, abstract index for Plan 147, GSU 197293, Archives of Ontario.

Chapter 9: I Ain't Got Long to Stay Here

1. Reprinted in the *Anti-Slavery Reporter*, April 1, 1858, 93–95; Canadian Black Studies Collection, File 4603, Special Collections, D. W. Weldon Library, University of Western Ontario. The doctor was surely A. T. Augusta and the medical student Anderson Ruffin Abbott. One of the two master builders must have been John M. Tinsley, while the other was the Abbott's brother-in-law Adolphus H. Judah. The Hickman family and the Judahs both owned upscale grocery stores, as did Grandison Boyd and William Watkins. James Mink owned the livery stable and Thomas Smallwood's son was a law student. The article mentions a visit to the home of a "capitalist" who came from Mobile and whose son was going to study medicine; this was certain to have been W. R. Abbott. Another grocer was probably William J. Watkins, who moved to Toronto from Baltimore in 1852, leaving behind his private school for Black children, the Watkins Academy, which had been in operation there for twenty-five years. Ripley, *Black Abolitionist Papers*, vol. 2, 234–35, 485n.

2. Both Rosedale and Parkdale were about three miles from Centre Street. There was no correspondingly close village with suitably wealthy white families within three miles east of the city at this time. However, if Cecelia meant three miles from the city limits, the place of her employment would have been either Etobicoke, to the west, or around the present Eglinton Avenue, to the north.

3. Fanny Thruston Ballard to Cecelia J. Holmes, January 25, 1857, Ballard Family Papers, Filson Historical Society, Louisville, KY. This letter suggests that Cecelia was corresponding with someone else in Louisville if her mother had "heard" in the autumn of 1856 that she was in Chicago, a dangerous practice.

4. The Northern Railroad had been inaugurated from Toronto to Collingwood, and four steamers made the daily run to Chicago. See "Storms and Shipwrecks—Great Destruction of Life and Property—The Commercial Distress in 1857," in John Ross Robertson, *Landmarks of Toronto*, vol. 2 (Toronto: John Ross Robertson, 1898), 246.

5. Mary Reynolds was indeed in a favoured position to be allowed to choose her next owner rather than being sold off privately, or sent to a trader's "pen," of which there were several in Louisville by this time.

6. "Washington Spradling," in "Interviews of Wilber Siebert," typescript, 173, J. Winston Coleman Papers, Special Collections, Margaret I. King Library, University of Kentucky, Lexington. Washington Spradling of Louisville admitted in later years that he had loaned thousands of dollars to people to buy their own freedom. Some had paid him back but others, he complained, had not.

7. Fanny Thruston Ballard to Cecelia Jane Holmes, January 25, 1857.

8. The last passage reads: "Aunt Emily Zane is now in Europe with her family; traveling for the benefit of her daughter Abby's health. The poor child has consumption and I fear will never return. Julia Churchill who still goes by the name of Puss is with her. They expected to remain two years, but I think Abby's health is such that they will find it necessary to return next summer." Both these women would one day have important Toronto connections. Emily Zane's daughter Abigail died three years after Fanny's letter was written, but Abby's sister, Mary Eliza (named for her aunt, Fanny Thruston's mother) later married Edinburgh-born Toronto educator George R. R. Cockburn. For more on Mary Eliza's life and family in Canada, see chapter 6, note 16.

   Julia "Puss" Churchill, while in Europe on the sad trip to which Fanny refers in this letter, met the widowed Dr. Luke Blackburn. He was a noted epidemiologist who, after the Civil War broke out, moved his family to Toronto's Queen's Hotel (owned by Captain Thomas Dick) and opened a practice on Adelaide Street. He spied for the Confederacy and was the mastermind of an early and diabolical effort at germ warfare. This was the "Yellow Fever Plot," in which infected clothing from an epidemic in Bermuda was shipped to Union officers and men, including a trunk filled with fine white shirts sent to President Lincoln. Blackburn was caught and tried in a Montreal court by a sympathetic judge who let him off, and he and his wife spent the rest of the war in Toronto. Luke Blackburn was eventually elected governor of Kentucky, an event warmly applauded in Toronto newspapers. He and his wife engaged in prison reform efforts and his tombstone bears the epithet "The Great Samaritan." Luke Pryor Blackburn to Major General D. H. Maury, Commanding the Department of the Gulf, June 23, 1863, Luke Pryor Blackburn Papers, Filson Historical Society, Louisville, Kentucky; "The Yellow Fever Plot," *New York Times*, May 16, 1865; "Yellow Fever Plot," *Globe* (Toronto), May 22, 1865. See also Adam Mayers, *Dixie and the Dominion: The Confederacy and the War for Union* (Toronto: Dundurn, 2003), 55; Claire Hoy, *Canadians in the Civil War* (Toronto: McArthur, 2005), 285–87, 268–69; Nancy Disher Baird, *Luke Pryor Blackburn: Physician, Governor, Reformer* (Lexington: University Press of Kentucky, 1979).

9. The question of Mamie's paternity was not settled by Cecelia's second deposition to the US Pension Bureau when she was trying desperately to gain access to her second husband's military pension in the 1890s. She told the commissioner, "I make my home with my daughter Mrs. Alex Reeves [Reels] my daughter [is] by Holmes [and was] born in Toronto before Holmes died." She may simply have been trying to establish her own respectability and therefore her credibility with the officials, however. Deposition A: 3-446, "Deposition of Cecelia J. Larrison, taken at Louisville,

Kentucky, May 6, 1898, in Case no. 631.101, service of William H. Larrison (Under-cook, Co. 'H,' 14th New York Heavy Artillery, Civil War)"; Civil War and Later Pension Files, Department of Veterans Affairs, Record Group 15; National Archives and Records Administration, Washington, DC [hereafter Case no. 631.101, Pension Bureau Files, NARA].

10. Benjamin P. Holmes to the Canada Permanent Building & Saving Society, deed 63844, September 12, 1856 (registered September 12, 1856), City of Toronto Copybooks, vol. 23, 706–7, County of York Land Registry Office, RG 61–64, Archives of Ontario.

11. Canadian currency was very complex. Banking and property amounts were calculated in "Halifax currency," each Canadian pound discounted to nine-tenths of a British pound. Dollars more or less equivalent to American dollars were also in use as day-to-day currency. In Halifax currency, one pound was equal to approximately four US dollars. Decimal currency was adopted after 1858. See Robert Chalmers, *A History of Currency in the British Colonies* (London: HMSO, 1893), 175–88.

12. See note 10, above. The tax assessment rolls for St. John's Ward, City of Toronto, 1856, were recorded on April 30, 1856 (City of Toronto Archives). Cecelia J. Holmes is shown as freeholder and occupant of the property on Centre Street, worth £12 per annum. Since the mortgage with Canada Permanent Trust was taken out on September 12 of the same year by both Benjamin and his wife, he had to have come home sometime that summer.

13. Tax assessment rolls for St. John's Ward, City of Toronto, 1857, recorded on April 30, 1857, show Benjamin P. Holmes, waiter, with a property valued at £24. He was living on the land and also had a tenant, presumably in the second house, named Alfred August, who was a twenty-seven-year-old carpenter. In the next year of assessment records, recorded on May 31, 1858, the currency changed. Benjamin was again the freeholder (now aged thirty!), the property was valued at $84 and his tenant was Mary A. Davis, living in a house valued at $78. The next year saw yet another tenant in the home, Margaret A. Brown. The high turnover was not unusual: in the 1850s this was the immigrant reception district for the city. Many stayed in Toronto for a short time before moving on to other parts of the province or locating relatives whose whereabouts they had not known before they arrived. For the probable builder of the Holmes' rental property, see Deposition of Joseph Buckner Lewis, taken at Toronto, October 1, 1896, Case no. 631.101, Pension Bureau Files, NARA. He was still living in St. John's Ward, at 65 Elizabeth Street at the time. I am inferring the friendship with Simpson because when he died in 1899, he was buried in a plot owned by Francis Griffin Simpson. See Toronto Necropolis, burial no. 27589: Joseph B. Lewis, plot adult, single grave C1, fence row, plot owner Francis G. Simpson; accessed October 6, 2016, https://familysearch.org/ark:/61903/1:1:KH6H-875.

14. Fortunately, the tax records for the City of Toronto provide an annual record of the name, age and occupation of each tenant as well as of the property owners. A comparison between street directories, at least for the period between 1857 and 1859, when Benjamin was still alive, suggest that either there was more than one tenant in 1859 or there were multiple renters at one time. In 1858 an Irish widow named Mary Ann Davis occupied the house, while in 1859 both Mary Brown (no occupation listed) and John Williams, the latter an upholsterer and paper-hanger, lived there; *Caverhill's Toronto City Directory for 1859–60* (Toronto: W. C. F. Caverhill, 1859), 205. By 1863 it was the home of Catherine Exinger, with number 31, Benjamin and Cecelia's old home, housing the family of shoemaker Thomas Wilson. Thomas R. Mann, shoemaker, was living just south of the Holmes properties, at 27 Centre Street.

15. The *Globe* of January 28, 1859, reporting a court case between Captains Dick and Heron and citing Benjamin's testimony, clearly states he is a steward, although he is listed as a waiter in the 1857 and 1858 directories. White recorders of directory data and census enumerators routinely downplayed the accomplishments of the city's Black residents: Robin Philips, who owned several properties, was a "whitewasher"; Thornton Blackburn, who owned the city's first cab and was the sixth largest landholder in St. John's Ward, was sometimes listed as a labourer; and Celestial Davis, who was a fine chef and catered events at Osgoode Hall and other elite white venues, was, according to some directories, merely a cook.

16. There is a painting by William Armstrong in the Trinity College, Dublin, Archives, showing the *Chief Justice Robinson* unloading passengers on the ice in Toronto Bay in the winter of 1851–52. See also Henry Scadding, *Toronto of Old: Collections and Recollections Illustrative of the Early Settlement and Social Life of the Capital of Ontario* (Toronto: Willing & Williamson, 1878), 575–76. The *Chief Justice Robinson* was lost in Richardson's bankruptcy and sold to Captains Dick and Heron in 1847. Alexander Grant, ed., *Grant's Upper Canada Chancery Reports*, vol. 3 (Toronto: Rowsell, 1853), 506; Scadding, *Toronto of Old*, 575; John Lovell, *The Canada Directory for 1857–58* (Montreal: John Lovely, 1857).

17. Richard Bonnycastle, "A Journey from Montreal to Toronto," in *Canada and the Canadians* (London: H. Colburn, 1849), reprinted in *Canadian Antiquarian and Numismatic Journal* 4/5 (1875): 60–64.

18. Fanny Thruston Ballard to Cecelia Jane Holmes, February 23, 1857, Ballard Family Papers, Filson Historical Society, Louisville, KY.

19. James L. Huston, *The Panic of 1857 and the Coming of the Civil War* (Baton Rouge: Louisiana State University Press, 1987), 24.

20. This account appeared in the *Globe* of January 28, 1859: "Toronto Winter Assizes *Dick v. Heron*: Benjamin Holmes had been on the *Chief Justice* as steward, while on the Niagara route. In the spring of 1857 he met Captain James Dick and Mr Heron together. The latter engaged him as steward for the *Peerless* about April in that year. The three were together in the street when witness told Mr Heron that he was expecting to go with Captain Dick in the *Peerless*. Mr. Heron replied 'Very well' and he added that the Captain would inform him when the *Peerless* would come out."

21. Kingston *Daily News*, March 28, 1857.

22. "Storms and Shipwrecks," in Robertson, *Landmarks of Toronto*, vol. 2, 246–48.

23. Mortgage from Benjamin Holmes and his wife Cecelia to Canada Permanent Building & Saving Society, deed 71754, March 9, 1858 (registered March 10, 1858), City of Toronto Copybooks, vol. 25, 643–44, County of York Land Registry Office, reel GS 6073, RG 61–64, Archives of Ontario.

24. The records of the Coloured Wesleyan Church in Toronto in the later 1860s show a "Sister Dunlop," also named as Mrs. Elizabeth Dunlop, probably Elijah's wife. Her son was living with friends by the time of the 1871 census. Guylaine Petrin, personal communication, October 7, 2016.

25. Don Papson and Tom Calarco, *Secret Lives of the Underground Railroad in New York City: Sydney Howard Gay, Louis Napoleon and the Record of Fugitives* (Jefferson, NC: McFarland, 2015), 94–95. The article was reprinted many times, *Frederick Douglass' Paper* adding in its February 2 edition: "He would like to return [to the US], but fears he might be arrested as a fugitive, and says he will not pay $1500 to get a title to himself . . . Such a man ought to have the privilege of living where he pleases, but he cannot so long as the leading policy of our government is the protection of slavery."

26. Mary Ann Boyd died on August 14, 1865, in Chatham. She is buried in the Toronto Necropolis with her Ross, Dunlop and other relations; Toronto Trust Cemeteries, Necropolis Cemetery burial register, vol. 3, entry 6096. Grandison Boyd died in Toronto on July 15, 1878, and was buried beside Mary Ann at the Toronto Necropolis.

27. Grandison Boyd remarried a year after Mary Ann died, his bride a twenty-year-old English girl named·Louisa Tigh. He was forty-nine and the wedding took place in Chatham on August 27, 1866. Kent County Marriages, 1866; Granderson [sic] Boyd, Census of Canada, 1871, Chatham, Kent County. By the 1870s Boyd had become a prominent miller and businessman in Chatham; he built the Boyd Block, consisting of a warehouse and mill, on downtown King Street. He was a founding member of Chatham's Board of Trade in 1872, one of very few Black men recognized by the town's white merchant elite. Chapter 47, 35 Victoria, *An Act to Incorporate the Board of Trade of the Town of Chatham* [assented to June 14, 1872]. He chaired a day of political protest in 1874 to bring attention to ongoing racism and to express the disappointment of Chatham Blacks with the Conservative Party's inability to bring about change. Natasha L. Henry, *Emancipation Day: Celebrating Freedom in Canada* (Toronto: Dundurn, 2010), 79; *Statutes of Canada* (Ottawa: Brown and Chamberlain, 1872), 184–85.

28. *Caverhill's Directory.* R. P. Thomas was president, F. G. Simpson first vice-president, E. J. Bailey second vice-president, W. H. Taylor treasurer, G. W. Carey secretary, G. W. Squirrel chairman and W. H. Taylor, E. J. Bailey, H. Jones and S. Stout on the council. Simpson was also on the executive committee of the Liberal Working Men at the May 30, 1878, "Address of the Hon. Alexander Mackenzie to the Toronto Working Men on the 'National Policy'" (Toronto: Globe Printing Office, 1878), accessed February 10, 2016, http://qspace.library.queensu.ca/bitstream/1974/10300/1/addressofhonalex00mack.pdf.

29. Over the years Simpson prospered and acquired considerable property, mainly in St. John's Ward. Francis G. Simpson was a familiar figure at city council meetings, such as the one protesting the potential extradition of Adam Morse, a Black man, to the United States in 1888. Morse was a former slave who had knocked down a Georgia railroad worker who injured his little boy. See "Adam Morse Set Free: The Savannah Negro Liberated by Judge McDougall," *Globe*, June 23, 1888, 13. The article, which names no other member of the Black community, identifies F. G. Simpson as present in the courtroom during the trial. (Interestingly, Morse first fled his Georgia pursuers to Rochester, New York, before coming to Toronto.) Francis Simpson was interviewed by Samuel Gridley Howe on behalf of the Freedmen's Bureau in 1863, when President Lincoln sent a delegation to Canada to examine the conditions and progress of the fugitive slaves resident there, in preparation for planning how best to prepare the South's four million enslaved men, women and children for freedom when Union victory was accomplished. See Matthew Furrow, "Francis G. Simpson," transcription of Samuel Gridley Howe interviews (unpublished), 330–41, from US Department of War, Letters Received by the Office of the Adjutant General, Main Series, 1861–70, microfilm reels 199–201, M619, RG 94, National Archives and Records Administration; these documents from his own research were kindly shared by Michael Furrow, for which I am grateful. Simpson died in 1900 in Toronto and was buried in the Necropolis; Matthew Furrow, "Samuel Gridley Howe, the Black Population of Canada West, and the Racial Ideology of the 'Blueprint for Radical Reconstruction,'" *Journal of American History* 97, no. 2 (September 2010): 344–70.

30. *Brown's Toronto General Directory* (Toronto: W. R. Brown, 1856), lii; W. T. Minter, *The Doctrine and Discipline of the British Methodist Episcopal Church*, 4th ed. (Toronto: William Briggs, 1892),

11–12; Robin W. Winks, *The Blacks in Canada*, 2nd ed. (Montreal: McGill-Queen's University Press, 1997), 356–59.

31. George R. Ure, *Handbook of Toronto* (Toronto: Lovell & Gibson, 1858), 199–120.

32. There are scholars who believe that the Dred Scott decision was instrumental in bringing about the Panic of 1857, by effectively opening western frontier lands to slavery and thereby devaluing both free labour and the land itself, by reducing its attractiveness to Northern migrants. See Jenny B. Wahl, "*Dred*, Panic, War: How a Slave Case Triggered Financial Crisis and Civil Disunion," Carleton College Department of Economics Working Paper Series 2009-01, July 2009, accessed Jan. 29, 2013, http://apps.carleton.edu/curricular/econ/assets/200901.pdf.

33. Eric Foner, *The Fiery Trial: Abraham Lincoln and American Slavery* (New York: W. W. Norton, 2010), 99–100.

34. Nancy A. Hewitt, "The Spiritual Journey of an Abolitionist, Amy Kirby Post, 1802–1889," Brycchan Carey and Geoffrey Plank, eds., *Quakers and Abolition*, (Urbana and Chicago: University of Illinois Press, 2014), 80.

35. "Gleanings of Canada West," in Dorothy Porter Wesley and Constance Porter Uzelac, *William Cooper Nell, Nineteenth-Century African American Abolitionist, Historian, Integrationist: Selected Writings from 1832–1874* (Baltimore, MD: Black Classics, 2002), 534–36.

36. *Caverhill's Directory*, 293, reports that in 1859 the president of the Elgin Association was Peter Brown (George Brown's father), and Reverend Willis was first vice-president. On the board were several African Canadian names randomly dispersed among the white directors: Wilson Ruffin Abbott; A. B. Jones, of London, Canada West; and John T. Fisher of Toronto. The Ladies' Colored Fugitive Association is listed on the preceding page, its stated purpose being to raise funds to assist incoming fugitive slaves. Equally prominent is the Moral and Mental Improvement Society (African), with its objective "the improvement of its members by means of essays and debates." Its first vice-president was Cecelia's friend Francis Griffin Simpson, and George W. Cary was secretary.

37. Toronto's "Crystal Palace," officially the Palace of Industry, stood at King and Shaw Streets just above the Provincial Lunatic Asylum. It was later moved to the present grounds of the Canadian National Exhibition. That the omnibus fare was considered inexpensive comes from the Jackson Webster Armstrong, ed., *Seven Eggs Today: The Diaries of Mary Armstrong, 1859 and 1869* (Waterloo ON: Wilfrid Laurier University Press, 2004), 97. Although Armstrong explains that a decimal monetary system came into use in 1857, adherence to older British, Halifax, and New York currencies continued for many years. See Armstrong, *Seven Eggs Today*, 190n63.

38. A. A. Den Otter, "Alexander Galt, the 1859 Tariff and Canadian Economic Nationalism," *Canadian Historical Review* 63, no. 2 (June 1982): 164; James L. Huston, *The Panic of 1857 and the Coming of the Civil War* (Baton Rouge: Louisiana State University Press, 1987), especially ch. 8.

39. Benjamin P. Holmes is listed as "waiter, Centre Street" in the Toronto section of the *Canada Gazetteer* for 1857, 794. He is listed in *Caverhill's Directory* as "labourer, 31 Centre Street."

40. Ure, *Handbook of Toronto*, 232–34.

41. Thomas Mann had assisted the Holmeses by managing their Toronto property while they were abroad. The City of Toronto tax assessment rolls for St. John's Ward, 1853, show Mann as the landlord of the Holmeses' Lot 7 on Centre Street. The will was also signed by Dougald McDougald Hearns, a law student living at 239 Queen Street East, who very likely assisted Benjamin in preparation of the will.

42. After the disastrous fire James Mink moved his livery stable to Teraulay Street, but his hotel never reopened; Rick Nelson, "George Mink: A Black Businessman in Early Kingston," *Historic*

Kingston 46 (1998): 111–29. Guylaine Petrin's exhaustive research has proven false the widely reproduced tale that Mink offered a $10,000 dowry to any white man who would marry his daughter, and that her new husband sold her into slavery in the Carolinas. Guylaine Petrin, "The Myth of Mary Mink; Representation of Black Women in Toronto in the Nineteenth Century," *Ontario History* (Spring 2016): 92–110.

43. Will of Benjamin Pollard Holmes, deed 3844, registered February 22, 1862, City of Toronto Deeds, vol. F, 35–36, York County Land Registry Office, RG 61–64, Archives of Ontario. James Mink, along with Thornton Blackburn, was also executor for the will of William Hickman, written in 1860. See Will of James Mink, Surrogate Court for York County, Canada West, Archives of Ontario.

44. Fanny Thruston Ballard to Cecelia Jane Holmes, August 11, 1859, Ballard Family Papers, Filson Historical Society, Louisville, KY. The letter has a handwritten note on the back: "Original letters from my Mother, Mrs. Fanny T. Ballard to her old maid servant Cecelia 1852 to 1859. RC Ballard Thruston." The signatory of the 1880s who collected the letters was the new baby, Rogers Clark, mentioned in the letter. (Fanny's youngest son had his surname legally altered at his mother's request to Rogers Clark Ballard Thruston, so the Thruston name would continue.)

45. A woman of about fifty is listed in the 1861 US Slave Census for Kentucky in the household of A. J. Ballard in Louisville. She may well have been Cecelia's mother.

46. Ontario, Toronto Trust Cemeteries, 1826–1989, Necropolis Cemetery, vol. 2, 1857–63, image 86, FamilySearch, accessed November 19, 2013, https://familysearch.org/pal:/MM9.3.1/ TH-267-11785-38572-34?cc=1627831&wc=M948-Q23:359768352.

47. James Taylor, *Narrative of a Voyage to, and Travels in, Upper Canada: With Accounts of the Customs, Character, and Dialect of the Country: Also, Remarks on Emigration, Agriculture, &c.* (Hull, UK: J. Nicholson, 1846), 37.

48. "I give and bequest [*sic*] unto my two sons Benjamin Alexander and James Thomas Holmes my house and lot situated on the East side of Centre Street in the said City of Toronto being the house and lot South of the one in which I now reside to [?] hold the same to their own use and benefit."

49. It is impossible to believe that Benjamin himself acknowledged such a relationship. It is telling that Ben Alexander and James Thomas Holmes seem to have severed relations with their stepmother and her little girl at this point, maintaining no more contact than was necessary for the management of their Toronto property. The rift in the Holmes family was complete. The two men did, however, retain ownership of the rental property, now numbered 29 Centre Street. It was rented out to a long succession of tenants, managed through an agent in the city who was responsible for collecting rents, paying taxes and maintaining the house on their behalf, for many years to come.

Chapter 10: I Am Seeking for a City

1. Frederick Douglass, *The Life and Times of Frederick Douglass*, rev. ed. (Boston: De Wolfe and Fiske, 1892), 333.

2. Deposition of Cecelia J. Larrison, Case no. 631.101, Pension Bureau Files, NARA. The date of Cecelia's removal is inferred from her statement in the Pension Bureau affidavit of 1898: "I went to Rochester not long after my first husband, Holmes died and had been there, not quite two years when I was married to [William] Larrison." She and Larrison married in April 1862,

suggesting that she had moved across the lake in the early summer of 1860. However, the dates Cecelia gives in official documents are often incorrect, and other evidence in depositions provided by her friends suggests she was in Rochester earlier. This chapter is substantially informed by Daniel J. Broyld's excellent "Borderland Blacks: Rochester, New York and St. Catharines, Canada West, 1800–1861" (PhD diss., Howard University, 2011). I am indebted to Dr. Broyld, who generously shared his thesis with me prior to publication of his own volume.

3. *Rochester City Directory, 1857–58* (Rochester, NY: D. M. Dewey, 1857), 21.

4. Ibid., 76–77. The old horse-car system that had carried steamboat passengers from Carthage, the river port at the Lower Falls of the Genesee to which the ships had at one time been towed, was in 1852 bypassed by this new rail route on the river's western shore.

5. Douglass, *Life and Times of Frederick Douglass*, 326. He wrote: "I did succeed in making tolerant the moral atmosphere in Rochester; so much so, indeed, that I came to feel as much at home there as I had ever done in the most friendly parts of New England."

6. Blake McKelvey, "Rochester's Near Northeast," *Rochester History* 29, no. 2 (April 1967): 1–23; Broyld, "Borderland Blacks," 21.

7. The small African American population was surveyed in 1834 by abolitionist William Bloss, editor of the *Rights of Man*; Victoria S. Schmitt, "Rochester's Frederick Douglass: Part 1," *Rochester History* 67, no. 4 (Fall 2005): 14n39.

8. US Census, 1860, Rochester, New York; Ruth Rosenburg-Naparsteck, "A Growing Agitation: Rochester Before, During and After the Civil War," *Rochester History* 46, no. 1/2 (January/April 1984): 1–40.

9. Cecelia Jane Holmes is listed as freeholder of 31 Centre Street from 1860 on. She personally handled the rental on her own house as well as that belonging to her stepsons (29 Centre Street) until Benjamin Alexander Holmes, who was the elder, reached his majority. He rented out both, sometimes with the help of an agent, until 1863, when James Thomas Holmes came of age. In some years Cecelia employed an agent to collect rents, pay the taxes and presumably maintain her property. In 1865 it was livery stable owner James Mink who assisted both her and her stepsons. Tax records for Centre Street, City of Toronto Diffusion Material, D 318, Archives of Ontario.

10. *Rochester City Directory for 1861–62* (Rochester, NY: Daily Union, 1862), 107, 270; *Rochester in History* (Rochester, NY: Wegman-Walsh, 1922), 149. John Craig died in 1872 and his wife in 1877. She was born in Bennington, Vermont, in 1805 and her death was reported in the Rochester *Democrat* with a very flattering obituary, reprinted in the Lockport, NY, *Daily Journal* of June 11, 1877. The couple had married in 1827 and lived in Middleport, New York, a town that owed its existence to the building of the Erie Canal. The Craigs owned a mercantile business there until 1855.

11. "Daniel W. Powers," in *Landmarks of Monroe County, New York* (Boston: Boston History Company, 1895), 56; and *History of Genesee County*, vol. 3 (Chicago: J. Clarke, 1925), 5–6. A banker, broker and real estate magnate, Powers had come to the city at nineteen all but penniless; he had worked his way from hardware clerk to exchange broker and private banker by 1850, at the age of thirty-two. He married his second wife, Helen M. Craig, in 1855 and they had five children. He was legendary for his contributions to Rochester. The stunning steel-framed Powers Building, which Daniel Powers began in 1865, was a monument to "Gilded Age" excess and the most prestigious business address in Rochester. He was both philanthropic and cultured. The Powers Building was attached to the Powers Fireproof Hotel, which had an entire floor devoted

to his thousand-piece art collection. The structure, to which he added several floors over the years to ensure that it remained Rochester's tallest building, still dominates the corner of State and Main Streets in the heart of the city. In interviews conducted in later life, Cecelia mentioned her connection with Powers in Rochester. Many years after she left Rochester, the son and daughter of Helen and Daniel Powers married grandchildren of wealthy wool merchant Aaron Erickson, whose family occupied the charming brick mansion just across the street from the Powers home, at 234 (now 474) East Avenue. The Pitkin-Powers home was for more than fifty years the head-quarters of Boy Scouts of America. Cyrus Hoy, "Mrs. Gilman H. Perkins and Her World," *Rochester Library Bulletin* 23, no. 1 (Autumn 1975), accessed Oct. 5, 2013, http://www.lib. rochester.edu/ index.cfm?PAGE=3511.

12. The 1865 New York State census notes, clearly written across the margins of the Craig and Powers address: "Two families live in this house." This was two years after Cecelia had left their service. Each family had a live-in servant, the Craigs Canadian-born Ann Martin and the Powers a young woman of Irish extraction born in Monroe County, Kate Brady.

13. Deposition of Caroline Ellis, taken at Louisville, Kentucky, May 3, 1898, Case no. 631.101, Pension Bureau Files, NARA.

14. Any uncertainty as to the ages of Mamie and Cecelia stems from their own very loose interpre-tations of the same in later life. Both women nearly always listed themselves in official documents as being years younger than they really were. The earliest and best corroborated records show Cecelia Jane Reynolds coming into the Thruston household at the age of five months in 1831, and her daughter born in Toronto in the spring of 1854.

15. Blake McKelvey, "Lights and Shadows of Local Negro History," *Rochester History* 21, no. 4 (October 1959), 6. See also Douglass, *Life and Times*, 331–33. Black female students in the mid-nineteenth-century United States were almost entirely excluded from higher education, except at Oberlin College in Ohio.

16. *Rochester City Directory, 1857–58*, 73.

17. For a discussion of the Cleggett, Nell and Francis families, see Monique Patenaud, "Bound by Pride and Prejudice: Black Life in Frederick Douglass' New York" (PhD diss., University of Rochester, 2012), 12–13, 101–117.

18. Rosenburg-Naparsteck, "Growing Agitation," 15. For the steamboat history of Carthage, see Blake McKelvey, "Early Rochester, Illustrated," *Rochester History* 5, no. 3 (July 1943), 10.

19. Tax records for Centre Street, 1861–67, City of Toronto Diffusion Material, D 318, Archives of Ontario. In 1865 Cecelia employed James Mink as her agent, while James Thomas Holmes took over renting the house for her in 1866 and 1867. Since Cecelia never mentions her stepsons or their children in her pension applications of the 1890s; the inference is that their relationship was very strained after the death of Benjamin.

20. Austin Steward, *Twenty-Two Years a Slave, and Forty Years a Freeman, Embracing a Correspondence of Several Years, While President of Wilberforce Colony, London, Canada West* (Rochester, NY: William Alling, 1857). Steward was first vice-president of the Black National Convention called by Reverend Richard Allen in 1830, while Abraham D. Shadd was secretary. Steward closed his business and moved to Upper Canada to help manage the Wilberforce colony, which had been founded in 1829 for the benefit of oppressed Cincinnati Blacks. The committee that organized the settlement was chaired by James Charles Brown, who later proved himself such a good friend to Hiram and Hannah Wilson in Toronto. With his extended family, Abraham Shadd was now living just outside Buxton, Canada West, and was newly elected reeve of Chatham Township.

His daughter Mary Ann Shadd Cary had recently moved her *Provincial Freeman* to Chatham, which had a very cultured Black community, of which Dr. Martin Delany was then a part. Dissension and fiscal problems at Wilberforce had sent Steward back to New York State in 1842.

21. Broyld, "Borderland Blacks," 27–28, 28n45; Douglass, *My Bondage and My Freedom*, 395–6.

22. Anthony's brothers Merritt and Daniel had fought with fiery white abolitionist John Brown against proslavery forces in "bleeding Kansas"; Rosenburg-Naparsteck, "Growing Agitation," 11.

23. There are numerous sources on this topic. See Judith Wellman, *Grassroots Reform in the Burned-Over District of Upstate New York: Religion, Abolitionism, and Democracy*, Studies in African American History and Culture (New York: Routledge, 2000); Whitney R. Cross, *The Burned-Over District: The Social and Intellectual History of Enthusiastic Religion in Western New York, 1800–1850* (Ithaca, NY: Cornell University Press, 1950); Michael Barkun, *Crucible of the Millennium: The Burned-Over District of New York in the 1840s* (Syracuse: Syracuse University Press, 1986). For specific information about the relationship between evangelical thought and abolition in upstate New York, see Milton C. Sernett, *North Star Country: Upstate New York and the Crusade for African American Freedom* (Syracuse: Syracuse University Press, 2002).

24. In the words of Booker T. Washington, "Douglass opposed the plan as wholly impracticable and fatal to all who might engage in it" but found Brown "not to be shaken by anything I could say," although he "treated my views respectfully." The Detroit meeting took place on March 12, 1859, at the home of William Webb, with George DeBaptiste and other Black abolitionists in attendance. The manifesto was printed by William H. Day, who was then living in St. Catharines. At Brown's convention in Chatham in early May 1858, he presented his plan to a mixed African American and Canadian crowd. Because of the cautionary intervention of Buxton's founder, Reverend William King, he garnered little practical support. Only one Rochester and two Canadian volunteers crossed the border with Brown in October 1859. See Gwendolyn Robinson and John Robinson, *Seek the Truth: A Story of Chatham's Black Community* (Chatham, 1988), especially ch. 12. The classic work is Franklin Benjamin Sanborn, *The Life and Letters of John Brown: Liberator of Kansas and Martyr of Virginia* (Boston: Roberts, 1891), ch. 12. Osborne Perry Anderson was the only Chatham man to go to Harpers Ferry. After his escape, Mary Ann Shadd Cary helped him publish his memoir of the events, *A Voice from Harper's Ferry* (Boston: O. P. Anderson, 1861); the minutes of the Chatham convention are on pages 10–12.

25. Booker T. Washington, "Many Roads to Freedom: John Brown's Rochester Connections," accessed December 17, 2013, http://www.libraryweb.org/rochimag/roads/johnbrown.htm.

26. *Globe* (Toronto), November 5 and December 2, 1859.

27. Douglass, *Life and Times*, 329.

28. The trustees of Rochester's Third Baptist Church were grocer Grandison Boyd, Harrison Powell, a whitewasher named Benjamin Foster, and George Frances, who was a cook on a packet boat; Papson and Calarco, *Secret Lives*, 94. Also involved was boatman William Moore, the man who became a used-clothing dealer in Carthage to help out Ralph and Margaret Francis's Underground Railroad operation there after the passage of the Fugitive Slave Law.

29. The Rochester Ladies' Anti-Slavery Society Papers are in the William L. Clements Library, University of Michigan. Susan Farley Porter was the first president, Julia Griffiths was secretary and Maria G. Porter served as treasurer from the time of the founding meeting on August 20, 1851.

30. Finding Aid: Rochester Ladies' Anti-Slavery Society Papers, 1851–1868, Manuscript Division, William C. Clements Library, University of Michigan.

31. Wesley and Uzelac, *William Cooper Nell*, 38. See also Rosie O'Keefe, *Historic Genesee Country: A Guide to Its Lands and Legacies* (Charleston, SC: History Press, 2010), and *Frederick and Anna Douglass in Rochester, New York: Their Home Was Open to All* (Charleston, SC: History Press, 2013), 38–39; Margaret Washington, *Sojourner Truth's America* (Chicago: University of Chicago Press, 2009), 214–17; Rosenburg-Naparsteck, "Growing Agitation," 12. A number of Sojourner Truth's letters to Amy Post are contained in the Post Family Papers Project, Rare Books and Special Collections, University of Rochester, accessed December 13, 2013, http://rbsc.library. rochester.edu/finding_aid. Amy Post was a cousin of fearless white abolitionist Lucretia Mott and was related to Reverend Lorenzo Thayer, who was in turn acquainted with Cecelia's stepsons in Lowell. There were circles within circles: when the Douglasses were unable to find a school to teach their daughter, Rosetta, in an integrated classroom, it was Phoebe Thayer who stepped in to tutor the promising child at the Douglass home. Swedish feminist Fredericka Bremner met her while visiting Rochester in 1850 and commented: "The governess is a white lady, who lives in the family. I can not but admire that force of character which enables her to bear those trials which, in such circumstances, she must have to bear from the prejudiced white people; and they are legion even in the Free States." Fredericka Bremer, *The Homes of the New World: Impressions of America*, vol. 1 (New York: Harper and Brothers, 1853), 585–86; Schmitt, "Rochester's Frederick Douglass, 19.

32. Marcy S. Sacks, *Before Harlem: The Black Experience in New York City before World War I* (Philadelphia: University of Pennsylvania Press, 2013), 116; Ira Berlin, *Slaves Without Masters: The Free Negro in the Antebellum South* (New York: The New Press, 2007).

33. Deposition of Cecelia J. Larrison, Case no. 631.101, Pension Bureau Files, NARA.

34. Thomas James, *Life of Rev. Thomas James, by Himself* (Rochester: Post Express, 1886), and "Summary," Documenting the American South, accessed June 15, 2013, http://docsouth.unc. edu/neh/jamesth/summary.html. Thomas James was born a slave in New York State but became a freedom-seeker who fled to Canada before settling in Rochester, where he learned to read and opened a Sunday School and then a school for Black children. He was ordained in 1830, was co-founder of the *Rights of Man* newspaper and helped establish Black abolitionism and Underground Railroad operations in Rochester before leaving for Syracuse and later New England. James was instrumental in assisting the *Amistad* mutineers, brought forth suits against railways that discriminated against Black passengers and, while minister of the AME Zion Church in New Bedford, ordained Frederick Douglass. During the Civil War Reverend James was in Louisville, where he was commissioned by the federal government to assist freed African Americans and protect contrabands there who had fled slavery. He returned to Rochester in later life and published his fascinating autobiography. See Broyld, "Borderland Blacks," 25–26.

35. Deposition of Cecelia J. Larrison, Case no. 631.101, Pension Bureau Files, NARA.

36. Ibid.

37. "Jany. 19th Wm Henry Larrison, from Newark Co. Del went to Wilmington on foot on Sat. 12th inst. Sent forward by Thos. Garrett. Was married a month ago, but his master proposed to sell him and the overseer giving him permission to go to Wilmington, he improved the opportunity, which he had long wished for, to escape." Entry for January 10, 1856, Record of Fugitives, Sidney Howard Gay Papers, Rare Books and Manuscripts Library, Columbia University; also cited in Papson and Calarco, *Secret Lives*, 159. My sincere thanks to Don Papson and Tom Calarco for sharing digital images of this passage with me.

38. William Still, *The Underground Railroad* (Philadelphia: W. Still, 1886), 336–37. I have been unable to locate a slaveholder in Delaware by the name of Francis Harkins, but it's possible that Larrison gave a false name to help conceal his trail, or that Still wrote it down incorrectly.

39. William H. Larrison is listed as "Lawrison" in the following: City of Toronto Archives. House of Industry Fonds Series 802, File 8. Register of aid recipients from the House of Industry 1837–1859, February 1858. His Delaware-born employer was Eliza A. (Carter) Ward (1832–1916). Slocomb himself was not born in Delaware but in Massachusetts. However, his adopted daughter, Eliza, was, on January 12, 1832. For details, see Joseph Buell Ward Family Papers, Department of Rare Books and Special Collections, Rush Rhees Library, University of Rochester Archives. Joseph Buell Ward (1827–1879) was a native of Rochester and was a nephew of Siba, William Slocomb's second wife. Joseph attended Marietta College (1846) as well as the Lane Theological Seminary in Cincinnati (1847–1848) and finally Auburn Theological School (1848–1849), but he was never ordained and entered into business in Rochester when he returned home. He and Eliza were married in Rochester on May 11, 1852. The Buells had come to Rochester from Marietta, Ohio, where Joseph's mother was born in 1804. They had originated in Connecticut, whence came several of the founding families of Marietta as well as a number of early Rochester settlers. See Albert Welles, ed., *History of the Buell Family in England* (New York: Society Library, 1881), 280. See also *General Biographical Catalogue of the Auburn Theological Seminary, 1818–1918* (Auburn, NY: Auburn Seminary Press, 1918), 109.

40. See Grove Place, accessed November 15, 2013, http://www.groveplace.org/history.html. Joseph B. and Eliza Ward's home is the only original house left standing in Grove Place today. The intermarried Slocomb, Buell and Ward families were well-to-do and had a number of servants. Grove Place was an extensive property at the eastern boundary of the city, according to the 1861 Rochester directory; this matches a description of William Larrison's employer's home given many years later. William always listed his occupation as farmer, and in his memoirs, Levi Ward's grandson mentions his father recalling the area when it was made up of fields of waving grain.

41. George K. Ward, "Grove Place and Its People in the Early Days" (unpublished manuscript, 1920), Department of Rare Books and Special Collections, Rush Rhees Library, University of Rochester.

42. Interestingly, a cartoon of Lincoln's fleeting visit to Rochester is held in the collections of the Lincoln Institute. It shows four Black spectators on the left side of the frame, including a little boy in a top hat clinging to the train's railing. Behind him stands an African American man in a ragged hat and loose shirt; he has both arms raised to hail the incoming president. Behind him and to the left, in the bottom left-hand corner of the drawing, is a clearly more prosperous Black man wearing a tidy white shirt and black vest and tie, with his arm about a well-dressed woman, presumably his wife, in a turban and scoop-necked flowered dress; she is wearing large hoop earrings and a beaded necklace. There are eleven whites in the picture, including two soldiers in Union blue and a woman on the far right side of the frame holding out her arms towards the president-elect. The tone is celebratory, and the presence of the relatively large number of Blacks, including two who are clearly well-off, suggests that Rochester's African Americans were visible and accepted in public spaces, that they especially supported Abraham Lincoln's election, and that the cartoonist acknowledged that Black Rochesterians included prosperous and respectable members of the community. Unlike many newspaper cartoons of the period, this is relatively lacking in the typical caricature and stereotypes with which Blacks were often portrayed. It shows a measure of respect for the accomplishments of Blacks in Rochester and also references

their special interest in the new president-elect because of his opposition to the expansion of slavery. Lincoln's short speech is recorded in Roy P. Basler, *The Collected Works of Abraham Lincoln*, vol. 4 (New Brunswick, NJ: Rutgers University Press, 1953), 222; also "Today, February 18, in Rochester History: Abraham Lincoln's 10 Minute Pop-in," *Rochester Subway*, accessed December 18, 2013, http://www.rochestersubway.com/topics/2011/02/today-february-18-in-rochester-history-abraham-lincoln/.

43. Born on a farm outside Louisville, Anderson was a hardline slaveholder and Charles W. Thruston's cousin. His father's first wife, Elizabeth Clark Anderson, was sister to Charles W. Thruston's mother and his daughter's namesake, Fanny Clark O'Fallon Thruston Fitzhugh.

44. Blake McKelvey, *The Story of Rochester* (Rochester, NY: Board of Education, 1938), 11, and "Rochester's Civil War," *Rochester History* 32, no. 1 (January 1961): 1–24.

45. St. Peter's Presbyterian was built in 1852 at the corner of Grove Street. The building in which William and Cecelia were married (with apparently very little ceremony) burned down in 1868. Their minister, John Townsend Coit, the third pastor of the church, was installed in June 3, 1860. A native of Buffalo, he served only three years; he died on January 23, 1863, at the age of thirty-nine and a memorial tablet was erected in the church. Ward, "Grove Place," 55–63.

46. The two misspellings of Larrison occur in the original. The marriage certificate that Cecelia filed with her pension applications is in the hand of Reverend Coit and gives the date of her marriage as April 3, 1862. She mistakenly says it was April 22 in her deposition but makes a point of saying that the certificate she has already provided has the correct date on it in case her memory is faulty. Deposition of Cecelia J. Larrison, Case no. 631.101, Pension Bureau Files, NARA.

47. Ibid.

48. Although some sources suggest that Harrison was William P. Powell's brother, the former had illustrious Revolutionary War antecedents in New York State, while Harrison Powell came from Virginia. He appears on the 1855 census of the United States as a resident of the northern part of Rochester's Tenth Ward. He was fifty, born in Virginia, and his wife, Sarah, was twenty-six and from Pennsylvania. Their children were Elmira, thirteen; William P. Powell, age three; and Delvira, just five months old, all born in Monroe County, New York, and all listed as Black.

49. Deposition of Cecelia J. Larrison, Case no. 631.101, Pension Bureau Files, NARA. In her first testimony to the Pension Bureau, Cecelia says she had lived on Tappan Street, where Harrison Powell resided. However, her second says she found herself unable to work very shortly after the marriage (she may well have been pregnant at the altar). There is no Maud Bailey listed in any directory, but Cecelia's 1896 affidavits show that she was often vague on both dates and names. Jacob Unglink, a carpenter, occupied a house at 86 St. Joseph Street in 1863, while a Mrs. Maria Bailey, widow of Stephen, lived at the corner of St. Joseph and Kelley Streets. In the 1864 directory Mrs. Bailey is listed in the Unglinks' former house at 86 St. Joseph Street, and the Unglinks had moved to 15 Hawkins Street. One suspects that Cecelia kept in touch with Mrs. Bailey, for she knew when she had died and she also was aware of her removal to the Unglink house. This was in Ward 6, in the northeast sector of Rochester, a largely immigrant district. It was a good distance from the Craig household and still farther from that of William's employers on Grove Square. See *Boyde's Rochester Directory for 1863* (Rochester, NY: Andrew Boyde, 1863) and *Boyde's Rochester and Brockport Directory, 1864–65* (Rochester, NY: Andrew Boyde, 1865).

50. This was Sarah Churchill, who, as Fanny informed Cecelia in her letter of March 11, 1852, had accompanied the newlywed Isabelle Churchill McCreary to her husband's home in St. Louis, Missouri. The US census of Rochester, New York, taken in June 1865 shows two daughters of

William and Cecelia Larrison (the census-taker mixed up the daughters' names and the ages are almost completely wrong). The family, which lived in a frame house worth $500, was made up of "William Lawrison, age 25, Male, Mulatto, born Delaware, married once, currently married, Laborer, works in Rochester, over 21 and unable to read or write, Formerly in Military; Cecelia G. Lawrison, age 30, Female, Mulatto, wife of Head of Household, born Virginia, Mother of 3 children[(?)], Married twice, Currently married; Sarah Lawrison, age 11, Female, Mulatto, Child of Head of Household, born Canada, single; Mary Lawrison, age 3 10/12, Female, Mulatto, born Monroe, single." It seems more likely that the daughter Cecelia bore to William Larrison was two years, ten months old, which would put her birth somewhere in the summer of 1862, just a few short months after the couple married in April. Finally, the census-taker lists William as resident in the household, but he had not returned from the war by June 1865; he was demobilized only in August at Washington, DC. One suspects that the census-taker began recording in June but did not finish until the end of August or later. This throws into question the exact month in which little Sarah was born; if the census was taken after William got home, then her birthday was sometime in June 1862, or only two months after the wedding.

51. Tax Assessment Rolls for Centre Street, 1860–63, City of Toronto Diffusion Material, D 318, Archives of Ontario. Her tenant for several years was a thirty-two-year-old shoemaker named Thomas Wilson.

Chapter 11: The Trumpet Sounds Within My Soul

1. The only record of Cecelia's employment in Rochester comes from her own statements to the Pension Bureau in the 1890s. She mentions Daniel W. Powers, whose children she cared for before her first child by Larrison was born, probably because he was very well known and the only one of her local employers who might still be alive by that time (he had in fact died in 1897, and when his daughter was questioned by US pension officials in 1898, she had no recollection of Cecelia). Her neighbour Aaron Erickson had been among those who tried to avert war by supporting the Crittenden Amendment, proposed by Kentucky senator John Crittenden in December 1860. It would have left slavery alone in the states where it was already established and confirmed the tenets of the old Missouri Compromise, but it was far too late by that point. The New Jersey-born Aaron Erickson may have risen from humble beginnings as a machinist, but he now owned Erickson, Livermore and Co., which controlled much of the wool market in the United States. Cyrus Hoy, "Mrs. Gilman H. Perkins and Her World," *Rochester Library Bulletin* 23, no. 1 (Autumn 1975), accessed Oct. 5, 2013, http://www.lib.rochester.edu/index.cfm?PAGE=3511.

2. John Lobb, Josiah Henson, *Uncle Tom's Story of His Life* (London: Christian Age Office, 1879), 176–68. In September 1861 the US government recognized the service of escaped slaves at Virginia's Fort Monroe and began paying the men eight dollars a month and the women four dollars, as well as providing what rations they could.

3. James, *Life of Rev. Thomas James*, 16–18.

4. Frederick Douglass, "Fighting Rebels with Only One Hand," *Frederick Douglass' Monthly*, September 1861. Some generals did recruit Black fighting units. The 1st Kansas Colored Volunteers were first blooded defending Island Mound, Missouri, from attacking Confederate forces on October 29, 1862, and General David Hunter enlisted contrabands.

5. James K. Bryant, *The 36th Infantry United States Colored Troops in the Civil War: A History*

(Jefferson, NC: McFarland, 2012), 67. Two of Anna and Frederick Douglass's sons fought in the 54th Massachusetts.

6. For superb accounts of Black Canadians in the Civil War, see Bryan Prince, *My Brother's Keeper: African Canadians and the American Civil War* (Toronto: Dundurn, 2015) and Richard Reid, *African Canadians in Union Blue: Volunteering for the Cause in America's Civil War* (Vancouver: University of British Columbia Press, 2014).

7. Obituary of Elisha G. Marshall, *New York Times*, August 4, 1883; Francis B. Heitman, *Historical Register and Dictionary of the United States Army, 1789–1903*, vol. 1 (Washington DC: US Government Printing Office, 1903), 690; Rochester *Union and Advertiser*, April 14, 1862. The Colonel had received a serious neck wound at Fredericksburg on December 13, 1862, and returned home, as reported in the Rochester *Union and Advertiser* of January 13, 1863. He mustered out the 13th New York on May 13, 1863. See Robert Marcotte, *Where They Fell: Stories of Rochester Area Soldiers in the Civil War* (Franklin, VA: Q Publishing, 2002), 223–24; David Lay, "Gen. Elisha G. Marshall," *Bivouac Banner* 5, no. 3 (Fall 2006), accessed June 15, 2008, http://www.bivouacbooks.com/bbv5i3s5.htm.

8. *Report of the Committee of Merchants for the Relief of Colored People, Suffering from the Late Riots in the City of New York* (New York: G. A. Whitehorne, 1863), African American Pamphlet Collection, Library of Congress; Larry Kincaid, "Two Steps Forward, One Step Back: Racial Attitudes During the Civil War and Reconstruction," in *The Great Fear: Race in the Mind of America*, ed. Gary B. Nash and Richard Weiss (New York: Holt, 1970), 45–46.

9. The process took time, for the officers were competing with recruiting officers for the 11th New York, who were also hard at work in Rochester. Colonel Marshall was subsequently criticized for enlisting men who had previously served with him in the 13th Regiment. This prevented them, of course, from re-entering service in the 11th New York when its officers began their own recruitment drive.

10. In the end William received the Monroe County and New York State bounties but not all he was entitled to of the federal one. For the amounts offered, see "14th Regiment Artillery (Heavy), New York Volunteers," Civil War Newspaper Clippings, accessed July 15, 2014, https://dmna.ny.gov/historic/reghist/civil/artillery/14thArtHvy/14thArtHvyCWN.htm.

11. Levi Parsons, *History of Rochester Presbytery from the Earliest Settlement of the Country* (Rochester, NY: Democrat-Chronicle, 1889), 43, 174. Reverend Thomas Bellamy had the Presbyterian church in Charlotte in 1851, being then the minister at Penfield. He returned to the church in June 1863, retired in November 1866 and died in Charlotte on April 31, 1867.

12. Tombstone inscriptions from Section G, Mount Hope Cemetery, Rochester, NY: "Hannah Viola Marshall, wife of Gen. E. G. and dau. Aaron & Hannah ERICKSON; Aug 7, 1844–May 25, 1873," accessed March 19, 2012, http://mcnygenealogy.com/cem/mthope-sec-g.htm. See also William Farley Peck, *Semi-centennial History of the City of Rochester* (Syracuse, NY: D. Mason, 1884), 167, 186, 195, 467, 697–700.

13. Caroline's sumptuous society wedding took place at Rochester's fashionable St. Luke's Church in 1856. When the bridal party drove up to the church in their carriage, they had difficulty navigating the crowd of well-wishers because "it was massed from the Savings Bank to the top of the bridge." Cyrus Hoy, "Mrs. Gilman H. Perkins and Her World," *University of Rochester Library Bulletin* 29, no. 1 (Autumn 1975), accessed July 10, 2010, http://www.lib.rochester.edu/index.cfm?PAGE=351. As Mrs. Perkins described her nuptials in a 1917 retrospective, "it was spoken of in the papers which was uncommon." Caroline, who became a leading figure in elite Rochester society, lost her husband, Gilman H. Perkins, but resided in the Erickson family home on East Avenue for the rest

of her life. Her son and daughter married the children of Daniel W. Powers and his wife, Helen Craig Powers, uniting two families important to Cecelia's Rochester experience.

14. Although Hannah V. Marshall is clearly identified as the daughter of Aaron Erickson and his wife on her gravestone (she died tragically young), there is no mention of her in the family genealogies. For instance, William F. Peck, *History of Rochester and Monroe County, New York: From the Earliest Historic Times to the Beginning of 1907* (New York: Pioneer, 1908), 628, states: "In the family were eight children, but only three daughters survived the father: Mrs. W. S. Nichols, of Staten Island; Mrs. Gilman H. Perkins, of Rochester; and Mrs. W. D. Powell, of New York." When Caroline Perkins wrote about her family, her younger sister was never mentioned. The family simply wrote her off.

15. General Orders, no. 323, War Department, 1863, Box1, 16, William A. Gladstone Afro-American Military Collection, Library of Congress. According to the Enrollment Act of 1863, section 10, "the President of the United States . . . is hereby, authorized to cause to be enlisted for each cook (two allowed by section 9) two undercooks of African descent, who shall receive for their full compensation $10 per month and one ration per day; $3 of said monthly pay may be in clothing . . . they will be mustered into service, as in the eases of other soldiers. In each case a remark will be made on their enlistment papers showing that they are undercooks of African descent. Their names will be borne on the company muster-rolls at the foot of the list of privates. They will be paid, and their accounts will be kept, like other enlisted men. They will also be discharged in the same manner as other soldiers."

16. Deposition of Chauncey Webster, taken at Truxton, NY, August 8, 1899, Case no. 631.101, Pension Bureau Files, NARA.

17. Michael Leavy and Glenn Leavy, *Rochester's 19th Ward* (Rochester, NY: Arcadia, 2005), 51; *Union and Advertiser* (Rochester), October 7 and 26, November 8, 1865; *Daily Democrat* (Rochester), January 18, 1864.

18. See, for instance, the two Depositions of Chauncey Webster taken on July 8, 1898, and August 8, 1899; and Deposition of Minor Lewis, taken at Louisville, June 19, 1898, Case no. 631.101, Pension Bureau Files, NARA.

19. Deposition A, before Special Examiner S. W. Cutler, Case no. 631.101, Pension Bureau Files, NARA. See also "14th Regiment Artillery (Heavy), New York Volunteers," Civil War Newspaper Clippings, New York State Military Museum, Saratoga Springs, NY, accessed July 10, 2012, http://dmna.ny.gov/historic/reghist/civil/artillery/ 14thArtHvy/14thArtHvyCWN.htm.

20. Marcotte, *Where They Fell*, 223–24; Lay, "Gen. Elisha G. Marshall"; George Levy and Paul Tynan, "Campgrounds of the Civil War," *Rochester History* 46, no. 3 (Summer 2004), 18–19.

21. Hannah Erickson Marshall lived for a time at Fort Union, New Mexico, where her husband was commanding officer, but he retired from active service in 1867 because of wounds sustained in the war. Theirs was a very happy marriage but she died young. Her obituary appeared in the Rochester *Union and Advertiser* of May 26, 1873: "In this city, on the evening of the 26th inst. of diphtheria, in the 29th year of her age, HANNAH V. MARSHALL, wife of Gen. E. G. Marshall, and youngest daughter of Aaron Erickson, Esquire." One-year-old Aaron died with her. Their little girl, Nora, had died of "brain fever" in 1865 at the age of seven months. Hannah is buried in the city's lovely Mount Hope Cemetery, along with her two children (see note 12 above). Marshall remarried in 1875. His bride was Jennie Rutherford and their wedding was announced in the Rochester *Union and Democrat* of September 25. They built a fine home in Palmyra, Pennsylvania, but the marriage failed and the couple separated. Elisha G. Marshall died

at his old home in Canandaigua; *Union and Advertiser*, August 3, 1883. He chose to be buried with his first wife and their children at Mount Hope Cemetery. Aaron Erickson, Hannah's father, died in 1880. Despite the fact that Hannah is left out of the Erickson family records, she may have reconciled with her father, for the Marshall grave is right beside the stunning monument erected to her father. Aaron Erickson and his wife lie beneath the famous "Weary Pilgrim," depicting a Crusader on pilgrimage, symbolized by the scallop shell mounted on his cloak. The monument, designed by papal sculptor Nicola Cantalamessa-Papotti (1833–1910), is now preserved in the Rochester Art Gallery. See also Hoy, "Mrs. Gilman H. Perkins."

22. Deposition of Chauncey Webster.

23. Judith E. Harper, *Women During the Civil War: An Encyclopedia* (New York: Routledge, 2004), 55ff.

24. RG 108, Letters Sent; DLC-USG, V, 45, 59, cited in John Y. Simon, ed., *The Papers of Ulysses S. Grant: January 1–May 31, 1864*, vol. 10 (Carbondale: Southern Illinois University Press, 1982), 335.

25. An excellent account of the life of an elite white woman in Washington during this period is Virginia Jeans Laas, *Wartime Washington: The Civil War Letters of Elizabeth Blair Lee* (Urbana: University of Illinois Press, 1999). Lee was the daughter of Francis Preston Blair and sister-in-law of Mary Jesup Blair, for whose wedding Fanny had taken Cecelia to Washington in the winter of 1845–46.

26. For a time Sojourner Truth lived in the Freedmen's Village on the grounds of Arlington, Robert E. Lee's former estate, and organized the relief effort there. She nursed the sick, visited orphanages, found clothing and food for the destitute, lectured on morals and supported the efforts of the new Freedmen's Bureau after its founding. After the war she worked to arrange new homes in the West for freemen and their families, sending large numbers to upstate New York, including Rochester, and to Michigan, where she prevailed on her network of friends, Black and white, to find them employment and assist in their resettlement. See Washington, *Sojourner Truth's America*, 311–30.

27. Harriet Jacobs had been working in Alexandria, Virginia, since 1862, teaching in a school, nursing and distributing food and clothing. She corresponded with the Posts in Rochester and embarked on a career in journalism, eliciting both funds and material comforts for the impoverished and terribly neglected freedmen in her care. Her first article appeared in the *Liberator*. Her report of conditions in the contraband camps was published in the *Freedmen's Record* of February 1865. Harriet Jacobs, "Life Among the Contraband," *Liberator*, September 5, 1862.

28. See, for example, Elizabeth Keckley, *Behind the Scenes, or Thirty Years a Slave, and Four Years in the White House* (New York: G. W. Carleton, 1868), accessed July 10, 2012, http://docsouth.unc.edu/neh/keckley/menu.html.

29. Laas, *Wartime Washington*, 1991; Reid, *African Canadians*, 257n.

30. Mrs. Marshall moved back to Rochester, where she gave birth to a little girl, Nora, in 1865. She lived in quarters rather than with her parents, who had not reconciled themselves to her elopement with her much older colonel, despite his stellar military career. A letter from General Orlando Willcox attests to Hannah Marshall's return to Rochester after the Battle of the Crater, and also that the birth of her child was the result of the couple's elopement: "Before Petersburg, Dec. 25, 1864. This evening I received a letter from Col. Marshall, one of the colonels of the old First Division, & a second cousin, in which he says that Mrs. Marshall wishes to exchange

pictures with you . . . write her a note, address Mrs. Col. E.G. Marshall, Rochester, NY. They have a little daughter—the product, by the way of a runaway match"; Orlando B. Willcox to his wife, Marie, in Robert Garth Scott, ed., *Forgotten Valor: The Memoirs, Journals, and Civil War Letters of Orlando B. Willcox* (Kent, OH: Kent State University Press, 1999), 597–98.

31. Deposition of Cecelia J. Larrison, taken at Louisville, May 6, 1898, Case no. 631.101, Pension Bureau Files, NARA.

32. Ibid.

33. Sojourner Truth and Oliver Gilbert, *Narrative of Sojourner Truth: A History of Her Labors and Correspondence, Drawn from Her "Book of Life"* (Battle Creek, MI: 1884), 176–78; also Washington, *Sojourner Truth's America*, 313–14.

34. McKelvey, *Rochester on the Genesee*, 84–85.

35. Deposition of Cecelia J. Larrison, Case no. 631.101, Pension Bureau Files, NARA.

36. The Muster Roll Abstracts for the 14th New York Heavy Artillery include two notices that William Henry Harrison [*sic*] had been hospitalized, both times for illness. The first time was in October 1864 and he was again treated in April 1865, just before his discharge.

37. "History of the Services, 14th NY Heavy Artillery," *Danville Advertiser*, September 17, 1865.

38. There are numerous volumes and articles on the Battle of the Crater, including Kevin M. Levin, *Remembering the Battle of the Crater: War Is Murder* (Lexington: University Press of Kentucky, 2012); Bryce A. Suderow, "The Battle of the Crater: The Civil War's Worst Massacre," *Civil War History* 44, no. 3 (1997), 219–24; and Richard Slotkin, *No Quarter: The Battle of the Crater, 1864* (New York: Random House, 2009).

39. Suderow, "Battle of the Crater," 221.

40. John Sergeant Wise, *The End of an Era* (New York: Houghton, Mifflin, 1901), 366.

41. Marshall spent time in South Carolina's Columbia Military Prison. In December he returned to Rochester after a prisoner exchange, as reported in the Rochester *Union and Advertiser* of December 19, 1864. He was promoted to brevet brigadier general in March of the next year. Levin, *Remembering the Battle of the Crater*, 18 and 147n19.

42. Slaney, *Family Secrets*, 66–67; Kate Clifford Larson, *The Assassin's Accomplice: Mary Surratt and the Plot to Kill Abraham Lincoln* (New York: Basic Books, 2008) provides the most recent account detailing the Canadian connection.

43. US Census, 1865, Rochester, Monroe Co., New York, Ward 13. "Well he was ruptured on his right side very bad, when he came home discharged. He got it in the army and was hardly able to walk. He said he got his rupture by having to walk so much and carry so many heavy things"; Deposition of Cecelia J. Larrison, Case no. 631.101, Pension Bureau Files, NARA.

Chapter 12: Climbing Jacob's Ladder

1. Part of the Kawartha Lakes system, Peterborough had been visited by Samuel de Champlain in 1615 and by the early eighteenth century was home to substantial Native populations. Sparsely settled by Europeans in 1818, the town's real foundation came with an 1825 experimental resettlement scheme funded by the British government. This resulted in the transporting of about two thousand impoverished Irish people to the region. They found a veritable paradise, although one requiring backbreaking labour and great diligence to bring under cultivation.

2. Some of the land opened up in this period included former clergy reserves. A letter signed by Commissioner of Crown Lands Peter Robinson denied sale of clergy reserves to Black petitioners for establishment of a new settlement but reassured the petitioners that land elsewhere could be purchased on the same terms as for whites. December 4, 1830, 58791–92, Upper Canada Sundries, RG 5, A 1, vol. 104, LAC microfilm C-6871, Archives of Ontario; Wendy Cameron, "Robinson, Peter" *Dictionary of Canadian Biography*, vol. 7, accessed November 12, 2015, http://www.biographi.ca/en/bio/robinson_peter_7E.html.

3. The *Kachewahnoonkah Herald* was a handwritten newspaper produced at irregular intervals in Lakefield, Canada West, by students at Colonel Strickland's Agricultural Academy; Kachewahnoonkah Herald fonds, 1855–59, Trent University Library and Archives, accessed November 13, 2013, http://www.trentu.ca/library/archives/83-004%20kherald%201858.

4. Ralph F. Johnson had been born in Canada West; in the census documents he is listed as a member of the family while James Thomas Holmes is not. Ralph Francis (Frank) Johnson was the son of Ralph and Margaret's daughter Julia Ann by her husband, Joshua Johnson. Census of Canada West, 186 Port Hope, Newcastle District. See also note 13.

5. She had been a slave of Nathaniel Hunt. The couple had several children who chose to leave New Jersey. Jacob Francis, Pension File W459, M804, Revolutionary War pension and bounty-land-warrant application files, 2,670 microfilm reels, National Archives and Records Administration, Washington, DC. Also see James P. Snell, *History of Hunterdon and Somerset Counties, New Jersey* (Philadelphia: Everts and Peck, 1881), 323, 330.

6. According to the 1850 US Census, Ralph and Margaret Francis, born in New York State, were both thirty-nine, their daughter Julia was fourteen and their son John was four. Ralph's parents, both sixty, shared their home, which had likely been purchased with their pooled resources.

7. Ena L. Farley, "The African American Presence in the History of Western New York," *Afro-Americans in New York Life and History* 14, no. 1 (Jan. 1990): 27–89. Ralph Francis was, according to Farley, "already well known for taking controversial public positions." See also Stanley Harold, *The Rise of Aggressive Abolitionism: Addresses to the Slaves* (Lexington: University of Kentucky, 2015), 67–70. The Buffalo convention was a landmark one, for it was there that Garnet presented his inflammatory "Address to the Slaves" for debate. Henry Highland Garnet (1815–1882) was a Maryland-born escaped slave who had been educated in New York. He took charge of the Presbyterian congregation in Troy, New York, in 1841. Garnet's views ran in direct opposition to those of William Lloyd Garrison. He favoured political and, if necessary, violent action, maintaining that slaveholders had declared war on slaves, which warranted a similar reaction on the part of African Americans. In 1848 he pastored a church in Geneva, New York, where he also ran a school for Black children. One of Garnet's major campaigns was on behalf of the Free Produce movement. Frederick Douglass and Henry Highland Garnet were less cordial with each other from the late 1840s on, partly because of Garnet's support for the violent overthrow of slavery. Against considerable opposition from Douglass and others present, Garnet argued at the convention that violent uprising on the part of the South's enslaved African American population was the only means to achieve an immediate end to slavery. Reverend Garnet was an ordained Presbyterian minister, and his address was eloquent and persuasive. He maintained that slavery was a sin against Christianity and therefore it was not a sin to rise up violently to overthrow it. Frederick Douglass rebutted the speech, and William Lloyd Garrison, who was also present, rejected the concept of militant action. However, Ralph Francis, who in the first round voted against the address, at its second reading found himself persuaded and supported Garnet.

8. Wesley and Uzelac, *William Cooper Nell*, 165–66. Charles Lenox Remond was also present. This organization came down somewhere between the Tappan and Garrisonian approaches. It espoused the views of William Lloyd Garrison and the American Anti-Slavery Society on including women on the podium and executives of antislavery events and organizations, but also supported political and more direct forms of opposition as well. See John R. McKivigan, ed., *The Frederick Douglass Papers*, ser. 2, vol. 1 (New Haven, CT: Yale University Press, 1999), 290n5, 303n2, 351n1, 383n5, 389n8, 425n5; Stanley Harold, *The Rise of Aggressive Abolitionism: Addresses to the Slaves* (Lexington: University of Kentucky, 2015), 67–70; Milton C. Sernett, *North Star Country: Upstate New York and the Crusade for African American Freedom* (Syracuse, NY: Syracuse University Press, 2002), 58–63; Wellman, *Grassroots Reform*, 181, 156.

   In January 1850 Ralph Francis joined with Frederick Douglass, white abolitionist William C. Bloss, George W. Clark, abolitionist minister H. E. Peck (born in Rochester and studied at Oberlin), and J. P. Morgan in protesting the segregation of children into one of two "colored schools" and calling for integration of the Rochester school system. Both Douglass and Samuel D. Porter, a noted Underground Railroad stationmaster, whose barn was sanctuary for dozens of fugitives on their way north, addressed the school board on the matter. The movement was denied, but by 1857 the coloured schools had been discontinued and children attended the public schools. See S. A. Ellis, "A Brief History of the Public Schools of the City of Rochester," *Publications of the Rochester Historical Society* 1 (1892): 71–89. For Reverend Peck's biography, see ibid., 106; Patenaud, "Bound by Pride and Prejudice," 106 and 186n1.

9. The Steamboat Hotel did rather well in the two years of Ralph and Margaret's sojourn there. Ralph likely hosted some of the delegates to the Colored National Convention held July 6 through 8, 1853 (Black guests were far from welcome at downtown Rochester hotels), and the *Liberator* of September 8, 1853, describes a "sumptuous repast" that he and Margaret prepared for that year's Emancipation Day celebrations. Speeches were made at the hotel by Frederick Douglass, and toasts were proposed by other representative members of the Black community, including Benjamin Cleggett, who hailed the memory of the great British abolitionists, starting with William Wilberforce, and later "William Lloyd Garrison, Wendell Phillips, and compatriots," and Ralph himself spoke of "William H. Seward, the liberal and enlightened statesman." In a delightful note, the article mentions that the party, which included representatives from Buffalo and other nearby cities, then moved to the ballroom for the "mazey" dance.

10. Papson and Calarco, *Secret Lives*, 94. At exactly the same time William Moore, who was also a member of the Western New York Anti-Slavery Society, moved to Carthage, a village at the top of the two-hundred-foot cliff above Kelsey's Landing. Moore had played a role in the Rochester Vigilance Committee since the 1840s. He had been listed in the Rochester directories as a boatman but was now a used-clothing dealer. Before the invention of sewing machines, providing clothes for fugitive slaves was a major problem. Dealing in used garments gave access to a supply without arousing suspicion from unsympathetic observers. Several important Underground Railroad operators dealt in used clothing, including David Walker, whose 1829 *Appeal* caused such consternation in Southern circles.

   There is a historical plaque regarding its importance as an Underground Railroad stop at Kelsey's Landing in Rochester. It seems no coincidence that Isaac Moore (no relation to William) was also at Carthage Landing, operating the Union House hotel. He was abolitionist-minded Governor William Seward's friend as well as brother-in-law to William C. Bloss. The latter was one of Frederick Douglass's strongest white supporters and in 1834 co-founded with Reverend Thomas James the *Rights of Man* newspaper. William Bloss (1795–1863) was born in Massachusetts but moved to upstate New York in 1816. He moved to Rochester in 1830, started the first antislavery organization in the city in 1833 with Thomas James, and was involved in temperance, anti-Masonic and other reforming causes. The Bloss family lived on East Avenue and operated an Underground Railroad Station near the Craig home, where Cecelia worked. Sernett, *North Star Country*, 182, 322n, 68. See also Daniel Broyld, "Rochester: A Transnational Community for Blacks prior to the Civil War," *Rochester History* 72, no. 2 (Fall 2010), 3.

11. Quote from Sernett, *North Star Country*, 181; Russell, "Frederick Douglass in Toronto," 25.

12. They also had a son who disappears from the records about this time.

13. Joshua Johnson operated his "Fashionable Hair-Dressing and Shaving Saloon" out of his three-storey home on Walton Street, "east side of the Bridge," the first advertisement for which appears in the *Tri-Weekly Guide* of August 14, 1855. His new bride was talented as well. The *Port Hope Directory for 1856–'57* contains a separate listing for "Mrs. Johnson, dressmaker," at the same Walton Street address. By 1861, in a move characteristic of the Black barbering tradition, Joshua had taken a second barber into his shop, Robert Sipples, and he and his wife lived with the Johnsons. By this time Joshua and Julia Ann Johnson had two children, John A. Johnson, age two, and Ralph F. Johnson, four. (It was the latter who was staying with his grandparents, Ralph and Margaret Francis, when James T. Holmes moved to Peterborough in the fall of 1860.) Robert Sipples, twenty-six, and his wife had one child; all were US-born and listed as Baptists. They seem to have shared the Johnson home above the barbershop. *Tri-Weekly Guide*, February 9, 1858, 1, 3. By 1862 the *Port Hope Directory* shows J. Johnson still operating his "Fashionable Hair-Dressing and Shaving Saloon."

14. This was, according to the 1861 census, the family of R. Baskerville, an American-born hairdresser of forty-one who with his wife, Sarah, and their six children attended the Baptist church. They had been in the country since at least 1856 (their nine-year-old daughter was the first of their children born in Canada West). By the time the 1865 directory was published, William H. Baskerville, age twenty, was operating his own "Haircutting, Shampooing and Shaving Emporium" on George Street in Peterborough, "two doors south of the Huffman House." See *Fuller's Counties of Peterborough & Victoria Directory, for 1865 & 1866* (Toronto: Blackburn's, 1866), 4; and Census, Peterborough, Canada West, 1861, 6.

15. James T. Angus, *A Respectable Ditch: A History of the Trent-Severn Waterway, 1833–1920* (Montreal: McGill-Queen's University Press, 1998), 47–48, 107–8.

16. "Marriages performed by H. A. Graset, Asst. Minister, Feb. 19, 1839, by license, William Robinson Johnson, of the city of Toronto, bachelor, and Anne Alexander, of the same place. Witnesses, George Williams, Mary Stephens." Marriage Registers of St. James Anglican Church/ Cathedral, York (Toronto), 1800 to 1896, in John Ross Robertson, *Landmarks of Toronto: A Collection of Historical Sketches of the Old Town of York from 1792 until 1833, and of Toronto from 1834 to 1895*, vol. 3 (Toronto: J. Ross Robertson, 1896), 395.

17. Enumeration District 38, North Monaghan Township, County of Peterborough, Agricultural Census for Canada West, 1861. According to the census, William Johnson, of mixed Black and white ancestry, was forty-six and his forty-four-year-old British-born wife was white. Their eldest child, Mary Ann, had been born in Upper Canada, as had her three sisters, Emma, fifteen; Martha, thirteen; and Rebekah (Rebecca), twelve. The census shows both William and Ann Johnson as having been born in England. This appears to be an error, for William is consistently

shown in other sources as a native of the West Indies. It is tempting to suggest a relationship between Julia Ann Francis's husband, Joshua Johnson, and William Johnson of Peterborough, but there is no evidence of one.

18. James Douglass (1792–1870) was a Presbyterian minister from County Monaghan, Ireland. Immigrating to the United States in 1822, he served in Lisbon, New York, and then Pennsylvania before answering the call to come to rural Upper Canada, having in his charge Monaghan, Cavan and Emily Townships. He served as superintendent of schools for Monaghan and Cavan South, townships in Northumberland County to the south and east of Peterborough. "County of Durham," *Journaux du Conseil législatif de la Province du Canada* 13, no. 2 (1854), App. B; Upper Canada, Chief Superintendent of Schools, *Annual Report of the Normal, Model, and Common Schools in Upper Canada for the Year 1853* (Quebec: Lovell & Lamoreaux, 1853), 179; William Gregg, *History of the Presbyterian Church in the Dominion of Canada* (Toronto: Presbyterian Printing & Publishing, 1834), 452–53.

19. The Johnsons had probably migrated to Peterborough County to join the former Ann Alexander's extended family, of whom there were several members in the area, all white. On the western edge of town, right over the town line on Lot 11, Concession 13 of Monaghan Township, lived Ann Johnson's brother, Pennington Alexander. In 1861 he was fifty-five and with his Scottish-born wife, Isabella, had nine children, of whom the eldest, Ellen, was a contemporary of the eldest Johnson girl, Mary Ann. Pennington's family had been in Canada since 1820 and were some of the very earliest settlers in that part of the province. They had married on January 11, 1835, and had their last child, Isabelle, in 1855. At the time of their marriage he was living in Hope Township and she in Smith Township. Abstract Book for Lot 11, Con. 13, Monaghan Township, Northumberland County Land Records. For land ownership, see This Land Archaeology Inc. and Historic Horizon, "Report on the 2006 Stage 1 Archaeological Assessment of the Peterborough Regional Health Centre Road Improvements, Peterborough, Ontario" (report submitted to Ontario Ministry of Culture, May 2006).

There were other relatives living right next door, for on the second quarter of Lot 11, Concession 13, lived sixty-year-old John Redhead (1801–1877) and his wife, Martha Alexander Redhead (1814–1880), and their seven Canadian-born children. They had migrated from England in 1834. Their eldest daughter, Jane, who was twenty-two, and her sister Emma, twenty, were also contemporaries of the new Mrs. Mary Ann Holmes. The two Redhead girls were Wesleyan Methodist, while the rest of their family, along with the Johnsons and Alexanders, were Anglicans.

20. James T. Holmes has the only hairdresser's advertisement in Thomas White, ed., *An Exhibit of the Progress, Position and Resources of the County of Peterborough, Canada West* (Peterborough, ON: Th. White, 1861), 59.

21. For an example of an advertisement by "Professor" Holmes, see *Peterborough Examiner,* January 17, 1862, and Index to *Peterborough Examiner,* 1862, Trent Valley Archives, http://www.trentvalleyarchives.com/resources/online-resources/newspaper-indexes/peterborough-examiner/peterborough-examiner-1862. For use of the title "Professor," see Douglas W. Bristol Jr., "From Outposts to Enclaves: A Social History of Black Barbers from 1750 to 1915," *Enterprise and Society* 5, no. 4 (December 2004), 594–606: William Robertson, born in slavery in 1836 in Maysville, Kentucky, but whose freedom had been purchased by his mother, owned the well-known and extremely elegant Marble Palace "Bath Institute and Tonsorial Parlor," which boasted Russian, Turkish and "electric" baths, at the Lindell Hotel in St. Louis. He adopted the title

"Professor Robertson" in advertising. The electric baths were "a sovereign remedy for female complaints and nervous troubles."

22. Michael Wayne, "The Black Population of Canada West on the Eve of the American Civil War: A Reassessment Based on the Manuscript Census of 1861," *Histoire Social/Social History* 28 (1995): 465–85. In Appendix B, Wayne shows the following figures for African Canadians in individual townships in Peterborough County: Ashburnham 7; Asphodel 1; Ennismore 4; Minden 8; Monaghan 10; Otonabee 3; Peterborough 23; Smith 10.

23. *Caverhill's Toronto City Directory for 1859–60* (Toronto: W. C. F. Caverhill, 1859), 215. The shop was at 44 Church Street.

24. *Fuller's Directory*, 18.

25. Marriage Records for Peterborough, Ontario: "William Henderson Edwards [*sic*], of Peterboro, born Toronto, s/o William H. Edwards & Mary J. Neil, m. Alice Dutton, 17, of Peterboro, born Ogdensburg, d/o William Dutton & Hannah Nash. Witness: Robert Brown, Peterboro, July 23, 1867." Interestingly, the first wife of William H. Edwoods in Toronto was Catherine Truss, daughter of Benjamin P. Holmes's friend Matthew Truss, the eloquent and elderly exhorter in the Richmond Street Methodist Church.

26. Census of Canada for 1871, Newcastle District, Bowmanville. John Edwoods, age sixteen, was living with his elder brother and Alice, who was then twenty.

27. While the date of Mary Ann and her children's departure from Ontario is estimated, the 1900 US Census shows the Holmes daughters, Emma and Rebecca Ann, residing in Rochester, and notes that they had entered the United States in 1865 or 1866. This would put the date of their immigration within a year of Rebecca's birth.

28. US Census, Rochester, New York, 1865. The census was taken in June. Daniel Bloxom had been in Toronto since 1835 and in the 1846 Toronto directory is listed as operating the Tontine Coffee House at 150 King Street East. He died about 1857, but his widow Hannah remarried and remained in Toronto until she passed away in 1887. She and her second husband, Hugh Robson, were buried in St. James' Cemetery.

29. Frank Johnson also trained as a barber. He was twenty-six and operating his own shop in Cornwall when he married Ida Runions (born 1864, daughter of Catherine and Philip Runions) on February 4, 1884. He is listed as Presbyterian and his bride Church of England; Reg. 011342, County of Stormont, Division of Cornwall Town, Schedule A, 1884. No record of Ida Johnson's death has been found, but on October 14, 1908, Ralph Francis Johnson, son of Joshua and Julia Ann Johnson, age forty-six, was living in Bath, New York. Johnson worked there as a barber until 1909, when, in a good example of the fluidity of the United States–Canada border, he moved to Hamilton, Ontario. In that year he married a local girl named Rachel M. Berry. The Berry family were long-time members of the African Canadian community who had settled on the Niagara Escarpment above the city, in an area known as Hamilton Mountain. Rachel's mother kept the toll gate there "near the corner of Concession Street and Upper Wentworth." After his marriage, Ralph F. Johnson opened a barbershop in Hamilton.

The tollgate-keeping job of Rachel's mother is reported in Jane Mulkewich, "Little Africa: Settlement Goes Back to 1850's," in *Vanished Hamilton*, vol. 2, ed. Margaret Houghton (Burlington: North Shore, 2006), 106. See also Adrienne Shadd, "Little Africa: Where Do We Go from Here?" (report to Museums and Heritage Preservation, City of Hamilton, 2009), 14–16, accessed September 12, 2015, http://www2.hamilton.ca /NR/rdonlyres/C724DF1F-1C9E-4A38-820F-A97C31AAB05/0/Apr07EDRMS_n85765_v1_5_6__ CS10032__ Little_Africa_Plaque.pdf. At the time of his marriage, Ralph Francis Johnson was listed as living in Bath. He died at fifty-six of a sudden heart attack, on November 17, 1913, in Hamilton.

30. There are some discrepancies about his age in several of the census documents, so it is possible that his parents concealed the truth of his birthplace even from him, in an attempt to protect Ben Alexander from the dangers posed by the Fugitive Slave Law.

31. Marriage Records, Lowell, MA, 1861, 134. See also Minnesota, Deaths and Burials, 1835–1990, "Lucia A Holmes, Aug. 13, 1901," FamilySearch, accessed November 26, 2013, https:// familysearch.org/pal:/MM9.1.1/FD62-29V. The 1860 census shows Lucia A. Holt living in the Lowell household of New Hampshire natives, blacksmith David S. Gordin and his wife, Hannah. The family lived in Ward 5.

32. Lorenzo Rockwood Thayer (1814–1888) was a highly respected clergyman born in New Hampshire who lived out his life in Massachusetts. He was ardently antislavery in his convictions and in 1851 spoke out at the New England Annual Conference against the Fugitive Slave Law. Thayer was a near relative of Amy Post in Rochester, demonstrating further links between the Holmes family and that city. What is more, he was a cousin of Quaker teacher Phoebe Thayer. It was Phoebe who in 1848 tutored Frederick Douglass's children when he could not secure them education in an integrated school in Rochester. This suggests a further association between the Holmes family in Toronto, their Rochester associates, and abolitionists both Black and white in Lowell, Massachusetts. Thayer had pastored at Lynn in 1850, and then in Lowell in two different churches in 1862 and 1863, before returning to Cambridge and Boston and finally settling in Newtonville, Massachusetts. See Wendy Knickerbocker, *Bard of the Bethel: The Life and Times of Boston's Father Taylor, 1793–1871* (Boston: Cambridge Scholars, 2014), 289; Charles Cowley, *Illustrated History of Lowell*, rev. ed. (Lowell: B. C. Sargeant and Jerusha Merrill, 1868), 99–100.

See Nancy A. Hewitt, "Amy Kirby Post: Of Whom It Was Said, 'Being Dead, yet Speaketh,'" *Rochester University Library Bulletin* 37 (1984), accessed November 21, 2013, http://www.lib.rochester.edu/index.cfm?PAGE=4018; F. W. Nicholson, *Alumni Record of Wesleyan University, Middletown, Conn, 1881–1883* (Hartford CT: Case, Lockwood and Brainard, 1883), 47.

33. County Marriage Register for Peterborough, MS 248, reel 13, Archives of Ontario. The railway had reached Peterborough by 1854, so they probably travelled across Lake Ontario to Port Hope or Cobourg to board the train.

34. Susannah Strickland Moodie, *Roughing It in the Bush, or Life in Canada: Part I* (New York: G. P. Putnam, 1852), 175. Although the description is delivered in offensively racist language, she has this to say about the poor young man who was killed for his love of an Irish girl:

> Tom Smith was such a quiet, good-natured fellow, and so civil and obliging, that he soon got a good business. He was clever, too, and cleaned old clothes until they looked almost as good as new. Well, after a time he persuaded a white girl to marry him. She was not a bad-looking Irishwoman, and I can't think what bewitched the creature to take him. Her marriage with the black man created a great sensation in the town. All the young fellows were indignant at his presumption and her folly, and they determined to give them the charivari in fine style, and punish them both for the insult they had put upon the place . . . They went so far as to enter the house, drag the poor n——— from his bed, and, in spite of his shrieks for mercy, they hurried him out into the cold air—for it was winter—and almost naked as he was, rode him upon a rail, and so ill-treated him that he died under their hands. . . . The affair was hushed up.

35. "Lindsay," *Fuller's Directory*, 38.
36. This was the case for John Levy, who may have had a hand in both Ben's and James Thomas's training. He wrote in his memoirs regarding his time at Geneseo, New York, in 1853 that all those involved in a trial came in to be shaved over the course of the day. John Levy, *The Life and Adventures of John Levy* (Lawrence, MA: Robert Bower, 1871), 77–78.
37. Connor and Coltson, *County of Victoria Directory, 1869–1870* (Toronto: Hunter, Rose & Co., 1870), 2–3. "B. A. Holmes, barber" is still listed in the 1870 directory, but there is no separate advertisement in the volume.
38. "A Pleasant Trip" and "Summer Arrangements for 1856: Daily Line of Mail Stages Between Peterborough, Metcalf, Lindsay" (unattributed newspaper clippings), Ontario Genealogy, accessed November 3, 2015, http://www.ontariogenealogy.com/ontarionewspapers/kawarthal-akesnewspaper.html.
39. Russell Duncan, ed., *Blue-Eyed Child of Fortune: the Civil War Letters of Colonel Robert Gould Shaw and the 54th Massachussetts Infantry* (Athens, GA: University of Georgia Press, 1999), 52–55.
40. Watson Kirkconnell, *Victoria County, Ontario, Canada, Centennial History* (Lindsay, ON: Watchman-Warder, 1921), accessed October 10, 2015, http://www.canadiangenealogy.net/ontario/victoriacounty/conditions_of_life.htm.
41. David J. Bertuca, "The Fenian Raid and Battle of Ridgeway, June 1–3, 1866," accessed July 12, 2014, http://www.acsu.buffalo.edu/~dbertuca/155/FenianRaid.html.

Chapter 13: Steal Away Home

1. The business was conducted in person. The records for the dispute are fragmentary, suggesting that much of the back-and-forth was not committed to paper. Ben's name never again appears with Cecelia's in any direct transaction, and neither she nor her daughter seems to have had any contact with her two step-grandsons in Minnesota, even when in desperate straits. Both of those very successful men would have been in a position to help them financially. Nor do any of the pension records mention Lucia Holt Holmes, who outlived her husband.

    The Toronto tax assessment rolls for 1866 show Reuben Sanders as tenant of 29 Centre Street, renting from James Holmes, and William Hartup as Cecelia's tenant at 31 Centre Street, again with James Holmes as leasing agent. Both men had good trades: Sanders was a blacksmith and Hartup a carpenter. James Thomas Holmes disappears from view in about 1867, the only clue to what become of him the fact that his name no longer appears on any property records relating to Lot 7 on Centre Street after 1875, when he presumably died.
2. Nancy Disher Baird, "The Yellow Fever Plot," *Civil War Times Illustrated*, 13 (November 1974): 16–23.
3. Matthew Furrow, Interviews conducted by S. G. Howe, September 5, 1863, US Department of War, Letters Received by the Office of the Adjutant General, Main Series, 1861–70, microfilm reel 201, M619, frames 330–40, RG 94, National Archives and Records Administration [hereafter NARA], Washington, DC (unpublished transcription).
4. Scott Cummings and Michael Price, "Race Relations and Public Policy in Louisville: Historical Development of an Urban Underclass," *Journal of Black Studies* 27, no. 5 (May 1997): 615–16.
5. For Isabelle Churchill McCreary, see chapter 6, note 13. The US Census for 1870 lists a "Sarah Churchill, mulatto, age 55" in nearby Elizabethtown, Hardin County.
6. The classic works on this topic include E. Merton Coulter, *The Civil War and Readjustment in Kentucky* (Chapel Hill: University of North Carolina Press, 1926), 11ff, and Lowell Harrison,

The Civil War in Kentucky (Lexington: University of Kentucky Press, 1987). More recent works include Kent Masterton Brown, *The Civil War in Kentucky: Battle for the Bluegrass State* (New York: DaCapo, 2000).

7. Cummings and Price, "Race Relations," 617. See Anne E. Marshall, *Creating a Confederate Kentucky: The Lost Cause and Civil War Memory in a Border State* (Chapel Hill: University of North Carolina Press, 2004). David Blight's *Race and Reunion: The Civil War in American Memory* (Cambridge, MA: Belknap, 2001) is the most important recent analysis of the triumph of nostalgic traditionalist sentimentalizing of the Old South over the realities of Union victory and fact of Black emancipation.

8. James, *Life of Rev. Thomas James*, 16–22; Kleber, ed., *The Encyclopedia of Louisville*, xx.

9. For A. J. Ballard's slave-owning history, see chapter 8, note 28.

10. Julia C. Parke, "Locust Grove," in Kleber, *Encyclopedia of Louisville,* 524–25.

11. Jennings, *Louisville's First Families,* 63.

12. Will of John Clark, probated October 1, 1799, in James R. Bentley, ed., *Early Kentucky Settlers: The Records of Jefferson County, Kentucky* (Baltimore, MD: Genealogical Publishing, 1988), 230–31.

13. "Charles W. Thruston," *Memphis Daily Appeal*, December 2, 1865. His remarkably flowery obituary was reprinted from the Louisville paper.

14. A. J. Ballard's estate for tax purposes was presented on May 24 of that same year in the Louisville *Daily Courier* as greatly augmented from his previous listings. Thanks to his wife's large inheritance from her father (though it was completely tied up in a trust for herself and her children), Ballard's estate was now worth $137, 648. Apart from the fabulously wealthy James Guthrie—Fanny's cousin by marriage, a former federal politician and now president of the Louisville and Nashville Railroad—who was assessed at a staggering $618,608 the same year, there were only three other property-holders in Louisville's eastern district whose personal wealth exceeded Ballard's.

15. Will of Charles W. Thruston, Will Book 6, Jefferson County, Kentucky, 360–62. Fanny inherited a life interest in the farm her brother used to operate on the Salt River, as well as the property on which Charles W. Thruston lived in Louisville. In addition she received her father's "slaves, furniture, plate, pictures, books, carriages, harness, and horses." Interestingly, this was all for "her sole and separate use, freed from any claim thereto by her present or any future husband, with no power in him to alienate or encumber her interest therein or in any way to assign or anticipate by receipt, or sale, any of the rents, issues or profits thereof." It all went to her children in the event of her death. His other land outside Louisville was to be sold and the proceeds added to the estate. Finally, should Fanny die without issue, A.J. Ballard was to have use of half the estate during his lifetime; if she did have children, he would have an equal share with her issue. One of the three witnesses was Charles's old friend Judge Samuel Nicholas.

16. R. C. Ballard Thruston (Fanny's youngest son) reminisced about them in November 1929, in a handwritten note on a bill of sale dated November 1, 1846, for "Old Uncle Jack," age forty-five, who had previously belonged to J. B. Bland: "Jack became my grandfather's body servant. His wife's name was Susan and after the emancipation proclamation they continued to lived with and care for my grandfather until he died in November 1865, after which old 'Uncle Jack & Aunt Susan' were given a house and cared for by my parents until they died which was after I went to boarding school in 1872." See Thruston Papers, Filson Historical Society.

17. Louisville *Daily Courier*, November 1, 1866. Clearly the money was Fanny's. The first invoice, for $3,000, was issued to "Mrs. A. J. Ballard." It was dated April 28, 1866, "on account of works of her

house about to be built on Walnut Street" and signed by architect Henry Whitestone. The address was 241 East Walnut Street, Louisville. The bills for the construction date between April 1866 and August 1867; Andrew Jackson Ballard Papers, Filson Historical Society, Louisville, KY. Whitestone was also responsible for design of the new Galt House, Louisville's premier hotel, which was constructed in 1865 to replace an 1830s building on the waterfront that had been destroyed by fire. An advertisement in the Louisville *Daily Courier* of April 6, 1866, announces an auction of construction materials and equipment from the old Thruston home on Saturday, April 28. They range from an iron balcony to a "top buggy and harness," a cook range and a "No. 1 fresh cow and calf," plus "a lot of ice." The contents of each building are noted, including the main house; the "L to the house"; kitchen and washroom (laundry), both separate buildings, as was common in the South to avoid heating up the house in the summer months; and a carriage house and stable.

18. There is substantial correspondence regarding Mammoth Cave and other property matters in the Janin Family Collection, Huntington Library, San Marino, CA; the Blair-Janin Papers, Washington Historical Society, Washington, DC; Papers of the Blair Family, Library of Congress; and the Andrew Jackson Ballard Papers, Filson Historical Society.

19. Bland Ballard's appointment was made on October 16, 1861. Andrew Jackson Ballard was appointed Clerk of the US District Court on January 11, 1862. He would not resign the position until 1870.

20. Thomas B. Speed, *The History of the United States Courts in Kentucky: The Making of Modern Law* (Louisville, 1896), 1–8. A. J. Ballard's bench book and other documents relating to his work for federal courts survive in the National Archives and Records Administration facility in Atlanta, Georgia. His logbook shows a long series of legal cases where pardons were granted to Kentuckians who had fought for the Confederacy. Docket Books, Andrew Jackson Ballard, Records of District Courts of the United States, RG 21; Records of US District and Other Courts in Kentucky, 1790–1979, NARA [21.19 at http://www.archives.gov/research/guide-fed-records/groups/021.html].

21. Michael J. Rhyne, "'We Are Mobed and Beat': Regulator Violence against Free Black Households in Kentucky's Bluegrass Region, 1865–1867," *Ohio Valley History* 2, no. 1 (Spring 2002): 30–42.

22. For instance, see the Louisville *Journal*, August 15, 1867, for an account of charges brought before Commissioner A. J. Ballard against a man named Dan Connelly for "the murder of an old negro man" in Nelson County, and the Louisville *Journal* of March 29, 1868, on the murder of a Black man named Lewis Swan in Nelson County by Jack Hardy, John C. Owens and others, heard by Commissioner A. J. Ballard. In the same paper a notice appeared on August 17, 1868, of a case that Ballard heard involving the stabbing of a Black man named Robert Twyman, "with intent to kill" on the part of J. T. Wooten. It would not be until 1872 that Blacks could testify against whites in Kentucky courts. See Victor B. Howard, "The Black Testimony Controversy," *Journal of Negro History* 58, (1973): 140–65.

23. Kleber, *Encyclopedia of Louisville*, 356; Lowell H. Harrison, *A New History of Kentucky* (Lexington: University Press of Kentucky, 1997), 238.

24. Kleber, *Encyclopedia of Louisville*, 271. The hospital closed in 1868.

25. Jack Welch, "The Great Changeover," *Louisville Magazine*, March 2013, 30–37.

26. George H. Yater, *Two Hundred Years at the Falls of the Ohio: A History of Louisville and Jefferson County* (Louisville: Filson Club, 1987).

27. George C. Wright, *Racial Violence in Kentucky, 1865–1940: Lynchings, Mob Rule, and "Legal Lynchings"* (Baton Rouge: Louisiana State University Press, 1990), 21–22. It was not until 1871

that Kentucky courts moved to permit African American testimony against whites, taking the onus for such prosecutions off the US Federal Courts of Kentucky. However, by this time A. J. Ballard had resigned his position as clerk.

28. Records of the Field Offices for the State of Kentucky, Bureau of Refugees, Freedmen, and Abandoned Lands, 1865–72, M1904, 133 rolls, NARA; Records of the Education Division of the Bureau of Refugees, Freedmen, and Abandoned Lands, 1865–71, M803, 35 rolls, NARA.

29. Deposition of Cecelia J. Larrison, taken at Louisville, May 6, 1898, Case no. 631.101, Pension Bureau Files, NARA.

CHAPTER 14: INTO THE LION'S DEN

1. Chas. A. Roxborough et al. to Mr. President, President 1957, 1865, President & Executive Departments, Office of the Secretary of War, Record Group 107, NARA. Reverend Thomas James, formerly of Rochester, was one of the signatories.

2. Tax Assessment Rolls for the City of Toronto, Tax Records for Centre Street, 1866–82, City of Toronto Diffusion Material, D 318, Archives of Ontario. Cecelia continued leasing out her house through a series of agents, first Ben Alexander Holmes and then James Thomas Holmes; livery stable owner James Mink, who had witnessed Benjamin's will; then a man named John Leys; followed by her first husband's friend Benjamin Gross, whose son had gone off to Australia to seek his fortune; and finally an elderly Irishman named Robert Dodds, who resided around the corner on Osgoode Street. Her last agent was Francis G. Simpson.

3. Jonathan Clark (1750–1811) was a Revolutionary War veteran. One of C. W. Thruston's uncles, he married Sarah Hite in 1782 before immigrating to Kentucky.

4. In 1833 Abraham Hite (1799–1863) married Selena Cecelia Gray (1807–1871). They owned ten slaves, according to the slave schedules of the 1860 US census. Their home was at 102 West Broadway and, according to the 1860 census, their only daughter, Mary Irwin (Hite) Barrett, and her family lived with her parents. See *History of the Ohio Falls Cities and Their Counties*, vol. 1 (Cleveland, OH: L. A. Williams, 1882), 211. After Abraham Hite retired from business he served as secretary for the Franklin Insurance Company of Louisville until his death.

5. Deposition of Caroline Ellis, taken at Louisville May 3, 1898, Kentucky, Case no. 631.101, Pension Bureau Files, NARA.

6. Ibid. Caroline Ellis says Cecelia performed fine laundry and other services for Mrs. Clay, as well as for other residents of Galt House. Cecelia sometimes had so much work that she would send for Mrs. Ellis to assist her. See also Isabella Beeton, *The Book of Household Management* (London: S. O. Beeton, 1859–61). The 1880 US Census for Louisville shows Cecelia Larrison's occupation as "wash and iron." William is listed as a labourer and Mary (Mamie) went out daily to do domestic work.

7. "Louisville and Its Defense, 1864" (map), accessed Jan. 10, 2012, http://digital.library.louisville.edu/cdm/landingpage/collection/maps/.

8. Deposition of Caroline Ellis.

9. Susan Maria Jacob Clay was born in 1823 and died in 1905. The Jacob home was on the block bounded by 3rd and 4th Streets and Chestnut and Walnut. For details on the Clay family and the close relationship between Henry Clay and this favourite daughter-in-law, see Lindsey Apple, *The Family Legacy of Henry Clay: In the Shadow of a Kentucky Patriarch* (Lexington: University Press of Kentucky, 2011). See also John J. Jacob, *Kentucky: A History of the State*, 8th ed. (Jefferson County, KY: Perrin, Battle, Kniffin, 1888).

10. James Brown Clay (1817–1864) became a Democrat after his father's death and represented Kentucky in the US House of Representatives from 1857 to 1859. He served as US ambassador to Portugal and in 1861 attended the peace conference in Washington in a futile attempt to avert war. The younger Clays had found the poorly constructed Ashland impossible to repair and so tore it down to the foundations and rebuilt it. Sympathetic to the Southern cause, J. B. Clay was briefly detained during the Civil War as a suspected Confederate. He was subjected to ill treatment and his constitution never recovered. Eventually he was forced to leave the state because of his Confederate sympathies, travelling first to Cuba and then to Montreal, where he joined the Confederate contingent. He died of consumption (tuberculosis) in Montreal in 1864, with Susan at his side.

11. "Mrs. Larrison was living at Mrs. Clay's at 1st & Chestnut and I knew her husband at that time. Our wives occupied [the] same house for years & we were both home every night and Sunday afternoon." Deposition of Anthony Bland, taken at Louisville, KY, June 10, 1898, Case no. 631.101, Pension Bureau Files, NARA.

12. Robert Battey, "Extirpation of the Functionally Active Ovaries" [reprint from Gynecological Transactions 1 (1876): 4], in *The Biographical Encyclopædia of Kentucky of the Dead and Living Men of the Nineteenth Century*, vol. 1 (Cincinnati: J. M. Armstrong, 1878), 571–72.

13. In her Pension Board deposition, Cecelia says the family was living in this place at the time of the Chicago Fire, which was October 1871. Mamie was her only child destined to live to adulthood. Cecelia wrote of her losses in these years in her deposition of May 6, 1898: "Then, I got in a condition [and] I couldn't work as I was carrying a child and he got me a room on Main St; near Preston St. at Floyd & Preston. Dr. Leachman attended me in my 2nd. confinement, 28 years ago, last March. I was on Chestnut St; between Floyd & East St. 1870. Both these children died. One lived 5 years & 1 four months. I have no other children by Larrison that lived." Case no. 631.101, Pension Bureau File, NARA.

14. For Abby Ballard's health issues see Asher, *Fanny and Cecelia*, 155–56. The politics of the time were in such disarray that Andrew Jackson Ballard renewed his interest in the future of the Republican Party. As a former slaveholding state, Kentucky was unusual in that the Republican Party retained its strength following the Civil War. The *Louisville Commercial* was founded in 1869; see Kleber, *Encyclopedia of Louisville*, 655.

15. Darrel E. Bigham, *On Jordan's Banks: Emancipation and Its Aftermath in the Ohio River Valley* (Lexington: University Press of Kentucky, 2005), 195.

16. "Freedmen's Bureau," Kleber, ed., *The Kentucky Encyclopedia*, 356–57; E. Merton Coulter, *The Civil War and Reconstruction in Kentucky* (Chapel Hill: University of North Carolina Press, 1926); Harrison, *New History of Kentucky*, 237–39.

17. George C. Wright, *Life Behind a Veil: Blacks in Louisville, Kentucky, 1865–1930* (Baton Rouge: Louisiana State University Press, 1985), 37–38.

18. "The next place Wm. worked was to drive carriage for Mrs. Wilder. She was the wife of druggist Wilder. Then, he worked at the Welland [sic] Hotel, as a waiter a long time and Horse Hack for the Louisville Transfer Co. I think that was the last place he worked here." There was no Welland Hotel, but the Willard Hotel was at the southeast corner of Jefferson Street at Center. Deposition of Minor Lewis, taken at Louisville, June 19, 1898, Case no. 631.101, Pension Bureau Files, NARA.

19. Louisville *Courier-Journal*, November 27, 1874.

20. "Louisville Transfer Company's Packet Express," Louisville *Courier-Journal,* December 23, 1868.

21. Green Street was renamed Liberty Street during the First World War.

22. Herbert G. Gutman, "Trouble on the Railroads in 1873–1874: Prelude to the 1877 Crisis?," *Labour History,* 2, no. 2 (1961): 215–235.

23. They were passengers on the steamship *Oceanic,* in the company of Fanny's uncle John Churchill, Mrs. Meriwether Lewis Clark Sr. and her stepson, M. Lewis Clark Jr. Also on board was the *Courier-Journal* publisher, Henry Watterson, who though once an avowed Confederate had had a change of heart after the Civil War. A. J. Ballard and he would have had much to discuss during the voyage, for Fanny's husband had supported the Whigs, was a staunch Union man, and was now active in the Republican Party. See Nashville *Union and Advertiser,* May 11, 1873. The *American Register* of July 5, 1873, notes the arrival in Paris of the Ballard and Churchill parties, as mentioned in the Louisville *Courier-Journal,* July 24, 1873. M. Lewis Clark Jr. studied European horseracing and a few years later founded Churchill Downs and the Kentucky Derby.

24. The family spent part of the next season recovering at Grayson Springs, near Leitchfield, KY; see Louisville *Courier-Journal,* July 16, 1874.

25. No official record of Mary Reynolds' death has been found. However, Fanny youngest son, Rogers, wrote a document detailing his mother's relationship with her former maid, dated at Louisville on June 5, 1899. He recounts an anecdote regarding the visit of Adam Reynolds to the house in 1877, saying that he had missed seeing his former wife by only three years.

26. Louisville *Courier-Journal,* May 11, 1907.

27. Henry Watterson of the Louisville *Courier-Journal* voiced the attitudes that many Louisvillians held about African Americans. Marjorie M. Norris, "An Early Instance of Non-Violence: The Louisville Demonstrations of 1870–1871," *Journal of Southern History* 32 (November 1966): 487–504.

28. Lucas, ch. 8; Wright, *Life Behind a Veil,* especially pt. 1, "The Struggle for Freedom and Civil Rights"; George C. Wright, "William Henry Steward: Moderate Approach to Black Leadership," in Leon F. Litwack and August Meier, *Black Leaders of the Nineteenth Century* (Urbana: University of Illinois Press, 1991): 275–90; Kleber, *Encyclopedia of Louisville,* 190; Marcia Fleming, "Freedom's Main Line," in Teaching Tolerance: A Project of the Southern Poverty Law Centre, Montgomery, AL, accessed January 22, 2014, http://www.tolerance.org/article/freedom-s-main-line. See also Kleber, *Encyclopedia of Louisville,* 798. It would not be until 1899 that Cecelia and her family could access a hospital. The Red Cross Hospital was founded by a group of African American physicians and supported by donations almost exclusively from the city's Black community.

29. "Report to Mayor Jacob by Basil W. Duke, Commander in Chief of the City Forces, July 31, 1877," Louisville City Records, Metro Archives, Louisville, KY; C. Vann Woodward, *The Origins of the New South, 1877–1913* (Baton Rouge: Louisiana State University Press, 1971), 7.

30. Joseph A. Dacus, *Annals of the Great Strikes in the United States* (Chicago: L. T. Palmer, 1877), 430; Stephen Hoffman, "Looking North: A Mid-South Perspective on the Great Strike," in *The Great Strikes of 1877,* ed. David Omar Stowell (Urbana and Chicago: University of Illinois Press, 2008): 105–35.

31. The 1879 city directory reads "Larrison, William H. (col'd), coachman" and his address "rear 460 3d, nr Kentucky." By the time of the next directory, no occupation is given, and the address is even more bluntly described as follows: "r. al. betw. Breckinridge and Kentucky, w. of 3rd"

(between 3rd and 4th Streets). The US Census, 1880, Louisville, Jefferson County, KY, shows: "Larison, W. H.," Black, age thirty-nine, with occupation listed as "labor." His wife, "Larison, Leselia," is listed as mulatto, age thirty-nine, and for her work "Wash & Iron." Their daughter, Mary, is listed as age sixteen with no occupation. Unfortunately, the right edge of the form is damaged and birthplace and other information are not available.

32. Wright, *Life Behind a Veil*, 107.
33. It was in 1880 that Minor Lewis first came to know Larrison's wife, through working the steamboats, as per his deposition. The reference, however, is inaccurate in several ways, for it says he met the family while they were living in Cincinnati (Cecelia's own deposition states clearly that the only time she lived away from Louisville was while working for Miss Morton). He also says that William fought with a Michigan rather than a New York regiment. Deposition of Minor Lewis, Case no. 631.101, Pension Bureau Files, NARA.
34. "He was in the habit of going & coming, stay a week or a month in the country and on steamboats after he quit the army." Depositions of Sophia Alexander, taken at Louisville, June 11, 1898, and Anthony Bland, taken at Louisville, Kentucky, June 10, 1898, Case no. 631.101, Pension Bureau Files, NARA.
35. This is discussed at some length in Wright, *Racial Violence in Kentucky*, introduction, ch. 2 and 5.

Chapter 15: In the Bosom of Abraham

1. "Well Met," Louisville *Courier-Journal*, December 11, 1879, cited in Robert Bruce Symon Jr., "Child of the North: Louisville's Transition to a Southern City, 1879–1885" (master's thesis, University of Louisville, 2005), University of Louisville Electronic Theses and Dissertations, paper 1412, http://dx.doi.org/10.18297/etd/1412, 74.
2. Release of Dower from Cecelia Jane Larrison, Widow, to Francis Simpson, Toronto, Deed 19808 B, reel City 01-293, City of Toronto Deeds, Land Registry Office, Archives of Ontario. The release was dated at Louisville, June 6, 1876, and completed on July 7 of the same year.
3. County of York Land Registry Office, Abstract Index for Plan 147, east side, Centre Street, Toronto, GSU 197293, RG 61–64, Archives of Ontario. The sale of the property took place on January 12, 1876, and was registered under instrument no. 19122 B on April 17, 1876. While there is no record of James Thomas Holmes's death, the only signature for the sale is that of Benjamin A. Holmes, along with Cecelia's release of dower. Benjamin immediately paid off the mortgage that was still owing on both properties.
4. Patricia Marks, *Sarah Bernhardt's First American Theatrical Tour, 1880–1881* (Jefferson, NC: McFarland, 2003), 126.
5. Deposition of Mary Dickenson, taken at Louisville, June 11, 1898, Case no. 631.101, Pension Bureau Files, NARA.
6. Deposition of Mamie Holmes, taken at Louisville, May 6, 1898, Case no. 631.101, Pension Bureau Files, NARA.
7. Scott Cummings and Michael Price, "Race Relations and Public Policy in Louisville: Historical Development of an Urban Underclass," *Journal of Black Studies* 27, no. 5 (May 1997), 618.
8. "Louisville, Kentucky," *Frank Leslie's Popular Monthly* 20, no. 5 (November 1885): 513–33; Symon, "Child of the North," 30–35.
9. "The Louisville Industrial Exhibition of 1872," *The Telegrapher*, June 5, 1873; Yater, *Two Hundred Years*, 102.

10. Yater, *Two Hundred Years*, 112–13. Meriwether Lewis Clark Jr. (1846–1899) was a grandson of William Clark, who was Charles Thruston's uncle on his mother's side, and Abigail Prather Churchill, daughter of Samuel and Abigail Oldham Churchill, and thus Mary Eliza Churchill Thruston's sister.

11. Consolidated Lists of Civil War Draft Registration Records, Provost Marshal General's Bureau, Consolidated Enrollment Lists, 1863–65, Record Group 110 (Civil War Union Draft Records); ARC identifier 4213514, vol. 4 of 10. See also Deposition of Alexander L. Reels, taken at Louisville, KY, 1898, Case no. 631.101, Pension Bureau Files, NARA. Alexander Reels was born in Iberville parish, Louisiana, in about 1838. At the age of twenty-six he was listed as a farmer living on America Street in Baton Rouge when he was conscripted into the Union Army. He served in Company A of the 3rd Louisiana Infantry (Colored) Regiment from 1863 through to the end of the conflict.

12. The US Census for 1880 shows Eulalie Reels as eighteen years old and her brother, James A. Reels, as sixteen. Both were attending school. This is puzzling, as the 1870 census shows three children: Mary A. Reels, age nine, who would be the same age as Eulalie in 1880, and twins, Leticia and James, who were six. Leticia is nowhere else to be found and is presumed to have died, or perhaps she accompanied her mother to her new life in St. Louis. Eulalie simply disappears from the record at this point. It's possible she married and moved west, or else went to St. Louis to join her mother.

13. Deposition of Alexander Reels.

14. This today is Muhammad Ali Boulevard.

15. US Census, 1880, Louisville, Jefferson County, KY. The census page was recorded on June 11, 1880. He was born in 1838, so he was likely at least forty-two. The 1870 US census for East Baton Rouge, Louisiana, records Alexander Reels, a literate mulatto cook aged thirty-two, and his wife, Elizabeth, thirty-one, also mulatto and keeping house; she is listed as illiterate. They had three children, all of whom were in school (see note 12, above). Alexander's wife was the former Elizabeth Wonn, whom he married in East Baton Rouge on July 9, 1866. Thousands of former slaves were married after the war under the Freedmen's Bureau's auspices in order to formalize existing relationships; the date of their marriage and the ages of the children suggest that the Reelses' marriage was of this nature.

16. Elizabeth D. Leonard, *Men of Color to Arms! Black Soldiers, Indian Wars, and the Quest for Equality* (New York: W. W. Norton, 2010), 199–202.

17. The wife of Henry Fitzbutler (1837–1901), Sarah McCurdy Fitzbutler (1848–1923), became a doctor herself after bringing up their family, graduating in 1892. Fitzbutler's newspaper lasted from 1879 to 1904. See Lucas, *History of Blacks in Kentucky*, 317–20; and Gerald L. Smith, Karen Cotton McDaniel and John A. Hardin, eds., *The Kentucky African American Encyclopedia* (Lexington: University of Kentucky Press, 2015), 182–83.

18. Darrel E. Bigham, *On Jordan's Banks: Emancipation and Its Aftermath in the Ohio River Valley* (Lexington: University Press of Kentucky, 2005), 31. Gibson was a cashier with the Freedmen's Bureau Bank starting in 1868, then briefly a mail agent for the L&N Railroad, which caused friction with white railroad employees. He later received a civil service position in the US Treasury Department from President Ulysses S. Grant. See Smith, McDaniel and Hardin, *Kentucky African American Encyclopedia*, 203–4. Gibson authored the important *Historical Sketch of the Progress of the Colored Race, in Louisville, Ky* (Louisville: Bradley & Gilbert, 1897) and *History of the United Brothers of Friendship and Sisters of the Mysterious Ten: in two parts; a Negro*

Order; Organized August 1, 1861, in the City of Louisville, Ky (Louisville: Bradley & Gilbert, 1897), which includes his autobiography.

19. Smith, McDaniel and Hardin, *Kentucky African American Encyclopedia*, 119.

20. Wright, *Life Behind a Veil*, 181–82. Wright makes the point that after Reconstruction Blacks were elected to positions on Baltimore City Council; in Cincinnati and Cleveland they were elected to the state legislature through the turn of the twentieth century; and even Nashville politicians wooed the Black vote and saw to it there were positions for them on the police and fire services. None of this happened in Louisville.

21. Louisville *Courier-Journal*, April 29, 1884. Reels was elected as an alternative delegate to the state Republican convention, representing Louisville's Sixth Ward, in April 1884. The Sixth Ward lay between 1st and 3rd Streets and ran from the river in the north to the city limits in the south. He was living and operating a second-hand store at 100 West Green, in the heart of the downtown district of the ward, just three blocks from the Ballard home at Floyd and Walnut. Also at the meeting were "well known Republicans" from among the Black community such as prosperous barber Austin Hubbard and E. W. Marshall, who was a leader in the United Brothers of Friendship.

22. Wright, *Life Behind a Veil*, 181.

23. Her father was Theodore Harris, who was a very important banker in Louisville. Harris was from an old New England family that had immigrated to Nova Scotia in the wake of the Acadian expulsions, just before the outbreak of the Revolutionary War. He moved to Louisville in his youth and married into a prominent local family.

24. *New York Times*, May 7, 1884.

25. The auction of his assets was announced in the Louisville *Courier-Journal* on November 11, 1884, the same day that Buffalo Bill's Wild West Show gave its last Louisville performance at the city's Baseball Park. Despite his efforts to recoup his lost fortunes, Andrew Jackson Ballard would spend the rest of his life living off his wife.

26. *Mercantile Bank of New York v. Ballard's Assignees*, 83 Kentucky 48L, September 1885, in "Cases of the Court of Appeals in Kentucky," *American State Reports Containing the Cases of General Value and Authority . . . Decided in the Courts of Last Resorts in Several States,* ed. A. C. Freemen et al., vol. 4 (San Francisco: Bancroft-Whitney, 1889), 160–67.

27. The Ballard brothers had an excellent reputation. When Charles tried to resign as president of the Louisville Board of Trade at the first sign of trouble, the members voted unanimously to keep him in the chair. And the confidence of Louisville's business community in the Ballard brothers was not misplaced: they paid off every cent owing to the creditors and started over. The firm, reputed to be the largest flour-milling operation in the world, was very progressive in respect to labour relations. It began one of America's first profit-sharing schemes when it reorganized in 1889.

28. Rogers Clark Ballard Thruston, Thruston Record Book, Filson Historical Society, Louisville, KY, 52. The official cause was acute dysentery. According to his youngest son, A. J. Ballard had always inclined to be heavy, and "in his efforts to reduce his flesh he allowed an attack of diarrhea to run too long and it resulted in his death."

29. "Mrs. Ballard has been visiting in North Carolina, but arrived in the city last night"; "Andrew Jackson Ballard: Death Yesterday of a Prominent Citizen in his Sixty-Ninth Year," Louisville *Courier-Journal*, August 18, 1885.

30. Timothy J. Mullin, "The du Ponts in Kentucky: Louisville's Central Park, the Southern Exposition, and an Entrepreneurial Spirit," DLSC Faculty Publications, Western Kentucky University, paper 18, September 21, 2009, accessed Dec. 13, 2013, http://digitalcommons.wku.

edu/dlsc_fac_pub/18. The du Pont property at Central Park was purchased by the City of Louisville in 1904 and turned into a public recreational space. The house and remaining Southern Exposition buildings were torn down and the park layout redesigned, in part by Frederick Law Olmsted; ibid., 29.

31. The Louisville *Courier-Journal* mentions their prize peaches in the August 19, 1883, issue.

32. Symon, "Child of the North," 83.

33. "The Louisville Exposition," *Washington Post*, June 8, 1883, quoted in ibid., 84.

34. Kleber, *Encyclopedia of Louisville*, 674–75.

35. Louisville *Courier-Journal*, March 5, 1885.

36. Nina Mjagkij, ed., *Organizing Black America: An Encyclopedia of African American Associations* (New York: Garland, 2001) i.e., the Afro-American League: 315–16.

37. See, for instance, "The 38th Annual Exhibition of the Colored A. & M. [Agricultural and Mechanical] Fair Association, Lexington, Kentucky, September 10–14, 1907," University of Kentucky Libraries, Special Collections Research Center; "African American Baseball," in Kleber, *Encyclopedia of Louisville*, 9–11.

38. James Robert Saunders and Monica Renae Saunders, *Black Winning Jockeys in the Kentucky Derby* (Jefferson, NC: McFarland, 2003), 103–6.

39. Deposition of Anthony Bland, Case no. 631.101, Pension Board Files, NARA. Anthony Bland, a hack driver and chimneysweep, had known the Larrisons ever since they moved from Rochester to Louisville in 1865. Of William, Bland reported: "He was in the habit of going & coming, stay a week or a month in the country and on steamboats after he quit the army and finally he went away and never came back. He was a man [who] thought a great deal of his children. Had a little boy that died that he thought a heap of. No, he had no children living at the time he last left here. . . . I only recollect I was well acquainted with his wife. She and my 1st. wife were intimate friends, lived in adjoining rooms for years after marriage. Mrs. Larrison done up my wedding shirt when I married my 1st. wife in 1867 or 1868."

40. The date of his disappearance is a bit murky. In her deposition to the Pension Bureau in May 1898, Cecelia says it was fifteen or sixteen years earlier that he disappeared. Her grasp of the passage of time was always a bit shaky, and there are numerous discrepancies in her accounts. Alexander Reels seemed uncertain, too, made his own deposition in June 1898: "This claimant is my mother in law. I got acquainted with her about 19 years ago, at which time she lived on 3rd. St. bet [between] Beckinridge & Ky[?] Sts. Her husband, Wm. Larrison was living with her at that time. He was a coachman on Broadway, at the time, for some merchant. I married his step daughter in 1888. He had been gone from here some time before that. Accordingly to my prazment [appraisement], it is about between 14 and 15 years since he left here." Deposition of Alexander L. Reels, taken at Louisville, KY, 1898, Case no. 631.101, Pension Bureau Files, NARA.

41. "A heap of times a man gets knocked overboard from a boat or, falls over asleep and nobody knows his home or, what become of him and I think he must be dead." Deposition of Minor Lewis, Case no. 631.101, Pension Bureau Files, NARA.

CHAPTER 16: NOBODY KNOWS THE TROUBLE I'VE SEEN

1. Booker T. Washington, *Up From Slavery: An Autobiography* (Garden City, NY: Doubleday, 1901), 39.

2. The wedding had taken place on the seventeenth of that month. This church was heir to the First African Baptist Church, which had been founded in 1829 and operated under significantly less white supervision than other Black churches. By 1848 it was located on 5th south of Walnut Street. Smith, *Kentucky African American Encyclopedia*, 175.

3. He was fifty and his bride thirty-four.

4. The Reels store is clearly visible in "Green Street (now Liberty Street), at Third Street, Louisville, Kentucky, 1895," image no. ULPA P_00599, R. G. Potter Collection, University of Louisville, accessed January 15, 2013, http://digital.library.louisville.edu/cdm/landingpage/collection/potter/.

5. *Caron's Louisville Directory* (Louisville: Charles K. Caron, 1885), 627.

6. Jews were more sympathetic than other immigrants to the Blacks' conditions in Kentucky and in later years would provide substantial support in the struggle for African American civil rights. Louisville had had a small Jewish community since the time of its founding, but in the 1880s the city experienced a large influx, for the same reason that Toronto's St. John's Ward did. The anti-Jewish riots and pogroms that followed the assassination of Tsar Alexander II destroyed communities across Ukraine, Poland and the rest of the eastern part of Europe and sent thousands fleeing across the Atlantic to North America. US Census, 1880, Louisville, Kentucky, 1st Ward, taken June 1, 1880; Amy Shevitz, *Jewish Communities on the Ohio River: A History* (Lexington: University Press of Kentucky, 2007), 135–36.

7. Loren Schweninger, "Prosperous Blacks in the South, 1790–1880," *American Historical Review* 95 (February 1990): 50. Of the Black elite on the post–Civil War border he writes: "In urban areas, those who had previously carved out a niche in the local economies as artisans, draymen, livery operators, stewards, and barbers, or who had managed small businesses, were often able to expand their operations." Bigham says there were fifty-nine clergymen, eight lawyers, thirteen physicians, and more than a hundred teachers. That was more attorneys of colour than in the entire state of Georgia. Darrel E. Bigham, *On Jordan's Banks: Emancipation and Its Aftermath in the Ohio River Valley* (Lexington: University Press of Kentucky, 2005), 212. Because of de facto segregation, none of the doctors had hospital privileges.

8. George C. Wright, "The NAACP and Residential Segregation in Louisville, Kentucky, 1914–1917," *Register of the Kentucky Historical Society* 78, no. 1 (Winter 1980): 39–54.

9. Alexander Walters, *My Life and Work* (New York, 1917), 40.

10. G. F. Richings, *Evidences of Progress among Colored People* (Philadelphia: G. S. Ferguson, 1902), 303.

11. Bigham, *On Jordan's Bank*, 212ff.

12. This is reflected in the volume *Men of Mark: Eminent, Progressive, Rising*, published by minister and intellectual William J. Simmons. See also Mjagkij, *Organizing Black America*, for an overview of the incredibly active organizing efforts in these years, including the American Negro Baptist Convention, founded by Simmons and others in Louisville in 1888.

13. W. H. Gibson, *Historical Sketch of the Progress of the Colored Race, in Louisville, Ky* (Louisville: Bradley & Gilbert, 1897), 25–32.

14. Wright, *Life Behind a Veil*, 136; David Delaney, *Race, Place, and the Law, 1836–1948* (Austin: University of Texas Press, 2010), 110. Ballard left Hathaway a legacy of $100; after his employer's death he became the mayor's driver.

15. Grant from C. J. Larrison to Francis Simpson, Toronto, Land Registry Office, City of Toronto Deeds, Deed 1694 E, reel City 02-128, Archives of Ontario.

16. They were using the surname of their stepfather by this time, but they signed as Emma and Rebecca Holmes.

17. "Grant from Emma Holmes and Rebecca Holmes of Rochester NY, only children of James Thomas Holmes, deceased, formerly of the City of Toronto to Frank Simpson, Toronto," Land Registry Office, City of Toronto Deeds, Deed 6679 O, reel City 05-13, Archives of Ontario. The Minnesota branch of the family did not in fact relinquish their rights to the land until October 20, 1896, after Ben Alexander Holmes's death. Lucia, Walter, Eugene P. and Marie E. Holmes of Minnesota granted their rights to the lot on Centre Street in a deed registered on October 20, 1896; Toronto Land Registry Diffusion Materials, Archives of Ontario. (Marie was Eugene's wife.)

18. Roslyn Tereborg-Penn, "African American Women's Networks in the Anti-lynching Campaign," in *Gender, Class, Race, and Reform in the Progressive Era,* ed. Noralee Frankel and Nancy S. Dye (Lexington: University of Kentucky Press, 2015): 148–62; Wright, *Life Behind a Veil,* 152–53. The Louisville Women's Improvement Club, the Eckstein Daisy Club and a host of female societies based in the city's Black churches took on national significance with the 1895 Atlanta Congress of Colored Women; Karen Cotton McDaniel, "Kentucky Association of Colored Women's Clubs," in Smith, McDaniel and Hardin, *Kentucky African American Encyclopedia,* 299.

19. "I have known Celia [Cecelia] Larrison all of 20 years. I can't tell you nothing about her husband for I never saw him, but she had on her band. She belonged [to the] same society with me till [until] she got infinancial." Deposition of Caroline Ellis, taken at Louisville on May 3, 1898, Case no. 631.101, Pension Bureau Files, NARA.

20. Anne S. Butler, "Black Fraternal and Benevolent Societies in Nineteenth-Century America," in *African American Fraternities and Sororities: The Legacy and the Vision,* 2nd ed., ed. Tamara L. Brown, Gregory S. Parks and Clarenda M. Phillips (Lexington: University of Kentucky Press, 2012): 67–94. By 1892 the United Brothers of Friendship and the Sisters of the Mysterious Ten boasted more than 200,000 members "from the lake to the gulf," mainly in the western and southwestern states.

21. Wright, *Life Behind a Veil,* 131–35.

22. Gibson, *Historical Sketch,* 42–43. Their members had official duties, titles, ever more elaborate regalia and—most important for men and women frustrated by the restrictions on their ambitions, entrepreneurial capacities and intelligence by the dominant white society—an opportunity to advance through the ranks. These organizations mirrored the ethnic heritage of their membership, for secret societies had a long history on the African continent, and at least some of the enslaved men and women transported to the Americas must have brought these traditions with them; W. E. B. Du Bois and anthropologist Melvill J. Herskowitz, quoted in Joe William Trotter, "African American Fraternal Organizations in American History: An Introduction," *Social Science History* 28, no. 3 (Fall 2004): 359. See also Melville J. Herskovits, *The Myth of the Negro Past* (1941; reprint, Boston: Beacon Press, 1968), 161; Betty M. Kuyk, "The African Derivation of Black Fraternal Orders in the United States," *Comparative Studies in Society and History* 25 (October 1983): 559–92.

23. Bigham, *On Jordan's Banks,* 262–64.

24. Kleber, *Encyclopedia of Louisville,* 212, 514.

25. The classic works on this topic are C. Van Woodward, *Origins of the New South* (Baton Rouge: Louisiana State University Press, 1951) and *The Strange Career of Jim Crow* (New York: Oxford University Press, 1955). The "Woodward thesis" maintains that segregation evolved after the failure of Reconstruction, while Woodward's principal critic argued that it started immediately after the Civil War. See Howard N. Rabinowitz, "More Than the Woodward Thesis: Assessing the Strange

Career of Jim Crow," *Journal of American History* 75, no. 3 (December 1988), 842–44, and his important volume on postwar Southern cities, *Race Relations in the Urban South, 1865–1890* (New York: Oxford University Press, 1978).

26. Wright, *Life Behind a Veil*, 3–4.

27. Nettie Hance Oliver, "The 1890 Louisville Cyclone," *The Filson Newsmagazine* 5, no. 2, accessed August 28, 2016, http://www.filsonhistorical.org/archive/news_v5n2_cyclone.html; E. Klauber, *Louisville after the Cyclone* (Louisville: E. Klauber, 1890); Keven McQueen, *The Great Louisville Tornado of 1890* (Charleston, NC: Arcadia History Press, 2010).

28. Deposition of Caroline Ellis, Case no. 631.101, Pension Bureau Files, NARA.

29. She is listed separately at the 417 Floyd Street address of Alexander Reels's shop in *Caron's Lousiville Directory for 1893*, 664.

30. Michael Veach, "Grand Army of the Republic at the Filson," *Filson Newsmagazine* 2, no. 3, accessed August 3, 2016, http://www.filsonhistorical.org/archive/news_v2n3_gar.html. Ironically, from Cecelia's point of view, the commanding officer of the Louisville Legion was Colonel John B. Castleman, whose father, David Castleman, in 1837 had chased his slave Solomon Moseby all the way to Niagara, sparking a melee in front of the county jail that saw the death of two men. David Murray, "Hands Across the Border: The Abortive Extradition of Solomon Moseby," *Canadian Review of American Studies* 30 no. 2 (2000): 187–209.

31. Deposition of Caroline Ellis.

32. Particular favourites were her two Churchill aunts who were closest to her in age. Julia ("Puss") Churchill Blackburn was the widow of former governor Luke Pryor Blackburn and had lived in Toronto during the Civil War; she and her widowed sister Emily Ann Churchill Zane lived together in Louisville towards the end of their lives. Emily and Hampden Zane's daughter had married G. R. R. Cockburn, who was president of Upper Canada College in Toronto and then a member of Parliament. Their daughter, Emily St. Aubert Cockburn, became the wife of Thomas Tait, who was knighted after running the Australian railways. The Taits returned to Canada when he became vice-president of the Canadian National Railroad. Their summer home in St. Andrews-by-the-Sea, New Brunswick, is now the Huntsman Marine Sciences Centre. See, for instance, "GRR Cockburn to See Mrs. Zane at Louisville," *Cincinnati Enquirer*, November 6, 1904. Emily's brother, Hampden Zane Churchill Cockburn, one of only five Canadians to win the Victoria Cross in the Boer War, visited his grandmother in Louisville; see for example, Louisville *Courier-Journal*, May 13, 1888, and July 12, 1889.

33. "In Georgia," Louisville *Courier-Journal*, April 7, 1893; "Mrs. Ballard's Funeral," Louisville *Courier-Journal*, June 7, 1896.

34. Will of Fanny Thruston Ballard, RCB Thruston Papers, Filson Historical Society, Louisville, KY. The will, without the codicil to Cecelia, is printed in full in "Mrs. Ballard's Will," Louisville *Courier-Journal*, June 11, 1896. The quotation comes from Asher, *Fanny and Cecelia*, 161; he notes that Cecelia's letter of thanks for the funds included both condolences for the Ballards' loss and a mention that she had not received the promised shawl.

35. "The Pension Office," *Barton County Democrat* (Grand Bend, KS), May 22, 1890. The article attacks Raum for running an agency that collected fees for representing would-be pensioners to the Bureau, of which his father, Green Berry Raum, was commissioner. Similar articles appeared in Missouri, Indiana, Iowa and other newspapers, and the scandal went on for months.

36. Deposition of Cecelia J. Larrison, Case no. 631.101, Pension Bureau Files, NARA; also testimonies of Caroline Ellis, Minor Lewis and Sophia Alexander, cited elsewhere.

37. Deposition of Sophia Alexander, taken at Louisville, June 11, 1898, Case no. 631.101, Pension Bureau Files, NARA.

38. Deposition A, Case of Cecelia J. Larrison, Case no. 631.101, widow of Wm. H. Larrison, H–14 NY Art. re: Benjamin Pollard Holmes: Statutory Declaration of Francis Griffin Simpson, Death of client's first husband [sent via] John Rawn [Raum], Solicitor, Washington, DC.

39. Mamie and her mother were both inclined to shave years off their ages when questioned, and this time she gave her age as thirty-nine. She had been born in Toronto in 1854, so in 1898 she was actually forty-four. Mamie had been five when she and her mother crossed Lake Ontario to live in Rochester, and eight years old when Cecelia and William were married. She must have had clear memories of travelling with the 14th New York Heavy Artillery to Staten Island, life in the army camp at Fort Richmond, and then moving with the troops as far as Washington when her mother was in service with the Rochester-born wife of her husband's commanding officer. Perhaps she felt it would muddy the waters to speak of Benjamin Pollard Holmes, the man she thought of as her real father, whose painful death in the little house on Centre Street so marred her childhood memories.

40. This is suggested by Brad Asher and accounts for what he calls, in a lovely turn of phrase, Rogers's rather "grumpy paternalism" in dealing with his mother's former lady's maid; Asher, *Fanny and Cecelia*, 177.

41. This is discussed in Asher, *Fanny and Cecelia*, 14. He is quoting Rogers C. B. Thruston's 1899 account of Cecelia's relationship with his mother. Several states, including Kentucky, Virginia and Missouri, had laws that levelled heavy penalties against abolitionists who "enticed" slaves to run away. See, for instance, a Marietta, Ohio, abolitionist named David Putnam Jr., who was prosecuted by a Virginia slaveholder in 1847 on such a charge: *Henderson v. Putnam*, US Circuit Court, District of Ohio, June 25, 1849, accessed June 4, 2016, http://henryburke1010.tripod.com/id52.html. Free Blacks were particularly suspect. The *Liberator* of November 19, 1858, reported the conviction and sale into slavery of three men accused of enticing slaves to escape. Kentucky's laws were very specific and had different penalties for free African Americans and for white abolitionists suspected of enticing slaves; Richard Henry Stanton, *The Revised Statutes of Kentucky*, vol. 2 (Cincinnati: Clark, 1858): 371–76.

42. This was not in fact the house in which she had lived with his family while still enslaved. The old Thruston house was demolished after Charles W. Thruston's death to make way for the beautiful mansion designed by Henry Whitestone, which was completed on the same site in 1867.

43. Rogers Clark Ballard Thruston, June 5, 1899, Ballard Family Papers, Filson Historical Society, Louisville, KY.

44. William Henry Slingerland, *Child Welfare Work in Louisville: A Study of Conditions, Agencies and Institutions* (Louisville, KY: Welfare League, 1919), 70–72. The house was used through the 1920s as the Detention Home. It included "accommodations for white and coloured children, both dependent and delinquent," until responsible relatives could be located or the courts could make other accommodation for their care. The white children were kept in a separate building from the "coloured children," who may have occupied Charles W. Thruston's old "office" where he lived out the last part of his life. Both structures, particularly in regard to bathing facilities, were considered outmoded and woefully inadequate for the number of children who needed to use them.

45. Cecelia J. Larrison to Senator William Lindsay, September 22, 1899, Deposition A, Case no. 631.101, Pension Bureau Files, NARA. Drafted by an attorney, the letter is typewritten but signed in Cecelia's good hand "Cecelia J. Larrison." Born in Virginia, Lindsay had immigrated

to Hickman County, Kentucky, as a young man and made an honourable career for himself, first in legal practice, then as a noted jurist and finally as a politician.

46. Deposition of Charles A. Van Horne, taken at Binghamton, New York, September 22, 1899, Case no. 631.101, Pension Bureau Files, NARA.

47. This explains the variety of addresses given for Cecelia J. Larrison in Louisville street directories in the 1890s. Her legal correspondence, however, is addressed from the Reels home. Once a baby was past infancy her services were no longer needed and she would move on to another employer.

48. Rogers Clark Ballard Thruston, June 5, 1899, Ballard Family Papers, Filson Historical Society.

49. Cecelia Jane Larrison to R. C. B. Thruston, March 31, 1898, RCB Thruston Papers, Filson Historical Society.

50. Rogers Clark Ballard Thruston Account Book, February 24, 1887–April 18, 1898, Ballard Family Papers, Filson Historical Society, 345.

51. The bells were originally intended as a memorial only to Fanny. A. J. Ballard is not mentioned in the *Courier-Journal* article of February 11, 1898, announcing that "Mr. Charles T. Ballard and his brothers S. Thruston Ballard, and Rogers Ballard Thruston have ordered a set of bells from the Meneely Bell Company, of Troy N.Y., to be placed in Christ Church Cathedral, which will constitute what is known as the Westminster Peel. The peel [sic] is to be given in memory of their mother, Mrs. Fanny Thruston Ballard." Perhaps the sons disagreed about memorializing their father along with their mother, given his dissipated habits and very short adherence to the church. Too, they may have feared scandal if they left him out so very publicly. At the service a Communion cruet was also dedicated "by Mr. and Mrs. Samuel T. Ballard in memory of their child."

52. Mortuary Record for third week, ending September 21, 1899, Jefferson County Courthouse, 277.

53. Wright, *Life Behind a Veil*, 95.

54. Deposition of Charley Cottrell, taken at Louisville, June 19, 1898, Case no. 631.101, Pension Bureau Files, NARA.

55. Ralph A. Rossum and G. Alan Tarr, *American Constitutional Law*, vol. 2, *The Bill of Rights and Subsequent Amendments*, 10th ed. (Boulder, CO: Westview, 2017), 530.

Chapter 17: I'll Fly Away

1. Sojourner Truth, and Olive Gilbert, *Narrative of Sojourner Truth, a Northern Slave, Emancipated from Bodily Servitude by the State of New York, in 1828* (Boston: The Author, 1850), 18.

2. According to *Caron's Louisville Directory* for 1909, their lodgings were on the north side between 8th and 9th Streets. Just to the west were the station and yards of the Louisville and Nashville Railroad. It was a mixed-use block with a hotel, laundry, two saloons, a shoe store, an express office and several lodging and boarding houses, the occupants of which were mainly Black, although German and English names are listed as well. While a few of the older homes remained, probably broken up into flats, the area was dotted with industrial and commercial establishments, including the extensive buildings and yards of the Louisville Leaf Tobacco Company, which abutted the rear of the house in which Cecelia and her daughter were boarders. The neighbouring building, at 830 West Broadway, was the Broadway Hotel.

3. For increasing segregation of Louisville neighbourhoods by race in these years, see George C. Wright, "The NAACP and Residential Segregation in Louisville, Kentucky, 1914–1917," *Register of the Kentucky Historical Society* 78, no. 1 (Winter 1980): 39–54.

4. "Statement of Attending Physician, Dr. W. T. Hayes, M.D., 306 S First St, Louisville, Ky. Oct. 5, 1909, US Pension Office, Application for Reimbursement, Auditor for the Interior Department, US Treasury, Certificate No. 485092, Cecelia Jane Larrison, Claimant Mamie A. Reels," Pension Bureau Files, NARA.

5. *Chicago Tribune*, July 27, 1903; Louisville *Courier-Journal*, November 1, 1907; also Indianapolis *Recorder*, August 1908. The Quinn Chapel was founded in rooms over a stable at 2nd and Main Streets in 1838 and was at the time known as Bethel House of God. It moved to 4th and Green Streets and was known as "the old Fourth Street Church." It housed the first school for African American children in the city, under the patronage of influential whites recruited by then minister Reverend W. W. Revels. It was also known as the "Abolitionist Church" because of its history of resistance in the AME tradition, so many slaveholders prohibited "their people" from membership. It relocated first to 9th and Green and then, from 1854 to 1910, was at 9th and Walnut, until it was replaced with the building at 912 West Chestnut. In the 1870s it was renamed the Quinn Chapel after noted AME Bishop Paul Quinn visited Louisville for the first time. The church was the catalyst for Black civil rights agitation in Louisville: the streetcar strike for desegregation in 1870, the fair accommodations protests in 1961, and the open housing demonstrations in both 1914 and 1967. In the latter event Dr. Martin Luther King led a march from the Quinn Chapel to City Hall. The lovely old Gothic-style brick church is now abandoned and the congregation meets in a newer building on the western outskirts of the city. Walter E. Hutchings, "The Quinn Chapel," in Kleber, *Encyclopedia of Louisville*, 741; Gibson, *Historical Sketch*, 11–12.

6. "Application for Reimbursement, Auditor for the Interior Department, US Treasury, Certificate No. 485092, Cecelia Jane Larrison, Claimant Mamie A. Reels," Pension Bureau Files, NARA. T. H. Hankins ran an African American undertaking parlour at 1316 South Preston Street in Louisville. One of the witnesses for the affidavit that Mamie filled out was Nellie A. Hughes, principal of Louisville's Wilson night school, who was perhaps a friend from one of the women's organizations to which Mamie belonged. She is identified in "Past Week at Louisville," *Indiana Freeman*, October 14, 1911.

7. "Application for Reimbursement," August 21, 1909. Case of Cecelia J. Larrison, no. 631.101, Pension Bureau File NARA. Mamie collected on her mother's life insurance policy, held by the Metropolitan Life Insurance Company, in the amount of $59. The premiums must have paid in pennies per week, given Cecelia's penury in her last years. The undertaker's bill was $65, and there was still the livery for the funeral ($26) and the cemetery charges ($5) to pay on top of that. Nursing care had amounted to $50, a debt Mamie found herself unable to meet.

8. Daniel F. Littlefield Jr. and Lonnie E. Underhill, "Black Dreams and 'Free' Homes: The Oklahoma Territory, 1891–1894," *Phylon* 34, no. 4 (1973): 342–57.

9. The couple were married at the Beebe Chapel by T. M. Gatewood, minister of the Colored Methodist Episcopal church in Logan County, Oklahoma, on the same day the marriage licence was issued. (Mamie's new husband is listed as Newsome Alexander in some sources.) The CME Church was a Black denomination formed on December 16, 1870, in Jackson, Tennessee. It was established as a separate body by forty-one formerly enslaved members of the Methodist Episcopal Church, South, to remove their congregation from oversight by white church leaders. The Southern Methodists had in 1844 broken with the Methodist Church over slavery; they not only counted slaveholders in their midst but also approved slavery in principle. Today the Colored Methodist Episcopal Church in America is known as the Christian Methodist Church. Reverend

Gatewood was a respected pastor whom the *Oklahoma Guide*, the local African American newspaper, said in April 11, 1912, was "worthy of honor" as a "worker in home, city and community for the good and uplifting of the people. He believes in righteousness and preaches the same," and "His voice can be heard in behalf of the people in any just and righteous cause."

10. See, for instance, *Constitution of the National Grand Lodge, United Brothers of Friendship and Sisters of the Mysterious Ten, of the United States of America, Dominion of Canada, Districts, Territories and Foreign Countries* (n.p., 1886).

11. Newson Alexander was born February 1, 1848, the son of William Edward Alexander and his wife, Martha. The 1850 census for Wilson County, Tennessee shows baby "Nusom," age two, as the child of William (thirty-six) and Mary (twenty-one), with a five-month-old sister named Mary. It is possible that Martha Alexander's maiden name was Newsom and that she had once been enslaved by a white family of that name. The Newsom family were early pioneers of the Nashville area, operating a quarry from which many of the city's early buildings, including the Customs House, Union Station and parts of the state Capitol Building, were constructed. The ruins of the Newsom mill on the Harpeth River, constructed by Joseph Morton Newsom in 1862 to replace an earlier one destroyed in a flood, are visible at Newsom Station, where a modern subdivision is located west of the city proper; they are included on the National List of Historic Places. The Newsom plantation was nearby and had "numerous slaves." See Sarah Foster Kelley, *West Nashville: Its People and Environs* (Nashville, TN: Blue and Grey Press, 1987), 158–59; Patricia A. West, "Newsom Station / Newsom Mill, Williamson County, Tennessee, 2000," accessed August 21, 2014, http://www.websitewiz.com/genealogy/pdf/pl_newsom_mill.pdf.

   The 1860 census of the United States shows the Alexander family as free, all mulatto and living in the Fourth Ward of Nashville, Tennessee. The household was headed by Martha, a thirty-one-year-old housekeeper, who was illiterate. Newson was twelve and had three younger sisters, ten-year-old Margiana, six-year-old Mary F. and baby Sarah Jane, who was ten months old when the census was taken on August 29, 1860. None of the family is listed as attending school. It is possible that Martha's husband was a slave, since she is listed as married and has a ten-month-old child, but the father did not form part of the household either then or later. The 1870 census shows "Newsham," age twenty-two, and his three younger sisters, "Marchy" (Margiana, now twenty), Mary (sixteen) and Sarah (ten), along with a little boy named William Jitters, age five, listed as mulatto. "Mart[ha] Alexander," age thirty-nine, is listed as a married woman. Newson was employed as a labourer and his mother worked as a housekeeper. All three sisters were literate.

12. The Thirteenth Amendment led to the Civil Rights Act of 1866, which was passed over the veto of President Johnson. See Jodi Barnes, ed., *The Materiality of Freedom: Archaeologies of Post-Emancipation Life* (Columbia: University of South Carolina Press, 2011), 173–89; Sundiata Cha-Jua, *America's First Black Town: Brooklyn, Illinois, 1830–1915* (Urbana: University Press of Illinois, 2000). Rural areas near Alton with substantial Black populations included Hunterstown and Wood Station. To the south, directly opposite the city of St. Louis, was Brooklyn, founded by eleven families from St. Louis in 1827. It became the first all-Black Illinois town to be incorporated and was a major way station for freedom-seekers. Cheryl J. LaRoche, *Geographies of Resistance: Free Black Communities and the Underground Railroad* (Urbana: University of Illinois Press, 2014): 21–42.

13. The 1850 US Census for District 52, Macon County, Missouri, lists William's parents as Oscar D. Winn, twenty-eight, and Nancy Winn, twenty-two. William was two when the census was taken on November 20, 1850. He had been born in Tennessee but by then his parents were living in

Missouri. The marriage of William and Margiana took place on September 25, 1879. William P. Winn was active in the Grand Army of the Republic. He died on January 26, 1901, and was laid to rest under a USCT headstone in Mount Hope Cemetery, Urbana, Illinois, near a large memorial erected by the 1884 Champaign County Soldier's Monument Association; Find a Grave, accessed Aug. 21, 2014, http://www.findagrave.com/cgi-bin/fg.cgi?page=gr&GRid=73248280&ref=acom. Margiana, also known as Maggie, was eighty-seven at the time of the 1940 census and lived in Decatur, Illinois, where she rented her home and took in boarders.

14. Edward E. Comley Sr. is listed in the census as being born in September 1848, of Black complexion, with a mother from Massachusetts and father from Illinois. An E. Comley in Upper Alton, Illinois, age two, son of Pete, a labourer, and Cinthia [sic] Comley, both mulatto, is listed as a free Black child in the 1850 census. He died in Nicollet, Minnesota, on September 9, 1931.

15. The area is a major centre for ongoing research into Black engagement in the Underground Railroad along the Mississippi River. See C. Van Woodward, "Seeds of Failure in Radical Race Policy," in *New Frontiers of the American Reconstruction,* ed. Harold M. Hyman (Urbana: University of Illinois Press, 1966), 133. Alton, Illinois, was home to Abraham Lincoln's close friend Lyman Trumbull. The house where Trumbull, who was Senate Judiciary chairman, drafted the Thirteenth Amendment to the Constitution is still standing in this town on the bluffs overlooking the Mississippi River.

16. Even African American newspapers, such as the *Freeman* of Indianapolis, a paper that espoused W. E. B. DuBois's anti-segregationist views, warned on March 15, 1890, of the potential for a "race war" over Black settlement on the frontier.

17. See, for instance, "Colored Men Protest," *Guthrie Daily Leader,* September 25, 1894.

18. "Oklahoma Adopts Grandfather Clause," *Daily Illinois State Register* (Springfield), August 4, 1910.

19. *Oklahoma Guide* (Guthrie) 17, no. 32, January 7, 1909; *Oklahoma Guide* 21, no. 23, November 21, 1912.

20. R. Bruce Shepard, "Diplomatic Racism: Canadian Government and Black Migration from Oklahoma, 1905–1912," *Great Plains Quarterly* 3, no. 1 (Winter 1983): 5–16, and "Plain Racism: The Reaction Against Oklahoma Black Immigration to the Canadian Plains," *Prairie Forum* 10, no. 2 (1985): 365–82. The *Oklahoma Guide* of Guthrie City quoted a *New York Times* article on May 11, 1911, informing Oklahoma Blacks that they were not welcome in the former British colony: "Protest against Immigration: Race Prejudice Caused by Colored People in Canada."

21. *New York Times,* October 5, 1919, accessed September 19, 2016, http://www.muchgrace.com/HistoricPapers/NYT5Oct1919.pdf.

22. Terri Myers, "Enid, Oklahoma: Historic Resources Survey of the Southern Heights/East Park Neighborhood," Report to the State Historic Preservation Office, Oklahoma, for Hardy, Heck, Moore & Associates, October 1997, pt. 2, 65–66, accessed May 12, 2013, http://www.okhistory.org/shpo/architsurveys/SouthernHeights&EastParkPt2.pdf.

23. "A Dollar's Worth for a Dollar," *Tulsa World,* February 8, 1920.

24. A report written by Dr. George E. Haynes of the US Department of Labor suggests how the FBI under J. Edgar Hoover and the Department of Justice fanned the flames by providing newspapers with additional "evidence" of Communist influence from Black-owned publications such as *The Crisis,* produced by the NAACP, that resisted the violence and abuse heaped on Black Americans. The Tulsa Riots began on May 31, 1921. According to the report presented to the US Senate's Judiciary Committee, there were thirty-eight anti-Black riots in cities from New London,

Connecticut and Washington, DC, in the east to Omaha, Nebraska, in the west, and from Syracuse, New York—very nearly at the Canadian border—to Port Arthur, Texas. There were at least forty-three horrible lynchings across the South and Southwest. See Cameron McWhirter, *Red Summer: The Summer of 1919 and the Awakening of Black America* (New York: Henry Holt, 2011), and Philip Dray, *At the Hands of Persons Unknown: The Lynching of Black America* (New York: Random House, 2002). For an analysis of the media coverage, see Chris M. Messer and Patricia A. Bell, "Mass Media and Governmental Framing of Riots: The Case of Tulsa, 1921," *Journal of Black Studies* 40, no. 5 (May 2010), 851–70.

25. For a full discussion of this phenomenon, see Jack S. Blocker, *A Little More Freedom: African Americans Enter the Urban Midwest, 1860–1930* (Columbus: Ohio State University Press, 2008), especially ch. 1. A sociological study titled *Our Negro Population* was published in 1913, from an MS thesis by Asa E. Martin. Martin was a product of his time, and some of the language he employs and the assumptions contained in this volume, particularly in the foreword supplied by L. A. Halbert, superintendent of the Board of Public Welfare for Kansas City, are both antiquated and deeply racist. Still, the little booklet provides invaluable insight into the lives of Black Americans in Kansas City at the time of Mamie and Newson's arrival. There were 23,566 African Americans in the city, according to the 1910 census, and 224,815 white people, so 11.2 percent of the population was Black. By contrast, Louisville's white population was 186,406, with the Black community comprising some 18 percent of the population at 40,522 people. Asa E. Martin, *Our Negro Population: A Sociological Study of the Negroes of Kansas City* (Kansas City, MO: Franklin Hudson, 1913), 25. See also Coulter, *The Civil War and Readjustment in Kentucky* (1926), 51–52.

26. Martin, *Our Negro Population*, 56. Apart from the elite, the vast majority of Black women in Kansas City worked outside the home. A substantial proportion were cooks, maids, nursemaids and other types of servants either in private homes or in the city's hotels, hospitals and boarding houses. In 1913, according to Martin, some forty were trained nurses, fifty-four were teachers (they were unmarried, for married women could not be employed as teachers under school board regulations) and ninety listed their occupation as seamstress. More than a thousand undertook the age-old duties of washing and ironing, both in the city's professional laundries and in their own homes.

27. Charles Edward Coulter, *Take Up the Black Man's Burden: Kansas City's African American Communities, 1865–1939* (Columbia: University of Missouri Press, 2006), 28–38. A high school curriculum was added in 1887, after much agitation.

28. Marcia Fleming, "Freedom's Main Line," in Teaching Tolerance: A Project of the Southern Poverty Law Centre, Montgomery, AL, accessed January 22, 2014, http://www.tolerance.org/article/freedom-s-main-line.

29. Chester Arthur Franklin was born in 1880 and died in 1955. See Department of History, University of Missouri–Kansas City, *They Came to Fight: African Americans and the Great World War*, online exhibit, accessed July 2, 2014, http://www.theycametofight.org/kansascity.html.

30. See Historic American Buildings Survey, Star [Gem] Theatre, HABS MO-1924, accessed July 2, 2014, http://www.loc.gov/pictures/item/mo1270/. Such theatres flourished until the Great Depression, which had a devastating effect on the city's Black population, but continued in operation up to the Second World War.

31. Nathan W. Pearson Jr., "Political and Musical Forces That Influenced the Development of Kansas City Jazz," *Black Music Research Journal* 9, no. 2 (Autumn 1989): 181–92. According to Pearson, Thomas J. Pendergast, who was the political boss of the city and later of much of

Missouri, found interference in his machinations inconvenient; thus his reign permitted African American music to flourish.

32. The lodges and secret societies so popular among African Americans were strong in Kansas City. There was much intercourse between members of such organizations in cities and towns across the United States, and local Black newspapers frequently mention that one lodge official or another is visiting from another state to be present at, for instance, an event hosted by one of the Kansas City branches of the Household of Ruth. There were both adult and juvenile branches and the lodges were active in politics, at times openly supporting the candidate who seemed most favourable to African American interests. The female branches particularly supported health care, local charitable efforts and educational endeavours, and the lodges did a great deal of fundraising for such causes.

33. The Kansas City Monarchs signed the great Jackie Robinson in 1945. Despite Robinson's breaking of the colour bar with the Brooklyn Dodgers in 1947, after first playing for the otherwise all-white Montreal Royals, the Kansas team would continue to play as an all-Black team until 1965.

34. "Newsom [sic] M. Alexander, 06 Mar 1927"; citing Public Board of Health, Archives, Springfield, FHL microfilm 1613727, Illinois Deaths and Stillbirths, 1916–47, FamilySearch, accessed August 16, 2014, https://familysearch.org/pal:/MM9.1.1/N3FV-L9V. The remaining members of Newson's family moved there from North Alton.

35. "Ewald Spring and Radiator Company, Rear 822 South Floyd Street," ULPA 1998.09.366.1, Martin F. Schmidt, Photographs of Louisville, ca. 1956–66, Photographic Archives, University of Louisville, Louisville, KY.

36. Doctor E. E. Butter wrote on her death record that he attended Mamie Alexander from December 16, 1927, to March 16, 1928. Commonwealth of Kentucky, State Board of Health, Bureau of Vital Statistics, Certificate of Death, Jefferson County, Kentucky, file no. 6611, registration 1144. The death registration gives her place of birth as Rochester, New York, which was erroneous.

37. Here is another example of connections between Toronto and Rochester Black families. Rowsell's 1850 Toronto directory lists "Bloxom Daniel (coloured), 215 King-street east near Berkeley." He was naturalized in 1842, which means he was in Canada seven years earlier and was likely a migrant from Virginia following the Nat Turner Rebellion. He operated the Tontine Coffee House at 150 King Street East, which was a fashionable area, but in 1847 he was charged with operating a common bawdy house. He is buried in St. James' Cemetery. See Edwin C. Guillet, "Respectable Prostitution: An Account of the Conviction of Daniel Bloxsom, Toronto, on a Charge of Keeping a Bawdy-House and of the Consequent Charge that Mayor W. H. Boulton, Lessor of the House, Was Living on the Avails of Prostitution, 1847, to Which Is Added a Consideration of Recent Cases of a Parallel Nature," vol. 47 of *Famous Canadian Trials* (Toronto: 1948).

38. Isaac Post died in 1872 and Amy in 1889, within a year of attending the International Council of Women in Washington, exactly forty years after she signed the Declaration of Sentiments at the Seneca Falls 1848 Woman's Rights Convention.

39. The death of Mrs. William H. (Mary Ann) Coleman is reported in the Rochester *Union and Advertiser* of November 17, 1875, 3–5. Her husband had died on August 11, 1871. US Census, 1890, Syracuse, Onondaga Co., NY.

40. US Census, 1900 and 1910, Onondaga Co., NY; Margie Abell and Esther Slater, transcr., "Maple Grove Cemetery, Jordan, New York," accessed Dec. 2, 2016, http://www.rootsweb.ancestry.com/~nyononda/CEMETERY/maplegrove.html.

41. Kate Clifford Larson *Bound for the Promised Land: Portrait of an American Hero* (New York: Ballantine, 2004): 252–53, 276–77.

42. An African American woman named Mrs. Bailey had been Cecelia's landlady in Rochester in 1866, just before she and William moved to Louisville. Deposition of Cecelia J. Larrison, taken May 6, 1898, at Louisville, Kentucky, Case no. 631.101, Pension Bureau Files, NARA.

43. The town was named for Alexander Faribault, the Métis grandson of a French-Canadian fur trader of some renown. He was half French, a quarter Scots and a quarter Native; his wife was a Dakota. He constructed a trading post on the site in 1834 and lived out his life in Faribault.

44. The Peterborough–Lindsay area saw the only known murder of a Black man for marrying a white woman in all the history of what is now Ontario. The only recent published account is actually a very well-researched fictional volume, *Oonagh*, by Mary Tillburg (Toronto: Cormorant Books, 2009). See Moodie, *Roughing It in the Bush*, 175.

45. George and Miriam French, of Lowell, Massachusetts, moved to Sumner at some point before the 1860 census was taken. In the census their children Anna, eleven, and Hannah, six, are listed as born in Massachusetts, but George O., three months, was born in Iowa.

46. Alan A. Brookes, "Out-Migration from the Maritime Provinces, 1860–1900: Some Preliminary Considerations," *Acadiensis* 5, no. 2 (Spring 1976): 26–55. Brookes shows that leaving Atlantic Canada in the period immediately after Confederation was a popular move, as evidenced by a letter published in the *Nova Scotian* of December 16, 1869, encouraging families to immigrate to beautiful Minnesota.

47. Similarly to the Southern visitors at Niagara, the post-Civil War tourists from the South who stayed at Lake Minnetonka resorts preferred African American service. W.E.B. Du Bois spent at summer there raising funds for the Fisk Jubilee Singers. See James W. Ogland, *Picturing Lake Minnetonka: A Postcard History* (St. Paul: Minnesota Historical Society Press, 2001), 49–51.

48. William D. Green, "Race and Segregation in St. Paul's Public Schools," *Minnesota History* 55 (Winter 1996–67): 139–49.

49. David Vassar Taylor, *African Americans in Minnesota* (St. Paul: Minnesota Historical Society Press, 2002), especially chs. 8 and 9; William D. Green, "Minnesota's Long Road to Black Suffrage," *Minnesota History Magazine* (Summer 1998): 69–84.

50. Circa 1874 a man of about thirty named Benjamin F. Day arrived with his family. Originally from Wisconsin, he was also a barber. *Western Appeal*, August 28, 1915; May 6, 1916. Day came with his Ohio-born wife, Ella, and two little girls. Two more daughters were born after they came to Faribault, but the marriage ended in divorce.

51. Soon after their arrival, the Holmes family would have met the progressive Episcopalian Bishop, Henry Benjamin Whipple (1822–1901), and it was likely he who was responsible for their conversion to the Episcopal faith. Whipple was in his early church career "not particularly concerned about the plight of Black Americans. During the Civil War he opined that the abolitionists had exaggerated the horrors of the slave condition and driven a fatal wedge between North and South. He opposed immediate emancipation and called African Americans "unfitted for freedom," a view for which his more abolitionist-minded relatives berated him in letters that have survived. Fortunately he changed his views during Reconstruction, coming to see (with the characteristic paternalism of his day) the United States' African American population as one with unlimited potential for progress. Being naturally deeply religious, he took up their cause as a special mission for the Episcopal Church. Introduction to Finding Aid, Henry Benjamin Whipple Papers, Minnesota Historical Society, accessed October 10, 2015, http://www2.mnhs.org/library/findaids/P0823.xml; Andrew S. Brake, *Man in the Middle: The Reform and Influence of Henry Benjamin Whipple, the First Episcopal Bishop of Minnesota* (Lanham, MD: University Press of America, 2005), 27–29.

52. Ben Alexander Holmes was involved in organizations that were heirs of the Black convention movement of the antebellum years. The League had begun in 1887, and St. Paul African Americans formed a chapter in November 1889. It was the brainchild of Thomas Fortune, publisher of the *New York Age*, to rally legal support to break the expanding grasp of Jim Crow and combat lynching, along with abuse within the prison system and racial violence. *Western Appeal* (St. Paul), November 9, 1889; January 11, 1890. The national group disbanded in 1893 but the causes it espoused were taken up by a number of other organizations, first the National Afro-American Council, founded in 1898 and led by AME Zion bishop Alexander Walters of Kentucky, with Ida B. Wells as the first secretary, and most notably by the National Association for the Advancement of Colored People (NAACP).

53. Paul Nelson, "How a St. Paul Meeting of the National Afro-American Council Reshaped the Civil Rights Movement for Decades," *MinnPost*, February 17, 2015, accessed August 22, 2016, https://www.minnpost.com/mnopedia/2015/02/how-st-paul-meeting-national-afro-american-council-reshaped-civil-rights-movement-d.

54. *Little Sketches of Big Folks, Minnesota* (Minneapolis: R. L. Polk, 1907), 197. He was also a member of the University Press Club, served on the staff of the *Education Herald*, was elected class "quizzitor" in anatomy in 1892 and acted as prosector for the chair of pathology during the junior and senior years of his course.

55. John Turner and C. Knut Semling, *History of Clay and Norman Counties, Minnesota*, vol. 2 (Indianapolis: B. F. Bowen, 1918), 880–82.

56. A photograph showing the Grand Army of the Republic Arch under construction at Nicollet and Washington Avenues in downtown Minneapolis includes the sign "DENTIST, Dr. E. P. Holmes." "The Arch Celebrating the Grand Army of the Republic Encampment," 1884, Hennepin County Library, Minneapolis Photo Collection, image no. BR0269, accessed November 12, 2013, http://www.hclib.org/pub/search/mplsphotos/mphotosaction.cfm?-subject=Veterans%20Organizations.

57. *Marie E. Holmes v. Eugene P. Holmes*, Decree of Divorce, September 21, 1899, State of Minnesota, County of Hennepin. His second wife was Anna E. Jamme, daughter of Henry and Delphine Jamme. The wedding date was November 2, 1912, and the bride was twenty-nine years old.

58. The house was 1,200 square feet in size and had three bedrooms.

59. Iric Nathanson, "African Americans and the 1892 Republican National Convention, Minneapolis," *Minnesota History* 61, no. 2 (Summer 2008), 76–82.

60. Case 2635, Estate of Benjamin A. Holmes, County of Rice Probate Court, April 12, 1905. These were Lots 3 and 6 in the Cooper Addition, Faribault.

61. "Death Claims Esteemed Ada Lady," clipping from unidentified newspaper (March 1930), Norman County Historical Society, Ada, MN. Valborg was born in what was at the time actually part of Norway, since the kingdoms of Norway and Sweden were united from 1814 to 1905.

62. Joris Norby had been twice elected clerk of Norman County and twice county auditor. After a bout of ill health sent him on an extended trip to Europe, he purchased the *Norman County Herald* in January 1892. Formerly a Prohibition paper, he transformed it into the Populist Party organ for northern Minnesota. J. W. Major Wooldridge, *History of Sacramento Valley, California*, vol. 3 (Chicago: Pioneer Historical Publishing, 1931), 165–67, transcription accessed November 26, 2013, http://freepages.genealogy.rootsweb.ancestry.com/~npmelton/yunorb.htm; *Compendium of History and Biography of Central and Northern Minnesota* (Chicago: Geo. A Ogle, 1904), 187–88; *The Gopher* [University of Minnesota yearbook] (Minneapolis: University Press, 1915), 252.

63. Turner and Semling, *History of Clay and Norman Counties*, 881; *Little Sketches*, 197.

64. Turner and Semling, *History*, 882.

65. Karen Shoenig and her cousin Barbara Cosens, neither of whom I have actually met, with the help of Connie Ferris—all of whom descend from Valborg Norby and her first husband—kindly arranged to send me Walter B. Holmes's letters to his stepson Erling in Marysfield, California, and to Erling's wife and children. All dated in the 1920s, they provide insight into the mind of a truly remarkable man.

66. He died in 1978 in Brownsville, Yuba County, California.

67. Wooldridge, *History of Sacramento Valley*, 165–66; C. E. Wentsel, *Norman County, Minnesota, in the World War* (Ada, MN: Pfund and Wentsel, 1922), 57, 67, 85–86.

Epilogue

1. The construction occasioned yet another recalibration of house numbers. Cecelia's stepsons' old property south of her house became number 7 and her own house became number 11 on a street now known as Centre Avenue.

2. The Toronto Tax Assessment Rolls for 1845 show Benjamin and Cecelia's family as owning a dog.

Acknowledgements

1. Frederick Douglass to Sidney Howard Gay, December 8, 1852, Sidney Howard Gay Papers, Manuscript Collections, Columbia University Libraries.

ILLUSTRATION CREDITS

Interior Text Images

p. vi: The Filson Historical Society, Louisville, KY, Charles W. Thruston Papers, 1777–1865.

p. 234: Louisville *Bulletin*, September 24, 1881; Margaret I. King Library, University of Kentucky.

Photo Section Inserts

1. The Filson Historical Society, Louisville, KY; engraving from *History of Kentucky* by Richard H. Collins (1874).
2. The Filson Historical Society, Louisville, KY; PC20.0096.057, paired miniatures of Charles W. Thruston and Mary Eliza Thruston (Rogers Clark Ballard Thruston Family Photograph Collection).
3. The Filson Historical Society, Louisville, KY; PC20.069.056a, portrait of Frances Ann Thruston (Rogers Clark Ballard Thruston Family Photograph Collection).
4. Broadside Collection, Library of Congress, portfolio 118, no. 26 c-Rare Bk Coll, Rare Book and Special Collections Division; LC-DIG-ppmsca-19705.
5. Courtesy of Christopher Densmore; private collection.
6. Courtesy of Niagara Falls Public Library.
7. Courtesy of Niagara Falls Public Library.
8. Courtesy of Niagara Falls Public Library.
9. Geography and Map Division, Library of Congress; G3804.N7A3 1882 .W4.
10. Popular Graphic Arts Collection, Prints and Photographs Division, Library of Congress; LC-DIG-pga-02597.
11. Photo courtesy of King and Queen Courthouse Tavern Museum.
12. Reprinted with permission of the Royal Ontario Museum, © ROM.
13. City of Toronto Archives, fonds 1498, item 0016.
14. The Filson Historical Society, Louisville, KY; Mss. A/B189a/2, letter from Fanny Thruston Ballard to Cecelia Jane Holmes, February 23, 1859 (Ballard Family Papers).
15. The Filson Historical Society, Louisville, KY; PC20.069.051b, CDV of Charles W. Ballard.
16. Courtesy of the Toronto Public Library.
17. Courtesy of the Toronto Public Library; Toronto *Globe*, July 30, 1890.
18. Courtesy of the Toronto Public Library; Toronto *Globe*, August 27, 1859.
19. Courtesy of the Toronto Public Library.
20. Courtesy of the National Afro-American Museum and Cultural Center, Wilberforce, Ohio.
21. Trent University Archives, *Fuller's Counties of Peterborough & Victoria Directory, for 1865 & 1866.*
22. From the Collection of the Rochester Public Library Local History Division, rsg00009.
23. Trent University Archives, *Fuller's Counties of Peterborough & Victoria Directory, for 1865 & 1866.*
24. Frederick Douglass, unidentified artist, 1856, quarter-plate ambrotype, National Portrait Gallery, Smithsonian Institution; acquired through the generosity of an anonymous donor.
25. Courtesy of the Toronto Public Library.
26. Photo courtesy of Dan Papson.
27. Civil War Collection, Prints and Photographs Division, Library of Congress; LC-DIG-cwpb-02010.
28. The Filson Historical Society, Louisville, KY; PC20.069.065b, CDV of Frances Ann Thruston Ballard (Rogers Clark Ballard Thruston Family Photograph Collection).
29. The Filson Historical Society, Louisville, KY; PR675.0012, Print of Andrew Jackson Ballard (Print Collection).
30. The Filson Historical Society, Louisville, KY; 1929.8.60, portrait of R. C. Ballard Thruston by Jules C. Aviat.
31. The Filson Historical Society, Louisville, KY; HJC-106, Ballard family home (Subject Photograph Collection).
32. University of Louisville, Louisville, KY. Photographic Archives, R. G. Potter Collection, P.00599.
33. New York *Freeman*, April 10, 1886.
34. Prints and Photographs Division, Library of Congress; LC-USZ62-64013.
35. Margaret I. King Library, University of Kentucky.
36. Courtesy of the Minnesota Historical Society.
37. Courtesy of the Oklahoma Historical Society.
38. Courtesy of Connie Ferris (both images).
39. City of Toronto Archives, *Globe and Mail* fonds, fonds 1266, item 21000.
40. Courtesy of Timmins Martelle Heritage Consultants Inc. at the Museum of Ontario Archaeology.
41. Courtesy of Timmins Martelle Heritage Consultants and Fanshawe College.
42. Courtesy of Timmins Martelle Heritage Consultants and Fanshawe College.
43. Courtesy of Timmins Martelle Heritage Consultants and Fanshawe College.

INDEX